INNOVATING
VICTORY

INNOVATING VICTORY

NAVAL TECHNOLOGY IN THREE WARS

VINCENT P. O'HARA
LEONARD R. HEINZ

NAVAL INSTITUTE PRESS
Annapolis, Maryland

Naval Institute Press
291 Wood Road
Annapolis, MD 21402

Library of Congress Cataloging-in-Publication Data
Names: O'Hara, Vincent P., [date]– author. | Heinz, Leonard R., author.
Title: Innovating victory : naval technology in three wars / Vincent P. O'Hara,
    Leonard R. Heinz.
Other titles: Naval technology in three wars
Description: Annapolis, Maryland : Naval Institute Press, [2022] |
    Includes bibliographical references and index.
Identifiers: LCCN 2021052331 (print) | LCCN 2021052332 (ebook) |
    ISBN 9781682477328 (hardcover) | ISBN 9781682477335 (epub)
Subjects: LCSH: Naval art and science—Technological innovations—History—
    20th century.
Classification: LCC V53 .O33 2022 (print) | LCC V53 (ebook) |
    DDC 359.009/04—dc23/eng/20211102
LC record available at https://lccn.loc.gov/2021052331
LC ebook record available at https://lccn.loc.gov/2021052332
⊚ Print editions meet the requirements of ANSI/NISO z39.48-1992
(Permanence of Paper). Printed in the United States of America.

30 29 28 27 26 25 24 23 22   9 8 7 6 5 4 3 2 1
First printing

Figures by Vincent P. O'Hara

To the memory of
Captain Stephen F. Davis Jr. (1962–2008),
who some years ago encouraged
a rank amateur to persevere

CONTENTS

ILLUSTRATIONS

FIGURES

TABLES

ACKNOWLEDGMENTS

This is new territory for both authors, who approached this work on technology with nontechnical backgrounds and during a challenging period for learning new things. We have been sustained and inspired by a network of supporters and colleagues, particularly our friends in the Western Naval History Association. We would like to thank in particular Enrico Cernuschi, Trent Hone, John T. Kuehn, and Michael Yaklich for reading and commenting on the entire manuscript, and Michael Whitby, who has been generous with his research. Other readers include Robert C. Stern, Sam J. Tangredi, and Stephen McLaughlin. We thank our editor at Naval Institute Press, Glenn Griffith, and the wonderful people there for bringing this book to print in such excellent fashion. O'Hara thanks his family—daughter Yunuen, son Vincent, and wife Maria—for their past and ongoing support, while Heinz thanks his wife Meg, daughter Julia, son David, and granddaughter Maggie, who loves technology but prefers Minecraft to mines.

ACRONYMS, ABBREVIATIONS, AND CONVERSIONS

ACRONYMS AND ABBREVIATIONS

AIO	action information organization
ASV	air-to-surface vessel (aerial radar)
ASW	antisubmarine warfare
BEF	British Expeditionary Force
BIR	Board of Invention and Research
CIC	combat information center
cm	centimeter
CNO	Chief of Naval Operations
COS	chief of staff
DAT	Défence Aérienne du Territoire
DEM	Détecteur Electro-Magnétique
DF	direction-finding
ECM	electronic countermeasures
GHG	Gruppen-Horch-Gerät
GRT	gross register tonnage
HF/DF	high-frequency direction-finding
HVB	Handelsschiffsverkehrsbuch
IFF	Identification Friend or Foe
kg	kilogram
KHz	kilohertz
km	kilometer
kw	kilowatt
m	meter
MHz	megahertz

MTB   motor torpedo boat

PPI   plan position indicator

RAF   Royal Air Force

SIGINT   signals intelligence

SKM   Signalbuch der Kaiserlichen Marine

TNT   trinitrotoluene

UHF   ultra high frequency

UN   United Nations

VB   Verkehrsbuch

VHF   very high frequency

CONVERSIONS

1 nautical mile = 2,205 yards, 1,852 meters, or 1.151 statute miles

1 knot = 1.852 kilometers/hour or 1.151 statute miles/hour

1 meter = 1.094 yards

1 yard = 0.9144 meters

1 centimeter = 0.3937 inches

1 inch = 2.54 centimeters

1 kilogram = 2.205 pounds

1 pound = 0.4536 kilograms

INTRODUCTION

O for a muse of fire, that would ascend
The brightest heaven of invention.
—SHAKESPEARE, *HENRY V*, ACT 1, PROLOGUE

nimals fight with horns, teeth, and claws. Humans can bite and scratch as well, but to win, they use technology. The word *technology* is a compound of two Greek roots, *tekhnē* (craft) and *logia* (learning). In essence, technology is the practical application of knowledge expressed through the use of a device.

Shaped stones and sharpened sticks are Paleolithic examples of combat technology. A raft that transports warriors over water is one expression of naval technology; a nuclear-powered ballistic missile submarine is another. Modern naval technology is the sum of the elements involved in the invention, development, production, and use of specialized weapons, tools, and platforms to fight at sea. Superior technology can confer a powerful advantage. Greek fire, a weapon, allowed the Byzantine navy to repeatedly triumph over more numerous foes. The Confederate armored ship *Virginia*, a platform, destroyed the wooden vessels of the Union navy at will. Centimetric radar, a tool, allowed Allied aircraft during World War II to spot submarine conning towers at night. But it is the nature of technology that such advantages are rare and often fleeting.

The twentieth century was a time of profound technological change. In naval terms, this change came in four major waves, with the first three climaxed by a major naval war. The first wave started in the mid-nineteenth century as coal-fired steam engines replaced sail, armor was developed, guns and mines were improved, torpedoes appeared, and radio was introduced. This wave peaked in the Russo-Japanese War. In the second wave, which started in 1905 and ran through World War I, naval warfare became three-dimensional with the development of practical submarines and aircraft. The armored gunnery platform reached its acme of power and influence and imperceptibly began to fade in importance. The third wave, which lasted through the end of World War II, moved naval warfare fully into the electromagnetic spectrum as technologies such as radar and sonar expanded perceptions beyond the horizon and beneath the waves, revolutionized the collection and use of information, and saw the introduction of practical guided weapons. The fourth wave is under way. Naval warfare has entered another dimension—starting with the splitting of the atom and progressing to satellites, computers, drones, data networks, artificial intelligence, and a new generation of weapons using magnetic and directed energy. The fourth wave has lasted the longest, not because the pace of invention has slowed—it has in fact accelerated—but because since 1945 there has been no major peer-to-peer naval war—that is, a total war between opponents with similar technological resources—to prove these new technologies in all-out combat.

This book examines six specific technologies that came of age in twentieth-century naval warfare and considers the way navies applied these technologies and adapted to their use. Technical details are not the focus here. What matters is the process by which each technology's possibilities were first recognized, tested, and then used, or not used, to best advantage. This book will explore the principles that govern this process and consider whether these principles apply across platforms, nations, and technologies, and whether, if observed, they lead to victory regardless of the period or the technology in question and thus can be expected to apply to the technologies of today, as yet untested in peer combat. As part of this exploration, this book will also consider how human factors such as established practice, politics, and policy complicated the process.

Technology is constantly evolving, and the navies of the twenty-first century are juggling innovations that are likely to revolutionize naval warfare as profoundly as did the introduction of steam and steel in the nineteenth century or electronics in the twentieth. Forethought, strategic vision, and technical acumen might drive technological development in periods of peace, but it is a thesis of this work that navies learn the best use of new technology only through the medium of peer-to-peer combat. And within the chaos of combat, only those navies that innovate successfully discover the best uses of their own technology and the best counters to those of the enemy. To paraphrase Carl von Clausewitz, while the concept of innovation is simple, innovating under enemy fire is difficult.

We recognize that we are shouldering a vast subject but consider it worthwhile to collect and follow the threads of technological development over more than a century of time and the course of three major and several smaller wars. To the best of our knowledge, such a broad and structured look at naval technology as a process viewed through the lens of specific application has never been done. Our goal is to seek new perspectives and insights and identify the factors that accelerate or retard the process of technological development. To accomplish such an ambitious goal, this work strives to be a synthesis and a simplification without being simplistic.

This book focuses on six technologies grouped loosely into three broad categories. The categories are *weapon*, a technology designed to damage a target; *tool*, one to assist in using a weapon; and *platform*, one to deliver a weapon. Each of the technologies we examined transformed the practice of naval warfare in its own way. They include

- *Mines and torpedoes*. These weapons are nineteenth-century technologies of tremendous impact. Mines gave navies a way to shape geography, while torpedoes allowed the smallest platforms to defeat the largest.

- *Radio and radar*. Radio expanded the volume and range of naval communications, while radar allowed platforms to see at great distances and in poor visibility. Both tools aided navies in bringing weapons to bear on their opponents and (generally) increased the amount of available information.

- *Submarines and aircraft*. These platforms allowed navies to operate in new environments below and above the surface of the sea, confounding existing weapons and tactics and expanding the scope of naval warfare.

This work will

- briefly consider the nature and history of each of the six subject technologies

- consider the state of the technology when it was first used in war and how different navies expected to use it
- explore how major navies subsequently improved or modified their use of the technology
- examine the development of countermeasures
- discuss how navies developed doctrine and incorporated ancillary technologies to improve the core technology's effectiveness.

Clearly, synergy is involved, and all six of these technologies were deeply intertwined by 1945. Case studies will show how this synergy affected actual combat. The narrative will focus on the technologies of the first three waves. Fourth-wave technologies—that is, technologies invented or developed since the end of World War II—will be treated very lightly as they remain largely untested in peer-to-peer combat. It is not our intention to judge how such technologies might fare in a future war; instead, the purpose of this book is to consider basic principles.

This book is not intended to be a complete history of naval technology in the period covered. Many other naval technologies were developed in the same period, and several had revolutionary impact. Ship propulsion evolved from sail to steam, and fuel from coal to fuel oil to nuclear; guns progressed from muzzle-loaders to automated 8-inch cannons; mechanical fire control was invented and elaborated. Tremendous advances in electrification, naval architecture, armor and protection, and damage control occurred during this period. Such technologies are mentioned in passing to the extent they affected the subject technologies, but we make no attempt to examine them rigorously. We also realize that naval technologies are specialized and form just a slice of the pie. Other technologies such as analog and digital computers, jet and rocket propulsion, and nuclear weapons were also under development during this period and were competing with the subject technologies for limited financial, scientific, and production resources. Naval requirements often played second fiddle to the requirements of land and air forces.

Each chapter addresses a single technology and follows a similar structure. In broad terms, the technology is treated as passing through a *discovery* stage, in which navies first pursue a potential capability; an *evolution* stage, which typically sees further development of the technology combined with the creation of doctrine and infrastructure to accommodate it; and an *exploitation* phase, in which navies strive to maximize the value of the now-integrated technology. The reader will appreciate that these general stages are not precise, but they are nonetheless helpful in framing the story of each technology.

Each chapter begins with an account of the technology's early development, including its first adoption by navies and initial expectations surrounding it. Next, the chapter discusses the discovery phase. For mines, torpedoes, and radio, this is the Russo-Japanese War; for submarines and aircraft, World War I; and for radar, World War II. Once the discovery phase is covered, the chapter focuses on evolution. In most cases this occurred after the war in which discovery took place, although submarines passed through both a discovery phase and an evolution phase during World War I, and radar did the same in World War II. After evolution, the exploitation of the fully developed technology is examined. For five of the technologies, the exploitation phase occurred in World War II; radio was sufficiently developed by 1914 to be exploited in both wars. Countermeasures and further evolution are discussed where relevant. The section describing the exploitation of the technology in World War II is followed by a summary of postwar developments and a brief review of the technology's current state. Each chapter concludes with lessons to be learned.

This book employs certain conventions. Distances over sea are stated in nautical miles and over land in statute miles unless otherwise specified. Displacements are given in long tons of 2,240 pounds. The authors prefer the U.S. customary system of measurement and do not convert measurements given in one system to another, assuming the reader can navigate the metric and customary systems. A conversion table is included. Where the text refers to aircraft, it includes both aircraft relying on engines to remain airborne (airplanes) and aircraft relying on buoyant gases (airships). Seaplanes encompass floatplanes—airplanes kept afloat by attached pontoons—and flying boats—in which the airplane's fuselage acts as the float.

Technology was hardly the only force that shaped naval warfare in the twentieth century, but it was a force that navies always had to take into account. It affected naval warfare from the most tactical level to the grandest national strategies. This study, then, looks at how six technologies facilitated and frustrated navies in their pursuit of victory.

CHAPTER 1

USE, DOCTRINE, INNOVATION

Victory smiles upon those who anticipate changes in the character of war, not upon those who wait to adapt themselves after the changes occur.

—GENERAL GIULIO DOUHET[1]

The most famous naval action of the nineteenth century, the 1805 Battle of Trafalgar, was fought by the British and Franco-Spanish navies with wooden, wind-propelled line of battle ships and guns that fired solid shot weighing up to forty pounds out to four hundred yards. The 1905 battle of Tsushima between the Japanese and Russian empires featured steel, armor-plated ships with coal-fired triple expansion stream engines and guns that fired 850-pound explosive shells out to ranges of ten thousand yards. Naval technologies present in 1905 that had been unknown at Trafalgar included torpedoes, radio, moored contact mines, and (barely) practical submarines. Ten years later the turbine-driven ships of the British and German navies that fought the Battle of Jutland were twice as large as the triple-expansion battleships that clashed at Tsushima and fired shells that were twice as heavy to double the range. The admirals who fought World War I—children of the nineteenth century—had to integrate and master the increasingly sophisticated uses of other recent technologies, such as submarines, radio intelligence, and aircraft. By 1945, within the span of a Jutland officer's service career, basic naval technologies included radar and guided weapons. Effective ranges were those of the aircraft on board carriers, not ships' guns. The battleship, the preeminent naval platform of 1805, 1905, 1914, and 1939, had been superseded in general utility and overall importance by the aircraft carrier and the submarine, platforms that hardly existed at the turn of the century.

HMS *Victory* and HMS *Dreadnought*. With the ships built more than a century apart, the past meets the present in this 1906 photo. *(Gosportheritage.co.uk)*

THE TEST OF COMBAT

During the Cold War's long and grim decades, navies integrated new technologies such as nuclear power, missiles, and computers. The medium of naval operations expanded into space. As technologies matured, their potency multiplied—compare the first gasoline-powered submarines that went to sea with one torpedo, no radio, and no periscope with the nuclear-powered and -armed boats of today. But even as platforms and systems evolved, the era of certain knowledge—the knowledge that only comes from observing naval technology used in peer-to-peer combat—ended in 1945. It is true that some smaller conflicts and "incidents," such as the 1982 Falklands war, campaigns fought in the Persian Gulf and the Gulf of Sirte during the 1980s, and the Arab-Israeli and Indo-Pakistani wars, offered flickers of insight, but none of these involved first-tier naval forces facing each other in a state of total war. These lesser wars showed that modern technology defeats World War II technology—although, given the successes of Argentina's iron bombs and Iran's moored contact mines, it is a lesson with an asterisk. Since the conflicts of the 1970s and 1980s, as networked and distributed systems, drones, artificial intelligence, and directed energy and magnetic weapons have come into use or development, there has not been a single case of peer-to-peer combat between major navies. However, history has shown that combat, and combat alone, ultimately determines a technology's utility.

The dreadnought battleship provides an example of how combat experience can confound expectations. The dreadnought battleship was, in 1914, the alpha naval technology upon which victory at sea was supposed to depend. In the event, the technology produced results far different than those envisioned by politicians, admiralties, and the public: dominance without decisive victory for the British, and the seedbeds of revolution for the Russians, Germans, and Austro-Hungarians. Within forty years of its 1906 introduction, the dreadnought battleship had been supplanted. The last few heavily modified examples of the type are thirty years out of service while submarines and aircraft carriers dominate the seas of the twenty-first century. Why was the dreadnought superseded? Because it no longer had a use that justified its cost.

New technologies do not materialize fully functional as from Aladdin's lamp. History shows that a successful technology undergoes a process: invention, development, acceptance, deployment, and then a cycle of discovery, evolution, and exploitation. The capstone of this process is determining the technology's best uses and then combining those with best practices for best results. In every case, the goal is a combat advantage. In 1904, 1914, and 1939, navies went to war with unproven technologies and experienced steep learning curves in trying to match expectations with practical and effective use. Should war break out tomorrow, the learning curve will be even steeper.

The way navies integrate new technology varies according to differences in national resources, force mixtures, priorities, policies, perceptions, and missions. A navy never has an advantage over all opponents in all technologies. Victory can hinge on a navy's ability to quickly apply a new or superior technology directly against a weakness of its opponent on one hand while mitigating the enemy's technological advantages on the other. An advantage in information technology, unsuspected by the Japanese, facilitated the U.S. Navy's victory at Midway despite superior Japanese numbers, platforms, and weapons. Conversely, advantages in torpedo technology and night optics, unrecognized by the Americans, allowed the Japanese navy to win tactical victories in the night battles fought in the Solomons despite U.S. advantages in radar. Using technology well is difficult because technology can harm as well as help; one side's perceived technological superiority can be exploited by an adept opponent and turned to its own advantage. The Germans' use of radio in World War I facilitated their operations, but overuse gave their enemies critical information about those operations. New technologies can also be dead ends, and there are many examples of navies clinging to an inferior technology or not "getting" a new technology until too late. The German use of radar in World War II broadly illustrates this. The continued planning and construction of super-battleships in World War II (the Japanese completed two of four planned, the Germans began building two of six, and the Americans planned a class of five) illustrate it better.

THE ROLE OF INNOVATION

The difference between the 104-gun first rate ship of the line HMS *Victory* of 1805 and HMS *Dreadnought* of 1905 is a clear example of technological progress, but where is the innovation? If the capital ship represents a synthesis of many technologies, then one can easily argue that behind the technological progress that produced this synthesis, there was profound innovation. This is true if one considers only technical innovation. One can ask whether these innovations were driven by militaries or by society in general. For example, the steam engine transformed naval warfare, but first it transformed transportation and manufacturing in general and in the process changed the world economy. Society at large and not the military drove many of the improvements in steam technology. The same is true of electromagnetic technology and even of advances in the sciences of metallurgy and chemistry that had direct applications to armor and explosives. Militaries generally regard the goal of technological innovation as a matter of progressive improvement in a proven field: larger guns firing bigger shells to greater ranges, for example. In general, navies strive to win wars with better versions of existing weapons, tools, and platforms rather than use novelties in the front line. But the greatest power of new technology comes from innovative use. What are these improved guns being fired at, and to what purpose? If they are used in the same old way, it is legitimate to repeat the question that opened this paragraph: Where is the innovation?

Victory's tactical function as a capital ship was to maneuver in formation with her fellow capital ships to a position from which she could bombard enemy ships with her broadside of cannons. The tactical function of the dreadnought battleships that fought the Battle of Jutland, 111 years after *Victory*'s triumph at Trafalgar, was essentially the same. So too was the tactical goal of the commanding admirals: to concentrate their firepower through maneuver while preventing their opponents from doing the same. Naval professionals throughout the long decades of peace leading up to 1914 expended great effort trying to keep pace with the tactical implications of rapidly changing capital ship technology. Line-abreast formations were tried and discarded; ramming tactics went in and out of fashion; torpedoes and speed were heralded (by some) as revolutionary. Still, by 1914 fleets of gun-armed capital ships dominated naval thinking, much as the ship of the line had more than a century before. In terms of formations, objectives, and major weapons, John Jellicoe and Reinhard Scheer, the admirals at Jutland, essentially fought the same way that Horatio Nelson and Pierre Villeneuve fought Trafalgar. All sought to concentrate the power of their big guns. Jellicoe accomplished this by crossing in front of the German line and pounding its leading ships, while Nelson split the Franco-Spanish line and defeated it in detail, but both men had the same goal. The technical innovations in the capital ships of 1914 compared to those of 1805 were enormous, but the tactical goal was still to concentrate gun power more effectively than the foe.

Technological advances often have unanticipated consequences that become clear only in combat. HMS *Victory* had one critical advantage over HMS *Dreadnought*: she was practically invulnerable to all lesser weapons. *Dreadnought*, on the other hand, needed to fear mines and torpedoes in addition to other dreadnoughts. In 1914 the battle instructions of the British fleet specified tactics that were similar to those of a century before, at least in their most distilled form. Admiral Jellicoe, however, also worried about floating mines dropped by retreating enemy ships, moored mines prepositioned for ambush, and torpedoes fired by surface ships or submarines. He had to account for these threats with only speculation and imagination to inform his countermeasures. There was no experience in war to season his instructions, and this led him to adopt tactics that Nelson would have considered pusillanimous—the most famous example being his instructions for the fleet to respond to an enemy torpedo attack by turning away. And what was the reason for such caution in the face of a hypothetical risk? Just that the irreplaceable nature of capital ships had reduced the level of acceptable risk. Losing battleships to mines or torpedoes without inflicting similar losses on the enemy would give the enemy an advantage that could be overcome only—if ever—by years of costly naval construction. In net effect, technology had invalidated the only suitable tactics for fighting with dreadnoughts. The strategic implication, which admiralties were reluctant to grasp, was that combat between fleets of capital ships had become a defensive exercise. A weak fleet would never knowingly dare to challenge a strong fleet. A strong fleet would decline to take risks, as did Jellicoe at Jutland, even with the opportunity to win a major victory at hand. Under such conditions, stalemate was the natural result.

By 1914, with combat governed by caution, the capital ship's strategic function had come to dominate its tactical function. Basically, because cost had escalated to the point where relatively few nations could afford to construct capital ships in any quantity, their primary function became to exist rather than to fight. Their very existence in superior numbers was enough to guarantee sea control. There was no point in fighting. This strategic aspect of the dreadnought revolution, as expressed in World War I, caught navies by surprise when it was recognized at all.

The admirals who developed fleet tactics were busy men with little time to explore the possibilities of untested technology. They used their platforms in the way they knew best. Accepting new technology and integrating it into the naval tool chest were neither natural nor easy processes; doing so was risky and took conscious effort and dedication from advocates and supporters in the highest places. The ruthless pressures of war brought out the true capabilities of technologies. Under wartime conditions, apparently "weak" technologies such as mines could completely transform the use and even the raison d'être of an alpha technology, the dreadnought battleship. Even an alpha technology must be open to innovative use if it is to remain relevant.

THE ROLE OF DOCTRINE

The evolutionary path from *Victory* to *Dreadnought* implies that victory favors superior arms, but is it really that simple? If technology grants a superiority in weaponry, is that technology sufficient in itself? The short answer is *no*. As will be seen, the effectiveness of many technologies depends upon numbers. Also critical are the methods used to select and develop new technologies and the doctrines governing their use. Ask, for example, what is a weapon without a target, or a platform without a weapon, or a tool without a use? The English longbow is famous as the decisive *weapon* of the Hundred Years' War. Yet England had the longbow 250 years before the 1346 battle of Crécy. The longbow did not become a decisive weapon until it had a decisive *target*—in this case, clustered masses of French chivalry. But a decisive weapon must have not only a target, but also a hand to wield it properly—the practice and technique to properly bend the bow. A secret memorandum from a British destroyer captain to his superior officer dated 26 December 1942 noted that he had at his disposal Type 285, 286, and 271 radars, sonar, a radio interception device, very high frequency radio, shore radar plots, enemy reports from remote sources, an automatic plotting device, and several binocular-enhanced sets of eyes. Much of the information derived from these tools required instantaneous action, not to mention the fact that he had "many other things to think of and duties to perform in action, particularly under conditions of modern night action." However, "unfortunately, up to date, adequate provision for co-ordinating and handling such information . . . has been lacking."[2] In other words, the captain had a mighty bow, but he could not bend it. He required doctrine, training, and practice.

Because the uses of new technology are rarely straightforward, establishing doctrine can be a tricky business. A technology without a doctrine will be misused or neglected. The image of hidebound battleship admirals stifling the development of new technologies is common, but what admiral ignores a clear path to victory, even if that path bypasses a favored weapon or platform? The trick is having systems to light the way. As Professor Irving Holley wrote in the early 1950s, "The greatest stumbling block to the revision of doctrine was probably not so much vested interests as the absence of a system for analyzing new weapons and their relation to prevailing concepts of utilizing weapons."[3]

The process of introducing and integrating new technology only begins with the better bow. There is the matter of selecting the proper target, determining the best circumstances of use, and, finally, of bending the bow itself. And then begins the hard part. Was the proper bending technique employed? Was the correct arrow used? Is there a better string? Is area or aimed fire better? Consider the sinuous path of radar's development. Originally envisioned as a collision warning device, it became, in less than forty years, a way to trigger antiaircraft rounds in the proximity of a target. In the end, it comes down to results. And, in war, results can only be truly measured in combat. Doctrine must be based upon results obtained through use, and only from use can innovation follow.

THE LIGHTS THAT FAILED

This book relates the development and use of six important and successful technologies, but to focus on success might give the false impression that every invention has a use, or that every use has a lasting purpose, or even that technologies with the strongest pedigrees and the most clearly defined uses will continued to be relevant. For navies, the ultimate criterion is whether the weapon/tool/platform effectively advances the task of securing power at sea and contributes to ultimate victory.

The searchlight is an example of a tool that had a specific combat use, one that navies believed would be decisive, and a technology that navies invested considerable research and funds to improve. However, when used in combat, it revealed itself also to be a weakness. Searchlights could illuminate the enemy and allow guns to target the enemy at night, but they also provided a wonderful point of aim. They did have successful and very specific applications, such as aircraft illuminating submarines, but the extensive and powerful arrays of searchlights on warships in World War II must be considered a failed technology; their use was restricted during the war, and by the end of the war, many were being landed to preserve topweight for other uses.

Shipborne rockets are another example of a dead-end technology. Although the naval use of rockets is immortalized in the U.S. national anthem, they disappeared from warships with improvements in naval artillery. The British reintroduced them in World War II as an antiaircraft weapon called the Unrotated Projectile. This weapon was supposed to lay an aerial minefield, but there is no record of one actually damaging an aircraft, and the bulky and ineffective system was landed within a year of its introduction. Rockets only became effective weapons in a sea fight when they found a better platform (in aircraft) and better accuracy (through electronic guidance).

Another dead end was the ram. Norman Friedman wrote, "Underwater weapons usable at sea were deeply subversive. The torpedo was the most important, but in its early years some naval officers saw the ram as a viable alternative."[4] And this makes sense; a ram was innovative in that it was a way to weaponize a platform, and it had proved deadly in the 1866 Battle of Lissa and during the 1879 War of the Pacific. But, in fact, rams were only practical during the brief era of slow-firing guns and, even then, only in very specific conditions.

CHOICES AND CONSTRAINTS

Another factor that affects the introduction, integration, and development of new technology, and the policy and doctrine essential to its use, is the matter of choice and naval culture. Navies are conservative organizations for good reason. The leaders of navies are responsible for the efficient use of massive repositories of national treasure and power. An environment of accelerating technological change and an increasing variety of new weapons/tools/platforms have forced naval professionals and policy-makers to make hard choices from a large (and at times confusing) range of alternatives. With the benefits of hindsight, it is easy to criticize these choices—why some navies pursued certain technologies and others did not—but the image of shellback admirals favoring outmoded weapons systems out of reverence for past practice, while both popular and powerful, is wrong. An article written more than eighty years after the fact condemns the leadership of the pre–World War II Italian navy because it "embraced the logic that older but effective technology was better than innovative technology." The principle that evoked this judgment was contained in instructions circulated by Admiral Domenico Cavagnari in January 1934: "A weapon, a simple device, resistant and of reliable functioning is—at sea—preferable to another that [is projected] to be more sophisticated and faster [but] is [also] more complex, fragile and less reliable."[5] In fact, it is impossible to think of the head of any navy, at any time, disagreeing with Cavagnari's basic principle. The goal of technological innovation at sea, in peace or in war, is to complete missions, improve outcomes, and ultimately to win wars. Innovation is an end to this means; it is not the means itself.

Conservatism in militaries, however, does exist, and it has many sources. New technology can threaten powerful vested interests and provoke backlash. Personally and professionally, the familiar often seems more comfortable than the novel and untested. Most officers would hesitate to tie their careers to an unproven technology. From an organizational standpoint, new technologies seldom fit neatly into existing structures, which means that they can be easy to shunt aside. New technologies often make significant demands on limited assets. Such demands are hard to justify where the benefits are speculative and impossible to quantify in peacetime. The impact of cost, and not just in the sense of budgets and balance sheets, is seldom fully recognized by critics. The obsolescence of battleships due to cost is hardly the only example. Consider naval propulsion, where the adoption of steam technology required the creation of a complex system to ship coal, store it, and supply it as and where needed. Why is nuclear propulsion so rare in combat ships today, despite its many advantages? Because it is so expensive. And while wartime brings more resources to bear, it also greatly increases demand for all resources.

All that said, navies have embraced innovation. They are not monolithic organizations closed to outside ideas. To the contrary, the best navies are constantly seeking an edge against their opponents and are constantly wary that their opponents have found an edge against them. Navies contain a mix of personalities, some dead set against change, others eager to embrace the next new thing, and most somewhere in between. How navies explore and adopt new technology stems from several factors. One way to explore this is to look at the nature of the technologies being considered. Where the technology facilitates an existing function, adoption comes more rapidly. Radio and radar are two examples. In general, tools have comparatively low costs and often have commercial applications that spur development. They promise increased effectiveness without overthrowing vested interests, although they also may have profound effects not recognized until after adoption. Weapons are an intermediate case. Acquisition costs are generally greater, particularly if the weapon requires a new platform. It is harder to judge their effectiveness, and their widespread adoption often challenges interests invested in older technologies. Torpedoes stand out here, with their proponents proclaiming the end of the battleship and their detractors dismissing the weapon. The hardest cases for innovation are platforms. These cost more than weapons or tools and are the hardest to test. A new platform can take a variety of shapes, making it harder to identify the optimum form to develop—particularly in times of peace. The torpedo boat and the submarine are good examples. They more frequently challenge vested interests, threatening to displace older platforms in budgets or making them obsolete in combat. Their effectiveness is hardest to test, and their adoption has the greatest doctrinal and strategic implications. And in some cases, such as aircraft, new technologies can provoke bitter power struggles between a nation's armed services.

The process of making difficult and often ambiguous choices and of separating "nice to have" from "need right now" is core to this study. Navies make choices based upon resources available and perceived needs. In some cases, the choices have proven wrong, and in other cases, the choices were forced. Moreover, comparisons about how different nations approached the matter of technological development must stress that the playing field was (and is) hardly level. It is not a competition with referees; fairness is not a factor. The process is regulated by a nation's wealth and scientific and industrial resources. It is possible for a nation to concentrate its economy on military matters (as in Japan's interwar "guns before rice" approach), but such choices will eventually cause political or economic collapse, as the Soviet Union discovered in 1989. The rule is the defeat of the weaker power. Victory against the odds is much the exception.

Italy, a second-tier economic power, went to war in 1940 without radar and without sonar. These are two foundational naval technologies that proved important to the Allied victory at sea. In the environment of the mid-1930s, however, when Italy's leadership did not envision the need to supply a ground war in Africa and the major anticipated foe was the French navy, the perceived need for these tools was not great enough to elevate this technology ahead of other apparently more pressing needs. In the matter of radar technology, Great Britain was a leader because policy-makers saw it as a solution to an existential threat: bombing attacks on cities. This concern was not so great in Italy, and the navy focused on technologies to meet its perceived needs. These included, for example, a functional air-dropped torpedo, innovative refits to turn pre–World War I dreadnoughts into usable modern platforms, secure communication technologies, weapons and techniques for insidious warfare, a large fleet of modern submarines, and world-class modern battleships. These were all matters of choice, and for the most part the technologies Italy chose to develop served the navy well, although the technologies it did not pursue because of lack of funding or perceived need also would have served it well. In the same vein, a list of Japanese technologies investigated by the U.S. scientific teams that swarmed Japan in September 1945 included "balloon bombs, the 'death ray,' radar, rockets, and heat-homing bombs." As in the case of Italy, these choices reflect a high/low mix of technologies, although unlike the Italians, who were more concerned with communications and platforms, Japanese research was inclined toward weapons.[6] These examples illustrate both the sheer number of possibilities for naval technologies and the cultural and political filters that influenced the choices each navy made.

Choices regarding technologies are also limited by other factors. As the costs of weapons/tools/platforms have increased through time, they have increasingly become available, selectively but especially in mass, only to the richest nations. After Italy developed usable radar and sonar in 1942, its electronics industry had a monthly production capacity of only six sets of each. One of the reasons Great Britain shared the secret of the cavity magnetron with the United States in 1940 was because its leadership recognized that the United States had the capacity to produce the hundreds of units each month that would be required if advanced radars were to be available in mass. One of the reasons Japan put resources into producing nine thousand weaponized hot air balloons was because they had the distributed craft-shop system and material to produce exactly such a thing. While devoting resources to weaponized origami is a choice open to criticism on several levels, it at least demonstrates innovation, its cultural basis, and, perhaps even more, its limitations.

This discussion sets the stage for the first of the technologies to be reviewed: mines. While mines were an old technology, they came into prominence in the twentieth century and played a major and evolving role in the three major naval wars fought from 1905 to 1945.

CHAPTER 2

MINES
The Neglected Weapon

Mines owe no allegiance to their makers and will
blow up friend or foe with strict impartiality.
—ARNOLD S. LOTT[1]

The concept of the mine is simple: a container filled with explosives comes into contact with a hull and detonates, blasting a hole at or below the target's waterline. Dating back a millennium, mines are the oldest naval technology considered in this book but one that did not mature until the Russo-Japanese War, when improvements in triggers and explosives met the need for area-specific defensive and offensive sea denial operations. World War I, which followed a decade later, confirmed the mine's importance as an essential naval weapon system. In the twenty-first century, continuing effectiveness and relatively low cost make mine and countermine warfare as important as ever. Given their long history and utility, it is ironic that mines have been a neglected technology in times of peace and one that navies have been slow to embrace in times of war.

THE TECHNOLOGY DESCRIBED, EARLY USE, EXPECTATIONS

A mine's basic elements are a container, an explosive, a trigger mechanism, and (unless the weapon floats on the surface or sits on the bottom) an anchor. The trigger detonates the mine upon contact with, or from the influence of, a passing vessel. There are descriptions from China's tenth-century Sung dynasty of containers filled with gunpowder submerged ten feet deep in coves or rivers to block traffic or protect small harbors. However, the Chinese never solved the problem of a reliable underwater fuze.[2] Fast-forward to 1776 when an American, David Bushnell, devised a weapon to be used against the British navy. He packed gunpowder into a barrel and crafted a flintlock trigger mechanism. The problem was delivery; Bushnell tried floating the barrel downstream, hoping it would bump against an anchored ship. He also constructed a one-man, pedal-driven submersible he called *Turtle*. Its mission was to fasten a mine to a ship's bottom. In several forays, *Turtle* was able to maneuver to a target but not to attach her weapon.

Bushnell recognized that his delivery systems were inefficient, but the practice of floating mines on the current persisted for another ninety years—an eternity in the history of technology. Mine warfare's first major innovation was to address the delivery problem by targeting moving ships with stationary mines. An early instance of this technology (as well as one of the first uses of electromagnetic technology in Western war—see chapters three and four) was an electrically-fired battery of bottom mines that defended Kiel harbor in the First Schleswig War (1848–51). The Russians were also early adopters, using moored, chemically fuzed contact mines to defend Kronstadt in the 1854 Crimean War. However, these systems were never tested in action, and the delivery question remained open.

Contact mines collected at Santiago, Cuba, 1898. Mines had no successes in the Spanish-American War, although the sinking of USS *Maine* in Havana harbor, allegedly by a Spanish mine, pushed the United States toward war. *(Library of Congress, 4a15165a, https://www.loc.gov/item/2016804855/)*

Two other early mine delivery systems were the spar torpedo and the towed torpedo ("torpedo" being the word first used to describe an underwater explosive charge). The spar torpedo consisted of an explosive charge attached to a long pole (the spar) projecting from the bow of a small boat. The pole would allow the boat's crew to jab the charge against the target's hull beneath its waterline. Spar torpedoes were first used successfully in the U.S. Civil War, where the Confederates damaged ironclad *New Ironsides* and sank *Housatonic* and the Union navy sank ironclad *Albemarle*. In action, the spar torpedo proved as dangerous to the user as to the target. Towed torpedoes were charges meant to be dragged across the path of a target so as to explode against its hull. Deploying a towed torpedo was difficult, and there are no documented instances of its successful use.[3]

The Confederacy used floating and moored mines to block rivers and defend coastal ports. Throughout the war, mines sank thirty-six vessels (all but one Union, and most in rivers) and although they inconvenienced Union forces, the technology was too unreliable to significantly limit the North's naval superiority or defeat its operations against Southern ports. The weapon's limitations were captured in Adm. David Farragut's legendary order when confronted by a field of moored contact mines: "Damn the torpedoes, full speed ahead."[4] Immediately before this order, Farragut had lost *Tecumseh*, his most powerful ironclad, to one of those mines, but the rest malfunctioned and Farragut won the day. In 1866 during the South American War of the Triple Alliance, Paraguayan defenders sank the new Brazilian ironclad *Rio de Janeiro* with floating mines. Such a result was an anomaly, however, and although mines were also used in the 1870 Franco-Prussian War, the 1877 Russo-Turkish War, and the 1898 Spanish-American War, they gained no success.

The mines deployed up through the U.S. Civil War used black powder as an explosive and percussion cap fuzes as a detonator. In 1846 a chemist accidentally spilled acid on a cotton apron, which ignited while being dried. Thus was discovered nitrocellulose or guncotton, which had six times the explosive force of black powder. Better explosives meant more power in a smaller package. Additional refinements followed, and by 1900 the most common mine explosives were picric acid mixes (the Japanese shimose, the French melinite, and the British lyddite). Picric acid was more shock resistant than nitrocellulose and thus considered safer. The Russians used

Recovered World War I German contact mine showing the distinctive Hertz horns that, when hit by a passing ship, would detonate the mine. *(Naval History and Heritage Command, NH 60757)*

pyroxylin, a soluble, less nitrated form of guncotton. An issue with all these explosives was shelf life and stability, with spontaneous explosion during handling or storage always being a concern. Trinitrotoluene (TNT), being more stable, was first used by the Germans in 1902, forty years after its invention, and replaced most picric acid explosives following World War I.

A mine's trigger mechanism needed to be safe, reliable, and robust—difficult qualities to ensure in something that had to function after being submerged for months or longer. The first triggers were impact types, and by 1905 horn and inertia systems dominated. A horn detonator was a soft metal protrusion on the mine's body that protected a glass tube filled with an electrolyte solution. A vessel hitting a mine would bend the horn, break the tube, and release the solution. The liquid would close a battery circuit and fire an electric detonator. Some nations, such as Great Britain, considered this method unreliable and dangerous and preferred an inertia system that used the force from an impact to propel separate elements of the mine into motion at different speeds. The difference in relative motions triggered the detonator. After World War I, more exotic detonators came into use; these consisted of triggers activated by a ship's magnetic field, by changes in water pressure caused by a ship passing overhead, or by sound.

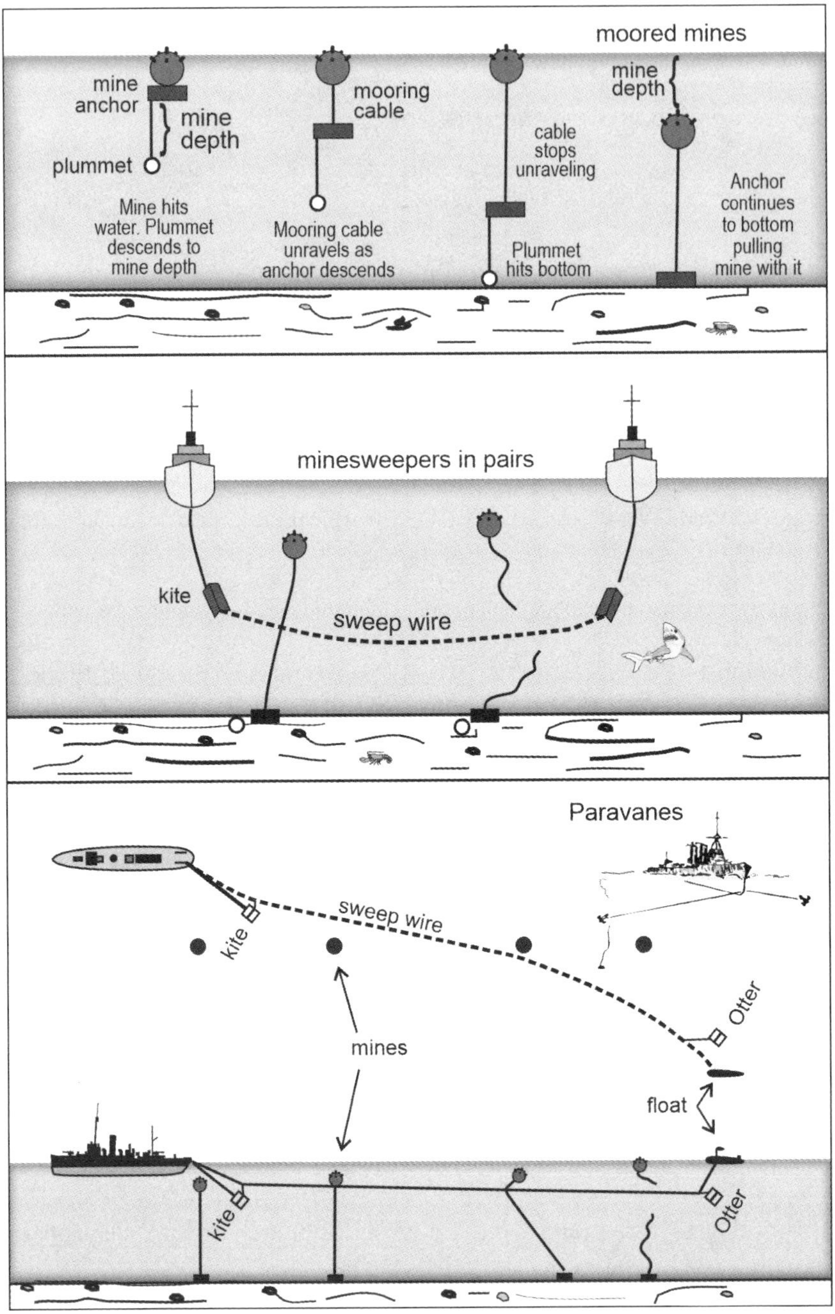

moored mines

mine anchor

mine depth

plummet

Mine hits water. Plummet descends to mine depth

mooring cable

Mooring cable unravels as anchor descends

cable stops unraveling

Plummet hits bottom

mine depth

Anchor continues to bottom pulling mine with it

minesweepers in pairs

kite

sweep wire

Paravanes

sweep wire

kite

Otter

mines

float

kite

Otter

FIGURE 2.1. Minelaying and Minesweeping. Shown are two techniques for sweeping moored mines and one technique for laying them.

The vast majority of mines used through the end of World War I were anchored contact types, and these remain in use today (see figure 2.1). Early types had mooring lines precut to the correct depth—practical only for defending friendly harbors. Where the water depth was not known, an early method of ensuring a constant mooring depth involved having a plummet weight hit the bottom first. This caused a claw to clamp down and stop the mooring line from further unraveling. The anchor would continue to descend, pulling the mine down with it to the depth set by how far the mooring line had already unraveled. This technique was later improved by a hydrostatic sensor that stopped the release of the mooring line at the desired depth. The British had an automatic anchor mechanism by 1890. Moored mines are always limited by the depth they can be anchored in, but this depth steadily increased as anchor mechanisms improved.[5]

Despite the development of better explosives and reliable detonators, several factors retarded the general acceptance of mine technology. Mines have a low unit cost, but they are expensive to store, maintain, and deploy in the numbers needed to be effective. More importantly, navies with powerful fleets shunned mine warfare. Throughout the nineteenth century, major navies considered mines a weapon of the weak and eschewed them as a hindrance to fleet operations. For these reasons, and because mines had not achieved any particular success in European warfare before 1904, general expectations were low. Most navies considered mines a coastal defense weapon, like shore batteries.[6] They were not generally recognized as being an independent weapon system with offensive capabilities that required a specialized branch of naval warfare to achieve the most effective use.

DISCOVERY: THE RUSSO-JAPANESE WAR

The first effective use of moored contact mines in combat occurred in the Russo-Japanese War (see figure 2.2). Japan was seeking to overthrow Russian power in China and Korea, and the first step in that process was to secure the sea lanes between Tokyo and the Asian mainland. Japan could only do this by neutralizing Russia's Asian fleet—its equal in capital ships—and, ideally, by capturing the main Russian naval base at Port Arthur (Dalian), Manchuria, before the Russians could send naval reinforcements from the Baltic. To this end, Japanese torpedo boats attacked the Russian fleet anchored at Port Arthur on 8 February 1904 without a

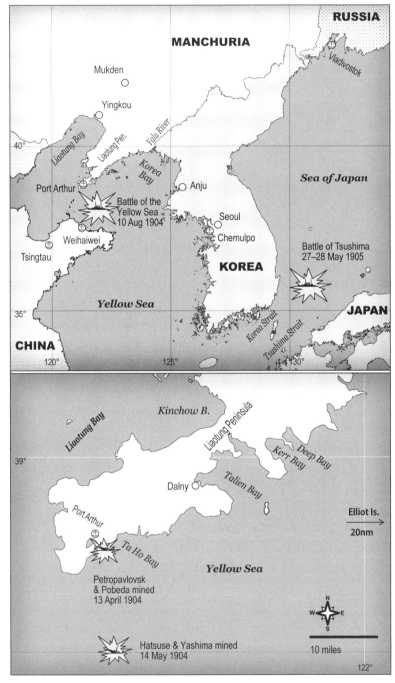

FIGURE 2.2. The Cockpit of the Russo-Japanese War. The Yellow Sea and the Sea of Japan, with an insert showing Port Arthur and environs.

declaration of war. The attack damaged two battleships and a cruiser and put the Russians on the defensive.[7]

Unwilling to contest Japanese landings with their diminished fleet, the Russians were forced to rely on mine warfare to protect their coasts and immediately sent minelayer *Yenisei* to lay a field off the entrance to Talien Bay thirty miles up the coast. This she did, but on the morning of 11 February *Yenisei* struck a drifting mine and sank with heavy loss of life. The cruiser *Boyarin*, coming to her assistance, was mined in the same field. These events suggest that the mines did not anchor as designed and that the barrage's placement was uncertain or hasty.[8]

The mines used by the two sides were state of the art. The Russians adopted a spherical mine in 1891 that was easier to manufacture, carried more explosive, and stored and handled better than its predecessors. It could be anchored at a set depth, and it used a reliable horn-type detonator. This mine initially carried 80 pounds of pyroxylin, increased to 140 pounds by 1897. The resulting M1898 was the basic mine equipping Russian forces in 1905. The Japanese deployed a spherical mine loaded with fifty pounds of shimose and detonated via an inertia trigger. A mechanical pawl mechanism regulated the mine's depth.[9]

After the loss of *Yenisei* and *Boyarin* in a "friendly" minefield, the Russians appointed a new admiral to head their mine warfare efforts and continued to mine potential landing sites, although not (at first) Port Arthur itself, where they relied upon the fleet and powerful shore batteries for protection. In this effort they created a mining force consisting of *Yenisei*'s sister ship *Amur*, an auxiliary, two torpedo gunboats, and two destroyers. This force thickened the barrage in Talien Bay. It then laid eight hundred mines in Deep and Kerr bays east of Talien and in bays to the west of the Liaotung peninsula and at Newchwang (Yingkou) at the head of Liaotung Bay—in other words, all likely landing sites from the Yalu River to the far side of the Liaotung peninsula.[10]

Japan pioneered the use of mines for offensive purposes. Concluding that the Russian fleet would not venture beyond the range of its shore batteries unless conditions heavily favored it, the Japanese decided to secretly mine inshore waters they had observed the Russian battleships sail through, an action accomplished on the night of 12 April by two divisions of destroyers, one division of torpedo boats, and the auxiliary minelayer

Koryo Maru. Although a Russian guard cruiser spotted the Japanese force, fleet commander Vice Admiral Stepan Makarov, who happened to be on board, believed that the unknown vessels were friendly destroyers and withheld fire.

The Japanese force laid forty-eight mines in two fields. The next morning a series of encounters ensued, first between a lost Russian destroyer and four Japanese destroyers, then cruisers, and then battleships. As Vice Admiral Makarov was leading his four battleships out to fight the six Japanese capital ships under the cover of his shore batteries, his flagship, the battleship *Petropavlovsk*, ran onto a mine that detonated the vessel's magazine. "A vast cloud of smoke and steam hung over the water, and when it lifted the *Petropavlovsk* had disappeared."[11] There were only 80 survivors from a crew of 632, and Makarov was not among them. The Russians continued the action, but thirty-five minutes later the battleship *Pobeda* hit a mine that exploded under her coal bunker. She was three months in repair. Japan's offensive use of mines was an innovation that surprised the Russians and tipped the naval balance heavily in Japan's favor. Moreover, this transformed the nature of mine warfare and greatly enhanced the weapon's general reputation. Navies realized that mines gave them a new capability: the ability to not just defend maritime geography, but to shape it.

Mines punished complacency. In the war's first months, Russia had suffered all the damage. This changed on 15 May when two Japanese battleships ran into a Russian minefield twelve miles south of Port Arthur. The battleship *Hatsuse* struck one, was taken under tow, and then hit a second mine, which detonated her magazine and destroyed her. *Yashima* also hit a mine and capsized while under tow. Throughout the war the Japanese lost nineteen warships, eleven of which were mined off the Liaotung peninsula. The Russians, meanwhile, faced intensive Japanese efforts to trap their fleet inside Port Arthur using mines and block ships. These attempts were never entirely successful, but they complicated Russian forays and required time and resources to sweep clear channels.

Improvements in mine warfare came from practice rather than from significant enhancements in material or techniques. Delivery methods also remained essentially unchanged except for one Japanese innovation that harkened back to the days of the towed torpedo. This was to drop a chain of four floating mines in the path of oncoming warships. One such chain, dropped at night by torpedo boats in the path of *Navarin* following the Battle of Tsushima, sank the Russian battleship. Although the weapon was considered top secret, the British naval attaché learned of it in 1909, and it sparked concern in London. Fear of floating mine weapons certainly affected the tactics the British fleet practiced in World War I. In the event, however, the mine chain proved difficult to deploy, and the occasions for its use were too rare to justify further development by any navy.[12]

COUNTERMEASURES

The unanticipated impact of mines forced both the Japanese and the Russians to improvise ways to remove them. An early technique was for specially reinforced ships to sail ahead of more valuable vessels to act as mine exploders—costly and uncertain, but still used by the Germans in both world wars and the United States in Vietnam. Another method was countermining, which involved detonating explosives in a minefield in the hopes of causing the mines themselves to explode. This practice was unreliable, however, and was easily countered with proper spacing. Yet another method used during the U.S. Civil War was an explosive mine-catching device that was attached to a float and pushed ahead of the minesweeping vessel. However, the best method against anchored mines, also from the Civil War, was to use a wire or grapple to snag the mooring line, or cut it altogether, and bring the mine to the surface. On 12 May 1904 the Japanese started clearing Kerr Bay using torpedo boats and grapples for the job and losing *T48* and supporting cruiser *Miyako* in the process. The Russians preferred to employ steam tugs; a single tug might tow a grappling hook, or a team of tugs might traverse a field with a hawser slung between them. The paired sweeper technique required precise coordination and good conditions and at first did not work well because the hawser tended to rise above the depth of the mines. Weights partially solved this problem. A further improvement was to use a kite, a device that streamed off the towing cable and dynamically regulated the cable's depth. This also allowed sweeps to be deployed at an angle from a ship's stern. The function of the sweep remained to cut the mooring cable and bring the mine to the surface, where it could be detonated or sunk with gunfire, or to snag the mine with an explosive charge. The best defense against floating mines was a sharp lookout.[13]

REVISED EXPECTATIONS

The world's major navies paid rapt attention to the events of the Russo-Japanese War and scrutinized the conflict for lessons about new technologies likely to influence the clash of fleets anticipated in a future war. In 1908 the Naval Institute *Proceedings* carried a French article reporting that "the Russo-Japanese war demonstrated in a striking fashion the danger of submarine mines. . . . As a result of this war, submarine mines have assumed a very important place in the considerations of various navies."[14] In 1910 the British likewise considered that "one of the most striking features of the war is the great development of the mechanical mine."[15]

By 1914 the major European navies had a variety of resources and policies relating to mine warfare. That they had some appreciation of the lethality of mine technology was demonstrated by both the accumulated mine stocks on hand and the fact that Great Powers had sought to regulate their use. The 1907 Hague Convention banned unanchored mines unless they had disarming mechanisms and anchored mines that did not "become harmless as soon as they have broken loose from their moorings." More importantly, it forbade the use of mines with the sole object of targeting commercial vessels. The United States, Japan, Austria-Hungary, Italy, and Great Britain unconditionally accepted these limitations; Germany, France, and the Ottoman Empire accepted them with conditions, and Russia did not accept them at all. Great Britain had tried to get mines banned altogether, but the Germans and Russians vetoed that idea. The restrictions that resulted were vague and unenforceable.[16]

In 1914 Russia was the world's leading practitioner of mine warfare. Fearing a German naval attack on Petrograd, Russia planned a massive mine barrage to bar entry into the Gulf of Finland. Heavy gun batteries on the flanks and the battlefleet waiting beyond to the east would support this barrier, while to the west, patrols of torpedo craft operating out of Moon Sound and submarines from Revel would shield it. The Russians also planned to lay offensive mine barrages off German Baltic ports. The Russians were well equipped to practice this coherent strategy, having 7,000 mines in the Baltic, 4,500 in the Black Sea, and 4,000 in the Far East. They primarily employed reliable Hertz-horned types and deployed purpose-built minelayers and minesweepers as well as destroyers readily convertible to minelaying. As a German submarine captain later wrote,

"No U-boat captain . . . willingly entered the Gulf of Finland. . . . everyone who had any say in the matter steered clear of Russian operations."[17]

Germany likewise emphasized mine warfare. As early as 1905 the imperial navy grouped old torpedo boats into specialized minesweeping units. Its inventory of mines consisted largely of Hertz-horned types. The navy deployed two small cruiser-minelayers and a larger auxiliary with plans to convert a dozen more mercantile vessels into minelayers. The Germans intended to mine major enemy ports in the Baltic, the west coast of France, and the British Isles. Mobilization plans included the formation of auxiliary minesweeping divisions of fishing trawlers and drifters.[18]

Great Britain expected less from mine warfare, although it did anticipate that Germany would mine British ports in the event of war, and the navy converted thirteen torpedo gunboats into sweepers in 1908. These used the method of slinging a hawser between two vessels and regulating depth with a kite. In 1909 preparations continued with the conversion of four trawlers into minesweepers. This was the basis for an auxiliary minesweeping force that was operating 250 trawlers by September 1914. The British also used seven old cruisers as minelayers. The major problem was that the primary British mine, the Elias, of which four thousand were in stock, used a flawed inertia detonation mechanism that was subject to premature detonation—when it detonated at all. As one senior British mining officer explained, "Our mine was developed by one Senior Staff Officer in *Vernon*, assisted by a draughtsman. . . . There were no proper trial facilities, and it took the outbreak of war to show that it was a most inaccurate depth taken [sic] that it might (and did) go off at any time except when it was struck by an enemy. It took two years of war, experimenting as we went along, before anything like a satisfactory mine was achieved."[19]

France had an inventory of 2,800 contact mines by 1911, half of which were obsolete. Delivery assets included two converted torpedo gunboats, two purpose-built vessels, a pair of light cruisers, and seven destroyers fitted with rails. The navy envisioned harbor defense as the major use for its mines. France began the war with four small purpose-built sweepers but expanded this force with requisitioned trawlers, thirty of which were on hand in August. The French navy preferred the Ronarc'h method of sweeping, named after the admiral who developed the technique in 1910.

This involved streaming two wires in the form of a *V* from the stern of a single sweeper using kites to maintain depth and keep the wires at an angle from the hull.[20]

Italy used four old torpedo cruisers and auxiliaries as minelayers. The navy's prewar planning for a war against France and Great Britain had to be redirected against Austria-Hungary after Italy abandoned the Triple Alliance. For a war against Vienna, Italy envisioned extensive minelaying in the upper Adriatic to deny the Hapsburg battlefleet access to the high seas. The country began the war with 3,700 modern mines in stock. Austria-Hungary's plans focused on defensive mine barrages to protect the empire's long coastline. The navy had one new and three old minelayers available in 1914. Old torpedo boats and five requisitioned auxiliaries comprised the dual monarchy's initial minesweeping forces.[21]

EVOLUTION: WORLD WAR I

Germany's first offensive naval action of World War I was to dispatch the hastily adapted auxiliary minelayer *Könige Luise*, disguised in the livery of a Great Eastern Railway steamer, into British waters to lay a barrage off the mouth of the Thames. On 5 August 1914 the light cruiser *Amphion* and a pair of destroyers encountered the German vessel and were fooled by her disguise until a fishing trawler reported seeing the crew throwing objects overboard. The British squadron returned and sank the German ship. Then *Amphion* ran across *Könige Luise*'s freshly laid field and was herself sunk. Thus, the first German and British losses in the war came as a consequence of mine warfare.[22]

In the following months the Germans also mined the approaches to the Humber and Lough Swilly in northern Ireland. The latter field caused the loss of the new dreadnought *Audacious* on 27 October 1914, demonstrating that the simple mine was capable of eliminating the most modern and powerful of warships anywhere and at any time.

The naval powers in 1914 faced a conundrum: to what extent was mining appropriate? Only the Russians had an overarching strategy, which they immediately implemented, using their preexisting minelayers to seed their large stocks of effective mines into their planned barriers. The questions of whether to mine, and where, were not so easy for the British or Germans. The major German North Sea naval bases lay at the southeastern corner of

The effects of a German mine on the hull of the passenger liner SS *New York*, damaged in the Mersey in 1917. This effect from underwater explosions enhanced the destructive force of mines and torpedoes, as had been demonstrated as early as 1805. *(Naval History and Heritage Command, NH 45137)*

Heligoland Bight, guarded by an outpost on the island of Heligoland itself. At the start of the war, the Germans laid fields directly in the approaches to these ports but elected to defend the bight with patrols of flotilla craft because they did not wish to complicate their navigation with minefields more than was absolutely necessary.[23]

The Germans learned in the 28 August 1914 Battle of Heligoland Bight, when the British surprised the patrolling flotillas with a superior force and sank three light cruisers and a torpedo boat, that navigational convenience came at a price. Spurred by their losses and the continuing wear and tear on their patrol forces, they began to mine the bight shortly thereafter.

The British began the war with a cautious attitude toward minelaying, both offensive and defensive. Although some advocates wanted to mine the Germans in, the British admiralty had a low opinion of offensive fields, was reluctant to impede navigation, and did not wish to unnecessarily aggravate any neutrals. Moreover, they wanted the German fleet to come out and did not consider desirable anything that impeded that goal. As late as 1915 Winston Churchill told Admiral Jellicoe that "we have never laid [a minefield] that we have not afterward regretted."[24] Like the Germans, the British initially preferred to protect their coast with patrols of flotilla craft and submarines, but these also proved unequal to the threat, as the Germans demonstrated in the war's first months by bombarding minor east coast ports, seemingly at will.[25]

The British laid defensive fields in August 1914 to screen the passage of troops to France and went on to sow 3,064 mines off Zeebrugge and in the Dover Strait by the end of the year. They did not place their first offensive minefield until 8 January 1915, when a field was laid off the Amrum Bank. As historian Arthur Marder expressed it, "Mines simply were not taken seriously before the war. They were regarded . . . as the 'weapon of the weak' and as 'rather expensive luxuries.'"[26]

Two campaigns in 1915 eliminated any doubt about the value of defensive mining. The first was the March 1915 Anglo-French naval attack against the Ottoman forts and minefields defending the Dardanelles. In this instance the Entente admirals believed they could force a fleet up the long and narrow passage—neutralizing shore batteries as they proceeded, landing shore parties as needed—and attack Constantinople with warships. They anticipated facing barrages of moored contact mines and perhaps floating mines and had collected a division of twenty-eight drifters to handle sweeping duties. These were manned by civilians and could only make three knots against the swift current that issued out of the strait. Searchlights frustrated attempts to sweep at night by illuminating the drifters for Ottoman shore batteries. The supporting battleships could not suppress the batteries because unswept mines kept them back. After several unsuccessful sweeping attempts, some navy critics concluded that the civilian drifter crews lacked courage. In another attempt, with the drifters under naval command and stiffened by an infusion of volunteer ratings, Ottoman batteries peppered most of the little boats with gunfire—despite a plastering from Entente battleships—and still few mines were swept. It was what one British officer called "a V.C. [Victoria Cross] sort of job."[27]

On 18 March, after a day of bombarding shore batteries and taking damage in return, British and French capital ships gave way to minesweepers. Ottoman mobile batteries shot them up and few mines were swept when, in a four-hour span, the predreadnoughts *Bouvet*, *Irresistible*, and *Ocean* were mined and sunk. *Bouvet* foundered in two minutes at 1354 and took 640 men with her. The modern battlecruiser *Inflexible* was holed as well but managed to avoid sinking by beaching off Tenedos with 1,600 tons of water in her. This disaster was caused by a hitherto unknown line of twenty mines laid by an Ottoman auxiliary the night before. Afterward, the commanders concluded that at least one shore would need to be taken before the minefields could be dealt with. Thus, the mines remained unswept, the passage remained blocked, and the Allies spent the rest of 1915 in a costly and futile land campaign. Thus did the simple mine exert power.

The other early war example came in the Baltic where the Germans tried to force entry into the Gulf of Riga. The German army was advancing on Riga at this time, and the German admiralty anticipated that a squadron supported by battleships could deal with the pesky Russian naval forces in the gulf while establishing a maritime line of supply to assist the army's advance. The Germans shifted units of the main fleet to the Baltic and established overwhelming surface superiority, but a thick mine barrage blocked Irben Strait leading into the gulf. The barrier was further supported by shore batteries and naval forces, including the predreadnought *Slava*. The Germans estimated the job of clearing the barrier would take three hours, but after five and a half hours of sweeping, starting on 8 August 1915, they had only opened a narrow passage at the cost of a light cruiser and destroyer mined and damaged and a minesweeper sunk. Then the Germans discovered another layer of mines when a second minesweeper exploded and sank. After that, running low on coal and worried about submarines, the Germans called it a day.[28] Over the next few nights, the Russians laid another 350 mines in the cleared areas. It took until 16 August for the Germans to organize another major minesweeping effort, and for that they allocated five days, not three hours. After additional losses, the Germans finally broke into the Gulf of Riga on 19 August and spent the day sinking a few minor Russian vessels and dodging enemy submarines, except for the battlecruiser *Moltke* torpedoed by the British boat *E1*. The Russians still retained secure bases on Moon and Ösel islands from which minelayers could sally each night, and the Germans had little appetite for continuing to expose valuable dreadnoughts to the perils of mine and torpedo. As was being demonstrated in the Dardanelles, breaching an enemy position defended by mines backed up by shore batteries and warships was far from easy, even with overwhelming naval superiority. After only a day the Germans abandoned the gulf to the Russians. The front lines stalemated, and Riga held out for another two years.[29]

In 1915 submarine and mine technology converged in two important ways. First, submarines became an important new mine delivery system. The Germans began this innovation with their small UC-type boats, seventeen of which were completed by May 1915. Although a UC boat could carry just twelve small mines, it could deliver these secretly and in places, such as the English west coast, where surface ships could not venture. The British did not realize that submarines were planting mines until they inspected the wreck of *UC-2*, which they raised after a coaster hit and sank her on 2 July 1915. Moreover, the impact of this delivery system was not just from the quantity of mines deployed or damage inflicted. As a minesweeping officer expressed it, "The small batches of mines constantly being discovered greatly hampered coastal navigation by the frequent stoppage and diversion of traffic." The minelaying submarines also brought the menace to French ports when a field was discovered off Calais on 14 July. The French official history noted that "this was the start of a campaign which, in the English Channel, would do much more damage than the direct attack of submarines."[30]

Mines threatened submarines as well. Mine barriers were the best way to protect friendly waters against them and were, until the appearance of the depth charge in 1916, the only practical way to sink a submerged submarine (see chapter six). In short, the growing utility of submarines gave all belligerents another reason to engage in offensive and defensive mine warfare, and the use of submarines to lay mines gave navies the ability to attack geography in places where surface vessels dared not venture.

As the war continued, the British overcame their original qualms about offensive mining, laying 4,538 mines in the Heligoland Bight during 1915.

Meanwhile, they laid many more in defensive fields.[31] This effort exposed some serious problems. First, the inventory of mines available was insufficient to meet the demands of defending British ports, maintaining blocking minefields off Dover and the Belgian coast, and overseas requirements (as in the Mediterranean). The defects of the British Elias model inertia mine have already been described, but the British technical agency responsible for developing mines, HMS *Vernon*, was slow to acknowledge its faults. As historian James Goldrick has written, "Too much time was taken to acknowledge the problems that British mines experienced and even more was consumed fiddling over alternative and unnecessary solutions." It took from May 1915, when *Vernon* first acknowledged the mine's faults, until mid-1917 before copies of the effective German Hertz-horned types began to appear in numbers.[32]

In the upper Adriatic, the Austro-Hungarians and Italians strewed minefields off each other's ports and coastlines. These, along with the submarine threat, slowed the tempo of naval warfare, at least for the larger warships. In the lower Adriatic, the principal mining activity was centered on the Strait of Otranto. The Entente powers calculated that this relatively narrow (but deep) passage could be closed to submarines with nets, patrols, and mines, but the barrier proved porous and only accounted for two confirmed kills. It acted more as an annoyance to Hohenzollern and Hapsburg submarine skippers while the Entente drifters patrolling it provided a soft and convenient target for frequent Austro-Hungarian raids.[33]

The year 1917 saw accelerated efforts to use the mine against submarines. In the Mediterranean, this meant more drifters and nets and patrol destroyers deployed to reinforce the Otranto mine barrier, all at great effort and expense but for minimal effect. After all but abandoning offensive minelaying in the Heligoland Bight in 1916 (only 1,782 mines laid), the British put down 15,686 mines in 1917 and 22,006 in ten months during 1918 (see figure 2.3).[34] This forced the Germans to constantly maintain swept lanes out to a hundred miles from the coast to get submarines and other warships to sea. These fields exacted a toll of minesweepers and scored an occasional success against a submarine or warship. Their greatest impact, however, was to make the sweepers themselves so important that they became the objective of fleet operations. The clearest expression of this

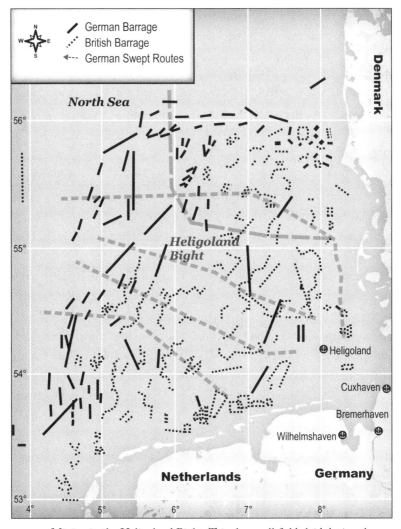

FIGURE 2.3. Mining in the Heligoland Bight. This shows all fields laid during the course of the war. Mining in the bight intensified throughout World War I, from simple defensive barrages in front of harbor mouths and occasional offensive fields to the point that the bight was clotted with mines.

transformation was the Second Battle of Heligoland Bight in which a British raid on German minesweepers operating 120 miles from the Elbe led to a running battle through mine-constrained waters, with capital ships on both sides engaged. By the end of the war, battleships were supporting minesweepers rather than the reverse.[35] In the Baltic, the Germans managed to sweep the Gulf of Riga defenses once and for all and capture the

TABLE 2.1

MINES LAID IN WORLD WAR I

Great Britain	128,652
United States	56,033
Russia	52,864
Germany	43,656
Italy	12,293
Austria-Hungary	5,650
France	4,700
Others	748

Sources: Dorling, *Swept Channels*, 337; O'Hara, Dickson, and Worth, *To Crown the Waves*, 74; Greger, *Russian Fleet*, 34, 70.

Baltic islands, but they never seriously challenged the massive barrages in the Gulf of Finland. A destroyer probe of the barrier's fringe cost the Germans seven destroyers in a single night.

History's greatest minelaying effort took place in 1918 when the United States conceived the plan of blocking entry into the Atlantic with a massive mine barrier running the width of the North Sea from Scapa Flow north of Scotland to near Stavanger in Norway. To this end, the Americans laid 56,033 and the British 15,093 mines between March and October 1918. The barrage probably accounted for less than one submarine sunk for every ten thousand mines laid, and the British admiralty never wholeheartedly supported the project, but the barrage was not completed so its effectiveness cannot be fairly evaluated. Nonetheless, the Northern Barrage is a powerful statement of how important mine warfare had become by 1918. Throughout the war, the major navies laid mines in the quantities shown in table 2.1.

COUNTERMEASURES, CONTINUED

The amount of minesweeping activity undertaken during World War I dwarfed anything before. Moored contact mines were the major threat; these were neutralized as they had been in the Russo-Japanese War, by cutting the mooring line with a towed wire and then detonating the mine when it came to the surface, usually with gunfire. Navies employed two major methods for engaging and cutting mooring lines: the first was the

Russo-Japanese War technique of using a sweeping wire run between two ships. An alternative method was the Ronarc'h method. These basic techniques were used by all navies with the British favoring the two-sweeper method. For them, it "was the means of destroying 30,000 mines during and after the war." The French, Russians, Italians, and Americans (after 1917) preferred the one-sweeper method.[36]

Of the wartime innovations, the British staff history of mine warfare considered the serrated wire "the greatest technical improvement in sweeping."[37] This came into general use in the British navy in 1916. It increased the likelihood that a sweep would cut a mine's mooring cable rather than merely dragging the mine along behind the sweepers. Another important countermeasure was the invention of the paravane—introduced into British service in 1916 as a towed explosive device for use against submarines but, as British author and destroyer commander H. Taprell Dorling wrote of its use in that guise, "We hated the contrivance, which was difficult to use, and always going wrong."[38] It was far more successful as a form of self-protection for vessels sailing in mined waters. It consisted of a pair of torpedo-shaped kites designed to be fitted on any ship, not just sweepers, and to be useable at higher speeds. It was fitted with a control vane to maintain depth and usually streamed from both sides of a ship's bow. The vessel's speed caused the line to extend laterally from the streaming vessel (and hopefully created enough of a wake to keep a mine from colliding with the ship head-on). By the end of the war, 188 British warships and 2,740 merchant vessels carried paravanes.[39]

Mines with more sophisticated trigger mechanisms that sat on the bottom could defeat traditional methods of sweeping, but such mines saw little use and then only at the end of the war. Sweeping was a repetitive affair. A field needed to be covered many times, and even then, all a minesweeper could do was lower the risk to an acceptable level. As shown at the Dardanelles, sweeping was virtually impossible at night or when under fire.

EXPLOITATION: WORLD WAR II

In the twenty years between World War I and World War II, advances in mine technology included the development of sophisticated trigger mechanisms activated by water pressure, sound, or magnetic fields instead of contact. The creation of new delivery systems such as aircraft expanded the range of mine warfare, but there was also a return to eighteenth-century methods brought up to date. Italy, which had sunk ex–Austro-Hungarian dreadnought *Viribus Unitis* with hand-delivered mines at the very end of World War I, refined the tools to deliver limpet mines using motorized two-man submersible sleds. The hand-delivered method was successful enough in World War II to be directly copied by the Germans and British.

In 1918 the British developed a bottom mine triggered by magnetic disruptions induced by a ship passing close by and deployed it in small numbers. They spent the interwar years trying to improve this weapon as the original model "behaved so capriciously that it had never been seriously pursued."[40] Along with investigating influence triggers, the British also considered ways to foil magnetic triggers, and they improved the anchoring systems on their contact mines. In 1923 Germany also started working on a magnetic exploder and perfected this device by 1936. Given that sweeping techniques remained those practiced in World War I, the Germans believed that effective countermeasures to their new, secret magnetic mine would take at least a year to implement and that the mine would cause a major disruption to enemy traffic once deployed. Moreover, because it did not require an anchor and cable, it was lighter and could be delivered by aircraft. Anticipating that their magnetic trigger would eventually be countered, Germany also started work on acoustic and pressure triggers in 1938, but these were not ready when war started.[41]

It is not possible here to sketch more than a brief outline of mine warfare as practiced in World War II. Mine stocks and reliability were generally better than in 1914, and all major navies possessed at least some specialized mine warfare vessels. Beyond this, mine warfare received relatively little consideration prewar, with the general attitude being that the tools and techniques of World War I would suffice. Only Germany and Great Britain spent any time working on influence mines between the wars, despite their potential for inflicting havoc. It might seem that Italy and Japan, in particular, would have been drawn to the advantages that mine warfare conducted with the very best weapons could have given them, but as with other navies, most of their available money went into capital ships or other pressing issues. The overall lack of attention to mine warfare in the interwar period was remarkable considering how effective it had been in World War I. In fact, admiralties disregarded this weapon because they considered it defensive, it was not a prestigious specialty like gunnery or aviation, and it endangered navigation. The professional head of the British admiralty even disdainfully compared minesweeping to "rat-catching."[42] Nonetheless, Great Britain laid 260,500 mines in World War II: 70 percent in defensive barrages and the rest offensively. This included 90,000 mines in a defensive barrier between Iceland and the Orkneys—a truncated version of the World War I Northern Barrage and one that produced even smaller results, sinking only three enemy submarines. Specialized minelayers accounted for 71 percent of the British mines laid, with aircraft contributing 21 percent, destroyers 3 percent, small craft such as motor launches 3 percent, and submarines 2 percent.[43]

The United States Navy deployed a specialized minelaying submarine in 1929, but she was never used for her assigned task when war arrived. According to one expert, "In 1939 the United States was more or less where it had been twenty years before with respect to mine warfare." However, once the fighting started in Europe and the U.S. Navy started to get information from the British and to see what the Germans were doing, things changed swiftly. The United States began developing influence mines in 1941; these included magnetic, acoustic, and pressure mines and dual-trigger systems to make the mines harder to sweep. The Americans considered and rejected triggers based on cosmic rays and gravitational, optical, and electric potential influences.[44]

France started the war with a large inventory of good quality moored contact mines and a fast minelaying cruiser, *Pluton*, along with six specialized minelaying submarines. France had, however, little opportunity to practice mine warfare, given the way its war developed. *Pluton* herself was destroyed in September 1939 at Casablanca when an explosion occurred as she offloaded mines.

Italy began the war with an inventory of 25,000 contact mines, the majority of which were the Bollo 1928 and the Elia 1925 models. They were reserved for defensive barrages. The Regia Marina preferred the more modern 1936 P200 for offensive barrages and to defend especially critical points such as Taranto, as it was considered more reliable, contained more explosive, and could be laid at greater depths. Italy did not start to develop magnetic and acoustic triggers until 1941, which was too late for its war, although the navy did receive some air-deliverable magnetic mines from Germany.[45] During its thirty-nine months of conflict against the Allies, the Italians deployed 54,457 mines. This, in fact, was the major activity undertaken by the Italian navy in the war's first five weeks, when it laid 10,928 mines in 223 barrages up and down both coasts, around its major islands, in the Aegean, off Libya, and in the Red Sea.[46] Once the navy had met basic defensive needs, it proceeded to lay offensive fields off Malta and in the Sicilian straits. Italian mines sank thirty-four vessels, including eleven British submarines. The greatest conventional mining success was the destruction of Force K off Tripoli on 19 December 1941, which cost the British a light cruiser and a destroyer with two light cruisers damaged. This came together on that same date with the attack on the main British naval base at Alexandria, Egypt, in which mines delivered by Italian naval swimmers disabled two battleships, a tanker, and a destroyer. The combined losses represented the single greatest triumph of mine warfare in any war, not because of the count of ships sunk and damaged but because of their profound impact on the struggle for sea supremacy in the Mediterranean and the land campaign in North Africa at a moment when the British were trying to conquer Libya.[47] Again did the simple mine exert power.

The Soviet navy maintained the mine warfare strategy of its czarist antecedents, and immediately following the German invasion, Red warships laid a number of defensive barrages off Sevastopol, across the mouth of the White Sea in the Arctic, along the Baltic coast, and to secure the Gulf of Finland. Two Soviet-era historians noted, however, that "mining the central position took eight days. Compared to the four and one-half hours it took the Baltic Fleet to mine the central position in 1914, the tempo of the June 1941 minelaying operation cannot be rated very high."[48] The Germans did not deploy major units in the Baltic until 1944, and the largest vessel lost to Soviet mines was the Finnish armored ship *Ilmarinen*, mined off Hangö on 13 September 1941. One significant mining action occurred in the Baltic when the German advance forced the Soviets to evacuate three divisions from Revel, Estonia, in August 1941. German and Finnish forces tried to seal them in with a barrier consisting of 2,828 mines backed by coastal batteries. The Soviets organized 170 ships into four convoys, carrying roughly 40,000 troops and civilians. The mine barrage, air attacks, and artillery cost the Soviets sixty-five ships and about 14,000 men. The Germans regarded this "as the most successful mining operation in the history of naval warfare."[49]

Japan also relied on contact mines but throughout the war did little mining beyond the Home Islands. The U.S. Navy found few fields in the Solomons, New Guinea, and the Pacific Islands. Even at Okinawa near the end of the war, the Navy only encountered six fields and swept just 184 mines and explosive devices. There were no influence mines.[50] As Mark Peattie, a top historian of the Japanese navy, concluded, the Japanese believed that "due to the navy's increasing emphasis on aircraft and to its protective improvements for surface warships, mines had become obsolete weapons."[51] As a Japanese mine warfare officer put it, "During the first years of the war little importance was attached to mine warfare. However, in 1945 when mines were used in quantity, they became of great concern to all leaders."[52]

In September 1939 Germany had in stock 20,000 contact and 1,500 magnetic mines of various types, including versions designed for aerial and submarine deployment. German submarines planted several fields of magnetic mines in September and October, and the results pleased Germany's naval staff. As early as 10 October Grand Admiral Erich Raeder gave Hitler a favorable report and urged the use of aircraft to drop mines. Over the war's first four months, German magnetic mines caused a sensation. A U.S. naval officer observing the situation in Liverpool wrote: "Ships broken in half in the middle lay around the harbor. There were victims of the new ground mines." Overall, mines sank seventy-nine merchant ships grossing 262,697 tons "and had dislocated the flow of [British] coastal shipping very seriously." Many other ships were damaged, including the battleship *Nelson*.[53] In five aerial operations conducted between 20 November and 7 December 1939 the German air force used seaplanes to drop sixty-seven magnetic mines in five locations off the east coast of Great Britain. However, they had to halt this campaign by 7 December because ice grounded the seaplanes, and the air force did not make wheeled aircraft available for the job until April 1941. Worse, the aircraft drops were not always well placed, and on 23 November the British recovered and disarmed two magnetic mines that had landed in tidal waters. Although the mines had a self-destruct mechanism that was supposed to activate if they did not sink to at least eight feet, it did not function in these instances.[54]

Once they had an example of an enemy magnetic mine in hand, the British quickly determined that they could render the device harmless by changing a vessel's magnetic polarity in a process called degaussing. These findings, as well as examples of German mines, were shared with the Americans. This kickstarted the U.S. development of influence mines and helped the U.S. Navy to establish its first underwater mine demolition and countermeasure school in April 1941. As the school's first director later recalled, "They taught us all they knew about these things."[55] This exchange is also an example of how Anglo-American cooperation accelerated their efforts to improve naval technology. It stands, as will be seen, in stark contrast to Axis practice.

Mine warfare in World War II unfolded in a tit-for-tat process common throughout the history of innovation. Along with degaussing, the British also developed a magnetic sweep, basically a long, insulated wire that generated a magnetic field to explode the mines. The Germans came up with several responses to these countermeasures. They made the trigger bipolar, they inserted a counter into the trigger so that a mine might not explode until it had been triggered a set number of times, and they sowed fields of mixed mine types. Safeguards against even the simplest type of magnetic mine were costly. In a purely prophylactic measure undertaken on the possibility a ship might encounter a magnetic mine, the U.S. Navy degaussed 12,693 ships—including 6,422 naval vessels—at an average cost of $23,357 per vessel.[56]

Some of the methods used to outfox and frustrate the enemy in the deadly game of mine-countermine were truly ingenious. Countersweeping devices included clocks, for example, that delayed activation of an influence mine for a period of a half hour up to six days. By the end of the war, the Germans were using clocks with delays of up to two hundred days. Devices delaying a mine's detonation until after a set number of activations have already been mentioned. Even more creative were devices that activated the mines for certain times of day only. Noticing that British sweepers worked in the mornings, for example, the Germans set their timers to keep the mines dormant during normal sweeping hours. The Germans also used booby traps designed to prevent capture, but after several accidents involving the loss of German personnel, these fell out of favor and during the latter part of the war were used infrequently.[57]

Dual-trigger (combination) influence mines were the next step in the technology's progress. The first dual-trigger mines that appeared in 1941 were magnetic/acoustic units. Pressure/magnetic and pressure/acoustic units followed in 1942. Having learned their lesson with magnetic mines, the Germans delayed the introduction of their acoustic and pressure influence mines to preserve their secrecy. The question of whether to use a new technology and risk disclosing it to the enemy is always a perplexing one. As will be seen, the Allies struggled with similar choices in the use of the proximity fuze and the cavity magnetron.

CASE STUDY: MINING THE NORMANDY INVASION

The use of advanced mines figured prominently in the greatest naval problem the Germans faced in World War II, which was how to defeat the coming Allied landing in northwestern Europe. To this end, Germany hoarded its most sophisticated mine, the DM-1 or Oyster mine, so that it would be used decisively and in mass at the moment of greatest need. The Oyster used a dual magnetic/pressure trigger that the Germans believed made it unsweepable, at least for a period. Having learned the lesson from the piecemeal early war misuse of the magnetic mine, they accumulated four thousand Oysters and, hoping for a decisive result, resolved to wait until they knew the invasion's location before using them en masse. In a parallel development, the German air force had developed a pressure/acoustic mine called the AD104 that was also to be held until the Allied landing. In the German way of doing things, mines delivered by air were an air force matter, and those delivered by sea were a naval matter. This duality extended all the way to separate development streams. Such dichotomies were not limited to mines, and they hindered Germany's effective development and use of new technology.[58]

In addition to the Oyster and AD104 mines, the German high command placed great reliance on the RMK (standard coastal mine): a simple, easy-to-construct concrete mine with a 70-kilogram charge embedded inside. In January 1944 there were hopes of having 25,000 such weapons by March.[59] These big plans were complicated by several factors beyond duplicate and uncertain responsibilities. For example, the navy's reluctance to use the Oyster mines too early was based in part on a fear that the Allies would learn the secret and start mining the Baltic with their own versions, interfering with the submarine training program there. But the decisive problem was that Germany lacked reliable intelligence. Not knowing where or when the Allies intended to land severely complicated the task of anti-invasion planning.

On 6 June 1944 German mines sank and damaged several ships of the Allied amphibious forces, but losses were insignificant, in part because the Oyster mines were still in storage. The German air force was eager to start minelaying immediately, but the local naval command objected because the pressure mines "might block" the navigation of its own meager forces. The naval high command overruled this objection, but the air force did not have the properly equipped aircraft available in any event. As for the navy, a 6 June entry in the staff war diary admitted, "The 600 DM-mines of the Navy were stored in the home area as ordered. Probably a fortnight will be required to transfer them into the operational area in the Channel."[60] As late as 17 June Hitler was asking the navy when the first mine operations with the DM 1 trigger would be possible. The air force was quicker getting into action and dropped 216 of its AD104 mines between 11 and 14 June. The use of the Oyster mine, when it finally came, caused delays and some losses, but by then the invaders were firmly established ashore. When the Allies recovered an Oyster mine on 20 June, they quickly determined that if a ship maintained a speed below four knots, the mine would not detonate. After the beginning of July, "there was no longer any risk that German minelaying would seriously impede the build-up."[61]

Facing its greatest challenge, Germany's greatest failure was not having the stocks of mines available to deploy en masse as quickly as possible when they might have played a decisive role. The fact that there were no Oyster mines in the water on the day of the invasion was a failure in intelligence. The fact it took five days to get the first special mines into the water was a failure of planning. The German squandering of this sophisticated technology greatly assisted the success of the Allied invasion. That the mines only functioned if a vessel exceeded four knots was a hidden vulnerability the Germans knew nothing about.

The mining campaign that historians credit as being decisive was waged by the Allies against Japan. In January 1944 U.S. Army Air Forces bombers out of India first mined the Menam River estuary near Bangkok, and throughout the year increasing numbers of U.S. and British aircraft and submarines mined ports in the South China Sea, throughout the East Indies, and even up the Yangtze River. In March 1945 the Americans turned their attention to Japanese home waters, using B-29s to deliver a variety of single and dual-trigger magnetic, pressure, and acoustic mines.

The differences between this campaign and Germany's 1939 aerial magnetic mining campaign in English waters were profound. The U.S. campaign represented a convergence of electromagnetic, mine, and aircraft technologies on a completely different scale. Rather than scratch navigating a slow seaplane carrying a single mine a hundred miles to a general location, the Americans precisely navigated very-long-range super-bombers more than 1,500 miles and dropped by radar location a dozen assorted types of influence and delayed action mines per aircraft. But even so, the Army Air Forces still scattered more than a thousand mines over land. While the British were able to defeat the German magnetic mine campaign by recovering one example, the Japanese at this point were focused on repelling an invasion, and the challenge of coming up with countermeasures, even with ample examples to study, proved unsurmountable in the time available. In a postwar interrogation, the head of Japan's central minesweeping section related that it took one month to solve the needle-type magnetic mine, two months for the induction type of magnetic mine, and two weeks for normal frequency acoustic mines, but low-frequency acoustic and pressure mines were never solved. The Japanese remarked that many of the U.S. mines exploded prematurely, but the Americans expended weapons lavishly. By the war's last year, the Japanese had to face mines everywhere they sailed in narrow waters, and by the end of the war, they could sail nowhere. In this case, the Americans offset technological flaws by saturating the enemy with numbers.[62]

THE TECHNOLOGY POSTWAR AND TODAY

Mines have played an important role in both major and minor postwar conflicts up to the present. Mines based on century-old technology continue to be used successfully. In fact, there has been a trend toward low-technology delivery systems as mines remain one of the most effective weapons available to less powerful navies and even nonstate entities. On several occasions, mines have embarrassed major naval powers.

Mine clearing operations off Wonsan, November 1950. A U.S. minesweeper prepares to stream a float that will mark one end of its cable-cutting sweep. North Korean minelaying caught the U.S. Navy unprepared. *(Naval History and Heritage Command, NH 80-G-425977)*

In the Korean War, during the heady days after the United Nations (UN) landed two divisions at Inchon and relieved the siege of Pusan, South Korean troops crossed the 38th Parallel and on 10 October 1950 entered Wonsan, an important east coast port. This preempted a planned UN amphibious assault there but, given jammed roads, the UN command decided to land two U.S. divisions at Wonsan for an advance farther north. However, Soviet naval advisors supervised the laying of three thousand old contact mines and more modern Soviet magnetic mines in Wonsan harbor and vicinity. An effort to countermine the fields by using bombs fuzed to detonate at twenty-five feet below the surface exploded many mines but could not completely clear an area. The U.S. Navy lost two minesweepers on 13 October and had to subcontract with civilian-manned Japanese minesweepers, still at work sweeping World War II–era mines from Japanese waters, to clear Wonsan. On this day the commander of the sweeping force informed U.S. Chief of Naval Operations Adm. Forrest P. Sherman that "the U.S. Navy has lost command of the sea in Korean waters." Sherman had to agree: "We've been plenty submarine and air conscious, now we're going to start getting mine conscious—beginning last week." It took two weeks before one channel was cleared into the harbor so that men and supplies could start landing. On the other coast, mines also retarded access to the port of Pyongyang.[63]

In May 1972 the U.S. military used carrier aircraft to lay a string of 1,000-pound Mark 52 mines in two minutes off North Vietnam's major port of Haiphong. These were set to activate in seventy-two hours to give shipping in port a chance to escape. Over the balance of the year the Americans laid 11,000 Mark 36 Destructor mines, an acoustic and magnetic triggered bottom mine loaded with 570 pounds of TNT, and 108 Mark 52–2 1,000-pound magnetic bottom mines in North Vietnamese coastal and inland waterways. This effectively halted all enemy maritime traffic and helped motivate the North Vietnam government to negotiate. One of the provisions in the settlement that ended the seven-year U.S. military intervention in Vietnam required the United States to sweep the mines it had sown. Helicopters did much of the work using towed sleds and other devices, but to ensure the Haiphong channel was clear, the U.S. Navy sailed an ex–tank landing ship loaded with buffering material up and down the waterway eight times to confirm it was free of variable trigger mines. The entire process required six months.[64]

The 1972 U.S. mining campaign off North Vietnam was conducted in accordance with the broad principles of mine warfare that were supposed to bring success: mines were used all at once in relatively large numbers and at critical chokepoints. The mines were replenished at need and were relatively difficult to sweep. Although few ships were sunk, the mining was highly effective and delivered political returns relatively quickly. The fact remains, however, that once used, mine technologies are compromised; once understood, the system can be cancelled by the application of countertechnology. This suggests that mines have evolved into a weapon with a limited technological shelf life. On the other hand, the application of countertechnologies requires time and resources. In the interim, the oldest and simplest of mines continue in effective use. In fall 2019 Iran engaged in another iteration of the Persian Gulf Tanker Wars in the Strait of Hormuz. The U.S. Navy established that Iranian personnel operating in small craft and even inflatable boats had planted moored contact mines, similar to those used in World War I, that damaged two super-tankers. The impacts were nonlethal and the damage was an annoyance, but the political ramifications were sensational.

There has also been a return to the original concept that the mine should travel to the target. This had been demonstrated at Alexandria on 19 December 1941 when Italian swimmers riding a motorized mine severely damaged a pair of enemy battleships. Delivery systems such as swimmers or motorboats might be low-tech, but that does not make them ineffective. The mines that sank *Rio de Janeiro* in 1866 are in essence the same as the mines that damaged the Argentine *Santissima Trinidad* in 1975 or the Sri Lankan *Edithara* in 1995. The decades after World War II have seen at least seven instances of mines being delivered by small boats or swimmers and not always by state players but by political dissidents and insurgent movements as well.[65]

WHAT THIS TELLS US

The importance of mine warfare and its associated technologies has not faded in the years since the mature weapon's first major uses in the Russo-Japanese War. Mine warfare's basic characteristics are as valid in the twenty-first century as they were in the nineteenth. These are:

- that navies do not prioritize mine warfare. They have a perception that mine warfare is (relatively) simpler and less costly than other types of naval technologies, such as dreadnoughts or nuclear propulsion, and the corollary of cheap and simple is that the capability may be developed or even improvised at need

- that mines are highly effective when properly used in the right circumstances and conditions

- that mine warfare has been a core naval weapon system over the past twelve decades as its fundamental use and nature remain remarkably enduring, and it seems likely to continue.

If all of this is true, there is a paradox here. How can the first characteristic be reconciled with the last two? Why would navies, with very few exceptions (like the Russians in 1914) collectively and repeatedly over the past century fail to prioritize a core capability?

This paradox is highlighted in the U.S. Navy's postwar assessment of the German mining effort from 1939 to 1945: "[German] [m]ining suffered consistently from its subordinate standing. No one in the Navy held operational control over mining; no one in the Mining Command possessed sufficient drive and grasp to present the case for mining with enough force before the High Command. As a result, the direction of mine warfare failed to rise above its second-rate position."[66] But this was hardly just a German problem. In 1946 the commander of the Pacific Fleet Minecraft complained that "service-wide 'knowledge of mining and minesweeping was generally poor to nil.'" Adm. Chester Nimitz agreed about "the low state of knowledge concerning mine warfare in the Navy" and recommended a "necessary emphasis" on mine warfare in the curriculum of the Navy's service schools and training establishments, including the Naval War College.[67] In the British navy, the situation in 1939 was similar: "[Mine warfare] was not formally recognised as a specialisation for officers. It was not a separate manning division like Submarines or Coastal Forces, it had no non-substantive badges and minesweepers generally were unglamorous ships."[68] Certainly, mines seemed less interesting to most naval professionals than other forms of naval warfare. How else to explain events such as the German reluctance to use top secret and potentially decisive Oyster mines against the Normandy landings because they might interfere with the navigation of the pitiful few torpedo boats and motor torpedo boats opposing the enemy's vast armadas?

Minelayers and minesweepers do not command the imagination like aircraft carriers and nuclear submarines do. Mine warfare at first glance appears incremental, passive, and incapable of achieving decisive results. Its main effects often come less from the outright toll of ships damaged or sunk and more from restricting the enemy's operations, limiting its geographic scope, and forcing it to devote resources to countermeasures. The study of mine warfare in the larger context of naval campaigns reveals its profound effects and potential. From this it follows that even a technology that is relatively accessible and enormously effective requires more than just success to earn the attention it deserves, at least from major navies.

There is a lesson here that applies to the development and use of technology. Some technologies are compelling, charismatic, and "sexy," and some are not. Some technologies, such as aircraft, have an emotional component that causes people to advocate for them. Aircraft technology was compelling, whereas the lurking, passive, ugly mine was not. Quantifying how emotional elements affect the use of technology might not be possible, but there is much anecdotal evidence, particularly in the history of mine warfare, to suggest that they do.

CHAPTER 3

TORPEDOES
The Long Arc

Torpedo. A fish which while alive, if touched even with a long stick,
benumbs the hand that so touches it.

—SAMUEL JOHNSON, DICTIONARY (1755)

As understood today, a torpedo is a self-propelled underwater explosive device that is launched from a platform such as a ship, submarine, or aircraft and that explodes upon contact with or in close proximity to its target. When Adm. David Farragut damned the torpedoes at Mobile Bay, he was actually cursing moored mines; when self-propelled torpedoes first appeared, they were called automobile torpedoes or (more colorfully) fish torpedoes to distinguish them from stationary mines, but the term "torpedo" came to mean a self-propelled weapon as they became more common. The distinction was one of delivery. The mine waited for its target or was carried to it, but the torpedo had its own motor. This difference between the mine and torpedo is both simple and profound.

INTRODUCTION: THE TECHNOLOGY DESCRIBED, EXPECTATIONS, EARLY USE

Robert Whitehead, an English engineer working in the Austrian Empire, developed the first practical automotive torpedo in 1866. He designed his weapon to operate underwater, a feature that gave two major advantages. First, it would strike beneath the waterline, increasing the chances of fatal damage, and second, it would be harder to see and avoid. Whitehead used a compressed air motor to power his invention and a damped hydrostatic mechanism to regulate depth. This latter device was truly innovative. Dubbed "the Secret" by Whitehead (although it became widely known), all successful torpedoes for decades to come would have it. Motor and depth regulator were crammed together with contact fuze, warhead, compressed air vessel, guide fins, and propeller in a streamlined cylinder. Whitehead's torpedo, with its intricate plumbing and motor, was cutting-edge technology at the time. Just producing tanks able to contain the required air pressures was a major challenge that many naval arsenals could not meet.[1]

Whitehead's 1866 prototype weighed 300 pounds, had an 18-pound warhead, and could cover 200 yards at 6 knots. By 1871 he was offering both 14-inch "small" and 16-inch "standard" torpedoes, with the former carrying a 26.5-pound warhead to 800 yards at 16.5 knots and the latter with a 67-pound charge and a 7-knot speed out to 1,000 yards. By 1896 a standard Whitehead torpedo weighed 893 pounds and carried a 110-pound warhead to 1,000 yards at 28 knots.[2]

The Austrian navy trialed the Whitehead torpedo in 1868 and gave the inventor a contract that year. The British followed in 1871, the French in 1872, the Italians and Germans in 1873, and the Russians and Ottomans in 1876.[3] The U.S. Navy balked at Whitehead's price and developed home-grown alternatives instead. Torpedo fever had clearly infected the world's navies, and despite the weapon's unproven nature, it is clear why: the torpedo seemed revolutionary. After studying and testing the weapon for three years, the British navy's "Torpedo Committee" concluded that "the most powerful ship is liable to be destroyed by a torpedo projected from a vessel of the utmost comparative insignificance." This would "reduce to one common level the Naval Power of the greatest and most insignificant nations"—not a reassuring prospect for the world's most powerful navy. In Britain, the principal line of enquiry was "the protection from offensive torpedoes of ships at sea." The gloomy conclusion was that no such protection could be assured.[4]

Navies embraced the torpedo before knowing how best to deliver it. Although Whitehead had designed the weapon to be launched from submerged tubes, navies quickly experimented with above-water launchers. These permitted torpedoes to be fitted to ships without major design changes. The British had so equipped steam corvette *Shah* by 1876; by the 1880s torpedoes were common on capital ships and cruisers. Navies also experimented with a wide variety of purpose-built torpedo carriers. The British navy commissioned *Vesuvius* (1874) as a 245-ton ship with low freeboard and muffled engines for slow, stealthy attacks and *Polyphemus* (1882) as a fast 2,640-ton torpedo ram with five tubes and thirteen reloads. *Rattlesnake* (1887) followed as a 550-ton torpedo-gunboat that resembled a miniature cruiser and was also tasked with fighting torpedo carriers. British builder Thornycroft produced *Lightning* (1876), a 32.5-ton boat with a single above-water tube and two reloads. She became the basis for a whole series of torpedo boat designs. Specialized torpedo craft also appeared in the Italian navy (*Pietro Micca*, 576 tons, 1876), the French navy (*Condor*, 1,229 tons, and *Bombe*, 369 tons, 1883), and the Russian navy (*Vzruiv*, 160 tons, 1876), among others.

Russia and France enthusiastically adopted torpedo boats as a way of cheaply countering British naval dominance. Proponents of the French Jeune École movement, which sought to overcome Great Britain's naval superiority though new technology, saw torpedo boats as an integral part of their strategy. Swarms of coastal torpedo craft would harass a blockading British fleet while fast cruisers attacked British commerce on the high seas. Torpedo boats also appeared in numbers in the British, Japanese,

TABLE 3.1

TORPEDO CARRIERS

NAME	TYPE	YEAR	NAVY	DISPLACEMENT (TONS)	GUN ARMAMENT	TORPEDO ARMAMENT	SPEED (KNOTS)
Vesuvius	Torpedo vessel	1874	Britain	245	None	1 16-inch	9.7
Lightning	Torpedo boat	1876	Britain	32.5	None	2	19
Polyphemus	Torpedo ram	1882	Britain	2,640	6 1-inch machine guns	5 14-inch	18
Épervier	Torpedo cruiser	1884	France	1,268	4 3/9 inch, 4 3-pounder	4 14-inch	17.5
TB15	Torpedo boat	1891	Japan (French design)	53	2 37-millimeter	2 15-inch	20
Ikazuchi	Torpedo boat destroyer	1897	Japan (British design)	305	2 12-pounder, 4 6-pounder	2 18-inch	31
Byedovi	Torpedo boat destroyer	1902	Russia	350	1 11-pounder, 3 3-pounder	3 15-inch	26

Sources: Gardiner, *Fighting Ships, 1860–1905*; Jentschura, Jung, and Mickel, *Warships of the Imperial Japanese Navy*.

The French torpedo cruiser *Épervier* ("Sparrowhawk"), launched in 1886, was an early form of torpedo carrier, with four 14-inch above-water torpedo tubes on a displacement of 1,268 tons. *(Naval History and Heritage Command, NH 74860)*

Austrian, Italian, and German navies. They were a weapon most navies could readily afford. Only the United States lagged behind.[5]

While torpedo launchers and torpedo craft proliferated, navies also considered countermeasures. Torpedo nets appeared, ship designers paid more attention to underwater protection and watertight integrity, and larger ships were festooned with machine guns and quick-firing light cannon to blast torpedo boats—a development mirrored sixty years later when aircraft became the threat.[6]

Potential and a record of effective use are two different things, and in action the torpedo was slow to develop such a record. On 29 May 1877 the British warships *Shah* and *Amethyst* engaged the armored Peruvian turret-ship *Huáscar*, which at the time was in the hands of political dissidents. When, two hours into an indecisive gunnery action, *Huáscar* closed to ram, *Shah* fired a Whitehead torpedo set to run four hundred yards at nine knots. The Peruvian came about, put on eleven knots, and easily outran the weapon.[7] In late 1877 during the Russo-Turkish War a pair of Russian launches fired two torpedoes at an Ottoman ironclad anchored in Batum harbor. Despite the sixty-yard range, both missed. The Russians returned on 25 January 1878 and aimed two small Whitehead torpedoes at the Ottoman revenue cutter *Intikbah* from eighty yards. They reported the ship sunk, but the Ottomans denied the loss. Sunk or not, this event encouraged Germany, France, and Italy to deploy torpedo-armed fast steam launches of their own.[8]

The next two attempts to use torpedoes in action involved the Lay torpedo, a huge and hugely expensive surface-running weapon controlled from the point of launch by an electric wire.[9] The occasion was the War of the Pacific, fought by Bolivia and Peru against Chile from 1879 to 1884. In August 1879 *Huáscar*, her mutiny long over, deployed one of her two Lay torpedoes against an anchored Chilean corvette from two hundred yards. The weapon began its run normally only to circle back toward the ironclad. Reportedly one of the officers jumped overboard and deflected the slow-running weapon, averting disaster. *Huáscar*'s captain buried the other torpedo in a cemetery rather than risk its use.[10] *Huáscar* was the target of a Lay torpedo attack in 1881, after the ship had been captured by the Chileans, but that one missed as well.

Incontrovertible success came for the Whitehead on 23 April 1891 during a Chilean civil war. Two rebel torpedo cruisers, modern twenty-one-knot ships that each mounted five 14-inch tubes, crept into Caldera Bay in the early morning of 28 January 1891, where they found a government armored frigate, *Blanco Encalada*, at anchor. The first cruiser missed with three torpedoes, but the second hit with one of two fired from 150 yards. The frigate sank in five minutes with the loss of 182 men. Three years later, during a Brazilian civil war, a government gunboat and three torpedo boats approached the anchored rebel ironclad *Aquidaban* at night. The torpedo boats missed, but the gunboat managed to hit from close range with one or two torpedoes, and *Aquidaban* slowly settled on the shallow bottom.[11]

When the Japanese and the Chinese fought the Battle of the Yalu in 1894, the Japanese fleet deployed thirty-two torpedo tubes and the Chinese fleet fifty, but Japanese quick-firing guns dominated the action. The Chinese fired five Schwartzkopf torpedoes (German versions of the Whitehead), but these did not maintain depth, with some skimming the surface and at least one plunging under its target. Chinese ships jettisoned other torpedoes for fear of fire or explosion. The Japanese had decided beforehand that torpedoes had little scope in a daylight gunnery duel and did not launch any during the action, although they did finish off a damaged Chinese cruiser with a spar torpedo.[12] While poor maintenance could have accounted for Chinese torpedo failures, most foreign observers sided with the Japanese in concluding that quick-firing guns were superior to torpedoes in daylight fleet engagements in open waters.

After the Chinese retreated to Weihai harbor, the Japanese subjected the defeated fleet to a series of torpedo boat attacks. Their first two forays failed but on their third effort on 5 February 1895, a bitterly cold day, five boats distracted the Chinese defenses while ten entered the harbor. A few of the attackers grounded and others had their torpedoes freeze in their tubes, but four managed to fire eight torpedoes. One struck armored turret ship *Ting Yuen* in the stern and caused progressive flooding. The Japanese lost two boats and suffered a third seriously damaged. A similar operation the next night sank a sloop, a protected cruiser, and the armored cruiser *Lai Yuan* with no loss to the Japanese.[13] While torpedoes had yet to be effective in a sea fight, they confirmed their worth in attacks on anchored ships. Japanese torpedo specialists absorbed both this lesson and the need to close quickly and fire from short range to be effective.[14]

Lay torpedo. A wire-guided surface runner, this torpedo was enormous, expensive, sophisticated, and ineffectual. It was the only torpedo to be (reportedly) deflected in combat by a swimmer. *(Naval History and Heritage Command, NH 82829)*

On the other hand, torpedoes saw little use and had no successes in the Spanish-American War of 1898–99 despite U.S. worries over Spanish torpedo carriers.

In their first three decades of existence, opportunities to use torpedoes in combat were rare. When employed against stationary targets at close range, torpedoes worked more often than not, with seven ships being sunk or damaged in five attacks. Only three attacks were complete failures. In actions against ships under way, however, torpedoes missed every time. Such limited usage in short, low-grade conflicts inhibited innovation and the development of doctrine. Despite significant technological progress, the best delivery platform and the most appropriate target remained debatable.

One lesson navies did draw from these early experiences was the need for a new type of warship to hunt down and destroy small and sneaky torpedo boats before they got within striking distance of valuable battleships. Torpedo gunboats had been a step in this direction but proved too slow. This need led to the evolution of the torpedo boat destroyer (the "destroyer"). In a quest for speed, destroyers were the first naval vessels to use turbine propulsion and, later, oil fuel. The destroyer's greater size relative to the torpedo boat brought advantages beyond heavier firepower. Torpedo boats were fair weather craft with limited range, but destroyers could accompany a fleet over longer distances in all weather. The British began ordering the type in 1892, and other navies soon followed. Russian and Japanese destroyers—varying in displacement from two hundred to four hundred tons—took an active part in the Russo-Japanese War with Japanese ships being faster and more heavily armed (see table 3.1 for details).[15]

TABLE 3.2
EARLY TORPEDO DEVELOPMENT

YEAR	DEVELOPMENT	SOURCE	EFFECT
1874	Contra-rotating props	U.K. Royal Laboratory	Higher speeds, balanced torque
1875	Radial engine	Brotherhood (U.K.)	More power, better reliability
1877	Servo actuation for depth-keeping	Whitehead	Better depth-keeping
1883	Rounded nose	U.K. Royal Laboratory	Higher speed, larger payload
1895	Obry gyro device	Whitehead	Reduced deviation from line of fire

Sources: Gray, *Devil's Device*; Branfill-Cook, *Torpedo*.

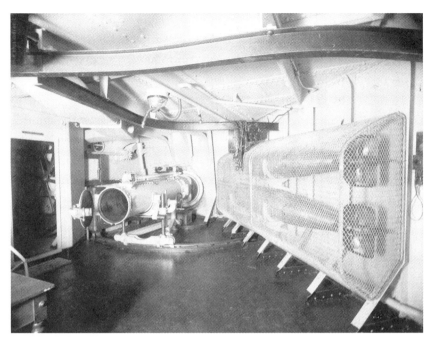

Torpedo room in USS *Oregon* (BB 3), above water and unarmored. Navies continued to equip their battleships with torpedoes through World War I, although battleships had almost no success in using them. Later battleship designs placed the torpedo rooms under armor and below the water line, which reduced the danger of shell hits detonating torpedo warheads but created large spaces that proved dangerous to a ship's stability when flooded. *(Library of Congress, 4a1461a, https://www.loc.gov/item/2016808090/)*

The years before the Russo-Japanese War also saw important developments in torpedo technology. These are summarized in table 3.2.

The last of these developments was the most significant. While Whitehead had invented a practical way to keep a torpedo at a set depth, maintaining a stable course remained problematic. Even in the best of circumstances, each torpedo had unique directional tendencies. This issue was compounded as launching speeds increased and torpedoes were deployed from amidships rather than from bow tubes, as the motion imparted by the ship made torpedo courses even more erratic. In 1895 an Austrian inventor, Ludwig Obry, came up with a solution: an internal gyroscope. This device sensed the torpedo's horizontal wanderings and corrected them through steerable vanes. Whitehead quickly adopted it, and enthusiasts heralded this device as greatly magnifying the torpedo's value.[16] The device proved challenging to adjust and maintain, but versions followed that could be serviced without requiring delicate recalibration in workshops. For example, the U.S. Navy introduced a second-generation gyroscope in 1903.[17]

Intrigued by the Obry device's possibilities, some navies began to consider attacks at ranges out to three thousand meters even though this meant accepting torpedo speeds as low as eleven knots. In the Russian navy Captain (later Vice Admiral) Stepan Makarov advocated this fundamental shift in tactics. Despite the objections of its own specialists, the Japanese admiralty adopted similar views and first practiced coordinated long-range attacks in 1902.[18] While longer ranges promised new capabilities, they also brought new problems. Torpedo fire control required a man on a low and lively platform to estimate the course and speed of a target a mile or more away.[19] The fact that a fifteen-knot torpedo fired from three thousand yards would take six minutes to arrive, giving the target plenty of time to maneuver, argued against the practice of long-range fire during the day, while in night attacks identifying a target and judging its course and speed were all the more difficult.

DISCOVERY: THE RUSSO-JAPANESE WAR

The Russo-Japanese War began with a surprise attack by ten Japanese destroyers on Russian warships anchored outside Port Arthur. British historian Julian Corbett called this "the first great torpedo attack in naval history."[20] The attack commenced with the Russians brilliantly illuminated, completely surprised, and unprotected by booms or nets. Theoretically, the results should have been devastating, but they were not. On their approach two Japanese destroyers collided, and several fell out of formation and got lost. Although the destroyers attacked at ranges varying from 400 to 1,500 meters, only three of the twenty torpedoes they launched struck home, being those fired at the shortest ranges and before Russian guns and searchlights could respond. Still, the attack damaged two battleships and an armored cruiser and gave the Japanese an important initial advantage.[21] The percentage of hits obtained was in line with other actions against anchored vessels in harbor, but the results were disappointing to the Japanese nonetheless.

As the war developed, torpedoes continued to be employed (mostly by the Japanese), and results continued to disappoint. The next major torpedo

action came four months later during a 24 June sortie by the Russian battlefleet. When confronted by the main Japanese force, the Russians turned
back to Port Arthur. The Japanese unleashed their torpedo craft against
the withdrawing enemy as night fell. Even though conditions were favorable, poor coordination, good visibility, and a fully alerted enemy caused
the Japanese difficulties. Three attacks against the rear of the Russian
formation failed. The only damage to the Russians came when battleship
Sevastopol was forced out of line by the maneuvers of the ship ahead and
struck a mine. She took on a thousand tons of water but kept up with the
fleet. The Russians then anchored under the cover of shore batteries and
searchlights. The Japanese continued sending in flotillas all night long,
making eight more attacks and expending sixty-seven torpedoes. The
attackers again reported launch ranges between 400 and 1,500 meters, but
in the midst of shell splashes and searchlight glare, it was easy to underes-
timate distances; in any case, every weapon missed. Russian defensive fire
damaged five Japanese boats.[22]

The Japanese torpedomen got another chance at the end of the 10 August
1904 Battle of the Yellow Sea. In this action the Japanese confronted the
Russian fleet as it tried to force passage to Vladivostok. As night fell, after
an hours-long gunnery action, most Russian ships again turned back.
Admiral Tōgō Heihachirō, the Japanese commander, ordered his eighteen
destroyers and twenty-nine torpedo boats to attack the retiring Russians.
Conditions were favorable, with a moonless night and the enemy disor-
dered by the gun battle. The Japanese launched seventy-four torpedoes,
but again all missed at a cost of one destroyer disabled and a torpedo boat
torpedoed, probably by one of her consorts. Several factors contributed to
this failure. The Russians used guns but not searchlights and maneuvered
freely to avoid attackers. The Japanese again found coordination difficult,
as group attacks quickly degenerated into individual actions. Some attackers could not even locate a target.[23]

After missing with 141 torpedoes in two actions, the Japanese began
to question the efficacy of long-range attacks against moving targets. The
next significant torpedo action occurred against the battleship *Sevastopol*
after Japanese siege guns forced her to anchor outside Port Arthur. Beginning on 10 December 1904 the Japanese expended 124 torpedoes in dash-
and-duck operations against this stationary target in often vile weather.

From this effort they obtained one hit and three damaging near-misses at a cost of two torpedo boats sunk and several others damaged—clear proof that an alert and well-defended enemy, even an immobile one, was not easy prey.[24]

The 27–28 May 1905 Battle of Tsushima gave Japanese torpedo forces a last chance to prove their effectiveness. They played little role in the daylight portions of the action. The Japanese battle line attempted a few torpedo shots but hit nothing except (possibly) an abandoned auxiliary cruiser. As the daylight action drew to a close, the Japanese dispatched two torpedo divisions against *Suvorov*, the already crippled Russian flagship. Destroyers first scored one hit, and a torpedo boat division finished the battered ship with two or three more. As the sun set, the Japanese next sent twenty-one destroyers and thirty-two torpedo boats into action against the rest of the fleet. They fired eighty-seven torpedoes for seven known hits, sinking or contributing to the sinking of a battleship, a turret ship, and two old armored cruisers.[25] While this was the best performance of the torpedo flotillas, it was far from perfect. Four divisions failed to find the enemy at all, and nine of the thirteen large Russian warships that survived the daylight battle also survived the nocturnal torpedo action.

REVISED EXPECTATIONS

Postwar analysis sparked debate about the torpedo's future role. The British confidential history of the war noted that the "Whitehead torpedo proved a somewhat ineffective weapon." It praised the training and efficiency of the Japanese torpedomen and ascribed Japanese failures to long-range launches, poor visibility, and attendant difficulties in estimating range, target course, and target speed.[26] British Admiral Cyprian Bridge, writing in Brassey's *Naval Annual of 1905* (before the results of Tsushima were known), concluded: "Perhaps nothing stands out more clearly in the campaign than the insignificance of the results effected by the locomotive torpedo."[27] Commodore Murray Sueter of the British navy instead emphasized the successes of the torpedo. To him, the Port Arthur attack "showed in a most effective manner the tremendous potentialities of the torpedo." He generously explained away the failures of the June and August mass attacks as due to the "neglect of a few minor technical details" in maintaining the torpedoes.[28] Sueter also alleged that many of the Japanese torpedoes lacked gyro gear, although the Japanese began ordering gyro-equipped torpedoes in 1897. It is more likely that the gyros suffered from maintenance problems.[29] As for Bridge's article, Sueter remarked that "this continual warfare between conservatives . . . and progressive specialists has restricted largely the development of torpedo warfare in most navies."[30]

Historian Julian Corbett took a more nuanced view. He acknowledged that the results of the Port Arthur attack were disappointing and ascribed this in part to Japanese overconfidence in their weapon's long-range accuracy. He cautioned that as a predictor of future results, the attack was "far from conclusive." As for the June action, he wrote that it demonstrated the unreliability of the torpedo for a "primary operation"—an attack that was neither a prelude to nor preceded by a main gunnery action—but also acknowledged that the Russians had been lucky to escape with only moderate damage to *Sevastopol*. In writing about the August action, Corbett still saw value in torpedo attacks, "particularly as the range and accuracy of the weapon itself are continually increasing," but felt that the Japanese

Russian torpedo boat destroyer *Byedovi*. Typical of early torpedo boat destroyers, originally mounting three 15-inch above-water torpedo tubes, an 11-pounder gun, and five 3-pounder guns, all on 350 tons. Completed in 1903, she was captured by the Japanese after the battle of Tsushima and later served in the Japanese navy as *Satsuki*. (Naval History and Heritage Command, NH 111653)

had reversed the logical order of events by not unleashing the flotillas to disorganize the Russians before the gun battle. In Corbett's view, the battle of Tsushima with its "slender results" simply confirmed his position.[31] In sum, analysis of the Russo-Japanese War produced no consensus on the effectiveness of the torpedo. What was clear was that no navy could afford to cast the weapon aside, as its capabilities continued to tantalize.

EVOLUTION: WORLD WAR I

The decade leading up to World War I saw range, speed, and warhead weight all increase. Compressed air propellant was stored at progressively higher pressures as metallurgy improved, but the breakthrough invention was the "heater" torpedo, patented in 1904. Initially, this involved heating compressed air to increase its energy before it was sent to the torpedo's engine. This was followed in 1905 by a refinement in which water was introduced, flashing to steam under heating. This "wet heater" or "steam" mechanism increased energy while cooling the gases being shot into the engine. The effect on torpedo performance was remarkable (see table 3.3), although it came at the cost of making the wake more visible.[32]

Before these improvements, effective gun range had been greater than torpedo range. This confined the torpedo to night attacks and the occasional target of opportunity. After 1905 gun and torpedo ranges increased in tandem. By the eve of World War I, when the effective range of big guns was still regarded to be 7,000 to 12,000 yards, torpedoes ranged 10,000 yards at close to thirty knots. Longer ranged torpedoes reinvigorated thinking about their role in gunnery duels—particularly as ten thousand yards exceeded normal visibility in the North Sea, the anticipated

TABLE 3.3
COMPARATIVE PERFORMANCE OF 17.7-INCH TORPEDOES— PROPULSION DEVELOPMENTS

TORPEDO	YEAR	SPEED/RANGE (KNOTS/YARDS)	WARHEAD WEIGHT (POUNDS)
Japanese Type 32	1899	28/1,100; 15/3,300	200
German C/03 AV Dry Heater	1903	31/1,650; 26/3,300	325
British Mark VII Wet Heater	1904	41/3,000; 30/6,000	200

Sources: Branfill-Cook, *Torpedo*; Friedman, *Naval Weapons of World War One*; Gray, *Devil's Device*.

cockpit of Britain's next naval war. While few went so far as a noted Italian constructor in advocating battleships armed primarily with torpedoes, perhaps the best evidence of the belief that torpedoes would play a role in a big-ship, big-gun battle was the fact that new dreadnought battleships and battlecruisers continued to be built with tubes.[33]

Admiral John Jellicoe was particularly concerned by the threat of long-range torpedoes, writing that an attack on a line of battleships could potentially hit with more than half of the torpedoes fired. While his arithmetic was suspect, other commentators espoused similar views, estimating that from one-quarter to one-half of all torpedoes would hit unless the line maneuvered radically, which would upset its gunnery. More generally, there was a lively debate as to whether the torpedo had replaced the gun as the dominant naval weapon, with the conclusion generally hinging on whether the debater thought that the gun or the torpedo would prove to have the range advantage.[34]

Jellicoe's worries over the efficacy of torpedoes drove his decision to turn the Grand Fleet away from a torpedo attack during the battle of Jutland, thus ensuring the German fleet's escape when he had it at a decisive disadvantage. Jellicoe's overriding priority was preserving his ships, but he was hardly the only officer to fight shy of torpedoes. At the earlier Battle of Dogger Bank, his aggressive subordinate, Vice Admiral David Beatty, sacrificed a superior position during a gunnery duel when he imagined German submarines were lining up to attack his battlecruisers. On balance, however, the experience of surface warfare in World War I showed that the big gun could hit at long ranges, and torpedoes used in surface combat remained the weapons most effective at short range and in bad visibility. Theory had again galloped past capability in judging the torpedo's long-range effectiveness. Throughout the war, the few massed torpedo attacks launched by flotilla craft against battleships scored just one hit. As in the Russo-Japanese War, such attacks proved hard to coordinate and execute. The only dreadnought battleship sunk outright by a torpedo delivered by a surface ship was the Austro-Hungarian *Szent István*, ambushed at dawn from close range by the twenty-ton Italian *MAS15*. Opposing flotilla craft were far more typical torpedo targets, and the threat of the weapon played a much greater role in naval combat than the weapon itself.

Despite this indifferent record in surface warfare, torpedoes proved critical, indeed nearly decisive, in World War I—but not in the way expected. Prewar thinking had not seriously considered the use of submarine-launched torpedoes as commerce killers. Nonetheless, in the submarine, the torpedo found its ideal platform; in the merchantman, it found its ideal target. The marriage of platform and mission magnified the technology's importance, much as the use of stationary mines to modify naval geography had made mine warfare a critical naval technology. Nothing about the technology itself was changed; rather, it was a matter of platform and target. Submarines (see chapter six) allowed torpedoes to be launched at close range from ambush—the best way to make a torpedo attack—at soft targets. Torpedo technology allowed the Central Powers' submarines to take a ghastly toll on Allied shipping: over 11,000,000 gross tons sunk (more than 4,500 ships), 95 percent by torpedo.[35] This is all the more striking given that merchant sinkings quadrupled from 1914 to 1915 and almost doubled again between 1915 and 1916. German submarine *U-35* alone accounted for 224 ships and over 536,000 gross register tonnage. While the victims of submarine-launched torpedoes were overwhelmingly merchant ships, warships were not immune. Older battleships and armored cruisers were frequent victims due to their slow speeds, inadequate internal subdivision, and employment in tasks where navies were reluctant to risk more modern ships. Submarines combined with torpedoes to sink nineteen of these ships but sank only one of their more modern counterparts (the French semi-dreadnought *Danton*). In all, the torpedo-submarine pairing vastly increased the torpedo's practical effectiveness.

EVOLUTION: BETWEEN WORLD WARS

Torpedo technology continued to evolve in the interwar period. Major developments included increasing range and power using pure oxygen, developing torpedoes purpose-built for aerial delivery, and increasing lethality with new detonators.

The French, U.S., British, and Japanese navies all experimented with pure oxygen as a torpedo propellant. Combined with wet heater technology, pure oxygen promised engines with significantly greater power to permit higher speeds, longer ranges, and bigger warheads. However, compressed oxygen is explosive and tricky to handle. The Americans and

French quickly concluded that the risks outweighed the benefits, especially as they had no overarching mission for such a weapon. The British, clinging to the pre–World War I concept of battleships torpedoing battleships, spent more time exploring oxygen for use in massive torpedoes intended for their first postwar battleship designs but ultimately abandoned pure oxygen as more trouble than it was worth and settled for oxygen-enriched air as a performance booster.[36]

The Japanese, however, had a specific and important mission for a super torpedo. Japanese tactical thought in the interwar period emphasized the need to defeat numerically superior enemies with more powerful weapons delivered from longer ranges. Framing victory in terms of a decisive action between battleships, the Japanese navy wanted a superior weapon to attrite an opponent's battle line with surprise long-range torpedo attacks before battle was joined. The Japanese had experimented with oxygen-enriched air in 1917, but reports that the British were pursuing pure oxygen encouraged them to explore that technology. Unaware that the British had in fact given up on pure oxygen by that time, the Japanese began development in 1928. Five years later they adopted the Type 93 oxygen-propelled torpedo for service. The Japanese solved the problems with oxygen by engineering the torpedoes to start on air and to switch to oxygen while under way, employing scrupulous manufacturing standards for the network of pipes and valves carrying the oxygen, and mandating meticulous servicing to make sure that the oxygen never came into explosive contact with oil or grease. The torpedo that resulted was so superior in its performance characteristics that opponents could not credit its capabilities (see table 3.4).[37]

TABLE 3.4

COMPARISON OF JAPANESE TYPE 93 AND U.S. MARK 15 TORPEDOES

	YEAR	DIAMETER (INCHES)	LENGTH (FEET)	OVERALL WEIGHT (POUNDS)	WARHEAD WEIGHT (POUNDS)	SPEED/RANGE (KNOTS/YARDS)
Type 93 Model 1 Mod 2	1935	24	29.5	5,952	1,080	48–50/22,000; 40–42/35,000; 36–38/44,000
Mark 15 Mod 0	1935	21	22.4	3,438	494	46/6,000; 34/10,000; 28/15,000

Sources: Campbell, *Naval Weapons of World War Two*; Wildenberg and Polmar, *Ship Killers*.

The Type 93 was a surface weapon designed to be fired from destroyers and cruisers in long-range attacks against enemy battleships. It seems ironic that the Japanese continued to pursue this mission so vigorously after their negative experiences in the Russo-Japanese War and the disappointments in World War I, but it also shows the role of mission (real or perceived) and platform in driving technological innovation. The Japanese did their utmost to ensure that this innovation would not be wasted; they shrouded it in secrecy, trained intensively, and developed excellent night optics to maximize its advantages.

The second major technical development of the interwar period was the airborne torpedo. Designing a torpedo that could be dropped from a height of fifty feet at a speed of eighty knots, hit the water, attain a preset depth, and run straight to a target was not a trivial matter. The British and the Germans undertook these efforts during the war, with the British adopting a purpose-made weapon in 1917.[38] By the start of World War II, most major navies (or, in some cases, air forces) had developed aerial torpedoes (see table 3.5). The British had continued their work from World War I, with the navy vacillating over its importance and the air force often uninterested.[39] The result was that in 1939 the navy's carriers had biplane torpedo bombers as their main antiship striking force, while the air force began the war with limited antishipping capability. They did, however, have a reasonably effective weapon despite problems with its magnetic exploder. The Italian navy lost the battle for control over naval aviation to the air force but still produced an effective torpedo by 1939 based on a

TABLE 3.5

COMPARISON OF AIR-DROPPED TORPEDOES

NATION	MODEL	YEAR	OVERALL WEIGHT (POUNDS)	WARHEAD WEIGHT (POUNDS)	SPEED/RANGE (KNOTS/YARDS)	DROPPING SPEED/HEIGHT (KNOTS/FEET)
Great Britain	Mark XII	1937	1,548	388	40/1,500	>150/100
Japan	Type 91 Mod 1	1936	1,728	330	42/2,200	250/1,000
United States	Mark 13 Mod 0	1938	1,949	404	30/5,700	115/50
Italy	S.I. 170/450 5.46	1934	1,995	441	41/4,400	160/120
Germany	F5	1940	1,625	441	33/2,500	75/80

Sources: Campbell, *Naval Weapons of World War Two*; Wildenberg and Polmar, *Ship Killers*; Branfill-Cook, *Torpedo*; Bagnasco, *Armi delle Navi Italiane*.

Norwegian prototype obtained in 1932. When war broke out, the French had a force of torpedo floatplanes with more on the drawing board and had adapted a small torpedo for their use (see chapter seven).[40]

The Japanese first tested air-dropped torpedoes in 1922 and immediately realized the need for a specially designed weapon. This appeared in 1931 as the Type 91. The Type 91 was the best in its class by the time Japan entered World War II thanks to a process of continuous development. At the outset, the torpedo could be dropped at speeds of up to one hundred knots from a height of 330 feet. Much work went into refining the weapon's aerodynamics and hydrodynamics, and much practice went toward honing the techniques of its use. By the start of the Pacific War launch heights stood at one thousand feet and speeds at 250 knots.[41]

The Treaty of Versailles constrained postwar German efforts to improve weapons or develop new ones, but after Adolf Hitler abrogated the treaty, the air force purchased a Norwegian weapon and resumed work on an aerial torpedo. This version went through a long trial period before being fit for service, and the Germans used Italian weapons in the interim (developed from the same Scandinavian prototype). German torpedo bombing operations got off to a slow start for the same reasons that dogged the Italians; the navy was interested but did not control the delivery system, while the air force guarded its prerogatives jealously and only gradually developed an interest in maritime operations.[42]

The weapon the U.S. Navy took to war in 1941, the Mark 13, sacrificed speed for range and a slightly heavier warhead. The Mark 13 was first tested in 1935 and entered squadron use in 1938. In its initial form it could be dropped from fifty feet at speeds no faster than 115 knots, which were poor characteristics for the time. The initial version of the Mark 13 was reasonably reliable, but the design's first modification, which appeared in 1940, sparked a chain of disasters that extended well into World War II. In one prewar practice the modified torpedo had a 90 percent failure rate. Adjustments followed, including jury-rigged plywood stabilizer fins, but without much success. At the Battle of the Coral Sea in May 1942 *Yorktown*'s torpedo bomber squadron used both original and Mod 1 torpedoes. The carrier's commander reported that "all of the Mark 13 Mod 1 made erratic runs."[43] As late as mid-1943 tests were still showing numerous defects and yielding a 69 percent failure rate. Only by October

1944, after help was sought from the California Institute of Technology, did the United States deploy a reliable weapon that could be dropped at speeds of up to three hundred knots and heights of eight hundred feet. It had taken four years to shake out all the bugs.[44]

In the third innovation, the British, Germans, Italians, and Americans each sought an edge by developing an effective magnetic exploder for torpedo use. This device used technology similar to that in magnetic mines but was designed to detonate as the torpedo passed under the target's hull, avoiding antitorpedo protection, tearing up vulnerable bottom plates, and hopefully breaking the ship's back. Enhanced lethality meant fewer torpedoes would be required to sink a target. This was particularly important in submarine warfare; submarines patrolled far from their sources of supply and carried limited numbers of torpedoes, so making each shot deadly translated into more attacks per patrol. Despite this advantage, the British abandoned magnetic exploders for submarine torpedoes in 1929 and focused their efforts on aerial torpedoes.[45] They contemplated using these to cripple fleeing battleships, which put a premium on getting the aerial torpedo's relatively light warhead to explode under the target's soft bottom rather than against its well-protected side. Their first magnetic exploder (technically, as with most of these devices, a duplex exploder with contact and magnetic elements) appeared in 1938.

The Germans and Americans focused on torpedoes for surface ships and submarines. The U.S. Navy first tested a magnetic exploder in May 1926. Lab tests and hundreds of trials with dummy warheads followed, but the Bureau of Ordnance conducted no more shots with live warheads in the fifteen years between the first test and the U.S. entry into World War II. The German effort was similar, with their magnetic exploder being declared operational after two unsuccessful tests.[46]

EXPLOITATION: WORLD WAR II

Navies entered World War II believing that the experiences of World War I and subsequent improvements to torpedo technology would give them lethally efficient weapons. Reality proved otherwise.

The British, Germans, and Americans quickly encountered problems with their magnetic exploders. The French recovered four unexploded British air-dropped torpedoes after the 6 July 1940 attack on Mers el-Kébir, while the Italians pulled three torpedoes in "*buone condizioni*" from the bottom of Taranto's Grand Harbor after a November 1940 air raid. The British were at first unaware of these problems, but a series of premature explosions seen when British torpedo planes mistakenly attacked the cruiser *Sheffield* during the *Bismarck* hunt alerted them to the detonator's issue. The premature explosions were likely caused by oversensitivity to the Earth's magnetic field. When attacking degaussed hulls, on the other hand, the exploder proved too insensitive and required the torpedo to be within two or three feet of the hull to activate. The British recognized the problems but took until 1943 to develop a reliable replacement.[47]

In a notable coincidence, two of the most technologically advanced nations, Germany and the United States, experienced the same set of problems with their torpedoes. Not only were their magnetic exploders defective, but unreliable contact exploders and faulty depth-keeping mechanisms confused their efforts to isolate and fix all the problems. For the Germans, issues with their magnetic exploders became evident shortly after the war began. Modified magnetic exploders distributed in November 1939 did not resolve the problem, as demonstrated by multiple torpedo malfunctions in the April 1940 Norwegian campaign. Distrust in the magnetic exploder shifted use to the contact exploder, but this also proved faulty due to an overly complex design. The Germans resolved the issues with their contact exploder after May 1940 by junking it and copying the mechanism on a captured British weapon. The depth-keeping issue contributed to the mess by making torpedoes run too deep for even the magnetic exploder to function or sending them skimming along the surface in plain sight. The German commander of submarines, Admiral Karl Dönitz, wrote that "the catastrophic technical deficiencies must be regarded as a calamity," while navy chief Grand Admiral Erich Raeder said that the torpedo defects were the navy's "most urgent problems." Nonetheless, fixes from the torpedo directorate were long in coming and then often ineffective. Despite being known as early as 1938 from experience in the Spanish Civil War, the depth-keeping problem was only completely resolved in January 1942. A reliable magnetic exploder did not appear until early 1943. These fixes took place against a backdrop of bureaucratic inertia and denial, until the submarine command demanded independent investigations. Courts martial followed.[48]

Combat also exposed problems with the American magnetic exploder. Disconnecting this device, however, still resulted in misses or duds as the torpedoes ran deeper than their set depths and the Bureau of Ordnance failed to realize that the contact exploder was also defective. As with the Germans, these problems led to an adversarial relationship between the end users and shore-based technicians. Finally, in June 1943 after field testing and numerous observed failures, the Pacific Fleet ordered the magnetic exploder disabled, with the southwest Pacific command following in December. By then, the depth-setting problem had also been recognized and addressed, while a modified contact exploder came into use in October 1943. Redesigned magnetic exploders were also provided to the fleet later in the war, but crews never trusted them, and the extent of their use is unclear.[49] What is clear is that U.S. torpedoes sank many more enemy ships during the war's last two years when they ran at the expected depth and exploded when they hit a target.

The Italians adopted a magnetic torpedo at the end of 1942. It proved more reliable than the current German version, and so it saw some use by the Germans as well. The Japanese had rejected the idea of magnetic exploders prewar but later reexamined the idea of an under-keel exploder, and in 1944 the navy produced a limited number of exploders that used a tethered hydroplane to trigger the warhead when it was under a ship's keel; the extent of its use is unknown.[50]

Why did the Americans and Germans experience such problems trying to improve a relatively mature weapon system? In both cases a central technical bureaucracy orchestrated interwar development and produced an immensely complicated weapon. The more complicated the weapon became, the more the central bureaucracy displaced end users in development and testing. Security concerns kept end users relatively uninformed about the complex mechanisms and their potential malfunctions, while the multiple flaws defied detection without rigorous testing under service conditions. Budget strictures limited testing. It was natural in this environment for developers to assume end users were doing something wrong, and for the users to think that developers had no grasp of operational realities.[51] Contrast this gulf between developers and users to the situation that pertained in aircraft design, which was an even more complex process. Here the product was operated constantly by users rather than being held in reserve for war. This revealed capabilities and design problems and fostered a more positive connection between flyers and designers. Contrast also the procurement process for aircraft, where private companies competed for contracts through hands-on testing, with that for torpedoes, which was monopolized—in these cases—by a single government bureaucracy. The lesson is that the more complex the weapon, the more rigorous must be the testing and familiarization processes, with users deeply involved in the process. This is easier said than done, because complexity naturally drives a divide between designers and users while cost inhibits testing. But one must note that the Japanese navy succeeded in this with the Type 93, while the U.S. and German navies both failed.

The Japanese never had the opportunity to attack a line of Allied battleships with their Type 93 torpedoes as they planned, but the torpedo actions in the 27 February 1942 Battle of the Java Sea give some indication of how such an attack might have gone. At Java Sea, the Japanese conducted two mass daylight torpedo attacks. The first consisted of thirty-nine torpedoes (including 31 Type 93s) fired against fourteen U.S., British, and Dutch ships at ranges between 15,000 and 22,000 yards. Twenty-one minutes after the last torpedo was fired, a Dutch destroyer blew up and sank. Surprise was complete, and the Allies were certain that a submarine or mine must have delivered the fatal blow. The second attack expended ninety-eight torpedoes (90 Type 93s) over twenty-two minutes at ranges between 10,000 and 27,000 yards. This entire barrage missed. The deadly stroke came later that night when two Japanese cruisers launched a dozen Type 93s from 14,000 yards and scored two hits, sinking both Dutch cruisers. In fact, no Type 93 ever hit an Allied battleship, although there were opportunities. Four separate torpedo attacks made from as close as four thousand yards failed to hit USS *Washington* (BB 56) and *South Dakota* (BB 57) on the night of 14–15 November 1942 during the Second Naval Battle of Guadalcanal. The big ships were sailing at speed and several Type 93s exploded around them. The Japanese had no trouble torpedoing enemy destroyers that night, suggesting that the underwater turbulence caused by the battleships was causing overly sensitive torpedo triggers to explode prematurely. Such results also suggest that the Type 93 might not have been the war-winning weapon the Japanese expected had it been deployed by surprise as planned against the U.S. battle line.[52]

Despite the lack of opportunity to fulfill its primary mission, the Type 93 was devastating when used in close-range night attacks. Alone or supplemented by gunfire, Japanese torpedoes—mostly Type 93s—accounted for just over half the Allied warships sunk in surface actions. At the 30 November 1942 night battle of Tassafaronga, twenty-four Type 93s caught a line of heavy cruisers by surprise, sinking one and maiming three. The Americans again blamed submarines. As their commander wrote: "It seem[s] improbable that torpedoes with speed-distance characteristics similar to our own could have reached the cruisers at the time they did if launched from any of the enemy cruisers which were observed to be present."[53] At Rice Anchorage on 5 July 1943 a Type 93 sank a U.S. destroyer after having been fired a half hour before from more than eleven miles away, completely mystifying the U.S. commander, Rear Adm. Walden Ainsworth. Over the next week Ainsworth went on to lose two more surface actions to Japanese destroyers wielding Type 93s, with one cruiser sunk and three more crippled. Ainsworth banked on radar and a tremendous gunnery superiority to deliver victory, but the speed and power of Japanese torpedoes, combined with excellent optics and well-trained crews, outmatched his technological advantages.

As late as December 1943 the U.S. Navy was basing its estimate of Japanese torpedo capabilities on an earlier 24-inch non-oxygen torpedo recovered from an old Japanese destroyer sunk in May 1942.[54] It was easier to imagine submarines or unseen ships than to credit the Japanese navy with its technological achievement. This was understandable given the general technological superiority that the Allies held in many other areas, but it reveals a dangerous, if common, assumption as well. General technological superiority is not absolute technological superiority, and a determined opponent can still achieve superiority of its own in an area where it concentrates time, thought, and effort.

Air-dropped and surface-launched torpedoes could bring tactical success, but the torpedo held the promise of being a war-winning technology in its own right only when paired with the submarine and directed at enemy trade. The marriage of the torpedo and the submarine had come within view of this goal in World War I, and with the objective of giving the technology added capabilities that might just take it to that goal, the Germans led the way in developing a family of homing torpedoes.

A U.S. TBF-1 Avenger drops a Mark 13-1 torpedo, October 1942. The combination of torpedoes and aircraft greatly increased the ship-killing capabilities of both, although the Mark 13-1 torpedo had a dismal reliability record. With the development of front and rear wooden boxes to cushion the shock of the torpedo hitting the water, it became a useful weapon. In this photo, the front box is not yet fitted. *(Naval History and Heritage Command, NH 80-G-19189)*

One of the principal benefits Germany expected from its quest to develop a "smart" torpedo, which began in 1935, was to allow submarines to attack without exposing themselves. The weapon was designed to steer toward the noise of the target ship's engines. The major problem was getting the acoustic guidance system to ignore the sound of the torpedo itself. Electric motors rather than compressed air propulsion helped, as did reducing the speed of the torpedo from thirty to twenty-five knots. A few production examples of the initial design, the T4 *Falke*, were issued to submarines in January 1943. A much-improved version, the T5 *Zaunkönig*, was in submariners' hands in September. *Zaunkönig*s were optimized to home on the propellers of convoy escorts, the idea being that the submarines could blast their way through the escorts with acoustic torpedoes and then ravage the convoy with conventional weapons.[55]

The Allies' response to the T5 was almost immediate. They equipped their escorts with towed noisemakers that distracted the torpedoes from their targets. There were serious drawbacks—the escorts streaming noise-makers were limited to slow speeds and could not use their sonars, while the noisemakers themselves had a short lifespan—but the rapid response went far toward neutralizing the German advantage. The Allied reaction was the result of good intelligence beginning in 1939 when acoustic tor-pedo development was mentioned in the "Oslo Report," a treasure trove of information on secret weapons programs received from an anti-Nazi German physicist. Continuing intelligence stoked British concerns and caused the naval staff to issue an alert in March 1943. The noisemaker was rapidly developed against the day that the torpedo entered service.[56] When compared to their continuing ignorance of Japanese oxygen torpedoes, the Allies' rapid detection of and response to the acoustic torpedo was striking. This can be laid to three factors: first, the Allies were developing their own acoustic torpedoes and so knew that it could be done; second, they possessed better intelligence on German intentions and activities; and finally, they respected German technological prowess more than they did Japanese abilities.

The United States began work on an acoustic homing torpedo in November 1941. It had a different purpose than the T5, being designed as an air-droppable antisubmarine weapon. Unlike prewar torpedo projects, which were handled solely by the Bureau of Ordnance's naval torpedo station, the Mark 24 mine (so dubbed as a security measure) was a collaborative effort. Torpedo bodies and rudder mechanisms came from the Bureau of Ordnance. Preliminary research was conducted at Harvard. Bell Telephone Laboratories contributed the guidance system and General Electric the electric propulsion system. The Navy's Model Basin assisted with body and propeller design. Western Electric got the production contract in October 1942, and the torpedo scored its first kill in May 1943. Mark 24 (also called Fido, after the project name) was a short, light torpedo that ran in a circular pattern at a depth of 125 feet. It would continue in its search pattern at twelve knots for up to fifteen minutes, homing on any submarine within a detection range of about 1,500 yards. Fido was credited with two submarines sunk and one damaged for every ten torpedoes dropped—an astounding success rate for an antisubmarine weapon.[57] Given the exquisitely sensitive hydrophones that equipped German submarines, it must have been sheer terror to hear a Fido circling ever closer.

THE TECHNOLOGY POSTWAR AND TODAY

Torpedoes have had a long development arc in their century and a half of continued use. And while Robert Whitehead would recognize the form of his original design in many of today's torpedoes, much of the technology would leave him mystified. He would have recognized wire-guidance, but active and passive acoustic homing, wake-following homing, modern propulsion systems, and warhead materials and designs would all confound him. He would be astounded by the speed, range, and depth capabilities of the modern weapons. And he might not even recognize the rocket-propelled Russian Shkval as a torpedo (although he might have recalled the various rocket torpedo designs of the late nineteenth century). Equally astounding would have been the shift in uses of torpedoes, with antiship weapons largely restricted to submarines and shipboard and aircraft torpedoes (the descendants of the World War II Fido) devoted to antisubmarine warfare. Although much about the torpedo has changed over the past 150 years, much has remained the same. The torpedo's best platform continues to be the submarine and its best target continues to be ships, although there have been scant opportunities postwar to put this to the test. A Pakistani sub fired three homing torpedoes in the Indo-Pakistani war of 1971; one malfunctioned and one missed, although the third sank an Indian frigate. Faulty torpedoes plagued Argentine attacks in the Falklands conflict. And when the British nuclear submarine *Conqueror* attacked the Argentine cruiser *General Belgrano* during the Falklands conflict, her commander opted to use updated versions of World War II–era straight-running torpedoes rather than modern Tigerfish guided weapons. This was a case of a heavy warhead and a time-tested design winning out over the sophisticated but suspect technology of the Tigerfish. Concern about reliability is the one aspect of technology that has endured the longest.

WHAT THIS TELLS US

More than with any of the other technologies discussed in this book, the development of torpedoes shows that the combination of the right platform and the right target transforms a technology of marginal application into one with war-winning potential. In this case, torpedoes started off as a weapon that proved suitable only for attacking anchored enemy ships on the rare occasions that such targets presented themselves. Nonetheless, the world's major navies believed from the start that this was a technology of tremendous potential. The French and the Russians seized on the torpedo as a way to even the odds in a confrontation with the dominant British navy, while the British worried that it would undercut that dominance. Navies were excited (or alarmed) by every incremental improvement: better engines, more powerful warheads, better depth-keeping mechanisms, gyroscopes for improved accuracy. They experimented with platforms to deliver this promising weapon, equipping with torpedo tubes vessels ranging from ten-ton boats to battleships. Special classes of torpedo carriers were designed and built in large numbers by many navies—all of this before the self-propelled torpedo had ever hit a moving vessel in combat. On one thing, however, all were agreed. The target for this potentially excellent weapon was other warships, and the best target was the battleship.

On the eve of World War I, the torpedo seemed poised to again transform naval warfare, and the perception that capital ships were the weapon's best target had crystalized into doctrine, although there was still no evidence to support its validity. The Germans hoped that torpedoes would give them the means to wear the British navy down before a climactic fleet action; the British, worried about the exact same thing, expressed their concern in combat doctrine aimed at reducing the threat from fast enemy surface craft. The awakening to the torpedo's true threat and potential came on 22 September 1914 when a German submarine sank three British armored cruisers. Suddenly the torpedo's best platform was revealed. In 1915, when German submarines began decimating Entente shipping, the weapon's best target became manifest.

Thus, the torpedo's main impact came in the submarine war, which almost defeated Great Britain and, by bringing the United States into the war, ensured Germany's defeat. An effective submarine-torpedo pairing was, of course, not even on the horizon when Whitehead's invention first appeared, but once submarines had matured sufficiently to make effective use of torpedoes, the integration of the two technologies immeasurably multiplied their significance and power. The aircraft-torpedo pairing, which was pioneered in World War I but only ripened to maturity in the interwar period, further increased the torpedo's significance. Aircraft proved an effective way to deliver torpedoes to warships at sea and in harbor, thus fulfilling two of the torpedo's early missions.

The interwar years also saw significant improvements in the torpedo—or at least attempted improvements. The development of oxygen torpedoes, airborne torpedoes, and magnetic exploders has been described here, but there were other types as well. The British developed very efficient "burner cycle" engines that squeezed the last efficiencies from piston engine technology, while the Germans revisited World War I developments to produce torpedoes propelled by electric motors. The latter lacked the performance of their steam-heater counterparts but were far easier to make and were stealthier in attack—both important considerations for a submarine war aimed at sinking large numbers of escorted merchant ships.

All this technological innovation had mixed results. The Japanese oxygen torpedoes were superb weapons that caught Japan's opponents completely by surprise. The Americans, considering (rightly) that the Japanese lacked their technological resources, struggled to understand that their enemy had succeeded with a technology they had judged unworkable. The obverse of this was the Allied anticipation of German acoustic homing torpedoes. Because they knew the technology was feasible and saw the obvious need, the Allies were well positioned to respond quickly and effectively when the T4s and T5s appeared.

The ultimate irony in Japan's accomplishments is that its navy had applied revolutionary enhancements to the technology in pursuit of a tactical dead end. The Type 93 was a superb weapon designed for winning a certain type of battle that never happened. Given U.S. superiority in resources, and other balancing technologies, the night actions that the Japanese did win with the Type 93 were cul de sacs well off the road to victory. And while Japanese submarines also had excellent torpedoes, the Japanese navy never unleashed them against the targets that really mattered: the cargo ships transiting the long and vulnerable supply lines leading to the Allies' Pacific bases.

The problems that the technologically advanced Germans and Americans had with torpedoes developed in the interwar years show the dangers of pushing technology too far without adequate proofing and testing and of creating barriers between developer and user. Both nations were operating on the forward edge of technology in straitened circumstances: in the German case, from a hurried development program during a chaotic rearmament, and in the American case, from parsimony and misguided priorities. In both cases, recognition of the problems was hampered by the fact that the torpedoes worked some of the time, enabling bureaucratic shore establishments to resist user complaints.

Airborne torpedoes presented other novel issues that required long development cycles to resolve. The British, Japanese, and Italians invested the time and effort needed to develop satisfactory weapons. The Germans, hampered by a lack of resources in the navy and a lack of enthusiasm in the air force, did not. The Italians faced the same problems as the Germans but still managed to produce a reasonably good torpedo. The U.S. efforts were compromised by uncertainty over the role of torpedo bombers generally and the proper design parameters specifically. They produced a substandard but functional torpedo and modified it into ineffectiveness. Only a prolonged development that ultimately drew on outside resources solved the problem. External resources played an even more important role in the development of the Mark 24 acoustic torpedo. The collaboration that produced that weapon was a remarkable testament to just how effectively the United States could draw on academic, industrial, and military resources once a need was identified.

The torpedo has gone through many twists and turns in its long development. It is likely to be a part of naval arsenals for years to come and to experience more permutations before the concept is finally obsolete.

CHAPTER 4

RADIO
The Mixed Blessing

Twenty years ago we abandoned radio telephones because of their abuse.

—OFFICE OF THE COMMANDER IN CHIEF, UNITED STATES FLEET,
COMMENTING ON THE USE OF RADIO IN THE 1942
SOLOMON ISLANDS BATTLE OF TASSAFARONGA[1]

T he story of radio and sea power is, at face value, a story of communication; communication is, at heart, the exchange of information. The purposes of communication are to inform, to organize, to persuade, and to direct. This story of radio, however, also includes the ramifications of expanded communications in naval affairs and the spillover into matters of information management, command and control, strategy, and tactics. It is a tale of new capabilities, unexpected consequences, and new vulnerabilities.

THE TECHNOLOGY DESCRIBED, EARLY USE, EXPECTATIONS

Guglielmo Marconi produced the first practical wireless radio set in 1896. For the world's navies, Marconi's invention raised the possibility of tactical communications at sea beyond the horizon and, strategically, of supplementing the rapidly expanding worldwide communications network of telegraph lines and undersea cables with a mode of communication that could directly contact vessels under way.

The Italian navy trialed shore-to-ship transmissions in 1897 using a Marconi spark transmitter powered by a 250-watt battery to communicate with a cruiser eleven miles offshore. The transmission could not be fine-tuned, and so the transmitting antenna determined the frequency and the receiving antenna's size and configuration had to match. The broadcast was blasted over a wide bandwidth. The receiver displayed the signal on tape but could not filter out static. Simultaneous transmissions resulted in gibberish.[2] Nonetheless, the Italians began equipping ships with radio in 1898. By 1899 Marconi was transmitting radio signals across the English Channel, and the British navy was testing Marconi sets. Radio's first wartime use came in the Boer War and by 1901 the British had ordered fifty sets and planned to equip every battleship and cruiser on the home, Mediterranean, and China stations.

Marconi became the sole provider of radio equipment to the British navy in 1903 with a ten-year exclusive contract. The Japanese produced their own version of the Marconi set, but the U.S. Navy, rejecting Marconi's restrictive license terms, looked elsewhere. It judged the German Braun system most capable of transmitting on a discrete frequency, but changing frequencies was hard. The French systems were not tunable. The German Slaby-Arco system that the Navy ultimately decided to buy in 1903 gave the longest effective ranges—seventy-four miles.[3] The German navy likewise purchased Slaby-Arco equipment. The Russians got off to a quick start with a ship-to-ship demonstration of a Popov design in 1897. The navy tried a variety of sets but eventually settled on the Russo-French Popov-Ducretet system. The French first tested shipboard radio in 1900 and installations were widespread by 1904, but the domestic sets adopted were bulky and fragile. Austro-Hungarian ships began to carry Siemens-Braun sets in 1903.[4]

Early sets used the spark system. Transmissions were made by a key that sent the dots and dashes of Morse or other telegraphic codes. A dotter on a paper tape recorded the result. Over earphones, transmissions produced a staccato crackling or whistling noise that could be hard to distinguish from the static often present in the low frequencies used. The spark systems broadcast on broad bands over a wide range of frequencies, which meant that transmitting sets often interfered with each other. The instruments themselves were delicate and relied on long, fragile antennas. Moreover, any properly tuned receiver, whether friend or enemy, within range of a transmission could listen in. A 1903 assessment summarized general expectations for this technology. As prominent radio engineer A. Frederick Collins noted, "Wireless telegraphy has advanced with wonderful swiftness from the position of a scientific curiosity [however] it is apparently destined not to supplant pre-existing agencies except to a very limited extent; but rather to perform new functions for which preceding

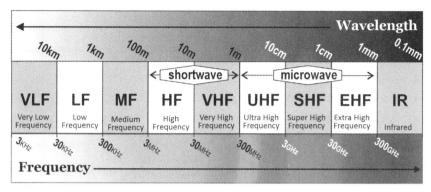

FIGURE 4.1. The Electromagnetic Spectrum. This shows the correspondence between wavelength and frequency, plus the terms commonly applied to different ranges of wavelengths.

means of electric communication were not adapted"—in short, to communicate where wires could not go and when visual signals could not be seen.[5]

Navies tolerated early radio's many shortcomings because it allowed communications from beyond the line of sight, a capacity heretofore unthinkable for a ship at sea. Nonetheless, its awkwardness in use, unreliability, and lack of security meant that navies continued to rely on flags, semaphores, and searchlights for short-range communications, especially in battle. There were even issues with acceptance of this technology as a source of orders: After the admiral commanding the U.S. squadron off Veracruz, Mexico, refused to contact the Navy Department before occupying the city in 1914, Robert Bigelow later noted that "there were Admirals and Captains who were unalterably opposed to it, who believed that when a ship was out of sight of land she belonged in the hands of her master, and that orders from the blue were an outrage and an affront to dignity."[6]

DISCOVERY: THE RUSSO-JAPANESE WAR

In the Russo-Japanese War of 1904–5 the contending navies used radio extensively. The Japanese navy faced three major tasks: to blockade the Russian battlefleet at Port Arthur, to contain a cruiser force at Vladivostok, and to counter any relief forces steaming from the Baltic. Radio played a role in all three tasks.

Blockading Port Arthur required continuous surveillance, a task made perilous by mines, torpedo boats, and shore batteries. The Japanese cruisers and destroyers that patrolled offshore relied on radio and a back-up system of courier ships to summon the main fleet, which waited safely tucked away in a nearby harbor. This spared the heavies the risks and their crews and machinery the wear and tear entailed by a close blockade. The Japanese considered the reliable range of their sets to be about sixty miles and deployed accordingly. Initially only cruisers carried radio, but destroyer flotilla leaders began to receive sets after the war began.[7]

This system worked reasonably well. A Japanese destroyer reported the Russian fleet sortie in June 1904 to a cruiser that then radioed an alarm in time for the battle squadron to intervene. A cruiser first spotted and reported by radio the August sortie that led to the Battle of the Yellow Sea. The Russians realized what the Japanese were doing, and Vice Admiral Makarov complained as early as March 1904 that long-range radio allowed the enemy to concentrate against him whenever he attempted to sail. The Russians, of course, also used radio to report Japanese activities, and when they heard strengthening Japanese signals, they often sortied their destroyers in response. But as the blockaded force, they found radio less useful than did their opponents.[8]

Radio was not so successful against the Russian cruisers at Vladivostok. The Japanese lacked bases to maintain scouts off the Siberian harbor, which allowed the Russians to repeatedly dispatch ships down the Korean coast and as far east as Tokyo Bay. During an April 1904 sortie each side intercepted the other's transmissions at close range, but fog prevented contact. In mid-June the Russians raided south to the Tsushima Strait, where an enemy cruiser spotted them and radioed an alarm. In trying to get her signal acknowledged, the Japanese ship had to break contact and close a shore station. Her enciphered report was garbled, but Vice Admiral Kamimura Hikonojō, commanding the force tasked with intercepting the Russians, finally reacted when he received a plain language message. Kamimura never got within visual range and spent a frustrating hour trying to get the scout to report the enemy's course.[9] Julian Corbett, in his confidential history of the war, ascribed the delay to "some unhealthy excitement" that caused "a reckless use of wireless."[10] Navies would discover that whether excited or dispassionate, communications in combat would naturally expand to overload available channels.

The next two raids saw more use of radio, but again Kamimura failed to engineer an engagement. He found himself greatly hindered by a flood of inaccurate reports and imaginary sightings, especially after a Russian appearance off Tokyo Bay caused Japanese shore stations to panic. A final raid conducted shortly after the Battle of the Yellow Sea found Kamimura's communication channels swamped in the aftermath of that action where "the organization of the radio and cable communications left much to be desired."[11] Nonetheless, Kamimura finally brought the Russian cruisers to battle. Radio proved useful in allowing him to concentrate his ships, but it was not decisive in establishing contact or managing the battle once it began.[12]

The arduous journey of the Russian Baltic fleet to its destruction off Tsushima is an oft-told tale. Radio allowed Vice Admiral Tōgō to position scouts off the straits between Korea and the Home Islands while the battlefleet waited in a Korean anchorage. One scout radioed the Russian fleet's presence as it approached Tsushima Strait, and, although her first report gave the wrong position, she broadcast clarifications. The Russians intercepted this traffic, but when asked for permission to jam the transmissions, the fleet commander, Vice Admiral Zinovy Rozhestvensky, preferred to preserve strict radio silence. This may have delayed his eventual detection, but did not prevent it. Eight and a half hours after the initial sighting, Tōgō got a definitive report that the Russians were making for the straits' eastern channel. He deployed his heavy ships accordingly and won a decisive victory. The admiral summarized radio's role in his official report: "The information thus received enabled me at a distance of several tens of miles to form a vivid picture in my mind of the condition of the enemy. I was thus able, before I could see the enemy with my own eyes, to know that the enemy's fighting sections comprised the whole of the Second and the Third Squadrons . . . that the enemy's rate of speed was about twelve knots; that the enemy were continuing to steam in a north-easterly direction; and so forth."[13]

The Russians, on the other hand, using newly installed Slaby-Arco units, had become disillusioned with their equipment during the long voyage east: "Admiral Rozhestvensky complained that after strenuous efforts over eight months to perfect wireless telegraphy in the fleet, the results were hopeless." It appears that many of his problems were due to poor maintenance and undertrained operators.[14]

The Russo-Japanese War demonstrated the utility of radio. In just five years, the technology had gone from experimental trials to being an essential tool that greatly facilitated certain types of operations. Without radio, the Japanese would have worked much harder and taken greater risks to contain the Russian fleet at Port Arthur or to intercept the Baltic fleet. Radio was less effective in dealing with the Russian cruiser raids, but the contrast between the Yellow Sea and Tsushima battles showed how wartime practice increased efficient use. All this was accomplished with crude sets of limited range and vulnerable to interference from weather conditions and enemy action. The war also demonstrated that radio needed more power to increase range and improved frequency discrimination to handle greater traffic loads.

There were concerns beyond the merely technical. The Russians had effectively swamped radio transmissions from Japanese shore stations trying to direct naval bombardments of Port Arthur. Both sides tried to gauge the other's location from the apparent strength of radio signals but Vice Admiral Kamimura noted that the conclusions drawn were often wrong. Finally, radio provided new insights into enemy operations because every radio message was available to a sufficiently sensitive receiver tuned to the same frequency. The only safeguards were codes and ciphers, but considerable information could be gleaned even without decryption. Rozhestvensky surmised that his force had been spotted, for example, because the enciphered Japanese contact reports were rebroadcast by many Japanese ships and "proclaimed themselves of an entirely different character" than previous Japanese signals.[15]

The use of radio also raised more subtle issues. As Kamimura discovered, it was difficult to get a scout to transmit the information he needed to accurately determine the enemy's location in relation to his own. Often, the scout could not be sure of its own position unless it was operating off a known coast. Nor could it know with absolute surety the position of its own fleet. Moreover, the Japanese discovered on several occasions that their radio network could carry only so much traffic and, if the net became overloaded, it could effectively carry no traffic at all.

EVOLUTION: TO WORLD WAR I

Radio technology improved in the decade between the Russo-Japanese War and World War I. The 1903 invention of quenched spark sets, which broadcast a distinctive musical tone rather than a crackle or whistle, enhanced clarity and range, and they came into general use after 1910. Arc transmitters, another 1903 invention, broadcast a continuous wave that gave greater ranges while using less power. Receivers increased in sophistication as well, first with crystal sets and then primitive vacuum tubes.[16]

Equipment improvements led to a global communications revolution. The major European powers and the United States constructed huge transmission stations to supplement cable systems and reach distant colonies. The Germans built a massive station outside Berlin, with a 200-kilowatt transmitter and two square kilometers of antennas. It could broadcast across the Atlantic or to Germany's African colonies. The Americans,

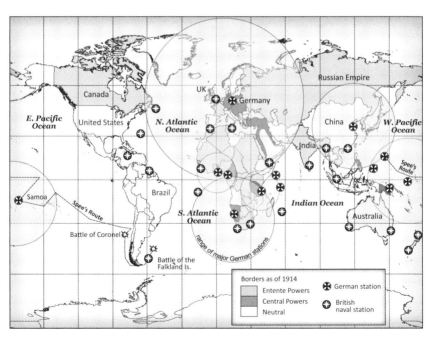

FIGURE 4.2. German and British Radio Networks, August 1914. The large circles show the nominal ranges of the German stations, which were built as insurance against the British severing German cable links. The map also shows Spee's route across the Pacific and into the Atlantic.

French, and Italians constructed similar longwave stations for distant communications. Admiralties supported this work, being anxious to establish routine communications with ships in distant waters. Germany saw radio as a means of maintaining communications if denied access to overseas cables, most of which were controlled by Great Britain. The British, in turn, regarded control of the world's communications network as a means of maintaining imperial hegemony and their supremacy at sea.

Although ranges grew, atmospheric interference still affected even the most advanced transmitters, and maximum ranges remained unpredictable. The inability to tune to precise frequencies was another problem; operators still experienced interference from nearby transmitters or even from distant stations. In an effort to minimize interference afloat, navies assigned different frequencies to different uses. Such assignments reduced but did not resolve the problem, particularly given the limited number of sufficiently separated frequencies available. In 1907, for example, the British employed eight frequencies, the Germans four, and the Japanese and Italians three each. The British discovered in 1906 peacetime maneuvers how easy it was to overload radio nets with unnecessary traffic.[17] One participant reported: "It is remarked that the workings of W/T [wireless telegraphy] was most inefficient, not because it didn't work but because of the enormous number of useless and obsolete messages transmitted which had to be received and decoded."[18] Warships from various nations sent to protect citizens during the 1912 Balkan war found the mutual interference so impenetrable that the captains held a meeting to "apportion certain hours of the day to the ships of each nation."[19]

Further complicating the military use of radio was the need to keep many messages secret through the use of codes and ciphers. Codes used arbitrary groups of letters and numbers to symbolize concepts and commands. Using the word *roger* as the command to open fire is a code. By contrast, a cipher, which was often added to encoded messages to provide an additional layer of security, involved substituting letters or numbers for other letters or numbers. The word *roger* could be enciphered by substituting the next letter in the alphabet for each letter in the word, producing *sphfs*. Navy codebooks were gigantic, with thousands of entries covering a wide variety of words and concepts. The German SKM (Signalbuch der Kaiserlichen Marine) codebook included more than 34,000 code groups.

Radio masts of the U.S. Navy radio station at Chollas Heights, San Diego. The powerful longwave radio stations of the era required enormous antennas; the buildings give a sense of scale. *(Naval History and Heritage Command, UG 21–11.03)*

Senders and recipients had to have the same version of the book, which meant any revision to a code required a massive distribution exercise. The laborious process of encoding, enciphering, deciphering, and decoding even a simple message took time and allowed ample scope for human error. It also caused congested communication networks (for example, by forcing the retransmission of coded messages garbled on receipt) and required navies to balance the needs for security and speed.[20]

By 1914 every large navy had equipped its major warships with radio, and most had at least a decade of experience in its use. The U.S. Navy used a variety of quenched spark sets but was switching to continuous wave. The German navy started the war with continuous wave sets in its battleships, flagships, and coastal stations and quenched spark sets in other vessels. The British largely made do with spark transmitters, albeit with a modification that produced a more musical note than the original crackle. They did fit continuous wave sets in some cruisers intended for long-distance radio work and installed them more generally starting in the second half of 1916. In general, German equipment outperformed British material in range and clarity; early German submarine sets could reach as far as three hundred miles compared to a British limit of sixty. This was significant; it meant that German submarines could report British vessels in much of the North Sea, but British boats watching German anchorages needed repeater ships, or carrier pigeons, to reach English bases. In 1914 the French were already using radio as their major form of ship-to-ship and ship-to-shore communications and seldom resorted to visual signals. The Italian navy had 250 land and shipborne sets in 1914 and introduced a Marconi voice telephony system in 1914. Austria-Hungary continued to prefer German equipment and had fifty-five shipborne sets in operation in 1914. In some respects, Russia's radio setup was the most sophisticated, based on its experiences in the Russo-Japanese War. A specific doctrine was in place to use radio to warn of German incursions, to jam enemy transmissions, to overcome enemy attempts to jam, to intercept enemy transmissions, and to gather intelligence.[21]

EXPLOITATION: WORLD WAR I

Six hours prior to the outbreak of war in 1914 Germany demonstrated radio's strategic utility by broadcasting an order for all shipping to seek shelter in neutral ports. Some of Great Britain's first actions were against Germany's global communications network, cutting the cables running through the North Sea and then attacking the radio stations at Dar-es-Salaam (Tanzania) and Yap and Samoa (in the Pacific) in August and Nauru, Rabaul, and Augaur (in the Pacific) and Douala (Kamerun/Cameroon) in September.[22]

These attacks isolated Germany's most powerful overseas force, the East Asiatic Squadron commanded by Vice Admiral Maximilian von Spee and based at Tsingtao (Qingdao), China. Motivated in part by the need to reestablish contact with his superiors, Spee proceeded to operate across two oceans and into a third effectively using radio for strategic command

and control. While Spee himself steamed across the Pacific with his main force of two armored cruisers, he detached light cruiser *Emden* to raid west into the Indian Ocean, another light cruiser to Honolulu, and two more to attack Entente facilities in the Pacific, including the cable relay station on Fanning Island. *Emden* operated independently, but Spee communicated with his other detached forces and supply ships via radio. Notably, the admiral summoned light cruisers *Dresden* and *Leipzig* over a distance of 2,500 miles to a rendezvous at Easter Island. As Spee approached the South American coast, he received information via a round robin chain of radio messages sent from Berlin to German consuls in eastern South America, who cabled them to ports along the west coast. German merchantmen in the ports then radioed the messages onward. The British relied on radio as well. Messages went by cable to Montevideo and then by radio to a low-power station in the Falkland Islands for transmission to ships at sea (see figure 4.2).

On 1 November Spee reached the Chilean coast and encountered four ships of an inferior British force off Coronel. Each side had taken the precaution of using only one ship to transmit radio messages, which led both commanders to think they were stalking solitary prey. The British commander accepted combat despite poor odds, and the result was the loss of two armored cruisers with all hands. The surviving ships ran south to get beyond German jamming range so they could broadcast news of the disaster to other British units in the area, which then fled to the British base in the Falklands.

The British admiralty reacted by dispatching battlecruisers to the South Atlantic, the Caribbean, and the Pacific side of the Panama Canal. They also sent two cruisers equipped with long-range radios: one to Ascension Island in the mid-Atlantic to serve as a link to the southern battlecruiser force, and the other to transfer its long-range set to the battlecruisers. Meanwhile, Spee sailed into the Atlantic, planning to destroy the British radio station in the Falklands as part of the tit-for-tat campaign against enemy communications.

Unfortunately for Spee, he encountered the battlecruiser reinforcements at the Falkland's Port Stanley. The big ships had maintained radio silence, and so their presence caught the German admiral completely by surprise. In the ensuing battle, Spee went down with his flagship, and only one of the five German cruisers escaped destruction. The British hunted the survivor, the light cruiser *Dresden*, with the help of intercepted radio messages and destroyed her in March 1915.[23]

In the Indian Ocean, *Emden* wreaked havoc. For three months her captain avoided the Entente warships hunting him by monitoring their transmissions while maintaining radio silence himself. In the end, however, he fell afoul of radio. In November 1914, when *Emden* attacked the Cocos Islands to destroy the British radio and cable station there, the operators transmitted an alarm. The larger cruiser *Sydney* was escorting a convoy nearby and rushed to the scene. She surprised *Emden* and sank her.[24]

Spee used radio mainly in a strategic context, to get information and control movement over long distances. As the war continued, radio served an increasing number of functions, including a significant role in tactical signaling. The Battle of Jutland provides an excellent illustration of the tactical use of radio in the midwar period where it acted in conjunction with traditional methods such as flag hoists, semaphores, and lights.

Jutland involved nearly the entire British Grand Fleet and the German High Seas Fleet—a combined total of 250 warships. It occurred after a series of intercepted and decoded radio messages regarding minesweeping, seaplanes, navigation, and other matters alerted the British admiralty to the likelihood of a German sortie. Combined with intercepted orders to the High Seas Fleet to raise steam and assemble, these messages also allowed the British to guess the German route and mission.[25]

This information helped Jellicoe intercept the High Seas Fleet with the Grand Fleet's whole strength. Vice Admiral Reinhard Scheer had planned to use radio-equipped zeppelin airships for reconnaissance, but poor weather grounded them and forced him to rely on submarines. These, however, mostly failed to spot the British ships as they left port. First contact came when the German scouting line collided with the British battlecruiser force, which had sailed from Rosyth to meet the rest of the Grand Fleet coming from Scapa Flow.

Both sides reported the initial contact via radio. The technology was up to the task, but procedures were not. An ideal sighting report would have included the enemy's position, composition, course, and speed. Few of the sighting reports at Jutland met this ideal, although the Germans did slightly better. Their method was to report the enemy's position directly, while the British gave the reporting ship's location with estimated range and bearing to the enemy. Thus, German reports contained fewer elements to omit or garble. Jellicoe was further hampered by being uncertain where his battlecruiser force was relative to his battle line. This meant that when his battlecruisers made first contact with the Germans, Jellicoe could not be certain how the positions being reported corresponded to his own location. This was critical, as he had to decide how and when to deploy the Grand Fleet into a line of battle as the High Seas Fleet approached. Jellicoe continued to demand information from the battlecruisers until he finally received a report, by searchlight, that gave the bearing to Scheer's ships. This was barely adequate given that reports from the battlecruiser force had been sporadic and that the report he did receive arrived fifteen long minutes after he first demanded it. Jellicoe immediately deployed his fleet, making the order by signal flags and radio. He made the right decision based on the incomplete information and famously succeeded in capping Scheer's "T." It easily could have gone the other way.[26]

During the battle, more than half of the German reports gave enemy position, and about a quarter also gave enemy course. The British made half again as many reports as the Germans, but fewer than one in ten included enemy distance and bearing (needed to determine enemy position based on the spotter's position), and only half of those gave enemy course. Determining an enemy's range and course is difficult when operating at the extreme limits of visibility. Nonetheless, the Germans were far more successful at this than the British. The disparity must be attributed to doctrine and training and underlined the role of these critical elements in the use of new technology. British reporting deficiencies had in fact been prefigured by similar failures when the German battlecruisers had raided three British coastal towns in December 1914. Tōgō was better served by his scouts at Tsushima than was Jellicoe at Jutland, for although Tōgō's scouts had a better sense of their positions (due to patrolling fixed locations), they had to cope with cruder equipment.[27]

The greatest British reporting failure came in the evening after the battle, when the retreating High Seas Fleet crossed behind the Grand Fleet. The failures began with a spotting report from the battlecruisers that was complete as to information but wrong as to position. More system failures followed. British light cruisers and destroyers clashed with the German battlefleet as it crossed the British wake, but few ships reported the contacts, and Jellicoe's flagship received only some of those messages. Battleship crews saw gunfire astern but maintained silence. Some battleship officers argued after the fact that the use of radio was discouraged; others maintained that it had been reasonable for them to assume that Jellicoe must have seen what they had seen. These explanations only make sense in the context of Jellicoe's battle orders, which focused on cruisers and battlecruisers making reports and on battleships fighting. Reconnaissance was not something Grand Fleet battleship officers regarded as part of their job—another demonstration of how doctrine and training affect the use and usefulness of technology.[28]

Both sides employed radio for tactical signals, but neither relied on it. Although flag signals suffered from the vagaries of visibility and a limited vocabulary, they had advantages over radio, particularly in communicating maneuvers. The use of flags in the British and most other navies followed a well-practiced drill in which the ships receiving the signal acknowledged receipt. This assured the force commander that his subordinate units understood the ordered maneuver and were ready to carry it out. With radio, recipients had to crowd onto the same frequency to acknowledge receipt, a process that could also be complicated by jamming, atmospheric disturbances, and equipment failures. Being subject to interception, such use could also provide intelligence to the enemy. In short, a flag hoist was more secure and usually faster.

Jellicoe had announced before the battle that once in action he would signal by radio and visual means. Although the battle orders also provided for maneuvering the fleet before contact by radio, Jellicoe elected, with one exception, to maintain radio silence and maneuver the fleet by visual means alone until contact was made. Once the action commenced, Jellicoe sent most signals to the main force under his command by radio and flags together. Fourteen of twenty signals were duplicated in this way. He relied on radio to communicate with his battlecruisers while they were detached, with one signal by searchlight at their closest approach. However, he maneuvered his destroyers solely by visual means. In practice, Jellicoe relied on the shortest-ranged signaling method adequate to the job: flags, then searchlights, then radio. Critical signals to his main body were duplicated by flags and radio.[29]

Scheer used a set of commander-only signals to maneuver his entire fleet. These were made by a combination of low-powered radio and one or two flags, with the maneuver communicated by radio and flag and made executive when the flags were hauled down. This method allowed Scheer to order his entire battle line to reverse course from rear ship to front ship, with the rear ship turning first and each succeeding ship turning thereafter—a difficult maneuver that his fleet successfully executed three times during the battle. Radio was an integral part of this system and not merely a back-up. When battleship *König* had her radios knocked out, she failed to understand Scheer's first order to reverse course and so steamed on despite the flag hoists. Scheer made slightly fewer signals than did Jellicoe to main formations in company, although he made a higher proportion of his signals by radio and visual means—sixteen of eighteen signals addressed to his main force and three of four signals to his torpedo boats. The German system was more susceptible to battle damage than the belt-and-suspenders British method but was superior when quick maneuver was essential.[30]

Moving beyond surface warfare, the Germans also integrated radio into their submarine operations. The massive radio station near Berlin proved capable of reaching submarines even thousands of miles away, which allowed the German command to control submarines in the Atlantic. Staff ashore even attempted to coordinate submarine attacks against Allied convoys late in the war—a foreshadowing of tactics practiced in World War II—but without notable success.[31]

German submarine communications were two-way. As noted, early war submarine sets had ranges up to three hundred miles, but by 1917 German submarines radios could reach nearly two thousand. Predictably, the ability to report soon became the requirement to report. Sinkings of merchantmen, encounters with warships, approaches to friendly minefields—all required radio reports. And while these reports were undoubtedly useful to headquarters, they also benefited the enemy. To further explore this, the issue of countermeasures must be considered.[32]

COUNTERMEASURES

All major naval powers attempted to impede or exploit enemy radio communications. Such measures took four forms. Most basically, navies could attempt to jam enemy traffic with their own transmissions. Second, radio direction-finding used enemy transmissions to locate the ship making the transmission. Third, interception of enemy transmissions led to cryptanalysis, the breaking of enemy codes and reading the content of transmissions. Cryptanalysis had long been a feature of military and naval intelligence, but the ability to intercept vast quantities of radio messages immensely broadened its scope. This unprecedented access to enemy communications also drove traffic analysis, the fourth countermeasure. This looked at the origin and pattern of transmissions to deduce enemy dispositions and intentions without unlocking the contents of each message. All these countermeasures had been prefigured in the Russo-Japanese War and were greatly refined in World War I.

Italy pioneered radio direction-finding (DF) when it tested a Bellini-Tosi system in 1908. This used a special antenna that took multiple measurements of the same signal, which could then be used to calculate a radio transmission's bearing. Initially this system was impractical for shipborne use, but it proved reasonably effective for land-based units. Even better, a network of DF installations could triangulate locations based on readings of the same transmission from different locations. The Russians established an effective three-station DF network in the Baltic by the end of 1914. The British established their first DF stations on the Continent to aid the land war, but by early 1915 they had established a chain of six stations in Great Britain and one in Flanders. The British stations, which used sensitive vacuum tube receivers, could typically locate a transmitter in the North Sea to within twenty miles and in the Atlantic to within fifty (see figure 4.3). The German North Sea DF network was in operation in 1915 but was less effective due to its shorter baseline. Austria-Hungary tested a Bellini-Tosi system in January 1914 but abandoned its use late that year and did not implement an effective DF network until 1916.[33]

Radio direction-finding was valuable in part because it was immediate and did not need to understand an intercepted signal. By 1917 any ship that used radio in range of enemy DF stations was potentially disclosing its location to the enemy. While the fixes DF yielded were too imprecise to guide attacks against individual vessels, they did allow convoys to be routed around submarine positions, give notice of enemy sorties, and help direct reconnaissance.

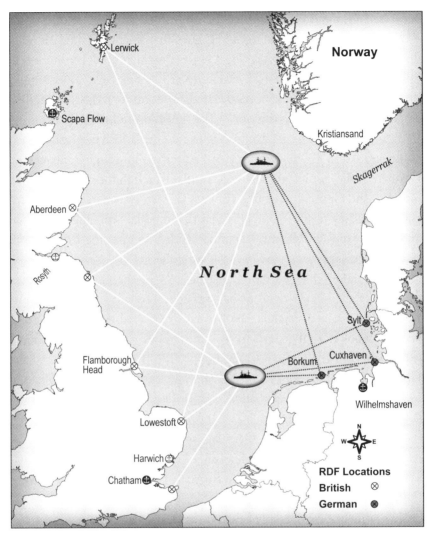

FIGURE 4.3. North Sea Direction-Finding Stations. The British, with more stations and a longer baseline, could get better direction-finding fixes on ships in the North Sea than the Germans could.

The content of radio traffic also became an important source of operational intelligence during World War I. At the start of the war the French Deuxième Bureau was the world's premier intelligence service and already had a network of radio interception stations focused on foreign military and diplomatic traffic. Vienna got a head start by acquiring two of Italy's major codes and practicing on the large volume of Italian transmissions between Libya and Rome during the 1911–12 Italo-Turkish war. Russia's Baltic fleet had three communications hubs that were charged with radio direction-finding and intercepting German radio traffic. The station at Spithamn, at the northwestern extremity of Estonia, began operating in 1914, originally to audit the fleet's own radio use and "to promote discipline among radio telegraph operators."[34] The transition to intercepting enemy traffic was natural and smooth. In August 1914 the British navy established a unit headed by the director of naval education to examine intercepted German traffic, but its progress was "antlike" through the war's first three months. The German navy likewise was slow to systematically intercept and read enemy traffic—a process that the imperial army initiated when an intercept unit in Belgium began decrypting and passing British naval traffic to the naval command in early November 1914.[35]

The situation changed rapidly, particularly in the North Sea, where the bulk of the world's naval power was concentrated, and in the Baltic, where, by a stroke of fortune, the Russians recovered the German SKM fleet codebook from the German cruiser *Magdeburg*, a bounty they shared with their British allies in October 1914.[36] The British also captured the German mercantile code (Handelsschiffsverkehrsbuch [HVB]), also used by light naval units and zeppelins), and in December they recovered the flag officer code (Verkehrsbuch [VB]) from a sunken torpedo boat. Even though the ciphers that the Germans applied to their codes had to be continually cracked, these codebooks jumpstarted both British and Russian decryption efforts. It took the Russians more than a month to solve the first cipher key, but with practice, they got to the point where they could routinely solve the daily key in three hours. On the other side of the hill, a German army unit cracked the British flotilla code in March 1915 and the fleet code in July, but the Germany navy was slow to establish an interception and deciphering organization. Not until December 1914 did the shore command ask the High Seas Fleet to begin monitoring British radio traffic, and not until February 1916 was the navy's decryption service, E-Dienst, formally established with three interception stations to cover the North Sea and Baltic. By this time the British service had ten interception stations and thirty full-time decoders working in shifts.[37]

British codebreaking efforts first bore fruit in December 1914 when they gave warning of a German battlecruiser raid against the English coastal towns of Whitby, Scarborough, and Hartlepool. The British decoded the German commander's request for aerial reconnaissance and, based on an operation conducted the month before, correctly guessed that a similar operation was in the works. The British almost intercepted the enemy with a superior force, being thwarted only by poor tactical signaling and bad weather. However, the British did not intercept signals indicating that twenty-two capital ships of the High Seas Fleet were following behind and so sent only ten capital ships to attack the raiders. This was exactly the sort of mismatch that the Germans had hoped to achieve, but the admiral commanding the High Seas Fleet grew concerned that he was about to meet the entire Grand Fleet. He turned away and missed the opportunity to overwhelm the British force.[38] Thus, this event illustrated the perils as well as the benefits of signals intelligence (SIGINT). It allowed the British to anticipate the raid but was not enough to give them victory. Because it gave only limited information about the enemy operation and led to bad assumptions, it also exposed the British to defeat. Over the course of the war, the general value of radio intelligence outweighed the danger of its use in specific cases, but the danger was always there.

By 1916 the British were eavesdropping on most German radio messages sent from their main bases. By 1917 the British believed they were intercepting all signals in the North Sea as well as some from the Baltic and Mediterranean. Likewise, the Germans thought, despite greater British security precautions, that they were aware of most British operations. Each side's codebreaking efforts became entangled with those of the other, as occurred in late 1916 when the British intercepted radio messages presaging a German destroyer raid into the English Channel. The Germans intercepted the radio transmissions repositioning the British forces in anticipation of the foray and so switched their own plans to raid shipping off the Dutch coast. The British in turn intercepted the change in German plans and laid a new trap for the Germans. An interception finally did take place, but it had no result.[39]

Under such conditions, it was not remarkable that the battlefleets came to blows only once. In fact, in the North Sea, SIGINT's main benefit came from predicting enemy movements. This aided the British in finding the Germans but also aided the Germans in avoiding superior British forces. The British, being in the position of blockading the Germans, benefited most from this type of intelligence. Without SIGINT, the only way the British could have reacted to German sorties in a timely fashion would have been by maintaining scouting forces constantly at sea. They had done this in the war's first months, and the strain had been tremendous. As Jellicoe himself said as early as January 1915, "While the intercepts last we can husband our strength and move only when there is a real cause."[40] The Germans would persist in their strategic vision of annihilating an isolated portion of the British fleet but would discover that neither radio intercepts, nor zeppelin reconnaissance, nor submarine patrol lines would give them the assurance that they were springing a trap and not steaming into one. They would always labor under the fear that the Grand Fleet lurked just over the horizon.

Some navies were more sensitive than others to the possibilities of radio intelligence and the need of an effective organization. Radio intelligence was, after all, new territory and between 1914 and 1918, admiralties were juggling many new technologies. The factors that contributed to effective radio intelligence included need, organization, luck (as in the recovery of enemy codebooks), persistence, and dedicated resources. Also important was a navy's approach to the problem. The British considered SIGINT a strategic asset to be guarded and nourished. The Germans regarded it as a tactical asset to be exploited. Two examples serve to illustrate the impact of "approach" and "organization." In November 1914 the German army broke a French codebook that included naval traffic and passed it along to the admiralty. The naval staff in turn instructed the High Seas Fleet to forward to Berlin for decoding any intercepted traffic that seemed to correspond to the code. The fleet then broadcast two hundred copies of this request to individual ships, effectively informing the French that their code had been compromised. The British, on the other hand, so closely guarded their penetration of German codes that they withheld information from their closest allies. David Kahn writes that when the director of the French cryptologic service was visiting his British counterpart, he asked why the British had not advised the French about a signal regarding danger to one of their vessels. His counterpart replied that it was better to lose the ship than to take precautionary measures that risked disclosing the cryptanalysis to the Germans.[41]

Inertia also played a part in facilitating SIGINT. Of the codes compromised by captured books, the German navy replaced the VB in May

1917, began the replacement of the SKM in 1916 but did not complete it until May 1917, and never entirely replaced the HVB—this despite the fact that the German navy learned in August 1915 from a prisoner of war about the SKM's capture. One specialist, Ivo Juurvee, recently wrote: "German ignorance toward cipher security seems to be amazing according to current standards and was rather amazing even by standards of 100 years ago."[42] But the Germans were hardly alone in this regard. An intercepted German signal tipped the British codebreakers to the fact that the British merchant code was compromised, but even the British, with their better sense of the vulnerability of radio communications, found that switching codes and ciphers in the middle of a war was a daunting task.[43]

Traffic analysis was another form of radio intelligence. The premise was that even if an enemy's messages could not be read, an analysis of the patterns and forms of transmissions could still yield useful information. A sudden uptick in the number of messages could presage a major operation or suggest that the enemy had anticipated a friendly operation. Further, traffic analysis had a symbiotic relationship with codebreaking. Recognizing patterns in messages yielded insights into the nature of the messages themselves—weather reports, reports of position, minesweeping reports—that could focus codebreaking efforts. Conversely, codebreaking could help to identify standard message formats, which could enable useful analysis even if codes or ciphers were changed.

The best antidote to direction-finding, codebreaking, and traffic analysis was radio silence. Short of silence, limited use was next best, especially because large volumes of intercepts facilitated successful decryption efforts. The German navy, for one, used radio profusely, even in port, giving Russian and British codebreakers a mass of material to work with. By contrast, the British ran landlines to ships in harbor, permitting communication by telephone or telegraph. In fairness to the Germans, they used low-power radio in harbor and mistakenly believed that the signals could not be intercepted, but this was not their only sin. Overuse also increased the probability of bad practices that could give insight into cipher and code changes. One of the most common mistakes was to transmit the same message in both an old and a new cipher or code; once a transmission was recognized as identical, it was a relatively simple matter to break the new format. For example, the SKM codebook was replaced in the North Sea in mid-1916 but not in the Baltic until May 1917. When a message needed to be transmitted to ships operating in both seas, it was sent in both codes, thus compromising the replacement code from the start.[44] Another poor practice was to send certain messages—weather reports, for example—in a standard format, allowing the codebreakers to divine the likely content from the form and attack the text from there.

The German navy improved radio discipline as results from its own radio direction network sparked a growing appreciation of the probable effectiveness of its enemy counterparts. Raids such as those against the Dover Barrage and Lerwick convoys in 1916 and 1917 caught the British by surprise because they were launched without radio chatter, but not until April 1918 did the Germans enforce strict radio silence for a major fleet operation.[45]

Unlike the Germans, the Austro-Hungarian navy recognized the dangers of radio from the beginning and practiced radio silence as much as possible. That they operated in a narrow sea and along a friendly coast whereby messages could be passed by secure landlines and cables and relayed to vessels by visual means made radio silence easier to practice; they even resorted to dropping message canisters from seaplanes rather than transmitting by radio. The repeated ability of Austro-Hungarian raiders to surprise Entente and Italian forces reflected this practice but there were still times when radio had to be used, such as when submarines returned from patrol.[46] The Italians also worked to keep their radio traffic to a minimum, their focus on security being reflected by their efforts to develop a short-range voice telephony system.

EVOLUTION: BETWEEN WORLD WARS

After World War I, the use of radio exploded. The first commercial stations began broadcasting, and during the 1920s radio receivers became common household items. In these years three major developments advanced the naval use of radio: voice radio, shortwave radio, and improved airborne radio and radio aids. Radio's ability to communicate with devices as well as with people also led navies to develop remotely controlled weapons, yet another new frontier in warfare.

Shortwave radio was the first of these developments to enter general use. In 1916 the Italian navy, seeking ways to improve the security of their radio traffic, experimented with shortwave transmissions to see if they could provide secure line-of-sight, ship-to-ship communications. These tests failed due to the limitations of available vacuum tubes, but better tubes led to the discovery of the "skip" phenomenon in which short radio waves are reflected from the ionosphere back to Earth. The skip, which both Marconi and the U.S. Navy successfully tested in the mid-1920s, provided relatively low-powered shortwave sets operating in the spectrum of 3 to 30 megahertz (MHz; ten to one hundred meters) with ranges rivaling those of the huge longwave stations then in operation. Navies seized upon shortwave as a cost-effective and reliable means of long-range communication. This evolution was complete before the start of World War II.[47]

The ability to broadcast voices over the electromagnetic spectrum (see figure 4.1) was demonstrated as early as 1907 when the U.S. Navy tested an innovative De Forest set that could transmit sound up to ten miles. The initial results were so encouraging that the Navy ordered twenty-six sets for use in the Great White Fleet's world cruise. However, these were constructed and installed in haste, and the operators were poorly trained. The experiment was considered unsuccessful, and the sets were unin-stalled when the fleet returned in 1909. A voice set built by the German firm Lorenz, also introduced in 1907, similarly found no purchase, while the British navy experimented with voice in the same year but stopped development when it proved unreliable. Along with immature technology, these sets met with resistance from captains reluctant to accept greater oversight. In the Great White Fleet, "ships often simply shut down their radios at sea so as to avoid receiving undesirable orders." This stands as an opportunity lost and as an example of how a lack of persistence can retard technological growth.[48]

Using continuous wave transmitters paired with improved vacuum tubes, practical voice telephony sets appeared toward the end of World War I when the U.S. Navy equipped its subchasers with sets that could switch between five different frequencies with the push of a button; these operated in the medium frequency band of 500 to 1,500 kilohertz. Voice telephony was particularly useful for antisubmarine warfare because attacking ships could use it to coordinate their movements in real time, but the equipment was soon in demand for all types of ships in both the

U.S. and British navies. Navies continued to develop voice radio, looking for systems to provide secure, limited range tactical communication as well as voice communications with aircraft. The U.S. Navy introduced its first very high frequency (VHF) experimental system in 1929, to be followed by the highly successful TBS set. TBS debuted in 1938 and operated with four watts of power in the sixty- to eighty-MHz range.[49] In essence, this unit enabled the sender to pick up a telephone handset and broadcast his voice over the selected frequency, which would then be heard on any receiver within range that was set to that frequency. TBS was a model designation rather than an acronym, but it was quickly dubbed "Talk Between Ships." Because higher frequencies paired with low power resulted in limited ranges, voice radio seemed ideal for tactical signaling, allowing quick communication with a minimal risk of enemy interception. The reality would be somewhat different.[50]

Interwar advances in radio multiplied the effectiveness of naval aircraft. Airborne radio direction-finders aided navigation, while the carrier navies developed radio homing beacons to guide aircraft back to flight decks. Aircraft could more easily carry shortwave sets and their smaller antennas, which allowed scouts to report sightings from great distances. These developments extended the capabilities of sea-based aircraft from barely over the horizon to hundreds of miles from their parent ships. The British and Americans went further still. Following the lead of the British air force's land-based radar interception system, they equipped their fighters with voice radios and, in the early days of World War II, pioneered radar-based interception with a controller guiding fighters to the enemy based on shipboard radar contacts. This development more than any other increased the survivability of carriers, which, packed as they were with munitions and aviation gasoline, many regarded as floating bombs.

EXPLOITATION: WORLD WAR II

After the experiences of World War I, navies accepted that their operations would inevitably generate radio traffic; they professed keen awareness of the attendant perils. Radio direction-finding had proliferated in the interwar period after the U.S. Navy introduced functional shipborne DF in 1917. British decryption successes had also been revealed, showing that codes and ciphers thought secure were vulnerable to attack. Nonetheless, different navies approached the problem of security differently. Some restricted their use of radios more than others and, by so doing, managed to keep their fleet operations largely secret. The Italians, who operated in a limited geographic area, centralized their radio communications out of fleet headquarters and prohibited the use of radio in port. They also strictly limited the use of radio while under way and benefited from the fact that the British never broke the Italian fleet codes.[51]

Italian restrictions on radio use, facilitated by the nature of their organization and operations, occupied one end of the spectrum. The Germans once again ruled the other extreme. Their situation and tactics required heavy use of radio communications. For example, inadequate air reconnaissance forced them to rely on submarine patrol lines to find convoys. Any submarine that spotted a convoy had to report to other submarines in the patrol line, potentially revealing its location. Combined with centralized command and the need to constantly report positions and coordinate "wolfpacks," the submarine war provided abundant radio traffic for the Government Code and Cypher School to digest. The German solution was to rely upon brief transmissions and more sophisticated encryption, adopting Enigma—a fiendishly complicated machine-based ciphering system that Berlin believed was impossible to crack. The German navy was the first to adopt machine-based mechanical and, later, electro-mechanical encryption, but they were followed by all major navies: the British with Typex, the Americans with SIGBA, the French with C35, and the Japanese with the Type 97 or B Machine. Decryption was no longer a matter of a mathematical genius, like with Germany's Ludwig Föppl, Russia's Ernst Vetterlein, or Italy's Luigi Donini puzzling over and then cracking a code in isolation; nor was it a matter of a room full of a few dozen professors and graduate students collegially solving ciphers as if they were crossword puzzles. Success now required organization, information sharing, mechanical assistance, and persistence on an industrial scale. Successful distribution and then exploitation of the mass of information gained was a completely different, and perhaps even more important, process.

The literature on the intelligence war in World War II is massive, and no attempt will be here to expound its details. Suffice it to say that while all navies practiced radio silence in certain situations, in general radio was too useful to restrict its utilization to the degree that would guarantee security. All major powers enjoyed successes in cracking their enemy's codes, and they also suffered much frustration, but the Allies enjoyed more and suffered less, especially as the war progressed. With help from the Poles and French, equipment captures, electro-mechanical calculators, and poor German signal practices, the British were reading some Enigma traffic from the beginning of the war, although with significant delays; by the end of the war, they were reading most such traffic with delays of hours, not weeks. The German navy proved to be a more disciplined and sophisticated user of Enigma than the other German services, such as the air force or state railroad, but this did not secure its communications from the efficiency of Allied codebreaking efforts. The Axis navies had their successes as well, with the Germans breaking into British naval codes at the beginning of the war and again at the start of 1942. The Italians too were privy to many British signals, often reading low-level radio traffic before the intended recipients.[52] In the end, however, it seems incredible that Germany should make the same or similar mistakes regarding the security of its radio communications in two consecutive wars, especially given its knowledge of both its own successes and those of its enemies in exploiting radio traffic prior to the second war. In the navy's case, the high command appreciated the importance of radio security, and it promoted the use of improved Enigma machines and more restrictive messaging rules. But it was also too invested in its tactical systems and too confident in its material and procedures. Strong evidence that the Allies had broken Enigma-encoded traffic led to a full-scale investigation in October 1941 and several more in the spring and summer of 1943. In the first case, the investigators "developed a hypothetical and completely unsubstantiated scenario to explain away an unsettling incident." In the second, the Germans completely exonerated Enigma because their base assumption was that it was impossible to break. "The investigators clearly set out to prove only [that Enigma] could not have been the leak."[53] The conclusion is that hubris, a lack of imagination, and wishful thinking marked the German approach to radio security and gave the Allies what proved to be an important advantage, especially as the war continued.

In the Pacific, the Americans had success against Japanese navy codes. The decoding of the Japanese plans for the invasion of Midway and the subsequent defeat of the Japanese carrier force was the best-known example of this. The Japanese, on the other hand, had little luck breaking U.S. naval codes or ciphers. Being on the sidelines of the action in World War I, they "lacked the appreciation of the importance of the 'intelligence revolution' wrought by radio communications and thus failed to devote sufficient resources—especially human resources—to the task."[54]

The British/U.S. assault on the German Enigma cipher is famous. Less well known is high-frequency direction-finding (HF/DF), another Anglo-American innovation, which provided first a shore-based capability to locate submarines and then a sufficiently precise shipborne capability to run them down. While direction-finding had proved itself extremely valuable during World War I, it struggled to deal with frequencies above 600 kilohertz (KHz). The Germans relied on this in building a naval communications network based on high-frequency radio. They believed that high frequencies and short transmissions would neutralize shore-based DF and that shipboard DF of high-frequency transmissions was simply impractical.[55]

Ongoing experimentation conducted in Britain and France during the interwar period showed the way to effective HF/DF through improved antenna design and a better understanding of where to put HF/DF stations. However, in the case of shipborne installations, the large antennas that were initially needed clashed with other requirements of a fighting ship; they impeded arcs of fire, limited the installation of other electronic gear, and compromised stability. The British navy's first experimental HF/DF unit (FH1), installed in March 1941 on a destroyer, required that the ship forego radar, for example. However, improvements in the system followed rapidly, and by January 1942 twenty-five ships had been fitted with an improved model (FH3). These models required highly skilled operators, but the next iteration (FH4) used a cathode-ray tube display, which was easier to operate and gave a better appreciation of range. This was first installed in October 1941, first tried in combat March 1942, and was in widespread use by May 1943.[56] The U.S. Navy was also conducting HF/DF experiments and approved a superior design (DAQ) in July 1942. A year later, these were rolling off assembly lines at the rate of twenty per month.[57]

The Germans were slow to appreciate the effectiveness of Allied HF/DF. In June 1941 submarines were ordered to restrict their radio use, but their tactical system still required them to transmit frequently. Headquarters required position reports to coordinate patrol lines and contact and combat reports to direct convoy battles. For example, during attacks on convoy SC118 in February 1943, the twenty attacking submarines made 108 transmissions over three days. Not until June 1944, well after the end of the great wolfpack-convoy battles, did the Germans realize that Allied escorts were using shipboard HF/DF to find and attack their submarines. More restrictions on transmissions followed. A procedure of systematically varying the frequencies that the submarines used, in place by early 1945, complicated the task of the Allied escorts but was countered by the growing prevalence of HF/DF equipment, which allowed an escort group's HF/DF-equipped ships to monitor a broad range of frequencies. The Germans also developed a "burst" transmission system, dubbed Kurier, that would have slashed HF/DF effectiveness; however, despite trials starting in August 1944, it was not in widespread use until the end of the war. By then, the British had recognized the threat and begun work on an antidote.[58]

Another technological leap in radio communications that flowered in World War II was radio telephony. The U.S. Navy had already adopted its TBS system for intership communication. The British relied on voice telephony sets of lower frequency but quickly adopted TBS once the Americans shared it with them. Not surprisingly, given its emphasis on radio security, the Italian navy explored microwave communications before settling on voice sets in the VHF range between 50 and 75 MHz. Other Axis sets also operated at lower frequencies; by 1943 the Germans employed sets operating in the 40 MHz range for communications between surface craft at sea and with aircraft, while Japanese voice radio used medium frequencies but special command sets reached 53 Mhz. Aircraft voice sets were widely adopted as well, with the best operating on VHF bands. As noted, reliable voice radio became a cornerstone of fighter interception systems.[59]

TBS and similar systems seemed to realize radio's promise of fast, effective, and secure tactical communications, but once again, better communications carried a hidden cost. Some of the more egregious examples of the dangers emerged during the naval battles fought in the Solomon

Radio room on board USS *New Jersey* (BB 62) with Captain L. Dow on the TBS radio telephone. Note the "cheat sheet" to the left with pertinent data such as time zone and formation chalked in. *(Naval History and Heritage Command, 80-G-469927)*

Islands in 1942. One problem was ambiguous terminology: during the 11 October 1942 Battle of Cape Esperance, a U.S. cruiser captain, confronted with a Japanese formation bearing down on him, urgently requested permission over TBS to open fire. The U.S. admiral, not appreciating the situation, answered "Roger," by which he meant "Request received, stand by." The cruiser captain took it to mean "Open fire" and started shooting.[60]

The requirement for a standard, unambiguous, servicewide radio vocabulary was relatively easy to address. Overuse of TBS was a more insidious problem; with ships, even down to destroyer size, equipped with multiple sets, voice radio's convenience invited excessive traffic that often confused and/or masked important orders and provided the enemy with information. The Italians addressed this problem by restricting their VHF system to one unit per ship and limiting use to the commander, although this was also a function of having insufficient sets to go around. The Allies preferred to address the problem with doctrine. A bigger danger was over-reliance on the system. When voice radio failed, the results could be cata-strophic, as in the Battle of Kolombangara. The U.S. commander lost TBS contact with a detached formation. When unidentified ships appeared, he hesitated before engaging for fear that they might have been his missing ships. They were Japanese destroyers, and they torpedoed two U.S. cruis-ers and a destroyer. As the U.S. Navy staff noted after the Second Battle of Guadalcanal, TBS was limited in range and subject to battle damage; commanders must be ready "to parallel TBS communication with keyed radio."[61]

The U.S. Navy also had a concern that the Japanese were eavesdrop-ping on their TBS conversations. This was not routinely the case, but it was a reasonable fear because the Allies eavesdropped on Axis voice com-munications. The British devised the QD monitoring system, nicknamed "Headache," for intercepting German VHF tactical voice transmissions, proving once again that assuming a system's security on the basis of one's own technological limitations was a bad assumption. The QD system allowed ships to identify the opposition facing them by the presence and type of "chatter" overheard. It had obvious benefits in tactical situations. For example, British operators quickly learned the German code term for "launch torpedoes," and several times during combat in the English Channel in 1943 and 1944 the British evaded German attacks even as the torpedoes were hitting the water. This was a powerful advantage that, when matched with effective radar and a lot of practice, erased a German advantage in night combat that had persisted through the war's first four years.[62]

One other aspect of radio deserves mention: the attempt to weaponize it by using radio frequencies to direct bombs, missiles, or even radio-con-trolled aircraft onto a target. Italy was the first to deploy a radio-controlled weapon: a standard S.79 trimotor bomber loaded with two specially fuzed 800-kilogram (kg) bombs set to explode under the ship's hull. The pilot would bail out once he pointed the aircraft toward its aircraft carrier tar-get. An accompanying aircraft would crash it against the carrier using a radio link for control. This method was used in August 1942 against a convoy to Malta. In the event, the aircraft did not respond to the controller and ended up running out of fuel over Algeria.

Germany was more successful with its radio-controlled weapons. It deployed the Ruhrstahl PC 1400FX (Fritz-X) and the Henschel Hs 293. The Fritz-X was a 1,400-kg armor-piercing bomb that was released from 20,000 feet down to 14,000 feet and steered to its target by a radio-linked controller on the aircraft using a joystick. This weapon began development in 1938, and the initial order of one thousand weapons entered production in April 1943. It was intended to be a battleship killer. The 1,045-kg Hs 293 was designed to be a stand-off weapon for use against convoys. It was, in effect, a radio-controlled, aircraft-launched, rocket-propelled cruise missile. Its design dated from 1940, and it entered service in 1943. Both used a VHF radio transmitting at one of eighteen frequencies between 48.2 and 49.9 MHz. This allowed up to eighteen aircraft in an attack to communicate with their weapon without interfering with each other.[63]

The Fritz-X scored its biggest success in September 1943 when two hit the Italian battleship *Roma* and detonated her magazine, sinking the ship and killing 1,352 men. Another caused moderate damage to *Roma*'s sister, *Italia* (ex-*Littorio*). After this the Fritz-X was used against the ships supporting the Salerno landings where it heavily damaged two cruisers and the battleship *Warspite*. The Allies were quick to devise countermeasures, even at Salerno, using a special jammer that could simultaneously attack all frequencies within a narrow bandwidth. The Fritz-X would not hit another Allied warship after September 1943. The Hs 293 premiered in August 1943 in an attack against two convoy escort groups in the Bay of Biscay. At first, it seemed to the ships that the distant bombers were jettisoning their loads. But then the apparent bombs, after dropping for a time, leveled out and came right at them. Even worse, they responded to evasive maneuvering with maneuvers of their own. In this attack eight missiles scored one hit and six near-misses. Fortunately for the Allies, the Hs 293 system also proved easy to jam, while both weapons required skilled operators plus a slow and steady flight path by the control aircraft. If the Germans had a generation of operators raised on video games, the outcome may have been different; as it was, the Hs 293 scored its last success in August 1944 when one sank a tank landing ship.

In World War II, as in World War I, radio silence could never be absolute. Navies tried to use radio communications with discretion and with safeguards, but the safeguards often proved illusory; particularly in the stress of combat as experienced in an aircraft cockpit or on a ship's bridge, the very human urge to communicate frequently defeated radio discipline. Each side believed that its own code and cipher systems and its codebreakers were much better than the enemy's. Interestingly, radio retained its core function throughout this period as attempts to weaponize it proved easy to counter once the initial surprise wore off.

THE TECHNOLOGY POSTWAR AND TODAY

Since the end of World War II, military applications of radio have continued to blend with commercial and civilian uses. Radio today is omnipresent in all three spheres—so omnipresent that it is sometimes not even noticed or named. Cellphones are highly developed radiotelephones, while Wi-Fi networks are deliberately short-ranged radio communications networks, the modern equivalent of TBS. The miniature radio frequency identification chips found in everything from shipping containers to pets to credit cards are distant cousins of the radio transponders developed in World War II to sort friend from foe on radar screens.

Radio miniaturization has been accompanied by a huge increase in the amount of information radios can handle. This trend was apparent through the end of World War II but accelerated greatly postwar, taking the form of systems to exchange digital data at high speeds. Digitized communications are now routed via satellites links. Encryption has become automatic as part of the process of sending and receiving messages. With current systems able to transmit huge quantities of data, huge quantities of data are sure to be transmitted, often regardless of their value. During the Falklands War, the commander of British naval task forces received about five hundred signals a day and had to employ a staff officer whose principal duty was to read them all and determine their disposition.[64] More than ever, with dispersed formations and concepts such as distributed lethality, navies need constant secure communication to function at peak effectiveness—and possibly to function at all. This in turn drives the desire to attack or exploit an opponent's systems, leading to the cyberwar revolution at sea.

WHAT THIS TELLS US

The time from invention to widespread use of radio by navies was rapid because this technology provided a powerful way to satisfy a universal core need. It also seemed to enhance the battlefleet strategy favored by the major navies at the turn of the twentieth century, unlike other technologies such as aircraft or submarines that seemed to threaten it. Better communications offered benefits such as conservation of force, improved scouting, and the coordination of strategic movements over long distances. Shortcomings such as clogged airwaves, limited ranges, and fragile equipment were regarded as areas for improvement, not evidence of unsuitability. Then there was the cost factor. Radio was relatively cheap. Navies had to budget for equipment, to train personnel, and to fund developments, but not at the expense of new battleships. In addition, outside factors pushed the development of radio. The technology was such that early on, even civilian hobbyists could contribute to its improvement. The creation and enormous expansion of commercial broadcast radio further accelerated radio developments in the interwar period. The pairing of radio with aircraft also drove innovation in civilian, military, and naval spheres.

Navies eventually came to realize that radio's utility had a price. Even during the Russo-Japanese War, intercepted radio transmissions alerted ships to the enemy's presence and, in some cases, provided useful intelligence. World War I saw widespread use of DF and SIGINT. Navies only gradually understood how radio communication could compromise operations as well as facilitate them. In World War I all sides were slow to appreciate the threat posed by DF. The Germans never seemed to appreciate how effectively and comprehensively the British and Russians had intercepted their radio communications and penetrated their codes and ciphers. The Germans in World War II built an entire operational system around radio, trusting that brief high-frequency transmissions would be immune from DF technology and that Enigma would defeat codebreakers. This proved disastrously wrong for the Germans but provided a marvelous example of thinking that something will work because it must work. The Germans were not alone in trusting faulty security measures, but they paid the highest price for it across two wars. The Japanese and Italians suffered as well. The British and Americans got off more lightly, although British codes were broken, and U.S. commanders fretted that enthusiastic use of intership voice radio was letting the Japanese get the drop on them in night battles. In short, radio was a very seductive technology; its apparent benefits were quite obvious, but its risks were harder to fathom and harder to control.

The dangers of direction-finding and codebreaking are obvious. A less obvious risk is that a system will be used to its maximum capacity regardless of whether that use is sensible. This problem predates radio. When Admiral Horatio Nelson began to make his "England expects every man to do his duty" signal at Trafalgar (which required extensive flag hoists), Vice Adm. Cuthbert Collingwood spoke for many modern commanders when he said, "I wish Nelson would stop signaling. We know well enough what to do."[65]

The ability to signal has other repercussions. First, the sheer volume of communications can slow and even overwhelm the decision-making process. Second, the ability to communicate over long distances tempts upper-level commanders to meddle with lower-level subordinates at the scene even though those subordinates may have better information. This dynamic affected Spee's victory at Coronel, when London gave orders to the admiral on the spot in the mistaken belief that he had more force with him than he did. Third, overused communication networks can substitute for doctrine. When the expectation is that the commander will be able to orchestrate all the actions of subordinates, there is no need for the subordinates to be briefed in advance or trained to a common doctrine. Battlefleets in World War I were particularly subject to this dilemma. Doctrine versus communication reappeared in World War II, as when U.S. commanders struggled to control improvised formations via crowded voice radio circuits in lieu of a common surface warfare doctrine and being able to trust that commanders would "know well enough what to do."

There is a final hazard inherent in every communications system: how can a navy continue to function if the system is taken away? Systems fail, either spontaneously or due to enemy actions. And even unimpaired systems can come with debilitating downsides. They may become avenues of attack through the insertion of false information or via cyberwarfare. Radio teaches the perils of rationalizing the use of a seductive technology by thinking that one's own capabilities to protect and exploit the technology are always superior to those of the foe. This may sometimes be the case, but it is always a bad assumption to make.

CHAPTER 5

RADAR
Magic Goes to Sea

*The key to the timing that turns a discovery or invention into successful
innovation lies in whether laymen can envision its possibilities.*

—ALAN BEYERCHEN[1]

Radar, like radio, is a technology constructed upon the electromagnetic spectrum, but its core purpose is detection rather than
communication. At first glance, it seems that navies embraced radar
as quickly as radio, with about half a decade elapsing between first service trials and widespread adoption, but in reality, the concept of radar
languished for three decades before militaries showed serious interest.
Even after naval interest grew, the first shipborne installations were just
the beginning of a process in which navies struggled to incorporate the
technology. This was, in some respects, a matter of naval professionals
unable to embrace an invention being thrust upon them by engineers and
scientists who, in turn, had limited appreciation of the conditions and
needs of naval warfare.

This tension was present from the beginning of the story. The principles
of radio wave reflection were discovered in the mid-nineteenth century.
But unlike radio—or torpedoes, for that matter—this capability did not
have a compelling application that appealed to naval professionals. For
example, in 1904 a German, Christian Hulsmeyer, successfully demonstrated a radar mechanism that rang a bell when it detected a nearby vessel.
He envisioned it as a way to avoid collisions in foggy conditions, but the
shipping officials and naval officers who saw his contraption thought that
foghorns worked just as well (not to mention being cheaper and easier to
use). In February 1916 two inventors tried to interest the German navy in
a device that used reflected radio waves to detect distant objects. The navy

listened but—looking for weapons with an immediate impact in the present war—lost interest when the inventors asked for six months to deliver an operational model.[2] In 1922 Guglielmo Marconi urged the exploration of reflected radio waves, and in the same year two U.S. naval engineers built a crude transmitter and receiver that used 5-meter (m) waves to spot a wooden steamer on the Potomac River. The U.S. Navy declined their proposal to develop this device.

The focus on applying existing technology to meet present needs was expressed by Admiral David Beatty in a 1922 remark to the Royal Air Force's Hugh Trenchard: "It is no use making our flesh creep with what may be done in 10 years' time. We want to know what is being done today. . . . We do not want to deal with imaginary things: we must deal with actualities."[3] Twenty years later Adm. Ernest J. King previewed a prototype centimetric radar installed on the destroyer *Semmes*. He purportedly said: "We want something for this war, not the next one."[4] These anecdotes demonstrate how naval professionals, busy people with many unmet needs, generally prioritized immediate threats and short-term results over innovation in both war and peace. Scientists, on the other hand, tended to focus on potential. Both had valid points of view, but the friction between potential and immediate use complicated the development of radar and inhibited both the development of best practices for identified uses and the development of new uses not envisioned by the scientists.[5]

The interwar period saw popular enthusiasm and scientific interest merge to push the frontiers of radio technology ever outward. Fed by improvements in radio transmitters and receivers, serious research in using reflected high-frequency electromagnetic waves to locate distant objects was under way by the early 1930s in Germany, Great Britain, the United States, France, the Netherlands, Italy, the Soviet Union, Hungary, Switzerland, and Japan. By 1939 the Germans, British, and Americans had developed deployable shipborne radar for detecting aircraft and ships and for gunnery ranging.

The outbreak of war accelerated radar development. Under the pressure of an immediate need for an improved air defense system, British radar capabilities soared. The Americans were not far behind and had surpassed the British by the end of 1941. German radar improved, but its use afloat never blossomed. As the war continued, the Japanese, Italians, and French deployed home-grown systems that lagged behind the technological curve but were better than nothing. The functions of radar also multiplied. The core naval uses of searching and targeting expanded to include navigation and station-keeping. Improved systems evolved functions that ranged from sea defense of entire coastal areas to the primary information source for a single ship's command center. Fire control radar progressed from passively providing range data to automatically controlling gunnery. Tiny radars inserted in anti-aircraft rounds converted every near-miss into a hit by detonating the round when close to a target. None of these applications were envisioned by the admirals of 1935, their imagination already strained by the idea of a device that could detect aircraft thirty miles away.

THE TECHNOLOGY DESCRIBED AND EARLY USE

Radar is an acronym for *ra*dio *d*etection *a*nd *r*anging. A radar system transmits electromagnetic waves and receives back the tiny portions of those waves that have been reflected off distant objects. The system calculates an object's range by measuring the time it takes for the wave to reach the object and return. As systems evolved, they could also determine with increasing precision the object's bearing (azimuth) and eventually its height. Radars have several basic characteristics.

Wavelength and Frequency

Electromagnetic waves radiate from a source in three dimensions. A radar system is often described in terms of its operating frequency or wavelength (see figure 5.1), which in turn determines its broad characteristics. Wavelength and frequency are inversely related: the shorter the wavelength, the higher the frequency. A longer wavelength requires less power to generate but is more diffuse and gives relatively poorer resolution. This made early sets operating in the VHF band good for detecting distant aircraft but useless for accurate target acquisition or gun laying. Shorter waves are more focused and show range, altitude, and bearing more accurately. Their drawback is shorter detection ranges. In effect, a lower frequency set with longer waves acts as a floodlight, whereas a higher frequency set with shorter waves is more like a spotlight. The major challenge with first-generation radars was generating the power required to operate at shorter wavelengths. Early radar sets were limited to wavelengths of half a meter

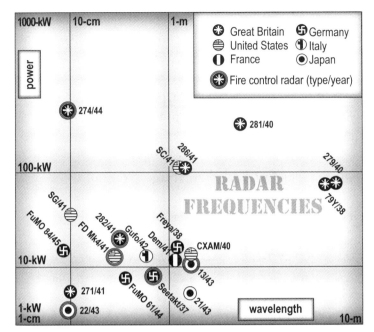

FIGURE 5.1. Major World War II Radars. The figure shows the type of radar (fire control or search), the designation of the radar, and the year of introduction, indexed against the radar's operating wavelength and peak power. In general, shorter wavelengths yielded better precision, and greater power gave greater range. The commanding lead that Allied radar technology achieved in World War II is apparent.

or more because power sources then available were too weak to generate useful high-frequency waves. Wavelength also affected antenna size and configuration. Although an ingenious design could save some space and weight, early radar antennas were cumbersome afloat and impinged on stability, a vessel's most precious commodity, particularly as they had to be situated as high as possible to improve effectiveness.[6]

Metric radars were adequate for air search, while a 40- to 60-centimeter (cm) wavelength sufficed for gunnery ranging. However, effective surface search—especially the ability to see through clutter—required wavelengths of 10 cm or less. These sets, operating in the microwave band, used a smaller antenna that could be fitted in an aircraft or a motor torpedo boat (MTB). Thus, the deployment of microwave radar sets in 1941 revolutionized the use of radar not just with their better resolution but also by allowing them to be carried on any platform.[7]

Pulse Frequency Rate

A problem that bedeviled the pioneers of radar was that when generating a continuous stream of radio waves, the output drowned out the returning target echo. Some (but not all) developers solved this problem by inserting a timed repeating pause in the transmission stream. This allowed undisturbed receipt of the return echo during these pauses. Pulsed radars could have their sending and receiving antennas close together (or even combined), an important feature for compact installations.

Power Output

In the 1930s developers addressed the problem of supplying enough power to a radar system by improving system components, but there seemed to be an upper limit beyond which frequencies could not be pushed. The development of the cavity magnetron, which multiplied power by a factor of a thousand, solved this problem. The cavity magnetron was an electronic vacuum tube developed in the United Kingdom in 1940 during an effort to improve 1.5-m airborne radar systems for surface search. The British shared it with the United States in August 1940, largely to obtain U.S. assistance in developing and manufacturing the device. Once developed to its full potential in August 1941 and supported by the integration of several electronic innovations, including the first solid-state electronic components, the cavity magnetron made radars operating in the microwave band feasible. These radars generated an order-of-magnitude improvement in target definition and gave more precise bearing and range. Shorter (more focused) wavelengths improved detection of targets in areas affected by sea or ground "clutter"—that is, echoes produced by unwanted returns from natural phenomena such as rain, a flock of birds, or nearby land. Shorter pulses allowed minimum ranges of hundreds rather than thousands of yards, permitting full radar control of anti-aircraft guns. Although a number of nations had developed magnetrons in the 1930s, the British design was enormously more powerful, representing a revolutionary scientific advance not duplicated by any other nation.[8]

Many factors affected the effectiveness of early radars. Atmospheric conditions could sometimes triple ranges, and sometimes they could shut a system down. Radar equipment was delicate and often failed when it was most needed. Even the shape of the radar pulse itself influenced important aspects such as bearing discrimination. Shipborne radar presented additional complications. As one British scientist so well expressed it, "Ships at sea roll, pitch, and yaw so that the radar aerials never point in a steady direction. . . . Everything on board a ship at sea is wet with salt water and it was most important to keep all radar equipment as dry as possible. . . . When the main armament of a capital ship was fired it produced intense vibration that could put radar equipment out of action. . . . All those and other problems were compounded by the fact that ships would be a sea for weeks, sometimes months, without being able to call on port or depot ship assistance for repair and maintenance."[9]

All these variables required research and experimentation in an ongoing quest to improve systems. But even the "robust" systems that appeared after 1943 were hardly perfect. As U.S. Navy radio technician Morgan McMahon expressed it: "Radar sets, being very complicated, would work fine for days, then suddenly behave like cranky camels. They would behave great during normal conditions, then might do strange things at the critical moment, when gunfire and concussion were shaking their innards."[10]

DIFFERENCES IN DEVELOPMENT BY NATION
On the brink of war, radar had developed differently in different nations. The degree and direction of development depended at least as much on perceived needs as it did on technological capabilities.

Germany
In 1933 the German navy began exploring electromagnetic waves as a means of determining gunnery ranges. Through 1934 scientists studied the characteristics of wavelength and demonstrated the need for power. They learned to pulse transmissions, allowing them to build more compact sets. In September 1935 Admiral Raeder received a demonstration of a working targeting apparatus. A scholar of German radar, D. E. Graves, notes that "from the outset, the navy's philosophy on the use of radar was an aggressive one—radar was seen as a quick means by which to acquire and range on targets for gun and torpedo fire from surface vessels."[11]

When the war began, Germany possessed two major radars: Freya and Seetakt. Freya was an air search device most widely used by the air force. It emitted 2.5-m waves with a range of one hundred miles and required

The German *panzerschiffe Admiral Graf Spee* in Montevideo harbor after the Battle of the River Plate. Her Seetakt radar antenna is clearly visible on the face of the director tower at the top of the bridge structure. It was of no use to her in the battle, but its presence told the British that the German navy had put radar into service. *(Naval History and Heritage Command, NH 59662)*

such large antennas that it was initially practical for land use only. The navy used the Freya system and its descendants ashore to support coastal units, particularly in the English Channel. Seetakt had a wavelength of 60 cm (later increased to 81.5 cm) and a range of 14–18 km. The armored ships *Graf Spee* and *Deutschland* deployed Seetakt operationally during the Spanish Civil War. At this point, German radar was state of the art, pushed by government patronage of rival private firms and fueled by a strong scientific establishment and generous funding.

German scientific talent was first rate, but the navy's strategic vision affected the role, and hence the development, of its radar capabilities. With a desire to change the global status quo to its own advantage, Germany's fundamental strategic outlook was offensive, but its military commanders perceived radar as providing a defensive capability, which in turn made it seem less useful in advancing their offensive capabilities. Moreover, Berlin squandered its early lead in radar technology by focusing more on its purely technical aspects rather than on how it could or would be used. For example, early experience with magnetrons revealed that they generated frequencies that fluctuated. This was a problem, as a receiver had to be tuned to the transmitter's precise frequency. Rather than solve that problem, the Germans focused on more precise but less powerful microwave transmitters, abandoning a road that might have led to centimetric radar had it been pursued. In contrast, British researchers were willing to attack the magnetron's problems in their quest for a more useful radar.[12]

Great Britain

The British saw the value of radar as a defensive aid. Radar development began when the air ministry—driven by the belief that bombers presented an existential threat to the nation—created a scientific group to examine new means of air defense. This in itself was an innovative response to the common view that "the bomber will always get through."[13] The group was tantalized by a report about aircraft reflecting radio waves, first observed during ionospheric research, and the possibility that this phenomenon might be parlayed into a means of detecting aircraft at great distances. A quickly assembled team first demonstrated an air search radar set on 15 June 1935, and even though the test failed, the air ministry persisted in its support. Subsequent tests succeeded, which led to the development of a linked air warning radar system. This Chain Home system transmitted on the 12-m frequency (22–25 MHz), which required bulky machinery and huge fixed antenna masts. The historian Walter Kaiser noted that, "The individual Chain Home station left much to be desired in comparison with a Freya Station. Yet centralized control made all the difference."[14] In Churchill's words, "It was the operational efficiency rather than novelty of equipment that was the British achievement."[15] This operational efficiency consisted of combining the input of all stations using a centralized plotting room and establishing communications links to air bases. It would prove vital to the nation's air defense.[16]

The British navy received a demonstration of a radar prototype in July 1935 and immediately commissioned work on a smaller shipborne variant. In December 1936 this resulted in the navy's first working device, the Type (T) 79X air search radar. After a nearly three-year development phase, the anti-aircraft cruiser *Curlew* received the first of thirty production models, the T79Z (7.5 m/70 kilowatts [kw], range 30–50 miles), in September 1939. The Type 282 (50 cm/15 kw), which began development in March 1938, became the first working fire control set. The T282 was specialized to meet a requirement for a short-range anti-aircraft gunnery director set while the Type 284, an equivalent set with refined bearing discrimination, became the main battery equivalent. The T284 first went to sea operationally in battleship *Nelson* in June 1940.

United States

The U.S. Naval Research Laboratory became interested in radar in 1931 after an experimental radio navigation device generated returns from passing aircraft. Priority was low and progress slow, and a primitive radar unit was not produced until December 1934.[17] In April 1937 the first test of radar at sea aboard the destroyer USS *Leary* (DD 158) detected an aircraft at twenty miles, which encouraged the Navy to pursue the technology. This led to the prototype Model XAF radar (1.5 m/15 kw) on the battleship USS *New York* (BB 34) in 1939. It was overenthusiastically reported as being capable of "air and surface detection of targets, of navigation, of spotting the fall of shot and or tracking the flight of projectiles."[18] The battleship USS *California* (BB 44), carrier USS *Yorktown* (CV 5), and three heavy cruisers received the initial production sets, dubbed CXAM, in December 1940. Five battleships, five aircraft carriers, a light cruiser, and two seaplane tenders got the slightly improved CXAM-1 throughout 1941. The heavy cruiser USS *Wichita* (CA 45) received the first specialized fire control radar, the CXAS Mark I, in June 1941.[19]

France

France had a growing electronics industry in the 1930s. In 1935 the Sociètè Française Radiotechnique developed a 16-cm continuous wave obstacle detection device for the newly built liner *Normandie*. Its power was inadequate, however, to reach beyond two miles, and it did not indicate a useful bearing.[20] More importantly, it did not spark any interest in the navy, even with an improved 1938 version that could detect a ship out to five miles. Instead, the French focused on a land-based electromagnetic air defense barrier system called the DAT (La Défence Aérienne du Territoire). In

1939 Great Britain shared with France its progress in radar development. This led the navy to begin developing the DEM (Détecteur Electro-Magnétique), a pulsed, metric air surveillance system. The battleship *Richelieu* received the first operational DEM in May 1941. The battleship *Strasbourg* and the heavy cruiser *Algérie* got improved sets in January and April 1942. *Jean Bart* and the cruiser *Colbert* received a higher-powered set in 1942, which extended the range to 150 km for aircraft and 25 km for ships.

Italy

Italian research into radio detection began in 1933. In May 1935 Guglielmo Marconi demonstrated to Benito Mussolini a device that could detect cars at two kilometers (km). This convinced the army to continue development, but compared to German, British, and U.S. efforts, Italian research was underfunded and small scale. The country's leading scientist said he would have saved two years of work had he immediately adopted the pulse system instead of persisting with continuous wave devices. By 1940, after several failed prototypes, the navy had two experimental pulsed sets. A larger land-based set completed in October 1939 generated a 70-cm wave with a range of twelve kilometers against aircraft. A shipborne unit in test from February 1940 through April 1941 had a wavelength of 1.5 m and an oscillographic indicator. Italy's official naval history noted some complacency with this situation: "We were not too worried because, in the absence of information from the Anglo-Saxon counties, due to the secrecy with which they worked, it was considered that they would not be significantly ahead of us." The radar-facilitated British naval victory at Cape Matapan in March 1941 shook Italian complacency, but by then it was too late. Italy's failure to realize a workable radar before the war was thus a function of underfunding, some poor choices when exploring how to deploy the technology, and inadequate intelligence. Noteworthy also was the fact that Germany did not share with its ally any of its own advances in shipborne radar until April 1941. Italy did not deploy its first effective home-grown radar system until spring 1942.[21]

Japan

Japanese scientists had concluded by 1936 that it would be possible to detect aircraft and ships using reflected radio waves, but the navy and army followed separate development paths. While the army tested a pulsed set in 1939 that spotted aircraft from one hundred kilometers, the navy's efforts consisted of "fragmented and isolated endeavors" and only resulted in a device with continuous wave signals that sensed ships at a range of three miles. Not until a Japanese mission inspected German radar installations in early 1941 did the navy learn that the European combatants were using pulsed radar, critical information that enabled Japan to produce a land-based air-search radar by the end of the year.[22] An eminent radio scientist, Yagi Hidetsugu, summed matters up: "The Army and the Navy certainly never cooperated with each other. . . . They treated [university] scientists exactly as if they were 'foreigners.'"[23] The type 21 *GO dentan*, Japan's first shipborne air search radar, installed on the battleship *Ise* in May 1942, detected an aircraft at fifty-five kilometers and a battleship at twenty kilometers. However, the Japanese admiralty did not place priority on this type of equipment until after the June 1942 Battle of Midway. By then, they were fatally behind the curve.

EXPECTATIONS

When considering the probable impact of new weapons such as torpedoes or new platforms such as submarines, most naval professionals had clear expectations (whether right or wrong) of how they would perform in combat. This was not the case with radar. The technology was too new and too secret for naval professionals to envision how best to use it or even usefully speculate on its impact. For many navies, it was a solution in search of a problem. The Germans had it pigeonholed as a useful enhancement to their existing weapon control systems; in the United States, it was "a vague answer to uncertain threats."[24] The U.S., German, and even British navies had no real appreciation of how best to benefit from shipborne radar during operations. Development would require some painful lessons, as these navies grappled with radar's strengths and weaknesses and began to comprehend the supporting infrastructure it needed to perform at its best.

Nor was radar seen as an unalloyed benefit. Because it generated electromagnetic waves at certain frequencies, its emissions were subject to interception just like radio broadcasts were. The fact that intercepted waves painted a target at much greater strength than return echoes meant that a target knew it was under scrutiny before the radar itself could receive the echoes—assuming that the target ship had an interception device tuned to the correct frequency. The Germans expected that the British would attempt to detect their radar and thus used it with extreme caution. This concern affected developmental efforts as well, with the Germans placing greater emphasis upon passive detection devices, just as they preferred hydrophones over sonar (see chapter six). The British and Americans generally accepted the possibility of interception to get the benefits of detection. This approach made sense; in most of the tactical situations they were likely to face, especially by 1943, the Allies would be more concerned with finding rather than avoiding the enemy.

DISCOVERY: WORLD WAR II

The first combat use of radar came on 28 November 1939 when twelve British Blenheim bombers raided the Borkum Island seaplane base. Freya radar detected the intruders from twenty-three kilometers. This was three minutes out, time enough to raise the alarm but not to man the anti-aircraft guns. The British reported that they achieved complete surprise. But the Germans sharpened their skills quickly. Radar gave five minutes' warning against a 3 December raid, and gunfire greeted the bombers. On 18 December a Freya station gave a half hour's warning of a raid on Wilhelmshaven. This gave enough time to scramble fighters, which jumped the raiders as they retired. They downed twelve of the twenty-two Wellington bombers participating in the attack. This result demonstrated to the British command that daytime raids against German territory would be costly—even if they did not completely appreciate the role of radar in the increasingly effective German response to their first feeble attempt at a strategic bombing campaign.[25] The Germans learned this lesson themselves during the Battle of Britain, fought from July through September 1940. This campaign provided an early and well-known example of radar detecting enemy attacks and aiding fighter direction. The equipment employed, the scale of the air battles, and the conditions under which they were fought had limited relevance to the war at sea, however. In discussing the use of radar at sea, its development and ever-growing impact can best be considered by starting with what developers generally considered to be the technology's core uses: detection and ranging.

In 1939 only the British, Americans, and Germans had shipborne radar; only the British had an airborne set. Within these three navies, there were few sets in operation. While prototypes could be effectively demonstrated by their developers, it was quite another matter to expect immediate results from operators tasked with learning and maintaining a sophisticated and cranky piece of equipment in wartime conditions. Experienced captains, presented with this new device, had little instruction in its use and were not always eager to add more complexity to an already complicated job. Moreover, it was one thing for a twenty-year-old operator to learn how to interpret green lights on a display or, depending upon the system's user interface, the significance of different pitched noises; it was another to collect and use radar information effectively. The captain of the cruiser HMS *Suffolk* noted that when he took command in 1941, radar was newly installed: "Not a soul could tell me a thing about its tactical implications. I had to figure it out for myself from such basic knowledge as I had or could add to experimentally at sea."[26]

Overestimating radar's capabilities could be more harmful than underestimating them. The 9 August 1942 Battle of Savo Island illustrates how some high-level commanders discovered the technology's limitations. In this action Japanese warships slipped undetected past two "radar-picket" destroyers to surprise Allied forces guarding invasion shipping off Guadalcanal and sink four cruisers. The U.S. destroyers had SC search radar (1.36 m/100 kw) and had been stationed expressly as "radar guard watch" to prevent a surprise attack. Nearby land masses baffled the equipment, which was unsuited for surface search in the first place. The after-action analysis noted "an apparent failure to appreciate the inherent deficiencies of radar operated in such a locality" and recommended: "Operating personnel must know its equipment, its limitation, and capabilities under all conditions."[27] Rear Adm. Richmond K. Turner, the U.S. commander, explained, "I received assurances that these two vessels ought surely to detect the approach of any enemy vessels up to twelve to fourteen miles. Knowledge possessed by me and the staff concerning radar was practically non-existent."[28]

The disaster at Savo shook the U.S. Navy; the fact that it occurred three years after *New York* put to sea with a prototype SC set suggests a lack of focus in the Navy's approach to using radar. And this was hardly just an American problem. The Australian navy served alongside the British in the

Atlantic, Mediterranean, and Indian oceans. The heavy cruiser *Canberra* took a centimetric Type 271 (10 cm/5 kw) radar into the Savo battle, top-of-the-line equipment for mid-1942. Yet, as the Australian author Bruce Loxton explained, "There was little knowledge . . . of its use in navigation or for plotting the movements of ships, both friendly and enemy. . . . At that time its value in surface warfare was generally thought to be the provision of information for the gunnery control systems. Officers returning from service or training with the Royal Navy were slowly indoctrinating their associates in its wider tactical uses, but this was a gradual process which had scarcely begun in June 1942."[29]

These events show that the process of discovering radar's basic uses, much less its best uses, was a matter of trial and error. As the U.S. Navy's Radar Bulletin Number 1 of 9 March 1942 put it: "It should be appreciated that Radar equipment is continuously undergoing further improvement and that the knowledge of its use is still limited. Officers and men associated with it should, therefore, feel that they have some latitude in exploiting its use, and the contents of this bulletin should be regarded as a guide and a basis for improvement after further experience afloat."[30] The discovery process can be illustrated by a brief survey of radar's use for detection and ranging.

In December 1939 the German armored ship *Graf Spee* went into action against British cruisers with a Seetakt FuMO22 radar installed (81.5 cm/ 7–8 kw). Some British authors have attributed the accuracy of the German ship's initial salvoes to radar ranging but, in fact, vibrations disabled the Seetakt when the ship accelerated to close the range. According to the ship's gunnery officer, the radar "was of no use for fire direction."[31] The next use of radar in surface combat occurred in a 12 October 1940 night battle in the Mediterranean between the light cruiser HMS *Ajax* and Italian destroyers and torpedo boats. The British ship carried a Type 279 air warning set, but human lookouts sighted the enemy first from just six thousand yards—twenty minutes after Italian lookouts sighted her. In his report the cruiser's captain noted, "Unfortunately, the R. D/F [radar] office was put out of action with the first salvo." The admiralty staff assessment concluded, "This action is felt to be a warning against too great reliance on R.D.F. control, as it is likely to be very vulnerable, especially at short ranges."[32] Clearly, the message was, "Do not trust radar."

The first effective uses of radar in a surface action occurred during the war's second year. During their Atlantic forays German cruisers and battleships used radar as opportunities arose. On 24 December 1940 *Admiral Hipper*'s FuMO 27 Seetakt detected a convoy and tracked it all night before the German cruiser attacked at dawn. At the Battle of Cape Matapan in March 1941, the Type 284 radar carried on *Valiant*, one of the three British battleships involved, detected an Italian ship at night. It was also used by the battleship for ranging in the subsequent surprise action. She "reported that R.D.F. ranges were used throughout, and that all broadsides hit." On 16 March 1941 *Scharnhorst*'s radar detected the British battleship *Rodney* and was able to break contact before *Rodney* could close range. In May 1941 radars carried by the heavy cruisers *Norfolk* (T286M) and *Suffolk* (T284 and T279) allowed the British to shadow *Bismarck* at night, although the British eventually lost contact when the German ship turned while in a "radar shadow." *Prince of Wales* and *King George V* used T284 for gunnery ranges while in combat against *Bismarck*. British conclusions were equivocal: "No doubt with practice in the use of [radar] and realistic training in rangefinding the accuracy of our opening ranges can be improved."[33] Even as late as March 1942 the British fought a major surface action, the Second Battle of Sirte, with only two of their five modern cruisers having T284 radar. The battle occurred in a rising storm, and the cruisers fired hundreds of shells but failed to score a single hit. Radar was used only for a short period to fire through a smoke screen but helped little in the conditions of reduced visibility.[34]

In its 1942 report on naval gunnery the British navy listed ten gunnery problems that required more information. Six concerned radar, including range accuracy, calibration, and barrage firing. It identified splash spotting and salvo correction as two important functions where radar needed to improve. The 1943 report provided tables giving values for expected variance when spotting salvoes by radar and the effective ranges by which salvoes of different sized guns could be spotted. The report had much to say about future capabilities once improved radars were deployed.[35]

U.S. battleship *Massachusetts* fought one of the longest-range surface actions of the war in November 1942 in the Battle of Casablanca. Her gunnery was excellent for a new ship in her first action. She hit stationary battleship *Jean Bart* at ranges out to 26,000 yards and sank one French destroyer and severely damaged two more at ranges out to 28,000. She did this without radar. Her third salvo caused a tube to blow on one of her two Mark-3 fire control radars. This was not repaired until the very end of the battle. Her second Mark-3's "ranges varied so greatly from optical spots that the gunners discounted its output. . . . Shooting was 'from the hip' with application of spots in ranges and deflection when salvo landed."[36]

Anti-aircraft fire control was expected to benefit from radar, and in some cases, it did. The 1942 British *Progress in Naval Gunnery* noted that "[radar] should assist early sighting, which leads to economical, rapid and intelligent distribution of gunfire. . . . [I]t must be realized, however, that many of our present [radar] sets do not give adequate warning against low flying aircraft."[37] The British found that radar-assisted gunnery could provide accurate height and range data, making it effective against level bombing. In the case of dive bombing, which was the much greater threat, the rapidly changing height of the attacker complicated fire control. In 1942 British warships began to use fire control radar to lay barrages against dive bombers, forcing them to fly through a wall of shell bursts to deliver their bombs. The British also experimented with using radar-equipped ships to control the barrage fire of vessels lacking radar.[38]

A use of radar that the U.S. and British navies had not anticipated prewar was radar-directed fighter interception at sea. The British first practiced this craft in April and May 1940 when two-seat fighters of the modern but radar-less carrier *Ark Royal* teamed with the T279-equipped light cruisers *Sheffield* and *Curlew*: "Direction of these aircraft at that time required the range and bearing of aircraft detected by [*Sheffield*'s] radar to be passed to *Ark Royal* by flag hoist to avoid breaking [radio] silence; this would be sent by Morse code to the observer in the fighter."[39] The fighter's navigator would calculate the enemy's location based on the signaled tracks and give the pilot the interception course. The carrier's signals officer, a lieutenant commander, devised this method. Although cumbersome, it was true innovation. It helped that *Sheffield*'s captain was a naval aviator.[40] In June 1940 *Ark Royal* and *Sheffield* were assigned to Admiral James Somerville's Force H operating out of Gibraltar. Somerville was a senior admiral who had helped in the prewar development of radar. He was also acutely aware of the limitations of the bootstrap system devised by *Sheffield* and *Ark Royal* and sought improvements. His war diary and correspondence complain that the lack of Identification Friend or Foe (IFF), an automatic system to separate friend from foe among the radar returns, made it necessary to check every contact. For example, he wrote to the First Sea Lord on 13 July 1940: *"Valiant's* RDF was reporting aircraft throughout the forenoon and early afternoon of 9 July, but owing to the absence of IFF in our aircraft, it was impossible to determine which were shadowing."[41] In the laboratory for carrier warfare that existed in the Mediterranean in 1940, radar demonstrated possibilities, but even in the hands of an air-minded admiral, primitive equipment and awkward communications limited capabilities. What is noteworthy in this example is the creativity and can-do spirit demonstrated by the British navy's early carrier force.

The first U.S. combat uses of radar for fighter direction, fleet defense, gunfire targeting, and even navigation occurred during the early 1942 carrier raids in the Marshall Islands and Southwest Pacific. *Yorktown's* radar reports allowed the gunners of her escort vessels "to be 'on' when the enemy plane emerged from the cloud." Based on experiences receiving radar data from the carrier, the captain of one escorting cruiser wrote, "The installation of a radar in this ship is considered vital."[42] *Lexington*, while on a mission to strike the Japanese base at Rabaul, repulsed two Japanese air attacks. Radar detected the first at seventy-five miles and the second much closer in; radar-directed fighters inflicted heavy losses, and the bombers scored no hits. In May 1942 at Coral Sea, however, despite American radar picking up the incoming Japanese attack from seventy miles, radar-directed fighters failed to break up the strike. Inexperience, ignorance of Japanese attack methods, and lack of IFF all blunted U.S. efforts. The lessons learned in these early attacks included the need for practice, a coherent fighter direction doctrine, better radios, the latest radar fire control installations, and IFF.[43]

This synopsis of radar at sea during the period of first use shows that progress in understanding and using radar over the war's first three years was slow but steady. As the statement of *Suffolk's* captain quoted above indicates, the accrual of knowledge was, at times, anecdotal, but in the U.S. and British navies, at least, staff began identifying the lessons that needed to be learned and formulating systematic ways to get answers. The German navy made less progress as the combat activities of its large surface units sharply decreased after May 1941 and submarines, the most active German warships, preferred passive rather than active systems because they believed such systems were safer. This masked the need (and potential) for improvement.

EVOLUTION: WORLD WAR II

It took two years for U.S. radar-assisted fighter direction and fleet air defense to become a fluid system that married efficient receipt, integration, and distribution of information with effective radars and experienced personnel. The Navy reaped the result of that system in the Battle of the Philippine Sea when four major Japanese air strikes were tracked by radar and intercepted as far as sixty miles from the carriers with fighters stacked at the correct altitudes. There were 33 interception attempts, 85 percent successful, resulting in 141 claimed kills for the fighters.[44] The U.S. Navy lost no ships. Pilot quality and better aircraft contributed to this result, but it started with effective fighter interception. Thus, fighter direction had evolved to the point that a carrier task force could use it to reliably defeat conventional massed air strikes. This facilitated the wide-ranging U.S. Navy carrier operations in the Pacific that decimated Japanese land- and sea-based airpower.

The U.S. Navy's use of SG air/surface search radar (10 cm/up to 50 kw) in the Solomons also illustrates the process of operational and tactical innovation. SG centimetric radar was first tested afloat in June 1941 and was installed on two cruisers and a carrier in April 1942. Its capability to spot large surface targets extended past forty thousand yards with an accuracy of 2 degrees and a resolution of 40,000 yards. The radar's most innovative feature was its display: the plan position indicator (PPI). The PPI presented a top-down view of all radar contacts on a circular cathode ray tube; a trace sweeping around the face of the tube like a watch's second hand showed contacts as luminescent "pips" in the wake of the trace. The PPI was a vast improvement over the "A" scope, previously the most common type of display, which showed contacts as spikes on a horizontal line. The Navy expected that SG radar would, in conjunction with fire control radar, permit accurate radar-assisted gunfire at night and facilitate command and control in low-visibility conditions. And it did, but the learning process was long and costly.

Throughout 1942 U.S. shipyards installed SG radar as fast as possible as ships were being refit, repaired, or constructed. SG-equipped ships were thrown into battle with inadequate training on the sets. Individual commanders struggled to forge doctrine for using this new radar, with hasty deployments forcing them to rely on what few exploratory exercises they could conduct before commitment to combat and whatever they could glean from the experience of others.[45]

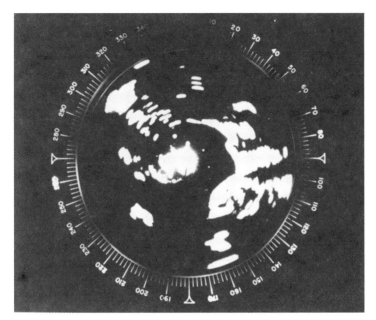

The plan position indicator greatly facilitated the task of deciphering radar returns. As USS *Cumberland Sound* enters Tokyo Bay in August 1945, the indicator shows ships and land, with *Cumberland Sound* at the center of the screen. It is set to a ten-mile scale, measured from the center of the screen to the edge. *(Naval History and Heritage Command, NH 80-G-344503)*

In the Battle of Cape Esperance, fought on the night of 11–12 October 1942, a U.S. cruiser/destroyer force ambushed a similar Japanese bombardment force. Just two of the nine ships of the U.S. formation, the light cruisers *Boise* and *Helena*, carried SG radar, which they were using for the first time in surface combat. The U.S. commander, Rear Adm. Norman Scott, flew his flag from the SC-equipped heavy cruiser *San Francisco*. He relied on TBS voice radio to receive information from the SG-equipped ships and to control his squadron (see chapter four). Striving for an easy-to-control formation, Scott arranged his ships in a long line with the cruisers in the center and destroyers ahead and behind. He ordered his ships to have their SC radars warmed up but not searching, as he had "highly secret intelligence . . . that the Japanese had radar receivers covering the frequency band employed by the SC."[46] *Helena*'s SG radar spotted the enemy at 27,000 yards. *Boise*'s set yielded a contact at half that range and malfunctioned five minutes into the action.[47]

Translating *Helena*'s sighting into actionable information was an involved process. It required entering the range and bearing of each contact on a plotting table. The table automatically displayed own ship's course and speed with input from gyrocompasses and a pitometer log while crewmen added the courses and speeds of other contacts based on the bearings and ranges shown on the PPI in relation to own ship course and speed. It was easy for a plot to become confused as pips bled into each other or separated, fell off the range scale in use, or went untracked while the radar focused elsewhere. Accurate plotting required effective communication between radar operators and plotters. This demonstrated the need for a team that was organized, trained, and equipped to plot and report radar contacts rapidly, accurately, and using a consistent vocabulary. In this respect, *Helena* was ahead of the curve, but it was still early days.

As *Helena*'s crew plotted and the two forces sped toward each other at a combined speed of a thousand yards a minute, the U.S. command system broke down—chatter overloaded the TBS circuit, and vague or undefined terminology caused confusion (did *bogie* mean an aircraft or a surface ship, for example). Scott's long line formation fell apart during a turn, leaving him uncertain as to whether the radar contacts reported soon afterward were friendly or enemy. The result was a muddled action marred by confusion and friendly fire incidents. The U.S. advantage came not from radar but from the Japanese commander's assumption that Scott's ships were friendly. The Battle of Cape Esperance was a U.S. victory in the sense the Japanese suffered greater losses and failed to accomplish their mission, but it was also a lost opportunity, and the Americans drew from it invalid lessons—for example, that a linear formation was the way to confront Japanese forces at night. Scott unwittingly exaggerated his success, as was common, and his superiors largely accepted his claims and concluded that "SG radar and fire control radars performed splendidly. . . . [radar] equipment for ships now being installed will prove to be extremely valuable in night operations."[48]

In the night surface action that followed, SG radar played an increasing role as more ships carried the device and commanders and operators grew more comfortable with its use. But it was a gradual process, and for every two steps forward there was a step back. The First Battle of Guadalcanal in November was a step back. Once again, *Helena* spotted the enemy at more than 27,000 yards, and this time she was much quicker to plot and report.[49] Nonetheless, Rear Adm. Daniel Callaghan, flying his flag in the ship with the biggest guns, not the best radar, steered his squadron into a collision with the Japanese before opening fire. When the smoke cleared, two Japanese destroyers had been sunk and a battleship crippled, against U.S. losses of four destroyers, one cruiser, and two admirals (Callaghan and Scott). The Americans had thwarted the Japanese bombardment mission, but it was an ugly victory that did nothing to leverage radar's advantage.

The Second Battle of Guadalcanal fought two nights later was a small step forward. U.S. commander Rear Adm. Willis Lee in the new battleship

SG radar installation in USS *Washington* (BB 56). The SG antenna is the smallest visible, on a platform stuck on the face of the battleship's tower bridge. The larger antennas are for the ship's fire control and air search radars, which operated on much longer wavelengths. The extemporized position of the antenna meant that it had a large blind spot aft. *(Naval History and Heritage Command, 19-N-32646)*

Washington used radar more effectively, and he was effusive in his praise of it. Still, Japanese night binoculars spotted the Americans first, while *Washington*'s SG followed a Japanese battleship but held fire for twenty minutes when Lee had lost track of his other battleship, *South Dakota*, after she disappeared in *Washington*'s radar shadow. Lee only reestablished contact when the Japanese opened fire and set *South Dakota* ablaze. The Americans sank a battleship and a destroyer but lost two destroyers and had other two others and *South Dakota* heavily damaged. It would have been a U.S. defeat had any of the many Japanese torpedoes fired at *Washington* hit.[50]

In the Battle of Tassafaronga, fought in the same waters, the Americans took into battle six destroyers and five heavy cruisers, three of each with SG radar. The destroyers without SG contributed almost nothing to the action, and the cruisers without it had to rely on information from the others to identify targets.[51] This battle also demonstrated another problem. All the cruisers' fire control radars fixed on the most prominent target, which they collectively obliterated. However, torpedoes from Japanese destroyers left unengaged then blasted four U.S. heavies, sinking one. Radar gave the Americans the advantage of surprise and it identified targets, but it could not deliver victory.

By the end of 1942, SG had proven itself capable of detection and contacts, coaching fire control radars onto targets, spotting the fall of shot, facilitating torpedo attacks, and assisting in coastal navigation. More importantly, it was reasonably reliable, even during battle. With each SG set spread between so many tasks, commanders argued for more radars and more scopes per ship. What followed was better methods and facilities to analyze radar data and pass that analysis on to commanding officers. Information management had been key to the successes of the primitive Chain Home system and was the foundation of fleet air defense. The same was true of surface combat. Enhancements began on the initiative of individual commanders, as when the destroyer *Fletcher* (DD 445) created a central location where radar data, sighting reports, and radio input could be collated, evaluated, and passed on to the captain. Thus was born the combat information center (CIC). In the British navy a similar process led to the action information organization (AIO). The captain of HMS *Cleveland*, a small *Hunt*-class destroyer, advised his commander in December

1942 that he had four sources of radar information: sonar, three radio feeds (one from enemy transmissions), an automatic plot, and several lookouts. The result was that "a state has now been reached where complication and confusion is liable to occur and the maximum value cannot be obtained from the many available sources of information."[52] These developments, which occurred independently on the initiative of the end users in both radar-rich navies, acknowledged the need for a dedicated facility staffed by specially trained personnel to distill the copious amounts of information provided by sources that had not existed just a few years before.[53]

By the end of 1942 many warships, such as *Fletcher* and *Cleveland*, were improvising ways to better use information. This happened at a different pace in the U.S. and British navies. In the case of Great Britain, a committee comprised of naval staff and area commanders met on 8 June 1943 and agreed to inform the fleet "of the arrangement envisioned in the destroyer of the future, in order that existing ships should have some idea of the system at which they should aim." As a result, AIOs were progressively implemented as vessels went into dock for repair or refit. In March 1944 the British started a five-day training course for AIO officers.[54] In the U.S. Navy, the method was different. *Fletcher* improvised a CIC mainly by reassigning responsibilities and streamlining communications and practiced this arrangement in combat during the First Battle of Guadalcanal. The Pacific Fleet command had already called for the establishment of a central facility to evaluate radar information, and it used *Fletcher*'s CIC as an excellent example of what could be achieved: it said what the CIC should do but left the "how" to individual captains. In a recent study, historian Trent Hone has assessed this approach as brilliant: "By allowing individual ships to experiment, Nimitz [the Pacific Fleet commander] fostered the development of more effective solutions."[55] The U.S. Navy as a whole mandated similar action in January 1943. The discovery and dissemination of best practices throughout the fleet were rapid, with the result that the U.S. Navy had CICs fleet-wide (albeit of varying quality) before the British navy had convened a committee to consider the matter. This is a clear demonstration of how innovation by the user can be more rapid and effective than innovation by fiat from the top, although at a cost in standardization.

The CIC and AIO were hardly panaceas. When surface combat resumed in 1943 Japanese torpedoes inflicted major losses on U.S.

cruiser-destroyer task forces in two night surface actions. The battles were remarkably similar. SG radar gave the Americans first sighting. It put the guns on the most prominent target, which was then annihilated. It also deluded U.S. commanders into overestimating the effectiveness of their gunnery as they assumed that a disappearing radar pip meant a ship sunk.[56] Often, though, the pip disappeared because it merged into another pip or a shoreline or just dropped off the scope due to a technical glitch. SG radar did not prevent the Americans from being surprised by Japanese torpedo ripostes when the Americans closed range and their gunnery could not swiftly neutralize all Japanese torpedo tubes. This caused commanders to question the validity of radar ambush tactics. But the Americans persevered and during the latter half of 1943, equipment, doctrine, and experience finally began to click—first in the August destroyer action in the Battle of Vella Gulf, then in the battle between two cruiser/destroyer forces at Empress August Bay in November 1943, and finally in the destroyer battle of Cape St. George later that same month. The Japanese failed to fulfill their objective in all three actions and in the process lost one light cruiser and seven destroyers without sinking any U.S. ships. It took nearly a year from the first use of SG radar in combat before the Americans were using this device effectively and routinely defeating the Japanese at night.

Taking 1 January 1943 as an arbitrary cutoff point (because from this date, nearly all large Allied surface combatants possessed some form of radar), Allied surface forces lost few naval battles. Of eighty-five surface actions fought between Allied and Axis forces from 1939 to 1942, the Axis prevailed in thirty-seven (43 percent), while the Allies won thirty-six (42 percent), with the balance having no clear victor. After 1942 there were sixty-eight surface actions; the Allies prevailed in forty-nine (72 percent), while the Axis won ten (15 percent). Radar was not the only factor behind these results, but it helped.

CASE STUDY: TECHNOLOGICAL INTEGRATION OFF THE NORMANDY BEACHES

The operations of the U.S. and the British/Canadian naval formations tasked with defending the flanks of the Neptune landings in Normandy between 6 June and 14 June 1944 provide a snapshot of the state of the art in both the U.S. and British navies and a demonstration of how electro-magnetic technologies worked together in action.

Off the western beaches U.S. destroyers supported by motor torpedo and gun boats provided the defense's surface muscle. The U.S. destroyers all had SG radar, CICs, and TBS. They were responsible for developing and engaging contacts on their own initiative. Captain Harry Sanders (commander, Destroyer Squadron 18) commanded this force from the normally equipped destroyer *Frankford*, which herself was also engaged in routine shore bombardment and patrol duties.

Rear Admiral Philip Vian commanded the British surface defenses in light cruiser *Scylla*. *Scylla* had Type 276 centimetric surface warning radar with PPI, specialized plotting equipment and personnel, and augmented communications facilities. She maintained a static position in the defense line, plotting friendly echoes 12 times and suspicious ones 120 times an hour. Radio silence was broken when necessary to vector MTBs toward a suspicious contact using a UHF (ultra-high-frequency) system. Captain A. F. Pugsley, acting as captain (patrols), filled a position similar to that of Sanders but commanded from a specially equipped frigate, *Lawford*, which carried a command and control suite like *Scylla*'s.

British and U.S. command practice and doctrine differed, and this affected the use of radar. For example, Destroyer Squadron 18's orders were four pages long, while captain (patrols) had twenty-nine pages of specific instructions to consider. The fact that an ordinary U.S. destroyer had better radar and communications systems than the two British command ships enabled the Americans to be less reliant on close supervision, although doctrine was also a factor.

On the first three nights British light forces successfully intercepted German intruders. However, when Pugsley's flagship was sunk on 8 June, defensive arrangements suffered. He was replaced by a new officer who, on his first patrol, nearly got into a firefight with a friendly destroyer. As he explained to Vian: "The situation was not clear owing to the confused enemy reports and congestion on the patrol wave. It was plain at the time and from subsequent reports, that many ships were missing many signals, and that orders issued by me were in contradiction to your own, origi-nated simultaneously."[57] In contrast, in her first action on 6 June *Frankford* detected German S-boats at 13,600 yards, plotted their advance to 8,000 yards, and opened fire at 4,500 yards: "This performance, particularly the SG radar, could not be matched by British destroyers."[58] No German surface vessels penetrated the U.S. screen.

EXPLOITATION: WORLD WAR II

If British practice lagged that of the Americans, it was far ahead of the Germans and Italians. The Italians, frustrated by ongoing problems in their own equipment, regarded naval radar as a secondary and futuristic technology until the Battle of Cape Matapan. Only after they learned that their enemy had working radar sets afloat and the Germans showed them a Seetakt did Italy prioritize radar development. The navy deployed an experimental (and unsatisfactory) ranging set in August 1941. The first Italian warship to carry an effective radar was the destroyer *Legionario*, which got a German FuMO 21/40G in the spring of 1942.[59] The Germans refused an Italian request for three more sets. On 9 June 1942 the German naval staff war diary noted: "the Italian Navy attaches very great importance to obtaining 3 German radar sets for 3 battleships. [But] it will not be possible to deliver these before autumn, all available manpower being engaged in meeting our own requirements."[60]

Italy's first effective combined air and sea search device, the EC-3ter "Gufo" (Owl), followed in September 1942. By April 1943 sixty sets were on order, but production was just three or four units a month.[61] This demonstrates another important aspect of certain types of technologies—the rich can outspend the poor. In this case, just having radar on a few ships was not enough; radar's effectiveness increased by more than the sum of the parts when deployed en masse—and when more personnel were familiar with its use. By September 1943 EC-3ter sets had been installed on three battleships, four cruisers, and seven destroyers (in addition to German sets on three torpedo boats), but the Italian navy was still in the early stages of learning how to use radar. In a 29 May 1943 memorandum assessing the performance of the first Owls deployed on a trio of destroyers, the Italian navy's chief of staff complained about equipment failures and lack of training. He could have been any U.S. or British admiral complaining about the same things in 1940–42.[62] After January 1943 a radar-equipped destroyer would lead most Italian sorties. The one confirmed use of the EC-3ter in combat occurred in July 1943 when the light cruiser *Scipione*

Africano tracked British MTBs while transiting the Strait of Messina and sank one.[63]

German radar had success stories. The function of naval radar as perceived by German naval staff can be illustrated by the fighting in the English Channel. The Germans began installing shore batteries and radar stations along the channel in July 1940. Over the next four years radar came to play an increasingly large role in how the Germans maintained their important coastal traffic and interfered with British operations. The Germans used shore radar stations to monitor Allied shipping, to vector attacking forces onto targets, and to forewarn German traffic. The German warships involved in this type of warfare, the torpedo boats, minesweepers, motor minesweepers, and S-boats, did not themselves carry radar (at least until April 1944) and relied on shore stations to locate the enemy for them. The German war diary cited a typical case that occurred on the night of 23–24 April 1942. British shore radar spotted a convoy bound down channel for Boulogne consisting of a seaplane tender and a *sperrbrecher* (mine breaker) escorted by large and smaller motor minesweepers. The South Foreland Battery's 9.2-inch guns opened fire, using radar for fire control for the first time. The radar was unable to detect the splashes, and although it was used for range, no shells fell close to the enemy.[64] The British then vectored five motor torpedo and gun boats to the attack. German radar spotted the enemy force and alerted the convoy. The British complained they were unable to reach an attacking position because of heavy starshell illumination. The German war diary exulted that "the speedy and effective defensive success of the German motor minesweepers and minesweepers was largely the result of the efficient radar location."[65]

In general, however, radar did not benefit the Germans as it did the British and Americans. German Seetakt and its various improvements were oriented toward fire control and target ranging rather than air or sea search. Moreover, the Germans believed the Allies had sophisticated radar detectors and that routine use of radar benefited the enemy more than them. There was never sufficient motive to develop a first-rate ship-borne equivalent of Freya. By February 1943, when Germany recovered a cavity magnetron from a crashed British bomber, the German navy was fighting the kind of war in which a good radar detector had more utility than a good search radar. Besides, radar detectors were easier to develop and produce while the Allied lead in radar was daunting. As Hermann Göring commented after learning of the Allied magnetron, "I did hope that even if we were behind at least we'd be in the same race."[66] By 1943 the Germans had been lapped and countermeasures were their best recourse. Even when German submarines received radar, their captains preferred to rely on passive devices—radar detectors and sophisticated hydrophones—to find or avoid the enemy. Detectors were seen as essential; *U-205* aborted her mission in the Aegean after hers malfunctioned. At the end of 1942 the Mediterranean submarine command considered its most urgent requirements to be improvements in anti-aircraft weapons and radar detection sets, "in which there are great weaknesses of performance at present." In May 1943 the submarine command was making the same demands, indicating little had changed during this most critical stage of the war.[67]

The Germans were equally slow to develop surface search radar for aircraft. A British bomber equipped with an air-to-surface vessel (ASV) Mark II metric surface search radar force-landed at Brest in June 1941, sparking an air force effort to develop airborne search radar but apparently exciting little interest in the navy.[68] The first two sets were deployed on FW 200s, and a 7 August 1942 entry in the German naval staff war diary notes: "At 1732 an FW 200, using a radar location-finding set, located a target presumed to be convoy PQ 18, *for the first time* in the fog, at a distance of about 20 km."[69] This was progress, but it came three years after the first British deployment of an ASV radar. The Italians went this route independently, recovering an ASV Mark II from a downed Wellington in January 1942 and developing a one-meter ASV copy called Arghetto in early 1943.[70]

One of the many ways in which the Allies exploited their radar edge was the proximity fuze, a small radar unit in a shell that triggered a detonation when the shell neared an enemy aircraft. Initially, it seemed that radar's greatest contribution to anti-aircraft fire would be to place shells closer to their targets by providing guns with a fire control solution. Miniaturization and ruggedizing changed that, allowing radar to be placed in the shell itself. According to researcher Louis Brown, "Of all the weapons in general use in 1939 none were improved in such a startling way by radar as was anti-aircraft artillery. When war broke out in 1939 the effectiveness of anti-aircraft fire ranged from thousands of 'rounds per bird' for daylight shooting to tens of thousands for night. . . . By 1945 an airplane caught in the range gate of an SCR 584 radar feeding the data to an M-9 director controlling an automatic tracking 90-mm gun using proximity fuzes simply meant that the plane was finished."[71] Radar-fuzed shells remained the exclusive province of the Americans and British, who were careful to keep them out of the hands of their enemies. The Germans were developing a radar fuze by the war's end, but it never entered production.[72]

The radar proximity fuze allowed an unguided projectile to detonate if it came near a target; the Bat glider bomb took this concept a step further, using a small radar set to guide a projectile to its target. It was a U.S. innovation that married a 1,000-pound bomb to a plywood airframe. An autopilot steered the bomb based on inputs from an on-board radar. The U.S. Navy used Bats in the closing stages of the war against Japan, where they were credited with sinking a number of ships and damaging an escort vessel, but the primitive radar seeker was easily confused when dropped on targets close to a shoreline. Judging overall results to be mediocre, the Navy dropped the weapon's development.[73]

COUNTERMEASURES

In May 1939, suspicious of the large antennas that had appeared along the southern coast of England, the Germans dispatched a specially rigged zeppelin to determine the electronic signatures and see if there was evidence of radar. This mission stemmed from the fact that, once armed with a radar set's frequency and location, countermeasures could be devised. The Germans came up empty in this instance and again in a second electronic reconnaissance conducted in August 1939.[74]

The most typical countermeasures to radar included jamming and spoofing. Jamming consisted of blinding the enemy radar so that it could not detect or track a target. One technique was to transmit disruptive patterns. An important jamming tool used by aircraft was called "snow," "chaff," or "window." It consisted of millions of micro-thin slips of metal foil, cut in lengths to resonate at the frequency of the defending radar. The result was that the radar operator saw a large cloud of echoes on his scope. Attacking aircraft would pop out of this cloud without giving time for defensive action. Spoofing took different forms. For instance, an aircraft using a special transponder to generate false echoes could register as an entire attacking formation. While defenders were occupied intercepting this bogus formation, the real attackers, flying low, could come in and conduct their strike unmolested. Alternatively, the Japanese aircraft disguised themselves with bogus IFF transponder responses to penetrate Allied aircraft carrier task forces.

German submarines also deployed decoy floats and balloons to distract Allied radars, but these had only limited effects because they were tuned to metric radar wavelengths. More successful were radar-absorbent coatings that the Germans employed on submarine snorkels late in the war. This was an early example of successful "stealth" technology and rendered the snorkels practically invisible to even the best Allied radar (see chapter six).[75]

The Japanese demonstrated that not all countermeasures needed to be technical. Starting in the Philippines in October 1944 the Japanese, by this time aware of U.S. radar and fighter direction capabilities, restored some effectiveness to their air arm by employing suicide (kamikaze) tactics that,

A kamikaze about to hit USS *Enterprise* (CV 6) off Okinawa on 14 May 1945—a brute force solution to the problem of radar. The strike sent the carrier back to Puget Sound for repairs. Using kamikazes, the Japanese strove to flood U.S. radar-controlled fighter direction with a series of attacks from all directions and altitudes. *(Naval History and Heritage Command, S-100-H.004)*

in effect, converted every aircraft so deployed into a guided weapon. Rather than attacking in massive groups, kamikazes followed erratic courses and attacked individually or in small groups at all attitudes. Such methods overloaded U.S. command and combat information centers. There were too many attacks coming in for effective fighter direction or even for effective plotting. This practice reached its height off Okinawa in April 1945. The Americans responded with radar picket ships, but the Japanese were still able to overwhelm U.S. radar technology and information management systems and inflict horrendous losses. How long Japan could have continued to employ such a solution is another matter, and the U.S. ability to use technology to devise an effective counter to the kamikazes—such as airborne early warning radar—was never fully tested.

One German electronic warfare triumph at sea was their subtle use of radar countermeasures to delay the British discovery of two battleships and a heavy cruiser transiting the English Channel in February 1942. The Germans began periodic jamming of British radar stations along the channel's north shore a month before the operation: "At dawn each day during January English radar stations had a few minutes of jamming deliberately made to appear like atmospherics. Every day the length of the jamming increased slightly. By February British radar operators were wearily accustomed to this interference."[76] This, and equipment failures in British ASV radar-equipped aircraft, allowed the German ships to make it nearly from Brest to the Dover Strait before a British aircraft discovered them.[77]

The Germans were fortunate to have a ready response to the first attacks by radar-equipped British aircraft on submarines transiting the Bay of Biscay. They had already put an effective radar detector on board their large surface ships, and they quickly extemporized a crude dismountable antenna for submarine use. The Metox detector had apparently eliminated the problem of radar-guided attacks by August 1942, only for these to start again in March 1943. This time, Metox gave no warning. Nor did Wanz, the next detector rushed into production. The Germans did not learn the key to this puzzle until they recovered a cavity magnetron. Neither Metox nor Wanz could detect the centimeter band emissions that the magnetron enabled. The air force launched the development of centimetric detectors but, despite the discovery, the navy concluded that the British aircraft were homing on Metox, which itself generated a weak signal. Discontinuing the

Conning tower of *U-3008* after her surrender. A Bali radar detector antenna crowns the submarine's snorkel while a Hohentwiel radar is located at its base. The radar was an adapted aircraft search radar operating on 54 centimeters. The Bali antenna was used with at least three different radar detectors, reflecting German concentration on this area. *(Naval History and Heritage Command, NH 96470)*

use of Metox in August gave no relief, however, and even after the navy appreciated that the British had developed airborne centimetric radar, an effective response took time, and the air force took priority. The navy got its first centimetric radar detectors in late 1943, but production was glacial, and the detectors were short-ranged and ill-adapted for naval use. Not until early 1944 did an effective detector come into general naval service, but by then Germany's submarine war had been all but lost.[78]

U.S. submarines also had radar detectors but relied far more on centimetric radar to find prey and avoid dangers. The report from USS *Barb*'s (SS 220) ninth war patrol, from August to October 1944, is instructive. She carried an APR detector, and her captain reported extensively on its use. Most of the report dealt with the technical characteristics and employment of the Japanese radars it detected. Little was said about enemy radar affecting *Barb*'s activities. The only significant protective measure the U.S. submarine took was to operate her radar periodically on the suspicion that the Japanese could home on the transmissions if its searches were too frequent or lengthy. The report notes that the Japanese aircraft apparently required a visual sighting to attack, which greatly reduced their effectiveness at night. Contrast this with the death struggles, day and night, that German submarines faced with Allied escorts and aircraft carrying centimetric radar, and it becomes clear why German submariners preferred radar detectors over radar.[79] The seesaw battle between radar and radar countermeasures during World War II continues to the current day and will extend into the future.

THE TECHNOLOGY POSTWAR AND TODAY

Postwar radar increased enormously in power and precision, but for navies the most remarkable development was its incorporation into guided weapons. As jets rapidly outpaced the capabilities of anti-aircraft guns and air-dropped stand-off weapons lengthened engagement ranges, navies combined radar with high-performance missiles to counter those new menaces. These missiles used radar in three ways. Beam-riders rode a radar beam to the target, active radar homers fixed on the reflections of their on-board radars, and semi-active homers used an on-board receiver to follow reflections from another radar. In time, most of these missiles incorporated ship-attack modes, although these were afterthoughts and the relatively small warheads of the missiles—designed to destroy aircraft—were of limited value.

The Soviet navy went a step further when it developed dedicated shipboard antiship missiles. The first of these, successfully tested in 1957, was a ground-launched weapon roughly adapted for shipboard use, but the Soviets quickly followed this effort with the P-15 Termit, a rocket with active radar homing expressly designed for antiship use. Termit could range out to twenty-two miles; it weighed 4,685 pounds with a 1,058-pound warhead. The rocket found its way onto a number of platforms, including the purpose-built *Komar*- and *Osa*-class missile boats. These latter two classes were reincarnations of the torpedo boats of the late 1800s—small ships with a big punch. A *Komar*-class boat carried two Termits on a displacement of 31.5 tons, while an *Osa*-class boat doubled the missile loadout on a 172-ton displacement. The Soviets calculated that two Termits would sink a destroyer and that twelve shots would assure two hits.[80]

In October 1967 two Egyptian *Komar*s fired their Termits at the Israeli destroyer *Eilat*. *Eilat* had been loitering outside of Port Said when lookouts spotted two streaks of light headed her way. Despite hasty evasive maneuvers, both missiles hit. *Eilat* lingered, burning, until a third missile detonated her ammunition magazine. The fourth hit the oil slick left by her sinking. Suddenly, the world's navies scrambled to develop surface-to-surface antiship missiles of their own, as well as antidotes to Soviet missiles. As the author of a 1969 article stated: "A new dimension, reminiscent of the appearance of the *Monitor* in Civil War days, had been added to naval warfare."[81] If confirmation was needed, it arrived in December 1971 when three Indian *Osa*s sank a Pakistani destroyer and minesweeper.

Even the U.S. Navy, which by that time relied on aircraft as its primary antiship striking force, began developing a dedicated shipboard antiship missile. The Israeli navy, which faced the most direct threat from Arab Termits, had begun its own development efforts even before the *Eilat* affair. This resulted in the Gabriel missile with active radar homing, sea-skimming ability via a radar altimeter, a range of twelve miles, and a 330-pound warhead.[82] The platform was the *Sa'ar II*-class missile boat, a craft of 220 tons displacement capable of reaching forty knots and carrying five Gabriels plus a 40-mm or 76-mm gun. Their gun armament would be used to sink opposing missile boats, while the missiles dealt with larger craft. It was only after operational testing that the Israelis discovered that the Gabriels could also hit targets as small as *Osa*s.[83]

This was validated in the Arab-Israeli War of 1973. First deployed against the Syrians, Gabriels sank two *Osa*s and a minesweeper. Attacks on Egyptian naval forces followed, with another two *Osa*s sunk by Israeli missiles.[84] The Termits had no successes in return. None of the approximately fifty fired at the *Sa'ar*s hit, a failure ascribed by the Israelis to the use of maneuvers, chaff, and electronic countermeasures (ECM), and by the Arabs to the inability of the relatively primitive radar homers in the Termits to hit small evasive targets.[85]

Whether one looks at the early Egyptian successes or the later Israeli ones, the wars in the Middle East validated the antiship guided missile concept. The Soviets were already true believers, having put into service five-ton carrier-killers with ranges exceeding 250 miles and sophisticated radar guidance. These were to be launched in strikes coordinated by a central command and control structure. Other navies hastened to adopt dedicated antiship missiles as well, albeit on a less grandiose scale. Examples included the turbo-jet Harpoon (a U.S. development), the rocket-propelled Exocet (a French effort), and the Franco-Italian OTOMAT. All used radar for target acquisition and to enable sea-skimming flight. Exocet proved its mettle in the Falklands conflict, where seven launches resulted in four hits and two sinkings. British shipboard air defenses struggled to cope with the threat; none of the Argentine aircraft attacking with Exocets were shot down, and air defenses destroyed at most only one missile. Even successes could turn into failures when confronted with effective radar homing. In one attack British warships managed to distract two of the missiles with chaff only to have them subsequently acquire, hit, and sink supply ship *Atlantic Conveyor*.[86] Harpoons had successes as well, with three (two air-dropped and one ship-launched) contributing to the 1988 sinking of the Iranian frigate *Sahand* during a U.S. Navy strike in the Persian Gulf.[87]

The history of radar-guided weapons shows that radar too has had a long development arc. Its air search capabilities were quickly manifest, but the technology needed to fit it into effective antiship missiles took twenty-five years to develop, and even more time was needed before all navies took it seriously. Even after thirty years, an established technology was able to surprise with a new application. Once navies recognized the threat of antiship missiles, countermeasures expanded beyond attempts to disable the launching platform or baffle its sensors. The weapon itself became the focus of both passive countermeasures—maneuvering, chaff, ECM—and active responses—guns and missiles. Of the two, the passive measures have proven the most effective. This puts a premium on accurately assessing an enemy weapon's characteristics and capabilities, a task that navies have found challenging.

The first application conceived for radar was as a means for ships to avoid collisions. Today radar is ubiquitous in military, civilian, and commercial applications. Cars have radar to warn if the driver is likely to hit another vehicle and to allow vehicles to drive autonomously. Radar tells where it is raining, shows how crops are growing, and forecasts storms. Radar tracks birds, wild animals, and pets. It monitors aerial traffic and helps aircraft land and avoid collisions. It guides missiles, shells, and projectiles. It can explore underground to find everything from mineral deposits to pipes. It is used to enforce speed laws. It can activate lights and open doors; it can track heart movements and sleep patterns. It is used to see through walls and as a security measure to detect concealed weapons or bombs. Radar signals map topography and land use; they measure soil moisture and the height of trees. It can trace subsurface structures or archeological sites. Radar is used to determine exact locations and can attach to cell phones to allow personal use and detection. In microwave form, it cooks dinner. Of all the technology that came into common use during World War II, radar and radio have had the greatest impact in nonmilitary applications.

WHAT THIS TELLS US

From the start, radar was a protean technology that could be shaped by each navy to meet perceived needs, and the technology's development hinged on the uses envisioned for it. Its early emergence was damped by the fact that most navies could not clearly see an urgent need for the technology, which resulted in promising leads remaining unpursued. The British fears of strategic bombing (and the determination to protect the nation from that threat) sparked and shaped radar's progress there, while other nations developed radar more slowly and for different reasons. When used at sea the Germans saw radar mainly as a fire control instrument and believed its indiscriminate use as a search device would, in fact, reveal more than disclose. Although the Allies certainly knew the dangers of using radar, it first demonstrated its value afloat as an aircraft detection device; as the war continued, they became increasingly less inhibited about using radar freely. Postwar, navies exploited radar's ability to guide weapons.

The improvements in radar made possible by the cavity magnetron were a triumph of Allied cooperation and industrial capability. At a time when the British and Americans were churning out thousands of miniature (for the time) radar sets to equip aircraft and motorboats, the Germans could not spare three sets for the battleships of their Italian allies. The way that the Allies were able to flood the oceans with small powerful radars in the air and afloat created an electronic environment that overwhelmed their enemies. The electronics suite of a German major warship late in the war had an extensive and capable array of passive radar detection devices that would alert the ship when it was being painted by enemy radar, but its radar suite was relatively skimpy. The Allies did not focus on passive detection devices because they did not need them. Thus, when the Germans innovated, they did so mainly as a defensive response to powerful Allied innovations. The Axis powers failed to share technology effectively. Cooperative research and development simply did not exist. Moreover, the Italian and Japanese navies came late to the realization of radar's value, and by that time they were riding the tiger's tail and could not recover the time they lost.

The history of radar's invention, implementation, and improvement also teaches lessons about technological development. The centralized British system of pushing development via a government committee proved more fruitful than the German approach of competing agencies and programs that did not even communicate, much less collaborate. In Japan, limited resources were squandered by the independent radar programs of the army and navy and a lack of cooperation with civilian scientists. In Italy, the underfunded craftsman approach was completely uncompetitive against the industrial and scientific might and organization of the British and Americans. Italy's leading radar scientist explained postwar that "the problem in Italian research was not the theoretical understanding, but the absence of an appropriate research infrastructure."[88] The limited resources available to the Germans were largely directed to land-based air defense, with the navy often making do with devices adapted from air force use. The Soviets largely relied on British and U.S. radar during the war but afterward developed both sophisticated home-grown radars and novel applications.

British and U.S. leadership also proved more receptive to and supportive of radar; some studies have suggested this was because the German political leadership was "anti-intellectual and scientifically illiterate."[89] Perhaps this was the case, but that same leadership aggressively promoted rocket technology, air-independent submarines, and jet aircraft. As radar technology spread, it required a certain type of culture to best explore the possibilities it offered; it required a freedom of communication and imagination more common in democratic than authoritarian states. So it was that experiments undertaken by a lieutenant commander on board *Ark Royal* in spring 1940 led to the creation of a coherent system for radar-directed fleet air defense; thus, the captain and officers of *Fletcher* teamed up to devise a system of collecting, analyzing, and distributing combat information that was, in turn, dynamically developed and propagated to the fleet. The fact that relatively low-ranking officers invented (or improved) new systems and uses for radar for the benefit of their individual ships was one thing; the fact that their navies in turn recognized the innovation and effectively spread it though the service is quite another. This was elemental to the Allied development of radar. And it was clear that this sort of innovation was critical to radar's success. It could not simply be grafted onto existing systems and processes; it demanded its own novel systems, processes, and support to reach its full potential. Even with their greater radar resources, the Allies spent the first half of the war discovering and then integrating the types of changes that radar demanded. An important aspect of this struggle was the need to absorb and quickly implement the lessons of combat. Radar was neither a panacea nor a plague, but navies could regard it as one or the other in the absence of effective analysis.

One other noteworthy element of the World War II "radar revolution" is the speed with which the capabilities and uses expanded. Canada, for example, started domestic production of an improved 1.5-m Type 286 radar in 1941. Meanwhile, in the United Kingdom, the 10-cm Type 271 was rushed into production in February 1941 before even being tested at sea and without advising the Canadians. Thus, when Canada started fitting its escorts with T286s in December, the British navy already had seventy-eight escorts equipped with T271s by the end of the next month. This was a problem in the Allied navies, but it was far worse for the Axis, especially given that they were completing against the British and Americans and not themselves. The Japanese Type 21, roughly equivalent to the Type 286, was not operational until August 1943—at which point it was plagued with poor reliability, run by insufficiently trained operators, and produced predictably poor results.[90]

American author Robert Buderi enthusiastically called radar the invention that changed the world and won World War II.[91] This is hyperbole, but radar did vastly expand the information available to a captain or a force commander on the tactical level, and it increased the lethality of his weapons. It remained the responsibility of commanders to effectively use this better information and these more deadly weapons in the completion of their tasks. With radar, as with all new technologies, it was a matter of better tools. In the case of radar technology, however, it is fair to say that it was a matter of much better tools—and lots of them. Still, in the end, technical innovation requires doctrinal innovation, and the story of radar demonstrates this truth plainly.

CHAPTER 6

SUBMARINES
The Mission Matters

It is possible to make a shippe or boate that may goe under the water unto the bottome, and so to come up againe at your pleasure.

—WILLIAM BOURNE, *INVENTIONS OR DEVISES* (1578)

The idea of underwater attack on warships, driven by the need for an affordable way to strike at stronger foes, dates back to antiquity. However, because it required the solution of many technical problems, such as effective means of propulsion, depth control, and suitable weapons, an effective submersible—one more deadly to the enemy than to its own crew—did not appear until the late nineteenth century.

THE TECHNOLOGY DESCRIBED, EARLY DEVELOPMENT

The first submersibles were all intended as blockade busters. The one-man *Turtle* of the American Revolutionary War is discussed in chapter two. France, exploring technologies to defeat the British naval blockade that proved so damaging in the eighteenth and nineteenth century world wars, flirted with a Robert Fulton design in 1800 and developed *Le Plongeur* in 1859. The boat was propelled by compressed air (anticipating the compressed air motors of Whitehead's torpedo) and was armed with a ram bow and a spar torpedo. She never made it past trials. In 1864 the Confederate States achieved the first successful use of a submersible when *H. L. Hunley* spar-torpedoed the modern screw-sloop USS *Housatonic*, which was blockading Charleston, South Carolina. *Hunley*'s eight-man crew, who worked the hand-crank drive, were all lost. This came after two years of development and two accidental sinkings with the loss of two other crews, so "successful" in this context is a relative term. The Russian navy, which experienced a British blockade during the Crimean War, commissioned the compressed air-driven *Alexandrovski* in 1866, but she proved less capable than *Le Plongeur*. The hopefully named *Resurgam* (Latin for "I will rise again") of 1879, brainchild of a British clergyman, used a steam engine for surface and latent heat for underwater propulsion. She foundered en route to trials with the British navy. Despite the lack of success, inventors and navies persevered. In fact, by the 1880s there were at least "forty-two separate submarine designs fifteen of which actually led to the construction of a submarine."[1] Among these were four steam boats constructed by the British-Swedish inventor Thorsten Nordenfelt. The Greek navy bought *Nordenfelt I*, which was armed with a 14-inch torpedo. She never became operational, but the threat alone caused the Ottoman Empire to double down by buying *Nordenfelt II* and *III*. Like their cousin, they never had enough volunteers to crew them operationally, but *Nordenfelt II* did test-fire a torpedo submerged. The Russians purchased *Nordenfelt IV*. She had severe stability problems (a common issue with these early designs) and foundered before delivery.[2]

Technological integration led to a practical means of underwater propulsion. The dry cell rechargeable battery was invented in 1859. During the U.S. Civil War, Samuel Alstitt designed an unsuccessful battery-driven submersible. The batteries could not generate enough power to keep the boat underwater and their fumes sickened the crew.[3] In the 1880s the Russians were the first to successfully use battery power when they converted two midget submarines from manual treadle drive to battery. In 1888 Isaac Peral, a Spanish naval officer, constructed an elaborate boat that crammed 613 batteries into a sixty-nine-foot hull. The Spanish government partially funded Peral's boat, and it demonstrated the ability to cruise and fire a torpedo underwater, but politics ultimately scuttled the project.[4] Throughout all this the French navy remained at the fore of early underwater technology. French designers launched three battery-powered boats and a steam-electric hybrid between 1888 and 1899.

Issuing a request for plans in 1887, the U.S. Navy Department made clear that it believed "that results already obtained justify the purchase of a submarine boat" and identified "desirable qualities," including the ability to recharge its underwater propulsion system while running surfaced.[5] This reflected the greatest deficiency of contemporary electric boats, which could only charge their batteries alongside a dock or tender. American John Holland was among the pioneers who addressed this problem; his

USS *Holland* (SS 1) in drydock circa 1900 and looking more like a torpedo than a submarine. The man standing on her deck gives a sense of the boat's diminutive size. *(Naval History and Heritage Command, NH 59)*

initial solution was to use a steam engine to recharge batteries and to drive the craft on the surface. However, it took a long time to raise steam, and even an extinguished boiler could heat interiors to an unbearable level. Holland then turned to a new technology, the gasoline engine. The result was the eponymous *Holland*, trialed in 1898 and purchased by the U.S. Navy in 1900; she influenced many of the next decade's designs, with the British and Russians building Holland boats under license.

By 1900 six navies had a total of ten submarines in service and another eleven under construction. France accounted for fourteen of these twenty-one boats.[6] Over the next five years navies advanced from experimental models to uniform classes for service use. A host of improvements attended this trend. Periscopes became better and more common, allowing for submerged attacks. New designs overcame the stability problems of the early boats. The French pioneered the use of diesel propulsion, which used less volatile fuel than gasoline motors and gave longer ranges.

The first combat use of an engine-propelled submarine came after the Russians shipped six boats to Vladivostok during the Russo-Japanese War.

These undertook several patrols in 1905, but only the ancient and tiny *Keta* (three tons with a two-man crew) came close to making an attack. She grounded while stalking a Japanese destroyer. The first underwater torpedo attack occurred on 9 December 1912 during the First Balkan War, when the Greek *Delfin* missed the Ottoman cruiser *Mejidieh* from five hundred meters.[7]

By 1914, after a long gestation and despite the absence of any proven results, the submarine had become an accepted component of every major and many minor fleets. At the same time, navies considered how to use their boats and debated their true level of threat. The head of the British navy, Admiral Jacky Fisher, was a fan. As early as 1904 he wrote, "It is astounding to me, perfectly astounding how the very best amongst us fail to realize the vast impending revolution in naval warfare and naval strategy that the submarine will accomplish."[8] German Grand Admiral Alfred von Tirpitz, on the other hand, "saw the new weapon as a threat to the battleship and himself" and made only feeble efforts to integrate submarines into the German navy.[9]

In 1914 the world's most capable submarines, the British *E* and the German *U-19* classes, had similar characteristics. Table 6.1 compares these to a Holland *C*-class boat of 1906 and shows how the technology had advanced in only six years.

The submarine of 1914 was twice the boat of a decade before in terms of speed, armament, and crew. And while the *E* class's range far exceeded the Holland boat, the German MAN two-stroke diesel engine, the world's best marine diesel, gave the German boat oceanic reach. Other differences were less obvious. German optics and radios outclassed British equipment; U.S. postwar assessments of German submarines lauded German workmanship. The British considered that their submarines handled better

TABLE 6.1

COMPARATIVE SUBMARINE CHARACTERISTICS

CLASS	YEAR	DISPLACEMENT IN TONS (SUBMERGED)	SPEED IN KNOTS (SURFACE/SUBMERGED)	TORPEDOES	RANGE ON SURFACE (MILES/KNOTS)	CREW
Holland C	1906	275	8/5	2 18-inch	800/8	15
German U-19	1912	837	15.4/9.5	4 19.7-inch	7,600/8	35
British E	1912	796	15/9	4 18-inch	3,000/10	30

Sources: Rössler, *The U-Boat*; Friedman, *British Submarines*; Gardiner, *Fighting Ships, 1860–1905*.

submerged. German or British, these early boats were noisy and cramped and lacked underwater sensors. They were not completely deaf, blind, and dumb, but near enough. French boats were not even standardized. When the Austro-Hungarians captured the French boat *Curie* in 1914, they found that some levers turned to the left to open a valve, others to the right, and that some handles went up to close a switch, others went down.[10]

EXPECTATIONS

In 1914 navies generally agreed that submarines had three basic missions: attrition, coastal defense, and fleet cooperation. Attrition consisted of patrol missions to find and destroy enemy warships. The German navy had come to regard the submarine as an important element in its *Kleinkrieg* doctrine—a form of naval guerrilla warfare by which German units would pick away at Britain's mighty fleet in a series of small actions. Once the odds had been balanced, Germany's battlefleet could sensibly risk a direct confrontation. Coastal defense consisted of patrolling off friendly ports, usually with the oldest and smallest boats, to deter enemy incursions. Fleet cooperation saw submarines as an integral component of the battlefleet, and Great Britain and Germany in particular promulgated tactics for joint surface/subsurface operations such as evolutions in which surface units would try to lure enemy vessels across submarine ambush points. The French explored using their submarines in a fleet scouting role, but their boats were too slow. In fact, France's reason for pioneering submarine technology—as a means of defeating a British naval blockade—evaporated when Great Britain became an ally.

No navy openly espoused using submarines for commerce raiding. Rules regulating this activity stipulated that a warship must stop and board a merchantman, examine it, and, if the ship or its cargo was subject to seizure, send it into a port with a prize crew aboard. Merchant ships were not to be sunk in the ordinary course of operations, but if they were, their crews and passengers had to be safeguarded, not a task a submarine could realistically undertake. And while navies might be tempted to bend the rules, sinking merchantmen on sight was casus belli and carried the risk of conflict with neutral nations. In any case, many doubted that the range, habitability, and endurance of even the "oceanic" boats in service would allow the long-range operations necessary for an effective war against shipping. The British had little reason to pursue a submarine war on trade; they would blockade Germany with surface ships. As for Germany, at the start of the war its civilian leadership regarded the political damage of waging unrestricted commercial warfare as "far greater than the military usefulness."[11]

The best submarines of 1914 were barely able to perform the missions naval staffs envisioned for them, and their limitations were underappreciated when the fighting started. Fleet cooperation was difficult, with battleships steaming at fifteen knots and perhaps twenty in action. In 1914 the most modern submarines could make sixteen knots, flat out on the surface, but less than ten knots submerged and that for a relatively brief time. Moreover, prewar radios were unreliable and underwater communications impossible. In the North Sea, coastal submarines could remain on station only for a day or two if they operated off the enemy shore and hardly longer off friendly ports. Targets were hard to find and, when found, hard to attack. Under perfect conditions, a lookout could see five or six miles—the periscope view was less. To conduct an attack, a submarine needed to take station ahead of the target and then fire, ideally leading the target by the correct amount from a position off the approaching ship's bow. In assessing the performance of submarines against warships, a postwar German commentator noted that "the means of luring the enemy warships into positions favorable for submarine attack were lacking, and many opportunities were missed by the fact that the low submerged and surface speeds of the submarines prevented their attaining a suitable position for attack."[12]

DISCOVERY: WORLD WAR I

In 1914 most of the major naval powers had substantial numbers of submarines (see table 6.2).

The first war lessons learned were baby steps. The Dover command assigned three *B* class submarines to guard convoys carrying the British Expeditionary Force (BEF) across the English Channel to France. These submarines, dating from 1906, were thought incapable of maintaining an underway patrol for an entire day, so they tied to buoys spaced along their patrol zone. It was hoped they would have time to slip their moorings and obtain an attack position should the Germans appear (which they never did).[13]

TABLE 6.2

SUBMARINES BY NATION, 1 AUGUST 1914

Great Britain	76
France	50
United States	32
Germany	27
Russia	22
Italy	18
Japan	13
Austria-Hungary	5

Sources: Gardiner, *Fighting Ships, 1906–1921*; O'Hara, Dickson, and Worth, *To Crown the Waves*; Sokol, *Austro-Hungarian Navy*; correspondence with E. Cernuschi and S. McLaughlin, 28 November 2020.

In Germany's case, "after a few weeks experience it was found that the larger boats, *U-19* and above, could remain at sea much longer than was supposed."[14] On 6 August, as the naval staff realized that the British were not going to conveniently lay off German harbors, they sent ten submarines north to find the enemy blockade line. The boats instead collided with the Grand Fleet, at sea in distant support of the BEF convoys. In the process, the Germans lost *U-13*, which may have been run down by a battleship, and *U-15*, rammed by the cruiser *Birmingham* after a mechanical failure forced her to surface. Nonetheless, these encounters, magnified by a slew of bogus periscope sightings, thoroughly spooked the British. Jellicoe withdrew his capital ships and ordered every available cruiser and destroyer to sweep the menace from the North Sea, without saying how this should be done.[15]

Some of the first German and British offensive naval operations involved submarines and surface warships working together. In an 18 August operation off the Dutch coast, the Germans dispatched two light cruisers to attack British destroyer patrols while stationing a pair of submarines to ambush enemy warships that tried to intervene. While surface forces made contact, the submarines came up empty-handed. A British raid into Heligoland Bight ten days later provides an even better illustration of the difficulties involved with coordinating submarines and surface ships. In this case, three British *E*-class boats were to provoke German

destroyers patrolling the bight into chasing them westward. Five submarines lurked near Heligoland and off the Ems to ambush reinforcements
emerging from the German ports. Meanwhile, eight light cruisers and
thirty-two destroyers would hit the Germans from behind. Due to their
limited communications and speed, the submarines had to leave a day
early with their activities predetermined by written instructions.

E9 attacked a German destroyer at 0500 28 August 1914, provoking a
vigorous response from ten others. At this stage, German antisubmarine
tactics called for flooding the area of a contact with surface warships to
keep the boat down until she had exhausted her batteries. Theoretically,
the submarine would then surface and be sunk by gunfire. The British
submarine *D2* sighted a German light cruiser emerging from the Ems
but was unable to attack. In fact, poor visibility and fast-sailing ships
frustrated the British submarines, and the unanticipated appearance of
British reinforcements led to some fraught moments as when *E6* attacked
Southampton and the British light cruiser tried to ram the "friendly" boat.
Fleet cooperation in a fast-moving and confused surface action produced
more close calls than target opportunities, and British surface units, which
sank an enemy destroyer and three light cruisers, garnered all the glory.
The British officer in charge of submarine operations, Commodore Roger
Keyes, expressed the early frustration experienced by all navies in a letter
written on 5 September 1914: "We have been in these waters [Heligoland
Bight] for weeks with considerable movement taking place and have only
once been within torpedo range of an Enemy's cruiser."[16]

Up to this point, a modern submarine had never sunk an enemy warship,
but this changed when *U-21* torpedoed the British scout cruiser *Pathfinder*
on 5 September. *Pathfinder* was patrolling off the Firth of Forth at six knots
when *U-21* ambushed her from two thousand yards. Lookouts spotted the
torpedo wake too late and the weapon detonated a magazine. *Pathfinder*
sank in four minutes, taking with her all but 18 of her crew of 268. The
submarine *E9* scored the first British success on 13 September when she
sank the German light cruiser *Hela*. Nonetheless, "The results of the first
seven weeks of the war seemed to justify the doubts of [Germany's] already
powerful anti-submarine party. With the exception of one old cruiser the
submarines had sunk no enemy vessels and they had suffered the loss of
two of their number. Although the British fleet had been constantly at sea,

the submarines had not been able to hinder their activity nor send much information as to their movements."[17]

The doubts of the anti-submarine lobby were, of course, premature. Submarines established their credentials nine days after the loss of *Hela* when the German *U-9* sank the British armored cruisers *Aboukir*, *Hogue*, and *Cressy*. The obsolescent cruisers were patrolling off the Dutch coast even though bad weather had driven their destroyer screen to port. First the submarine hit *Aboukir*. She took on a list and capsized a half hour later. *Hogue*'s captain, thinking that *Aboukir* had been mined, approached to rescue survivors, but *U-9* torpedoed her as well. Although *Cressy*'s captain now realized that a submarine was the culprit, he continued with rescue operations, and *U-9* torpedoed *Cressy* next. Nearly 1,500 British sailors died in this tragedy. After this "sensational success," as German Rear Admiral Arno Spindler remembered, "even some of the experts were prone to over-shoot the mark" about the capabilities of the undersea arm, and he noted that "to obtain a slight result a great expenditure of force was necessary."[18] With these successes under their belts, German boats started venturing beyond the North Sea and their cruises paved the way for subsequent operations. *U-18* penetrated the Dover Strait and then Scapa Flow on 23 November (and was sunk trying to exit). *U-20* circumnavigated Britain and Ireland. These operations established that any base in the British Isles was theoretically subject to submarine attack.

Admiral Jellicoe, who had already expressed deep concerns about mines and torpedoes, was one expert who overshot the mark. The British admiralty originally selected Scapa Flow as the main fleet base in part because it believed the far northern anchorage to be beyond range of German submarines, and it considered the tidal currents too strong for submerged entry. When Jellicoe discovered that both assumptions were false, he raced to secure the vast anchorage, keeping his fleet at sea as much as possible and using other harbors farther from German bases in the interim. On 5 September a lookout mistook a seal for a periscope and then for a torpedo. The fleet hurriedly raised steam and fled Scapa Flow while light craft crisscrossed the waters firing guns. The whole Grand Fleet did not return until 24 September. A similar stampede occurred on 16 October. In describing his concerns, Jellicoe said, "I feel we are risking such a mass of valuable ships in a place where, if a submarine did get in, she practically has the British Dreadnought Fleet at her mercy up to the number of her torpedoes."[19] Jellicoe's concerns reflected the *in terrorem* effect that submarines enjoyed, despite their lack of success against modern dreadnoughts.

Jellicoe was hardly alone in overestimating the capabilities of submarines. Fisher scolded Commodore Keyes after German battlecruisers bombarded Hartlepool on 16 December 1914 without interference from British coastal subs. Keyes afterward complained that Fisher unjustly believed "the 12 submarines under my orders should make it impossible for a German ship to show herself anywhere from St. Abbs to Harwich if I knew how to use them."[20]

EVOLUTION: WORLD WAR I

It took roughly six months of warfare for British and German naval commands to get a sense of what their submarines could and could not realistically do. Although operations such as the Heligoland Bight raid had illustrated the difficulties and dangers of surface and subsurface forces operating together, the German and British commands continued to explore joint actions with the Germans conducting a major fleet/submarine operation as late as August 1916 and the British launching large steam-driven submarines designed for fleet cooperation as late as 1918. The lurk-and-shoot patrol attrition mission produced some successes (generally against obsolescent targets) but fell far short of the German goal of attriting the Grand Fleet. Coastal defense submarines made no kills, and experience was teaching that mines were a better way to deter enemy incursions into friendly waters. As offensive minelaying by surface ships proved dangerous, coastal submarines were converted to the role. Submarine minelaying was first practiced by the Germans in May 1915. By the end of 1915 mines laid by an average force of six small boats were sinking twelve to fourteen enemy and neutral ships a month, disrupting traffic, and occupying more than one hundred British minesweepers and several dozen French ones.[21]

Despite few successful attacks against modern warships, submarines continued to affect surface operations disproportionately. The French fleet opened the war with a policy of aggressive operations in the Adriatic Sea but after the Austro-Hungarian boat *U-12* torpedoed the French dreadnought *Jean Bart* off Albania in December 1914, French battleships never

Austro-Hungarian boats *U-3* and *U-4* at Pola. These were small coastal boats but were suitable for operations in the Adriatic. *U-3* was rammed by an Italian armed merchant cruiser and then sunk by a French destroyer, but *U-4* sank Italian armored cruiser *Giuseppe Garibaldi* in July 1915 and survived the war. *(https://home.ilcorriereditrieste.agency /archives/610)*

again entered the Adriatic. Farther east, the German *U-21* sank the pre-dreadnought battleships *Triumph* and *Majestic*, which were supporting the Entente beachheads at Gallipoli in May 1915; this caused the battleships to withdraw, and subsequent submarine scares continued to disrupt fire support for the hard-pressed troops on the narrow beachheads.[22]

In 1915 submariners gained a new mission—attacking enemy commercial traffic. It was this mission that transformed the submarine into a strategic weapon of war. In a prewar study, one German officer estimated that the navy would need more than two hundred submarines to conduct an effective mercantile war under the customary rules of commerce warfare. Ignoring those rules was "virtually guaranteed to embroil Germany in difficulties with neutrals."[23] Nonetheless, on 8 October 1914 the chief of U-boats recommended that submarines should begin attacking merchant shipping. The commander of the High Seas Fleet, Admiral Friedrich Ingenohl, was still wedded to *Kleinkrieg* and so rejected this recommendation. The first mercantile ship sunk by German submarines was *Glitra* (866 GRT) on 20 October 1914, after eleven weeks of war. The submarine *U-17* stopped the ship, examined it, and allowed the crew to take to their boats.[24]

Once the land armies stalemated in the late autumn of 1914, it became clear that the quick triumph the German army had anticipated was now impossible. Seeking other paths to victory, especially in the face of Britain's increasingly effective naval blockade, Germany declared a submarine blockade of the British Isles to begin at the end of February 1915.[25] Submarines would try to verify nationality before attacking but would not otherwise respect the traditional prize rules. Neutrals' ships in the declared "war zone" might be sunk without warning due to British ships disguising their nationality by sailing under neutral flags. At the time, Germany had on hand thirty-seven boats of all types, including those in training and under repair. For the campaign's first three months an average of only six boats patrolled the operational areas at any one time. Nonetheless, in that quarter German submarines sank sixty-one British commercial vessels displacing 170,926 gross register tonnage (GRT) compared to eighteen vessels displacing 41,863 GRT in the quarter prior.[26] Such results convinced the German naval staff that a traffic war was the best use for its undersea forces and one that potentially offered war-winning potential, even if the new mission restricted surface fleet operations by denying the fleet submarine reconnaissance to supplement the often unreliable zeppelins.[27] The watershed event of the first unrestricted campaign was the sinking of the thirty-thousand-ton liner *Lusitania* on 7 May 1915. The death of 1,198 men, women, and children caught the world's attention and caused widespread outrage, particularly in the United States, which lost 128 citizens. The international censure—specifically a warning from Washington that "Germany could avoid war with the United States only by ending unrestricted submarine warfare"—led Germany to terminate its unrestricted campaign after six and a half months, except in the Mediterranean, where there were few U.S. ships to sink. Moreover, the navy was not delivering the results required because there were not enough submarines for the job.[28]

The British also embraced the antitraffic mission, sending three submarines into the Baltic in 1915 (two made it) and ultimately building a force of seven boats there. During 1915 they sank twenty-one transports and two cruisers and damaged the battlecruiser *Moltke*.[29] Entente submarines also targeted Ottoman shipping in the Sea of Marmara. In fifteen patrols involving thirteen British and French boats, they claimed the destruction of an old battleship, a destroyer, 5 gunboats, 55 merchantmen or transports, and 148 sailing vessels. Ottoman accounts credit the campaign with 39 steamers and transports and 135 assorted smaller vessels sunk. A total of

56,000 GRT was sunk or damaged. Reaching the Sea of Marmara was difficult, with the antisubmarine nets at Nagara being a particularly dangerous chokepoint, and the French and the British each lost four submarines in the campaign. Their depredations, however, forced the Ottomans to rely upon the longer and more difficult overland supply route down the Gallipoli Peninsula. In fact, the Gallipoli campaign is an example of how submarines could directly affect a land campaign: the Germans by driving off Entente ships providing fire support, and the Entente by complicating Ottoman supply. In the Black Sea, the Russians gave the Ottomans further anxiety by using a combination of submarines, destroyers, and minefields to blockade the Anatolian coast, particularly the vital coal traffic from Zonguldak to Istanbul.[30]

Some members of the German fleet command believed that the suspension of unrestricted warfare provided a renewed opportunity for conducting joint fleet-submarine operations, with the submarines providing reconnaissance rather than close support. This concept failed in the Battle of Jutland, as most of the submarines missed the signal ordering them into positions off the British ports. The two submarines that did take proper station managed only one unsuccessful attack, and while Scheer received their contact reports, he did not realize that the entire Grand Fleet was at sea.[31] An operation in August 1916 had better results as submarines sank two light cruisers, but in those post-Jutland days, that was hardly enough. After 1916 German and Austro-Hungarian submarines refocused on the war against commerce, with the Germans announcing the resumption of unrestricted submarine warfare in February 1917. Without large enemy merchant fleets to target, Entente submarines concentrated on coastal defense, patrol, and fleet cooperation. Their only added roles were as submarine hunters and even as convoy escorts. Through the end of 1916 submarines of all combatants worldwide had sunk or mined only thirty-eight warships and no dreadnought battleships (see table 6.3).

After 1914 Central Power submarines became the leading cause of loss for Entente and neutral shipping. Their share of merchant tonnage sunk rose from less than 1 percent of the total in 1914 to 90 percent in 1915 and 95 percent in 1916. This is even more remarkable given that merchant tonnage losses quadrupled from 1914 and 1915 and almost doubled again

TABLE 6.3

WARSHIPS SUNK OR DAMAGED BY SUBMARINES, 1914–16

NATION	OWN WARSHIPS LOST TO ENEMY SUBMARINES	ENEMY WARSHIPS SUNK BY OWN SUBMARINES
Germany	5	25
Austria-Hungary	0	5
Ottoman Empire	3	0
Great Britain	14	8
France	7	0
Italy	6	0
Russia	3	0

Sources: Gardiner, *Fighting Ships, 1906–1921*; "World War 1 Naval Combat" (worldwar1.co.uk); uboat.net.

from 1915 and 1916, to more than 2 million GRT.[32] In this same period the Germans lost forty-seven submarines: eight by unknown causes, eight by accidents, sixteen by enemy vessels, including Q-ships (faux merchantmen with hidden guns) and submarines, eleven by mines, three by nets, and one by depth charge. In return, they sank 2,391 vessels, including warships, or more than 50 ships per German submarine lost.[33]

Even before Germany's 1917 decision to launch an unrestricted campaign against shipping, the submarine's most important mission in World War I had become attacks on enemy commerce. This task had strategic, even war-winning, potential—if the enemy relied upon seaborne traffic—and important tactical implications as well, as shown by their impact on Ottoman logistics at Gallipoli. Throughout the war, German and Austro-Hungarian submarines sank 4,837 merchant ships, accounting for more than 11 million GRT of enemy and neutral vessels. On the other hand, submarines were hardly more effective in the attrition patrol and coastal defense missions in 1918 than they had been in 1914, and the fleet cooperation mission remained impractical, even with special high-speed submarines, due to communication difficulties. Thus, in 1918 the Central Powers were devoting nearly all their undersea strength to the mission against commerce while Entente submarines were continuing to patrol, obtaining occasional successes that at least kept the submarine threat alive in the minds of German admirals, and defending coastlines and ports that the enemy was never going to attack. When Admiral Beatty came to command of the Grand Fleet in 1917, he found that of eighty-six submarines available, the admiralty was holding back seventy-six to defend against a German invasion. Without many worthwhile merchant targets, the only new missions the Entente powers could find for their boats were as antisubmarine platforms and convoy escorts.[34]

Politically, the fact that unrestricted submarine warfare triggered a U.S. declaration of war suggests that submarines actually caused Germany's defeat. They were a poisoned chalice because using them in what seemed to be the best way violated international norms and enraged neutrals. Submarines were hardly the first technology to raise issues of ethical use. In this case, imperial Germany proved notably inept at addressing the problem and in the process provides a clear example of why considering military issues to the exclusion of nonmilitary matters in the use of new technology is a dangerous practice.

COUNTERMEASURES

The British navy first considered antisubmarine warfare (ASW) in 1904, but not until 1910 did it approach the subject systematically. Major exercises followed in 1912. Roger Keyes, participating in the exercises, wrote that "if a Submarine was sighted for two or three minutes on the surface, or even if her periscope was sighted prior to her attack, she was put out of action."[35] This came at a time when the principal shipborne antisubmarine weapon was a towed explosive charge. As one British destroyer commander commented, "Any German submarine who got caught in a fool device like that deserves to be sunk."[36] Buoyed indicator nets were the only means of detecting submerged submarines. ASW tactics emphasized blanketing threatened areas with small warships including trawlers, torpedo boats, and destroyers. The British divided their coastal waters into patrol zones and assigned vessels to each area. The Germans maintained a constant patrol in the Heligoland Bight. At the very least, they would force submarines to submerge. A surfaced submarine had to fear gunfire, torpedoes, ramming, and mines. Once submerged and at depth, submarines were invisible, and mines were their only worry. Even when surfaced, submarines were small and the ocean vast, making ASW patrolling a needle-in-a-haystack activity.

In 1914 the best defenses against submarines were speed and maneuver. Generally, warships zigzagging at fifteen knots or more were safe. Clouds of destroyers surrounded battleships to provide additional protection. Such measures, however, degraded the battlefleet's endurance because maintaining such relatively high speeds required more fuel and increased wear and tear on machinery. Mines were the best ASW weapons available in August 1914, but in the war's early months most navies, worried about their own mines limiting their freedom of maneuver and with limited stocks of mines on hand, did not rely on minefields as they later would (see chapter two). In fact, until the Germans started their war against traffic, British ASW lacked urgency inasmuch as submarines, limited by numbers and used in missions they were not suited to perform, did not at first cause the harm alarmists had anticipated. Even in August 1915, when German submarines sank 186,000 GRT of shipping—the heaviest losses in the war to date—British casualties were "only 1 per cent, which was half what the French privateers achieved in the Napoleonic wars."[37] Once submarines started sinking merchant ships in great numbers, however, the imperative to devise more effective ways of fighting them increased, particularly in Great Britain, which was suffering the greatest harm.[38]

The British admiralty had begun arming merchant ships prewar, but it now increased its efforts and focused on ships exposed to submarine attack. By May 1915, 115 of these vessels were armed, mostly with 12-pounder guns.[39] Such weapons were more effective in discouraging attacks than in actually inflicting harm. They did, however, increase the use of precious torpedoes as submarines became increasingly reluctant to surface and sink targets with their deck guns. Other countermeasures included instructing merchant skippers to ram submarines, introducing Q-ships and aircraft ASW patrols, and even towing old C-class submarines behind a likely victim to ambush the attacker. Through 1916 these methods sank eight enemy boats.[40]

In the quest to improve ASW methods and weapons, France and Germany took a centralized approach to the problem. France, for example, had a ministry of inventions to coordinate the military use of new technology. In Great Britain, however, various military and private research organizations worked independently and sometimes at cross purposes. The navy employed creative methods such as offering prize money to fishing boats for reporting submarines and sponsoring a contest for the general public to propose new methods of antisubmarine warfare. As historian Willem Hackmann commented, "The imaginative contribution was strong but the science was weak."[41] Not until July 1915 did the British establish a centralized Board of Invention and Research (BIR) headed by Admiral Fisher, returned from a self-imposed retirement. The admiral summarized his take on British efforts: "Man invents: monkeys imitate. Eleven months of war have shown us simply as servile copyists of the Germans. German mines and submarines have walked ahead of us by leaps and bounds."[42] This was not entirely true; his polemic approach, and the politics behind it, only compromised the board's effectiveness.

The first task the navy gave to the BIR was to evaluate the more than 14,000 responses to its submarine contest; suggestions such as dowsing for submarines or training seagulls to follow periscopes were all investigated and discarded. Mutual contempt and disagreements between methods and goals undermined cooperation between civilian scientists and military specialists on critical technologies such as underwater acoustics.[43] While navy and civilian-staffed boards did important work in a number of fields, technological enhancements such as better hydrophones, depth charges, and bomb-throwers all came slowly and, in the end, had little impact on the antisubmarine war then under way; "Much had to change before science and the military could work together with harmony and tangible benefit."[44]

The two areas in which innovation was most required were in detecting submerged submarines and in harming them once detected. When the war began no nation possessed an underwater bomb or depth charge, but the concept was obvious and before the year was out the Germans, French, and British were developing such a weapon.[45] Admiral Jellicoe first proposed a droppable antisubmarine mine in December 1914. The British navy approved the Type D depth charge in June 1915; it began to appear on vessels in January 1916. The Type D operated hydrostatically and could be set to detonate at forty or eighty feet. It packed either a 120- or a 300-pound Amatol charge (the mine with the smaller charge equipped drifters, which were not fast enough to escape the blast of the larger charge). The Germans deployed their standard depth charge, the C15, in April 1915 and used it in the Baltic and the Sea of Marmara (in Ottoman service), although to no effect. This weapon detonated mechanically after a preset time or after a set length of cord tied to a firing pin had run out. It was packed with 50 kg of TNT. In service it proved fragile and had a 50 percent dud rate. The Austro-Hungarians received some but choose to develop their own depth charge. Germany produced 2,256 C15s, equipping destroyers with four to six and drifters with two to four.

The French depth charge, the Guiraud, detonated hydrostatically at 50, 85, or 115 feet. It also came in versions with charges of 42 and 63 kg of ammonia perchlorate. The French found it delicate and unstable. The British refused a request for Type D charges, saying they needed all they could make, and so the French began using the Italian-made BTG charges in 1917. These carried a 50-kg charge.[46]

The Americans produced four marks of depth charges. The Mk I with a 50-pound charge began its production run of ten thousand in 1916 and was available in numbers when the United States entered the war. The Mk II and Mk III were modified British Type Ds. The Mk III increased the maximum depth to three hundred feet. The Mk IV, which carried a massive 600-pound TNT charge, appeared in late 1918. The United States produced 40,000 Mk IIs and IIIs and 1,000 Mk IVs from July 1917.[47]

The first submarine sunk with the aid of depth charges was *U-68*. Charges blew her to the surface during an action with the Q-ship *Farnborough* on 22 March 1916 whereupon the ship's guns provided the coup de gras. During the war the British issued 74,441 depth charges, nearly 70 percent in 1918. They expended 16,451 charges. These killed thirty-eight submarines, two-thirds in 1918, for an overall kill rate of one submarine per 433 charges used.[48] The number of kills jumped in the latter half of 1917 as the British improved the Type D, crews gained experience, and the number of charges carried increased. Like mines and torpedoes, depth charges were more effective when used profusely. As one British antisubmarine expert put it, officers had to put it in their heads that a depth charge was a round of ammunition, not the Bank of England.[49]

The only tool available for locating submarines underwater was the hydrophone, a technology that first appeared in 1893. In 1903 the Royal Navy torpedo school tested a hydrophone for detecting undersea craft but concluded it was too unreliable. Nonetheless, the technology had promise, and scientists of various nations continued to explore ways to capture and interpret underwater sounds. From late 1915 nondirectional hydrophones began appearing in numbers on British warships. This type was referred to as a "drifter" set because it was hung over the side of the patrol vessel, commonly a drifter. Although it was a crude device and required the ship to come to a complete stop to work, the navy purchased 4,534 units. Germany deployed two types of towed hydrophones. These had to be operated at very slow speeds and the towing vessels had to change direction to fix a contact's bearing. They were not very successful. The French and Italians also deployed various hydrophone systems that the British generally considered inferior to their own. Directional hydrophones dated from 1917 with the Royal Navy acquiring more than 3,430 sets.[50]

The biggest problems with hydrophones were their unreliability, especially in heavy weather or in crowded waters, and their need for highly trained and skilled operators. Even when they did detect submarines, however, they could not *locate* them in the final stages of an attack, when such information was most needed. The British deployed massive hydrophone-equipped patrol flotillas in the war's last year, but according to admiralty statistics, of 255 encounters between submarines and patrol boats in 1918, hydrophones played a role in only 54 cases.[51] Visual sighting resulted in far more contacts. Nevertheless, such poor results did not deter the practice of large ASW offensive sweeps, as the equipment was available and offensive patrolling satisfied the compulsion to do something active against the submarine menace.

Research into echo-sounding detection devices was also under way, with U.S. and French work being ahead of initial British efforts at least up through 1916. These devices emitted an ultrasonic wave underwater and measured the time it took for the wave's echo to return, thus measuring the distance to the object. In November 1918 a prototype obtained echoes from a submarine three thousand yards away, and had the war continued, the Entente powers would have deployed such devices in 1919.[52]

In summarizing the overall results of the efforts to innovate ASW technology in World War I, American author Philip Lundeberg correctly observed, "Although there was a frantic search for technological antidotes to the submarine, the only useful active weapon developed during the war was the depth charge, and it was hardly more successful in sinking U-boats than gunfire or ramming and far less successful than mines."[53]

It turned out that the most effective way to deal with submarines was to mitigate their impact rather than attack them directly. It was not better sensors or weapons; it was organizing merchantmen into escorted convoys, a practice from the age of sail. In 1915 British submarines operating in the Baltic disrupted German iron ore traffic from Sweden. In 1916 the boats enjoyed little success because the Germans implemented convoys. It took the British longer to adopt this practice, but when they did, the results were immediate—merchant ship sinkings dropped and submarine kills climbed. Convoys worked for several reasons. Given the immensity of the oceans, a convoy of three dozen ships was hardly easier to find than a single ship. Thus, with shipping concentrated into groups, the opportunities for German submarines to spot targets plummeted. Moreover, the British ability to read German codes and take fixes on radio transmissions enabled them to determine the location of enemy submarines well enough to route convoys around them. Finally, because convoys were escorted, every submarine contact with a convoy was also a contact with antisubmarine forces.

New ASW technologies and old practices proved capable of managing the German submarine threat in 1917–18, but it was never defeated. From start to finish submarines remained hard to detect and harder to kill. In the end, the most effective solution was resource management, not technology. The impact of convoying can be grasped by comparing the first five months of the second German unrestricted campaign (February–June 1917) to the next six months (July–December 1917), when convoying was in place. On average, during the second period the Germans kept more submarines at sea but with less success, as the rate of sinkings per submarine dropped from about six ships per month to three, while monthly submarine losses climbed from almost four boats per month to seven. Although more than 3,106,343 GRT (an average of 194,146 tons a month) of British-flagged shipping was lost to submarines in the sixteen months between July 1917, when convoying began, and October 1918, this compares favorably with the 1,768,015 GRT (353,603 tons a month) sunk in the first five months of the German unrestricted campaign—far from ideal, but tolerable.[54]

Although the Entente powers significantly reduced the rate of mercantile losses and sank more enemy boats in the war's final year, this should not obscure the fact that submarines continued to be deadly to the war's last day. By 1939, however, optimists in the British admiralty believed that the vastly improved tools of antisubmarine warfare would allow the British navy to contain the underwater menace in a new war. First among the new tools was echo-sounding detection, dubbed asdic by the British and sonar by the Americans. Stephen Roskill wrote that many believed "asdic had reduced the submarine threat almost to extinction."[55] Although nearly ready for deployment in 1918, sonar did not actually go to sea until 1927. The ten-year lapse reflects how the pace of specialized technological development can slow during peacetime. Nonetheless, by 1932 the British had equipped all their modern destroyers with sonar, and the first U.S. types were entering service.[56] The Germans, on the other hand, had different priorities and focused on hydrophones as a means for their submarines and surface vessels to detect ships, both above and below the surface.

Hydrophones had the advantage of being passive, so they did not disclose any information about the user, and they could detect at much greater distances than sonar. The most common German system, installed in submarines from 1935, was called Gruppen-Horch-Gerät (group listening device, or GHG). This used an array of hydrophones, initially eleven to a side on Type VII submarines, but in the case of cruiser *Prinz Eugen*, sixty to a side. Under ideal conditions GHG could pick up single ships from twenty kilometers and convoys from one hundred kilometers and give an indication of bearing but not range.[57] Regarding its effectiveness, *Prinz Eugen*'s captain noted that GHG allowed his ship to detect and avoid torpedoes throughout her career. For example, on 17 May 1942 twenty-seven Beaufort torpedo bombers attacked while she was returning to Germany. Thanks to her GHG and despite a jury-rigged rudder, she combed one spread of six torpedoes and wove her way through another. This she accomplished under perfect (for the aircraft) attack conditions. At the Battle of the Denmark Strait, the cruiser's GHG purportedly picked up the sound of the approaching British battleships twenty miles away, long before they came in sight.[58] The Allies first glimpsed the capabilities of GHG after the capture of *U-570* in August 1941. Upon examination, the British admiral commanding submarines claimed *U-570* "was six times as good with her multi-unit hydrophone as our submarines were with their asdic."[59] This may have been an overstatement but in any case, "these conclusions made no impact on British wartime asdic research because resources were not available to follow-up the findings."[60] German naval historians Gerhard

Koop and Klaus-Peter Schmolke noted: "The German GHG came as a complete surprise to the Allies, since their research into the frequencies used by the Germans had been abandoned as hopeless—an error parallel to that of the German scientists respecting radar centimetre technology."[61]

The Germans also had sonar, called Sondergerät für Aktive Schallortung (Special Equipment for Active Sound Location, or S-Gerät), installed on ships from 1938. This gave the range and bearing for underwater objects out to a distance of ten kilometers under ideal conditions. German submariners disliked it because they believed there were Allied detection devices that could hear it before it could hear them, and therefore it was seldom used.[62] It malfunctioned easily and had to be turned off for at least ten minutes during every hour. In January 1940 production was six units a month.[63] Italy, like Germany, focused on hydrophone technology. In June 1940 the Italian navy had one ship equipped with an experimental active echo-sounding device and two others with more refined prototypes. Germany began sharing its sonar technology in September 1941, sending Rome forty-one S-Gerät units over the course of several months. Italian-produced sonar appeared in late 1942 at a rate of six sets per month.[64] The Italian official history noted that although domestically produced hydrophones could filter noises and obtain bearings, sonar was superior, and its antisubmarine forces were equipped with sonar "as soon as possible."[65]

Indeed, sonar appeared to solve the problem of finding and fixing the submarine for depth charges to kill, within its limits. Like radar, it was a technology that required broad use for best results. Great Britain went to war in 1939 with 185 sonar sets at sea: 100 in modern destroyers, 45 in sloops and old destroyers, and the balance in trawlers. By March 1945 the British navy deployed nearly 3,200 sonars, including 904 in motor launches and another 559 in trawlers. Sonar was nearly ubiquitous. Italy, in contrast, had sixty-seven sonars afloat by September 1943. Given that using a sonar required special skills, widespread distribution also required a pool of highly trained personnel to operate the device effectively.[66]

Sonar had a critical but unappreciated limitation: it only worked against submerged objects. Given this obvious fact, it is hard to understand Britain's prewar confidence that sonar gave ASW a decisive advantage. German submarine tactics, up through the advent of Allied centimetric radar, were to operate on the surface and at night. This rendered sonar

useless unless the submarine could be forced to dive. Thus, sonar was the
solution to a problem the Allies anticipated based upon their World War I
experience. However, due to the German strategy of using radio communications to achieve concentration and night surface attack tactics, sonar
was not the solution the British had hoped for, at least in the war's first
three years. It was a better tool, in fact, for the type of antisubmarine war
the Italians waged against the Allied, mostly British, submarines in the
Mediterranean in 1940–43.

EXPLOITATION: WORLD WAR II

As table 6.4 shows, the major navies of 1939 embraced the submarine as a
weapon of war, and they envisioned for it roles identical to those of 1914:
coastal defense, antiwarship patrol, and fleet cooperation missions, all of
which had been only marginally effective in World War I. Additional missions included commerce warfare, mine warfare, and special operations.

The British navy actually had fewer submarines in 1939 than in 1914,
while French growth was modest. Based on their Great War experiences, the British had little interest in advancing submarine technology,
and they even tried to get submarines banned at the 1922 Washington
Conference and again at the 1930 and 1935 London Naval Conferences.

TABLE 6.4

SUBMARINES AVAILABLE BY NATION AT THE START OF WORLD WAR II AND GENERAL MISSIONS

NATION	NUMBER OF SUBS	PERCENTAGE COMPARED TO 1914	MISSIONS IN 1939
Great Britain	71	97	Patrol/coastal defense (P/CD), antiwarship (A/S)
Germany	57	211	Commerce warfare (CW), P/CD, mines
France	80	160	Fleet cooperation (FC), P/CD
Soviet Union	213	1,121	CW, P/CD, A/S, mines, special operations (SO)
Japan	58	446	A/S, FC
Italy	115	547	CW, P/CD, SO
United States	111	505	FC, A/S, P/CD

Source: O'Hara, Dickson, and Worth, *On Seas Contested*. Any submarine could theoretically perform
any mission. This table specifies missions emphasized in prewar naval policy and training.

USS *Tambor* (SS 198), the basis for a series of successful fleet-class submarines. Launched in 1939, she had ten 21-inch torpedo tubes and a 3-inch deck gun. Her range of 11,000 miles made her suitable for Pacific operations, where she and boats like her gutted the Japanese merchant marine. *Tambor* mounted twelve war patrols and was credited with sinking fourteen ships—eleven with torpedoes, two by mines, and one with her deck gun. She also caused two heavy cruisers to collide when evading her, leading to one being sunk by carrier aircraft. *(Naval History and Heritage Command, USN 278118)*

Table 6.4 shows, however, that the genie was out of the bottle, and given past history, there was no reason to believe that rules limiting the use of a naval technology would be respected in a new conflict. In fact, the powers that challenged the status quo, Germany, Italy, and the Soviet Union, all embraced the anticommerce mission, as reflected by the number and types of submarines they constructed between the wars.[67] The French, British, Japanese, and Americans made missions against enemy warships a primary function of their submarines, although the Western democracies were clearly hedging their bets by building types suited for a trade war. In an examination of British naval policy, Stephen Roskill wrote about submarines: "Both we and the Americans regarded attack on heavy ships as their primary function. . . . Yet the fact is that the multifarious duties performed by our submarines in World War II (ultimately in disregard of all treaty obligations) bore little relation to their peacetime tactical training."[68] The same applied to the U.S. submarine force. The Japanese took the antiwarship mission more seriously than any of the other nations. The general battle instructions for their submarine force stated the primary goal to be "surprise attack on the enemy's main force."[69] The French also continued to view submarines as an antidote to an opponent's larger surface navy, although the identity of their projected opponent and the effectiveness of submarines in this role were both obscure. Their main employment after the 1940 armistice was in a coastal defense role. They enjoyed one major success off Dakar in September 1940, when a French boat torpedoed a British battleship, which proved the decisive event in defeating an amphibious assault. They also had failures off Morocco and Algeria in November 1942, when French submarine torpedoes missed U.S. cruisers and USS *Massachusetts* (BB 59). The mission set envisioned by the Soviet Union was the most extensive; behind the accumulation of so many submarines was the general belief that they could enable a weaker power to confront a foe with stronger surface forces.

The German submarines that went to war in 1939 were improved versions of those that fought in 1918 in terms of size, speed, and armament. Stronger hulls allowed for diving depths of 150 meters compared to the 80 meters of 1918. Hydraulic systems allowed rudders, valves, and air vents to be controlled automatically. In general, submarines had better sensors and better radios. They were quieter and more habitable. In theory, they had better weapons. They remained, however, submersible torpedo boats with limited underwater endurance and speed.[70]

Germany, once again, went to war with an insufficient number of submarines. Their boats achieved results, however, even against improved ASW and immediately applied convoying. There was no prolonged learning period as in 1914–15, and while depth charges and sonar were better than explosive sweeps and indicator nets, they were ineffective against submarines attacking on the surface, while submerged submarines remained extremely difficult to find and destroy. And the British were hardly the only ones to have learned lessons and developed solutions. The German "solution" to the problem of submarine effectiveness was, as noted in chapter four, largely doctrinal. Its essence was a switch from the lurk-and-shoot tactics most common in World War I, and against which the sonar was the most effective, to a radio-controlled, hunt-and-slash "wolf-pack" approach designed for attacking convoys. And from the start of the war through 1942, German submarines inflicted staggering casualties on Allied shipping (although monthly losses never reached the record set in April 1917).

Other nations did not do so well with their submarines. The immense Soviet submarine fleet was ineffective, proving deficient in essential areas such as maintenance and training, and it lacked targets. Italy's fleet also struggled, being hampered by conditions in the Mediterranean (which likewise affected British and German operations in that narrow sea), a shortage of targets (and the few available being very well defended), and boats that proved ill-suited for the tasks at hand, although they did much better operating in the Atlantic. The large U.S. submarine force in the Pacific at first caused the Japanese little discomfort, being handicapped by defective torpedoes and captains conditioned by conservative peacetime

The ten-thousand-ton Japanese tanker *Toa Maru* taking on oil at San Pedro, California, in 1934. Merchant ships proved most vulnerable to submarine-launched torpedoes, and tankers were priority targets. Dependent on foreign oil, the Japanese built a modern tanker fleet in the 1930s and lost almost all of it to U.S. submarines and carrier aircraft in World War II. *Toa Maru* met her end at the hands of U.S. submarine *Searaven* in November 1943 while serving as a fleet oiler. *(Naval History and Heritage Command, NH 111675)*

training. British submarines enjoyed isolated successes against Germany's surface fleet in the war's first year but suffered heavy losses in the Mediterranean and required a year of warfare before they began inflicting significant casualties in that relatively target-rich environment.

As the war continued, the opponents applied new measures and countermeasures in a back-and-forth struggle. The British, for example, invented operational research, which stemmed from the work of a shore station that studied German tactics and gamed out possible solutions.[71] By the spring of 1943 the Allies had smothered Germany's submarine force with a long list of countermeasures: massive production of escorts (as well as merchant ships), improved air coverage, centimetric radar, HF/DF, better weapons, better training, attrition of skilled German crews, and, from time to time, advantages in code-breaking. Yet this was a victory in large part against German methods, not against the basic concept of the submarine. What this array of Allied countermeasures did was to drive the Germans to minimize the time their submarines spent on the surface. ASW tools improved over time, with better sonars, quicker- and deeper-sinking depth charges, and projectors to fire ASW weapons ahead of attacking escorts; nonetheless, finding and sinking a submerged submarine was still more a matter of skill, luck, and brute force than technological finesse. This was particularly true after the Germans introduced the snorkel. Only

TABLE 6.5

SUBMARINES AND COMMERCE:
TWO WARS COMPARED—BRITISH, ALLIED, AND
NEUTRAL SHIPPING BY CAUSE OF SINKING

CAUSE	WORLD WAR I		WORLD WAR II		PERCENT CHANGE FROM WORLD WAR I TO WORLD WAR II
	SHIPS	TONNAGE	SHIPS	TONNAGE	
Submarine	4,837	11,135,460	2,828	14,687,231	132
Mines	497	1,044,456	534	1,406,037	135
Warships	177	553,826	336	1,557,767	281
Aircraft	5	8,039	820	2,889,883	35,948
Other			632	1,029,802	
Total	5,516	12,741,781	5,150	21,570,720	169

Sources: Admiralty, *Defeat of Enemy Attack on Shipping*, vol. 1B; Roskill, *War at Sea*.

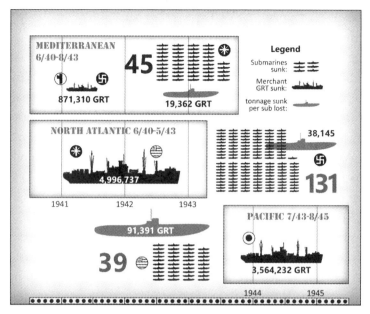

FIGURE 6.1. The Great Submarine Antishipping Campaigns of World War II. German submarines exacted a high toll on Allied shipping, but the cost in submarines sunk ultimately became prohibitive. Operating conditions hampered the efforts of Allied submarines in the Mediterranean. By way of comparison, Axis submarines (nearly all German) sank 101 ships and 472,599 GRT in the Mediterranean between June 1940 and June 1944 (excluding vessels grossing less than one hundred tons). The Germans, like the British and Italians, suffered heavy submarine losses in the Mediterranean—up to eight times their loss rate in other areas. In the Pacific, Japanese antisubmarine warfare failed to meet the challenge of Allied submarines, with the massacre of the Japanese merchant marine the result. The statistics for the Pacific campaign begin in July 1943, when U.S. submarines became fully effective. Battle of Atlantic sinkings are for North Atlantic convoy areas in the period indicated. German submarine losses also include boats sunk in the Bay of Biscay, moving to or from combat areas. Sources: Hezlet, *British Submarines*; Parillo, *Japanese Merchant Shipping*; Blair, *Silent Victory*, app. L; Joint Army-Navy Assessment Committee, *Japanese Naval and Merchant Shipping Losses During World War II by All Causes, 60–99*; Admiralty, *Defeat of Enemy Attack on Shipping*, table 21; U-boat.net records of sinkings.

the acoustic homing torpedo, which made aircraft a deadly foe, was a true breakthrough in ASW technology.

In the Pacific, the Americans solved their problems with faulty torpedoes and integrated their ever-growing advantage in signals intelligence to demonstrate what a modern submarine force could do against technologically stagnant ASW. By 1945 they had almost completely driven Japanese shipping from the seas. In terms of strategic impact, there was nothing else to match the scale and results obtained by the German Atlantic and U.S. Pacific campaigns against commerce, although the submarines of other nations had their successes. The British conducted a three-year campaign against Axis traffic in the Mediterranean that began to bear fruit in the latter half of 1941, but it also proved relatively lethal to their submarines.

In World War I submarines sank an almost unimaginable amount of merchant tonnage. In World War II they sank more (see table 6.5).

CASE STUDY

The ever-changing alchemy of new weapons, new tactics, and new technologies that the combatants applied to submarine warfare is easiest to put in context with a brief case study that highlights the progress of not just submarine technology, but also torpedoes, radio, radar, and aircraft as well as the way these technologies were integrated in action.

By June 1944 it seemed that submarines were no longer an existential threat to the Allies. They had apparently been managed by May 1943, especially in the transatlantic convoy routes. The truth, however, was more complicated. Through the summer and fall of 1943 and into 1944 Germany responded to Allied ASW successes with the following measures.

- *Improved torpedoes*: T1 (wet heater) and T3 (electric) torpedoes with functional magnetic pistols (August 1943); T5 *Zaunkönig* acoustic homing torpedoes (July 1943); Fat I and II devices that caused a torpedo to follow a circular or zigzag path (early 1943).[72]

- *Changed weaponry*: The 88-mm deck gun was discarded on most boats and replaced with 20- and 37-mm anti-aircraft weapons. There were variations, but from early 1944 the standard mix was a single 37-mm and a pair of twin 20-mm flak guns.

- *Improved sensors*: These included the FuMB 7 Naxos (late 1943) and the FuMB 26 Tunis (May–June 1944) centimetric radar detectors.[73]

- *Snorkels*: This was a simple idea that allowed a conventional diesel-electric submarine to run on diesel power while underwater by using a tube to suck in air and vent exhaust. More than two hundred boats were equipped with snorkels starting in early 1944.

- *Sensor countermeasures*: Bold noisemakers were containers that released hydrogen bubbles to simulate a submerged submarine and fool sonar while the submarine left the area at slow speed. A rubber coating to absorb sonar echoes called Alberich was developed and tested in August 1944 but required adding five thousand to six thousand work hours to the production of a boat when time was a commodity Germany no longer possessed. By late 1944 the Germans did begin to use special coatings to mask snorkels, already difficult radar targets, from centimetric radar detection.[74]

Germany had 444 submarines available in June 1944, 180 of which were operational, and these needed to be used.[75] The innovation that made continued use feasible was the relatively low-tech snorkel. This greatly enhanced the boat's survivability since it baffled radar, but a boat could only travel at five or six knots while snorkeling. This is the background to the two sorties of *U-247* (see figure 6.2).

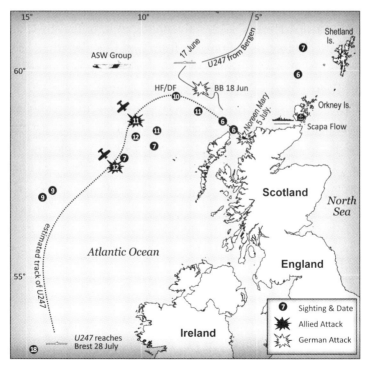

FIGURE 6.2. The Odyssey of *U-247*. Despite the overwhelming resources concentrated against the submarine, she made port safely, but the results of her cruise were meager.

U-247 was a Type VIIC submarine. This was the most common class of boat that fought in World War II with 661 examples constructed. At this point in the war she was armed with the usual mix of flak guns and five 21-inch torpedo tubes. *U-247* also had a snorkel and a FuMB 26 Tunis radar detector. The standard load of torpedoes would have been three T5, two T1 Fat I, and three T3 Fat II for the forward tubes and two T5 aft.[76] The boat was commissioned on 23 October 1943 after which, in accordance with a rigorous training program, she underwent seven months of work-up in the Baltic, a period lengthened by the weather and the war situation. The boat departed Bergen, Norway, on her first war cruise on 31 May 1944 under a twenty-four-year-old captain.

On 8 June the Government Code and Cypher School intercepted radioed orders to *U-247* sending her to the northwest coast of Scotland in response to the 6 June Normandy landings and alerted the British area command to expect her appearance. Although *U-247* reported firing upon and missing a *King George V*–class battleship on 18 June, there is no British record of such an incident. As long as the submarine kept her head down, evading the area defenses was easy. But on the evening of 5 July *U-247* surfaced and attacked a group of trawlers fishing off Cape Wrath in Scotland. Apparently, the submarine had fired three torpedoes but all missed, and so she sank *Noreen Mary* (209 GRT) with her flak guns.

The reaction was immediate and overwhelming. Within an hour a force of antisubmarine trawlers led by a corvette was in the area; three large and modern destroyers were en route from Scapa Flow, a long-range ASW-equipped Liberator bomber was overhead, and a strike force of Hurricanes and Swordfish, the latter equipped with the new ASV Mark XI 3-cm radar—which, it was hoped, would be able to locate a snorkel or periscope from relatively long range—was inbound from an escort carrier group just eighty miles to the west. All this force was available to hunt a submarine off the remote northwestern Scottish coast even though the Normandy buildup was in full swing and both ends of the English Channel were under attack by snorkel-equipped submarines.[77]

U-247 had two escape routes. Although her top speed was that of a leisurely jog, it was a big ocean, and *U-247* did indeed escape. False contacts gave the impression of two submarines in the area, including one north of the Orkneys, and this confused the British. With every minute, the search area grew. Nonetheless, the British hunters were reinforced and they persisted. Then, at 0116 on 10 July *U-247* surfaced for a half hour to take a navigational fix and radio a report of her activities. The British DF chain picked up low-quality bearings that had a potential radial error of sixty miles. The resulting estimated location was nearly two hundred miles east of where the antisubmarine search was focused. As an official British naval history put it, "It is much the same as looking in a dark room for a black cat that isn't there."[78] The search was recentered, and Swordfish and Liberators saturated the new area as another escort carrier group arrived. A Liberator obtained a likely sighting and made an attack on the morning of 11 July. By that evening ten Swordfish and nine Coastal Command aircraft were scouring the seas within thirty miles of the point of the Liberator's attack with two escort carrier groups nearby. A Sutherland flying boat attacked a suspected periscope or snorkel wake on the morning of 12 July, adding more intensity to the hunt but producing no results.

The British searched along the track *U-247* would need to take to reach Brest, her ordered destination, until 20 July although by 16 July it was clear that the trail was cold, and Coastal Command had turned its resources to other tasks. *U-247* arrived at Brest on 28 July 1944 after nearly two months at sea. Other than keeping large enemy forces occupied, she had achieved little. On the other hand, seven of the eleven snorkel-equipped boats that departed Norway in May and June 1944 for French waters were lost, and *U-247* tallied one of only two kills these submarines made.

Given such statistics, it is not surprising that the Canadian frigates *Saint John* and *Swansea* sank *U-247* on 1 September, a week into her next sortie from Brest. She had been laying quiet on the bottom, but sonar in the hands of experienced and patient operators and a pattern of conventional depth charges destroyed her.[79]

This incident illustrates how technological innovation had come to play a major part in even the smallest and most routine operations. The German boat had been modified to enhance her lethality and survivability, and the fact that a single boat under a new captain on her first war mission could evade squadrons of aircraft and specialized hunter-killer groups testifies to the effectiveness of her defensive technology. On the Allied side, every time the submarine used her radio, British DF fixed her approximate location and signals intelligence disclosed the boat's destination and supply status. Her enemy could scour her route with old biplane ex-torpedo bombers equipped with the latest radar and with high-endurance bombers and seaplanes that could linger over a contact for hours deploying sonobuoys—a new technology that provided, via a radio link, a way for aircraft to listen underwater.[80] The British were able to send specialized surface ASW hunter groups that were equipped with the latest sonar and a variety of antisubmarine weapons such as depth charge mortars and forward-firing spigot charges to the location of contacts. *U-247*'s initial success and ultimate fate demonstrated, however, that the very best technology available for a specific task still required practice, training, and most of all, persistence.

EVOLUTION: GERMAN SUPER SUBMARINES

The Germans responded to the growing superiority of Allied antisubmarine technology by trying to develop a true submarine: one that could travel underwater a relatively long distance at high speeds, run down a convoy, attack, and escape without surfacing. The German road toward such a submarine started in 1934 when the inventor and engineer Hellmuth Walter submitted plans to the navy for a small, single-engine boat propelled by hydrogen peroxide that could reach twenty-five knots submerged. However, "Walter's proposal seemed like a flight of fancy and [the high command] showed little interest."[81] After the war started, Walter approached Captain Karl Dönitz with an improved design. The first eighty-ton test boat, V-80, sailed in April 1940 and hit a submerged speed of twenty-three knots. Such performance commanded attention, but the advanced Walter boat was not rushed into production. The boat was extremely complicated and expensive to manufacture, and its fuel was costly and difficult to produce. Even worse, like the oxygen in Type 93 torpedoes, hydrogen peroxide reacted explosively to impurities. None of this would have mattered if there had been a compelling mission for its high underwater speed, but in April 1940 it seemed imprudent to upset the production of the technologically adequate and desperately needed Types VIIs on such a speculative venture. Instead, planning and design work continued.

In February 1942, with British ASW more effective than in April 1940, the navy authorized two 305-ton and two 260-ton test Walter hydrogen peroxide boats. Construction began that summer. Two were operational by November 1943, the others in April 1944. *U-794* famously took Dönitz and four other admirals on a test run off Hela in March 1944. The boat reached twenty-two knots submerged, and Dönitz was so impressed he complained that a lack of courage and confidence in his own staff had delayed these boats by as much as two years. The Großadmiral naturally lamented lost time after Allied ASW had established absolute dominance over the Type VII, but this was wisdom after the fact. An order for twenty-four small coastal boats had been made more than a year before. Because they were "phenomenally complex and expensive to build and operate," the navy never regarded them with enthusiasm.[82] In mid-1943, even after three years of development and with several experimental versions on hand and more in production, the Walter boats remained a next-war type of project.

A more practical and less advanced compromise was the Type XXI *Elektroboot*. This project originated in March 1943 when an engineer suggested that the large and streamlined hull being developed for an oceanic Walter boat (the Type XVIIB) could be used with a conventional battery/diesel propulsion system. The size would allow the number of batteries to be tripled, giving submerged speeds of just over seventeen knots. The boat's hull and size would allow it to dive deeper, and the sophisticated Balkon (balcony) Gerät hydrophone—an improved GHG—allowed it to "track, identify and range multiple targets at a range of 50 miles while the boat was totally submerged."[83] There was also a coastal version capable of twelve knots submerged but armed only with a pair of torpedo tubes and no reloads.[84]

None of the Walter boats ever engaged in combat. Four of the coastal Type XXIII *Elektroboot*s made war patrols and sank several small merchant ships. By war's end the first of nearly one hundred Type XXIs were just entering operational service: several deployed during the war's final days but were recalled. *U-2511*'s captain reported that during his return to port, he encountered a British cruiser force. The boat's enhanced performance allowed him to get inside the screen, make a simulated attack, and escape without being detected. Some authors have taken this as proof that the new submarines would have reestablished German dominance in the undersea war. This was possible but extremely unlikely, even if the captain's report was in all senses accurate. The Type XXIs were dogged by a chaotic development process and production difficulties stemming from not just Allied bombing but also political infighting and the use of inexperienced subcontractors. If the experience of the snorkel boats was any guide, the Type XXIs would have required an extended shaking-out period. The finished boats fell well short of their potential.[85]

The story of advanced German submarines is important to this work in two respects. The development of the Walter boats supports the principle that new technology must have a compelling mission from the beginning. It is another example of the Axis navies hesitating to develop new technology until the need was urgent. It is also an example of why they hesitated. Even a practical compromise, the *Elektroboot*, which used off-the-shelf technology and whose production was given every priority, took two years from concept to deployment. In the end, the greatest strategic effect of the super submarines was to keep a German army group tied down in Latvia trying to preserve the Baltic as a testing and training site when the troops were desperately needed to defend Berlin.[86]

In World War II, as in World War I, the submarine was managed but never absolutely defeated. The Allies managed it with a huge influx of technology and resources; the Japanese, with much less technology and far fewer resources, failed in the same task. Fortunately for the Allies, German counterresponses were either inadequate to tip the balance or too long in development.

THE TECHNOLOGY POSTWAR AND TODAY

The most significant technological improvement to the platform since the end of World War II has been the introduction of nuclear power. Combined with streamlined hull designs, this allows boats to sail more quickly submerged than surfaced and to stay down indefinitely. Other air-independent propulsion systems—particularly hydrogen fuel cells—have been introduced as well, although their capabilities are inferior to those of the nuclear boats. Submarines still fire torpedoes, some with greatly enhanced capabilities, while many are also armed with ballistic and cruise missiles. Such weapons give them strategic and tactical attack dimensions undreamed of a century before. Nuclear submarines—in terms of speed, power, range, and stealth—were a game changer. They appeared in operational numbers during the 1960s. The world's major navies have been conceiving, developing, and deploying an ongoing stream of nested technologies trying to solve the problem of how to spot and destroy enemy submarines while making their own submarines deadlier and more survivable. There has, however, never been a war of nuclear submarines, so it is impossible to say how effective these technologies, doctrines, and platforms would be when the waters start to boil and the horizons turn black.

The experiences of the Falklands War suggest that at that time submarines held the advantage over ASW technology. The British nuclear boats dominated the Argentine navy, as expected, and forced it to stay in port. More surprising was the fact that Argentina's one operational diesel/electric boat, *San Luis*, which had just completed basic sea training, "was able to operate for almost two months in the vicinity of the British fleet and could not be eliminated either by surface ships, nuclear submarines or ASW-helicopters." She made two attacks with SST-5 wire-guided torpedoes against surface targets. In both cases, the fire control system malfunctioned and the target data was calculated manually; in both cases, she lost control of the torpedo several minutes into its run. The third attack was with an Mk-37 torpedo. The captain was not certain of the target type, but it was probably a whale. The British navy, for its part, expended hundreds of antisubmarine munitions and counted 2,253 helicopter sorties chasing false contacts—without detecting *San Luis* either time she closed within firing range. Ironically, in the only attack made by a British nuclear boat, *Conqueror*, against the pre–World War II vintage cruiser *General Belgrano*, the submarine skipper's justifiable concerns over the small warhead and questionable reliability of his state-of-the-art Mark 24 Tigerfish torpedoes meant that he used a salvo of three Mark VIII torpedoes, which first entered service in 1927, to sink his target.[87]

In terms of contemporary relevance, the experiences of submarine warfare in the Falklands harken back to a time the when the IBM 3380 2.5-gigabyte hard drive weighed 550 pounds and cost more than a house. How will the reliance on networked-distributed warfare and satellite communications play out in a future submarine war? Are submarines becoming stealthier more quickly than sensors are becoming more acute?[88] Will underwater laser communications be a next step? Will chemical or biological sensors play a role? How will fully autonomous, unmanned (but smart) submarines change tactics and strategies? The history of the submarine over the course of a century in two major conflicts and several small ones suggests that in a future conflict, many more questions will arise. All that is certain is that weapons will not all function as they are designed—that naval commanders, their staffs, and fleets at sea will need to adapt quickly to the challenges that new and refined technologies will present, but they will probably respond in the context of their past practices and expectations. In World War I the British navy spent more than two years developing inadequate technologies and barely adequate doctrines to counter what proved to be an existential threat. In 1939 the British navy went to war against the submarines in a similar campaign with all the experience and tools from the first war and still required more than three years to muster the forces and techniques needed to contain the threat again. One never knows what the future will bring, but these time scales will unlikely be available to combatants in a future war as they grapple with the advanced submarines of the twenty-first century.

WHAT THIS TELLS US

The record of submarine operations in World War I—as examined through the lens of technological innovation—is one of missed opportunities. When the war began both the Germans and British followed best professional practice in the use of their submarines. There was little else they could have done, especially in the absence of wartime experience or even realistic peacetime exercises. In some respects, it was a race, with each side given the opportunity to assimilate experience faster and put it to best use most quickly, but also to perceive the nature of the threat and develop countermeasures. The fact that it took two years for the British to develop and deploy a depth charge is an example of a lost opportunity. That it took another year to learn how to use it effectively demonstrated the failure to apply a systematic approach to the problem of technological management and integration, even though the establishment of the Board of Invention and Research showed that elements in the navy and government recognized the need for such a process.

The Germans were first to send their submarines after commercial traffic, at least systematically and in force, but they did not stick to this strategy.

The historiography assigns political reasons for this lack of consistency, but in truth, if Berlin had had enough platforms the political consequences would not have mattered. The Entente submarines had far fewer targets but British, French, Russian, and Italian submarines attacked traffic where they could. By 1916 German, Austrian, and Ottoman ASW, which included convoying, combined with difficult operating conditions, narrow waters, and a lack of targets, shut down most of these Entente efforts. The British political and naval leadership lost the opportunity presented by the pause in Germany's trade war to integrate the nation's scientific and military talents and bring them to bear on the problems of antisubmarine warfare. The British sank more German submarines in the last year of the war but were never able to drive them from the seas or even reduce their operating numbers. Extreme measures, such as the massive Northern Barrage and, to a lesser degree, the Dover and Otranto barriers consumed enormous resources but did not deny submarines access to targets. Overall, they symbolized the ineffectiveness of existing ASW practice and technology. German effectiveness per boat expressed in terms of average tonnage sunk only dropped after the Entente powers implemented comprehensive convoying.

The North Atlantic submarine war of 1939–45 resembled the 1917–18 campaign in many respects, but in others it was far different. Of interest was the way the British, in particular, integrated a wide range of technologies and eventually developed a system that neutralized submarine technology as it then existed. These included new platforms such as escort carriers and frigates, specialized weapons such as forward-firing spigot mortars, improved and more abundant tools to pinpoint submarines on the surface and direct attacks from the sea and air, the mechanization of radio intelligence, and operational research to refine tactics and develop doctrine. The German response to Allied countermeasures—new sensors, stealth technology, and air independent submarines, among others—was likewise impressive but in the end, too late. It is an open question whether all of this, even if fully implemented, could have allowed a renewed submarine campaign. In the Pacific, the Japanese failed to deploy similar resources and efforts against U.S. fleet boats. Once the Americans fixed their defective torpedoes, the destruction of the Japanese merchant marine quickly commenced.

Most discussions of submarine effectiveness focus on merchant tonnage sunk, but their effect on warships has likewise been great. While submarines were largely unsuccessful against modern warships in World War I, they were deadly against older types such as armored cruisers and predreadnoughts. In World War II numerous destroyers and cruisers fell victim to submarines, and they accounted for half of all fleet carriers sunk during the war.[89] There is reason to think that they would be even more effective now, given the relative states of submarine and ASW technology.

A war of nuclear-armed boomers will have but one sad and tragic outcome, but in nonnuclear conflicts the submarine has the weapons, power, and range to guarantee utility in every mission envisioned for it and doubtless in some not yet envisioned. These still include attrition, fleet cooperation, war on commerce, and area denial as well as strategic deterrence. But in the next war, the submarine will have the power to conduct all these missions simultaneously with lethality unimaginable in 1914. It is likely that the techniques and countermeasures to manage the threat will prove ineffective, at least initially. Certainly, this is the outcome suggested by the 120-year development of this technology and its use in several wars.

CHAPTER 7

AIRCRAFT
Vision and Competition

Those who are engaged in the development of aviation for war purposes
do not pretend that it is going to revolutionize warfare, but it has been fully
demonstrated that of two opposing forces, the one which possesses superiority
in aerial equipment and skill will surely hold a very great advantage.
—CAPT. W. IRVING CHAMBERS, USN, 1912[1]

A viation is the most transformative technology considered in this work because it elevated naval warfare into a third dimension, it greatly extended the reach of navies, and it blurred the distinction between land and sea. Before the advent of aviation, warships had naught to fear from land forces once they were outside the reach of coastal artillery; nor could they attack any targets on land beyond the range of their own guns. That began to change in the second decade of the twentieth century, albeit slowly. The transformation was progressive over the course of two world wars as aviation technology improved. Aircraft are generally credited with overthrowing the battleship's reign as queen of the seas, and while this might be debatable—cost and the erosion of its core mission were making the battleship obsolete in any case—aviation, blended with the right weapons and tools and put to the right uses, proved more versatile than any other platform in the history of naval warfare. At the same time, the story of naval aviation demonstrates how subjecting control and use of a technology to the dictates of ideology, theory, and untested doctrine can compromise effectiveness at sea.

THE TECHNOLOGY DESCRIBED, EARLY DEVELOPMENT

Barring Icarus and Daedalus, people first took to the skies late in the eighteenth century. The method was the hot air balloon. Floating free, balloons had no military applications. Tethered, they served as observation platforms. In the Russo-Japanese War the Japanese navy deployed a land-based balloon detachment to warn of Russian ships leaving Port Arthur. Navies experimented with tethered inflatables telephonically linked to ships. The Italian cruiser *Elba*, for example, used such an arrangement in 1907 tests to successfully spot minefields. The Germans invented a more stable kite balloon called the *draken*, which became the preferred observation platform for the Italians after 1908.[2]

Effective naval work required a self-propelled aerial vehicle that could go where it was needed and return to base. The internal combustion engine provided good power in a relatively lightweight package and quickly found a place in airships. As the nineteenth century turned to the twentieth, airship technology branched into three forms: rigid, nonrigid, and the less common semirigid. Rigid airships were built on metal or wooden frames, while nonrigid airships relied mainly on the pressure of the gas inside their envelopes to retain their shapes. Nonrigids might seem easier to build, but they still needed to be aerodynamic. Designing an appropriately stiff envelope without an internal frame proved challenging.

In 1900 Ferdinand Zeppelin pointed the way to practical rigid airships with his LZ1. It was underpowered and unwieldy but Zeppelin persisted, constantly improving his design, and the German army accepted its first zeppelin in 1909. The German navy ordered a zeppelin in 1912. Zeppelin refused to sell to foreign customers, so the British navy ordered its own rigid airship domestically in 1908, in part to judge how effective zeppelins might be in the hands of an enemy. His Majesty's *Airship No. 1* was overweight when completed in 1911 and never flew. Other navies also pursued airship designs in the years leading up to World War I with limited success. In all cases, reconnaissance was the anticipated function of these platforms.

While pioneers such as Zeppelin developed powered balloons, others, such as the Wright brothers, added internal combustion motors to gliders. The Wrights achieved the first powered heavier-than-air flight in December 1903. Over the next five years the Wrights and other designers improved their flying craft by combining more powerful motors with a better understanding of aerodynamics. Militaries followed these developments closely. The British navy and the U.S. Army purchased military airplanes in 1909. In 1910 the U.S. Navy launched an airplane from the deck of the cruiser *Birmingham*, and France established an army air service. Most major European militaries followed suit over the next two years. British naval officers led the way in developing seaplanes, which appeared in 1910. Airplanes first carried radio that same year, while in 1911 airplanes trialed dropping torpedoes. The end of 1911 saw the first war missions, when Italian aircraft scouted and bombed in a war against the Ottoman Empire. Machine guns went aloft in 1912. Thus the stage was set for naval aviation.[3]

EXPECTATIONS

By 1914 aviation seemed poised to affect naval warfare profoundly, and every major navy already had an aviation component (see table 7.1). Naval air forces grew tremendously during the course of the war. Many navies also deployed specialized vessels to take aircraft to sea.

France had become the preeminent prewar innovator in heavier-than-air flight, and French companies, among them Bleriot, Farman, Voisin, Nieuport, Gnome, and Le Rhône, dominated the industry. The navy experimented with aircraft in a maritime scouting role in 1913 and was the first to deploy a seaplane tender.[4] The British formed a combined army and naval air service in 1912, with the two separating in July 1914. In addition to its role of fleet cooperation, the naval air service was tasked with

TABLE 7.1

NAVAL AVIATION IN WORLD WAR I

NAVY	AIRPLANES AUGUST 1914	AIRPLANES NOVEMBER 1918	AIRSHIPS AUGUST 1914	AIRSHIPS NOVEMBER 1918	FIRST AIRCRAFT
France	8	1,264	0	37	1910
Great Britain	93–95	2,949	6	111	1909
Italy	30 (May 1915)	638	2 (May 1915)	36	1910
Russia	24	200+ (November 1917)	0	0 (November 1917)	1911
United States	4	2,107	0	20	1911
Austria-Hungary	22	249–268	0	0	1910
Germany	24	1,478	1	19	1912

Source: Layman, *Naval Aviation in the First World War*, appendix 1.

Striking from the sea. Russian seaplane tender *Almaz* hoists on board a Grigorovich M-5 seaplane at Novorossiysk. Along with the British, the Russians became active practitioners of using seaplane carriers to mount attacks on land targets. The need to hoist seaplanes out at the start of the operation and retrieve them at the end made such operations cumbersome. *(Naval History and Heritage Command, NH 100143)*

the air defense of Great Britain. At the start of World War I, the navy quickly recommissioned a prewar seaplane tender and converted a series of cross-channel packets to supplement its shipborne aerial capacity. The Russian navy also adapted several merchant vessels as seaplane carriers once war began.[5] The Italian navy established a naval air service in 1913 and converted a protected cruiser into a seaplane carrier the next year. In Japan the first naval flights occurred in 1912. The navy committed a seaplane tender and four seaplanes to the siege of Tsingtao after Japan's entry into the war, where they flew bombing and scouting missions and even had an air-to-air encounter with a German aircraft.[6]

Germany was the world's leader in airships with the ponderous metal-framed zeppelins and their wood-framed cousins, the Schütte-Lanzs. With ranges exceeding two thousand kilometers, these airships seemed well suited to scout the North Sea, and the British feared that zeppelins would not only give the Germans an enormous reconnaissance advantage but also allow them to freely bomb British bases. At the start of the war, however, the German navy deployed only one zeppelin, having lost two others to accidents—a foreshadowing of things to come.[7] The Austro-Hungarian navy focused on aviation for reconnaissance and had two air bases, one servicing the northern and the other the southern Adriatic.[8] The U.S. Navy had operated airplanes with the fleet, in maneuvers and during the 1914 intervention in Veracruz, Mexico, but made little progress in increasing numbers or improving the types of aircraft it operated. In August 1914 the U.S. Navy had four flying boats and fourteen pilots.[9]

Airplanes and airships each had their advocates and their critics. Airplanes were cheaper to build and easier to support, and due to their small size and greater speed, they seemed harder to defend against. On the downside, their payloads were small, they could accommodate only short-range radio transmitters, and unreliable motors caused many crashes. A postwar assessment of U.S. naval aviation cited, as an example of "efficiency," a rate of one in seven patrol flights terminated due to forced landings.[10] This meant that navies regarded seaplanes as necessary for extended operations over water, forcing them to accept the performance penalty that their floats or boat hulls inflicted compared to wheeled aircraft. Airships could lift far larger payloads to greater ranges and could carry more powerful radios. They were better suited for night work and could hover if needed.[11] However, they were vulnerable to storms, high winds, and fire, even when on the ground. The German navy fielded seventy-one rigid-framed airships during the war; it lost thirty-four to accidents and only twenty-two to enemy action, despite a costly campaign to bomb Britain.[12] Airships remained in service after the war (and continued to be lost in spectacular accidents), but they proved a dead-end technology. No mechanical enhancements could mitigate their base faults whereas the constant development of bigger and more reliable aero engines overcame many of the problems with aircraft.

Navies had specific expectations for naval aviation. Primarily, they expected an enhanced set of eyes. As one British commentator noted in 1913: "Just as the introduction of the torpedo and submarine put more proportional power into the hands of the weaker powers, by increasing the chance of a surprise attack, so the introduction of the aeroplane tends to again equalize the condition of affairs. Reconnaissance, then, is the first duty we require our aeroplanes to perform." The author also foresaw the need to have aircraft attack land and sea targets, act against submarines and commerce, and operate from ships. Ideally, "one should be supplied to each large ship for reconnaissance purposes."[13] Captain Rene Daveluy of the French navy, writing that same year, advocated the seaplane as the ideal naval platform and identified reconnaissance as its primary duty: "The attacker—that is to say, the blockader—will require aviation to reveal the whole system of defense of the enemy's position. . . . The defense—that is to say, the blockaded force—will require no less important service of its aeroplanes." He likewise agreed that "it has not been a question of assigning a ship specially constructed for transporting aeroplanes to the fleets; on the contrary, we have urged the embarking of two apparatus on each ship of large tonnage."[14] German naval constructor Felix Pietzker, writing in 1913, advocated airships as the naval platform of choice: "They are especially qualified for scouting at sea, inasmuch as, contrary to the conditions over the land, there is no possibility of hiding at sea."[15] In 1912 Capt. W. Irving Chambers (the first head of the U.S. Navy's aviation section) considered the primary function of aircraft as scouting, with ancillary tasks including locating and destroying mines, submarines, and airships, cooperating with submarines and torpedo boats, bombing enemy bases, and transporting messages. In 1914 Lt. Richard Saufley, another U.S. Navy aviation pioneer, added to that list the roles of attacking ships at sea and directing naval gunfire.[16] Yet despite this unanimity of opinion, in 1914 machines capable of reliably and routinely carrying out such duties did not exist.

DISCOVERY: WORLD WAR I

In the effort to determine the strengths, weaknesses, and best uses of a new technology, aircraft presented a special case. This was because they were both platforms and weapons. They were platforms in that they used weapons in combat—ranging from handheld darts to 1,000-pound torpedoes—and there was a process involved in learning which weapons worked best and how use them to best advantage. But airplanes were themselves weapons in that they could be delivered by a larger platform—in this case, an airplane-carrying vessel—to increase their range and utility. In naval use the nature of an aircraft delivered by ship was

NOV 18 · 10 · 1000 (8")

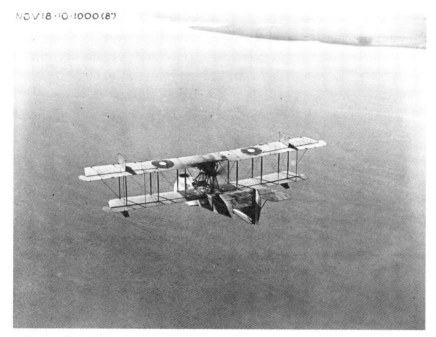

A Curtiss Type H flying boat in flight. In World War I, aircraft such as these proved especially useful in escorting convoys and patrolling against submarines—a lesson that many seemed to forget or ignore after the war, when newly independent air forces often neglected maritime patrol in favor of strategic bombing. *(Naval History and Heritage Command, NH 2872)*

fundamentally different than one that operated from a land base, even if the target and the missions themselves were identical. This was a subtle but fundamental distinction that some navies grasped better than others. Pursuing it opened entirely new vistas of technology, techniques, and tactics. This was, naturally, also a matter of debate. Some theorists promoted the concept of specialized aircraft-carrying vessels, while others believed that ships throughout the fleet needed to carry their own aircraft, much as they carried guns or torpedoes, and that the notion that aircraft must be operated only from a special parent ship or shore bases was fallacious.[17]

Problems that needed to be solved for aircraft-carrying vessels were, first, how to get the aircraft from the ship to the air and, second, how to get the aircraft back on the ship. The original solution was to launch from a long, inclined ramp projecting down over the vessel's stem. The British,

Americans, and Italians tested this method prewar using wheeled aircraft and ramps mounted on cruisers or old battleships. The first British seaplane carrier, *Hermes*, refined this technique by launching seaplanes on wheeled trolleys. The French carrier *Foudre* and the Italian *Elba*, both converted from protected cruisers, used the drop and stop method, where a crane set the seaplane on the water for takeoff and lifted it on board again after it landed. The British and Russians also adopted this technique. The British even conducted experiments with a submarine-launched seaplane. As the war progressed, navies discovered that small, wheeled fighters could get airborne from a ramp as short as forty feet—short enough to be fitted onto a light cruiser. Once launched, however, wheeled aircraft had to be flown to land bases or ditched at sea and the pilot rescued (hopefully), although some had inflatable bags so they could float long enough to be recovered.[18]

In June 1917 the British deployed their first ramp-equipped cruiser, *Yarmouth*. On 21 August 1917 *Yarmouth* launched a Sopwith Pup that shot down zeppelin *L23*.[19] Success encouraged further experimentation, which in turn yielded the innovation of a rotating platform mounted on a turret top or other convenient location. This allowed aircraft to be launched without the ship having to turn into the wind, at least under ideal conditions, and made it practical to put aircraft on battleships, which were required to keep formation. By August 1918 sixteen battlecruisers and cruisers had been fitted, and by the end of the war the Grand Fleet carried 103 aircraft on such platforms, realizing the vision of the 1913 author who advocated an aircraft for every major warship. Towed barges also served as aircraft carriers, and on 11 July 1918 a barge-launched Sopwith Camel shot down *L53* off the Dutch coast. The United States began testing catapults as a means of hurling aircraft into the air in 1915 and the British followed suit in 1916, but neither navy deployed a practical catapult during the war.[20]

Recovery of wheeled aircraft remained a problem. The light battle cruiser HMS *Furious* was reconstructed to have a flying-off deck forward and a recovery deck aft of her superstructure, but tricky air currents and funnel gases made landings unacceptably dangerous. The main problem was not stopping the airplane's forward progress, it was keeping it from being flipped off the deck by cross-currents when slowing. The solution was threefold: an unobstructed flight deck with an offset island super-structure (or no superstructure at all), funnel gases vented away from the flight deck, and a series of arresting wires strung fore and aft to keep aircraft on the deck. The British navy put the solution into practice with *Argus*, constructed from the incomplete hull of an ocean liner, *Eagle*, built on a battleship hull, and *Hermes*, the first ship built from the keel up as an aircraft carrier. But only *Argus* was commissioned before the end of the war, and she saw no action.[21]

Aircraft were too new and too few in 1914 for any navy to go to war with a settled doctrine, and thoughts varied wildly within different services on their likely effectiveness. As the war progressed, navies made larger or smaller efforts in accordance with their needs and the resources available to them to use their aviation assets in a variety of roles. By 1918 six general missions had evolved. These included

• scouting and patrol

• gunnery spotting

• attacks on ships and shipping

• strikes from the sea against land targets

• antisubmarine warfare

• air defense.

All of these missions save the second were still important at the end of World War II and remain relevant today, but the process of arriving at the right mix of platforms (wheeled airplanes, seaplanes, airships), weapons (guns, bombs, torpedoes), tools (aiming, navigation, communication devices), and delivery systems (ship-, water-, or land-launched) was slow, and in nearly every respect, the difficulties of implementation were far greater and the results far less than predicted by prewar enthusiasts. As with other technologies, the biggest challenge was identifying a need and the technology that could potentially meet it and then mustering the required resources.

Scouting and Patrol

This was the major use navies anticipated when they established air ser-vices. Upon the outbreak of war, all such services deployed land-based

HMS *Hermes*, the first carrier to be laid down as such in 1917 but not completed until 1924. She was also the first operational carrier to be sunk by carrier aircraft. Displacing 10,850 tons and with an aircraft complement of twenty, her small size hampered her usefulness, and by World War II she was used mainly for patrol and escort duties. The flight deck layout shows that with the aircraft of the day, landing was a far greater challenge than taking off. *(Naval History and Heritage Command, NH 60467)*

aircraft to patrol their coastlines and offshore as far as capabilities and weather permitted. Assigning routine reconnaissance to aircraft saved wear and tear on ships and crews and reduced the danger to flotilla craft that would otherwise be doing the job. The advent of radio made fast, effective communications between air and ground a possibility, although early airborne sets were unreliable, short-ranged, and capable only of transmitting. It rapidly became apparent that aerial reconnaissance over water involved special issues that did not apply to land operations. Aerial navigation, once out of sight of land, was essentially a matter of dead reckoning that often left an aircraft's crew uncertain of their position. Further, aircrews struggled to properly identify what they saw; mistaking friends for foes and reporting merchant ships as battleships were common errors.

Even when reports were accurate, responding to them was difficult. Ships were relatively speedy compared to land forces and, in open waters at least, were not constrained as to course. A vessel traveling at ten knots could be anywhere within an area of 315 square miles within an hour of being spotted; at fifteen knots, the area would be 705 square miles. Chasing down a distant contact was usually hit or miss, more so when compounded by delays in receiving or responding to sighting reports. Finally, patrolling over water, particularly in the mechanically unreliable aircraft available in 1914, was dangerous. Effective maritime reconnaissance required special training and brave flyers.

Germany, with its zeppelin technology, initially seemed to hold the advantage, but the stormy North Sea made zeppelin operations a matter of luck. Weather prevented airships from scouting in three of the five battlecruiser raids the Germans conducted against the English coast. Nor could airships accompany the High Seas Fleet in the May 1916 operation that led to the Battle of Jutland. In the two major fleet operations in which zeppelins participated, the airships accomplished little. In an August 1916 operation, for example, the German admiral received seven reconnaissance reports from three of the ten zeppelins deployed to scout for the fleet. Four of these were wrong as to ship type, location, or both. The most consequential report misidentified five light cruisers as five battleships, luring the German fleet into a futile chase. The mistake saved the Germans from the British Grand Fleet, which had been approaching unseen from another direction, but that was serendipity and not effective scouting.[22]

Using shipborne aircraft to scout in direct support of a battle force seemed logical but proved difficult to execute. The first instance of a British carrier-launched aircraft successfully reporting an enemy contact at sea did not come until May 1916 when the Grand Fleet was on its way to the Battle of Jutland. The carrier *Engadine*, which carried two radio-equipped seaplanes (and two smaller antizeppelin fighters), sailed with the British scouting force. Prior to contact, Admiral Beatty, the scouting force's commander, ordered *Engadine* to make an aerial search. After seeking calmer waters unroiled by the wakes of the large warships around her, the carrier managed to get one of her two scouting aircraft airborne in just twenty-seven minutes. Twenty minutes later the aircraft sighted three German cruisers and correctly reported their composition and location to *Engadine*. Then a mechanical problem forced the aircraft down. The carrier tried to pass along the information, but two separate battleships ignored her signals by searchlight and there is no record of a radio message—perhaps because *Engadine* did not have a frequency assigned or because any such message was lost in the "welter of signals pouring into *Lion* [Beatty's flagship] at this time."[23] These events showed that the technology required for effective shipborne aerial scouting was still inadequate for the task midwar; it continued so to the end. Effective shipborne aerial reconnaissance would require technological advances such as catapults, more robust aircraft, more reliable radios, better navigation tools, and better training. Even with all those improvements, and radar to boot, aerial reconnaissance remained hit or miss throughout World War II.[24]

Gunnery Spotting

Using aircraft to direct gunfire was another mission that proved problematic during World War I. Accounts of gunfire spotting early in the Gallipoli campaign verge on the comic. Either the spotting aircraft broke down or the bombarding ship did. If multiple ships were on station, too many fired at one time to permit effective spotting. Radios malfunctioned or, if they worked, the Ottomans jammed them or shot up the spotting aircraft. When everything was working, the weather failed to cooperate.[25] There were successes, however, at Gallipoli and elsewhere. In July 1915 aerial spotting allowed British monitors to sink the German light cruiser *Königsberg*, which had been cornered far up a river in East Africa. After many failures an aircraft successfully directed the fire of the monitor *General Craufurd* off the Belgian coast in January 1916.[26] Technical innovations such as a two-way radio light enough to be carried aloft helped, but the technique never reached the point where an aircraft spotted the fire of a ship against another ship while both were under way. Such a capability remained a future promise.[27]

Attacking Ships

Attacking ships from the air was a goal from the first days of aviation. In February 1913 a Greek Farman floatplane bombed the Ottoman fleet with four grenades; in July 1913 an airplane crewed by Mexican revolutionaries dropped dynamite-stuffed pipes in the vicinity of an anchored government gunboat off Guymas.[28] These attacks alarmed but did not harm their targets. Hitting ships, especially warships under way, proved difficult. German airplanes recorded the first success, striking British cruiser *Attentive* off the Belgian coast in 1915. But on the whole, the results were trivial considering the thousands of bombs dropped. Even stationary targets were difficult to hit.[29] In eleven attacks against the anchored Russian battleship *Slava* in 1916, the Germans dropped numerous bombs but scored only three hits, none of which inflicted serious damage.[30] British bombers rained more than fifteen tons of 65-pound and 112-pound bombs on the stranded Ottoman battlecruiser *Yavuz* in 1918 for two inconsequential hits. Aircraft attacked with machine guns as well, but these were at best a harassment weapon unless used against light craft such as MTBs.

Prewar, the British, Americans, and Italians investigated dropping torpedoes from aircraft, and during the conflict Britain and Germany modified seaplanes to carry single torpedoes between their floats. On 12 August 1915 a British Short 184 seaplane torpedoed an Ottoman merchantman. Only slightly detracting from this achievement was the discovery that the target was aground, having earlier been torpedoed by British submarine *E14*. British torpedo bombers reported two more successes in short order but these went unverified. The British produced a purpose-built torpedo bomber, the Sopwith Cuckoo, in 1917. They planned a massed torpedo attack on the German fleet in harbor but could not gather the necessary material to pull it off before the end of the war.[31]

The Germans first tested torpedo bombing in September 1916 as part of an operation designed to sink the troublesome Russian battleship *Slava*. Three seaplanes dropped torpedoes against *Slava*, with level bombers overhead to distract the enemy. One torpedo malfunctioned, and the other two missed fore and aft.[32] After this the Germans shifted their focus to merchant shipping off the British east coast. Torpedo bombers sank freighters in May, June, and September 1917, but the need to provide aerial escorts, as well as growing shipboard antiaircraft defenses and the difficulties of operating the lumbering torpedo bombers, caused the Germans to abandon this type of attack as being not worth the effort. On 20 September 1917 the Italians sent a torpedo-armed Caproni tri-motor bomber on an unsuccessful raid of Cattaro in the Adriatic, and

TABLE 7.2

SHIPS SUNK BY AIRCRAFT IN WORLD WAR I

NATION	SURFACE WARSHIPS LOST/METHOD	SUBMARINES LOST/METHOD	MERCHANT SHIPS LOST/METHOD
Great Britain	1 (bomb), 3 (gun)	3 (bomb–1 in error by a French airship)	3 (torpedo)
France	0	1 (bomb)	0
Russia	1 (bomb)	0	0
Germany	3 (bomb)	3 (bomb)	0
Austria-Hungary	1 (bomb)	0	0
Ottoman Empire	1 (bomb)	0	1 (bomb), 1 (torpedo; 2 others unverified)

Source: Layman, *Naval Aviation in the First World War*, appendix 3.

the Italian navy was training a torpedo bomber squadron when the war ended.[33]

Throughout the course of the war, air attacks sank twenty-two vessels (see table 7.2).

Striking from the Sea

The most versatile form of air attack is one delivered from ships, exploiting their mobility, to strike targets that are outside the range of land-based aircraft. The Japanese demonstrated the power of this type of strike at Pearl Harbor in 1941, just thirty-eight years after the first heavier-than-air flight. In World War I a strike from the sea was one of the first offensive naval actions undertaken; on 25 October 1914 two British seaplane carriers with six aircraft closed to within eighty miles of a German zeppelin base to launch an attack. Heavy rain prevented four seaplanes from taking off; one struggled aloft only to suffer engine failure, and the bad weather forced the last to abort.[34] This was the first of two raids attempted in 1914, with an additional six attempts in 1915 and four more in 1916.[35] All were conducted using the laborious stop and drop method of getting the seaplane into action. The British clearly felt that these risky operations deep into enemy waters were worth running despite the difficulties and the paltry results. They had to wait until 7 July 1918 for their first success. That raid was conducted by wheeled Sopwith Camels carried to the German coast in *Furious*. *Furious* launched seven Camels, each carrying two 50-pound bombs, against the zeppelin sheds at Tondern eighty miles away. The raid put six planes over target and achieved complete surprise, destroying two zeppelins.[36]

The other practitioner of air strikes from the sea was the Russian Black Sea fleet. The Russians gradually accumulated a force of six seaplane carriers and mounted at least eight raids from 1915 through 1917, targeting the Ottoman Bosporus defenses, the Bulgarian and Romanian coasts, and the Anatolian coal port of Zonguldak. They enjoyed better weather and less opposition than their British North Sea counterparts but still struggled to achieve meaningful results. Their biggest success came on 6 February 1916 when a raid on Zonguldak sank the collier *Irmingard* (4,211 GRT). This was the largest vessel sunk by shipborne aircraft in World War I.[37]

Antisubmarine Warfare

Antisubmarine patrol was one of the two primary tasks of the British naval air service in 1914, and the threat from German submarines made this mission increasingly important to the Entente nations, especially after Germany started its first unrestricted submarine campaign in February 1915. Antisubmarine patrol miles flown in British home waters alone rose threefold from 1917 to 1918, to more than six million over the two years. Aircraft rarely killed or even attacked submarines, but they did force them to submerge and so limited their radius of action. The start of convoying in 1917 enhanced the value of aircraft as patrols could focus on convoys and call upon the escorts. Airships were found to be particularly good escorts, weather permitting, especially since they could hover over contacts for a long time. As patrols increased, they forced submarines to seek targets beyond the range of aircraft or to attack at night when aircraft were grounded. The former cut into the time that the boats could remain on patrol; the latter blunted their effectiveness. By the end of the war, more than five hundred aircraft based in British home waters were devoted to coastal patrol and convoy escort; they averaged 14,000 hours aloft per month for the last six months of the war, a total not exceeded in World War II until mid-1943. According to one British officer, "Only five ships were sunk out of thousands sailed in convoys with air escort and threatened by U-boats."[38]

Air Defense

The best defense against aircraft proved to be other aircraft. This seems obvious now, but at the start of the war it was by no means clear that the slow and underpowered aircraft had the ability to attack their opposite numbers, particularly at sea. However, once the war began, aircrews quickly began to carry weapons aloft, and some even unofficially mounted machine guns. Because of the zeppelin threat, the British led in taking fighter airplanes to sea and making air defense an important mission for sea-based air.

INFRASTRUCTURE NEEDS

The infrastructure required to maintain just a dozen airplanes in service was considerable. To maintain thousands during combat operations involved enormous effort. Airplanes, especially in their early days, were truly expendable platforms. The British calculated monthly wastage rates from 66 percent (for single-seat fighters at the front) to 20 percent (for home defense and training squadrons). At the higher wastage rate, an air force had to replace the entire flying strength of its combat forces every six weeks. This called for a major manufacturing base just to maintain frontline strength. And while casualties among aircrew were somewhat less than airframe write-offs, they were still tremendous: "During most of World War I, pilots stood a greater chance of being killed during training or in accidents than in combat."[39] All air services thus required extensive training programs to provide skilled pilots in the quantities needed. And flyers and flying machines were just the tip of the iceberg—pilots were only 2 percent of personnel in the British Royal Flying Corps.[40] Aircraft required consumables, spare parts, and trained mechanics; they were temperamental and needed constant repair and maintenance. They required specialized fuel and ordnance. Airships had their own needs, including huge sheds to protect them from wind and weather and large ground crews to move them in and out. Because weather had a profound impact on air operations, the science of meteorology was expanded to include conditions aloft as well as at the surface. This required specially trained personnel and newly created instruments.[41] In other words, to begin to explore the combat potential of aircraft, navies had to make a significant investment in men and resources.

COUNTERMEASURES

Navies began contemplating countermeasures for aircraft even before World War I started. Armies had already developed artillery shells with time fuzes that could shower shrapnel down on land targets, while navies had quick-firing guns of up to 4-inch caliber to deal with enemy torpedo boats. These technologies could be combined to (hopefully) shoot a line of bursting shells into an aircraft's path. Machine guns were common and could be adapted as short-range antiaircraft weapons. But while the basic means of defending against aircraft were available, making them effective proved hard. The larger guns particularly required the rapid solution of a complex three-dimensional time and distance problem to get bursting shells close to a target. No satisfactory solution was found during the war or indeed for a long time afterward, and larger guns generally used a barrage technique in which they fired a wall of shells to discourage attacking aircraft. As the war progressed, more ships sprouted more antiaircraft guns until even submarines and some merchant ships were so armed. *Slava*, for example, received a pair of 3-inch high-angle guns and a 40-mm Vickers machine gun in her first refit after suffering a string of air attacks in the spring of 1916.[42] Guns provided some defense and could discourage attacking aircraft regardless of their actual effect, but as discussed above, aircraft would become the best defense against aircraft.

EVOLUTION: BETWEEN WORLD WARS

More than nine thousand aircraft were devoted to naval aviation at the end of World War I, and many more had been expended in the course of the conflict. Engines had grown far more powerful, albeit still prone to breakdown. Payloads had increased, which meant more fuel, bombs, and guns. Two-way radios were common. Vast infrastructures serviced the needs of the air forces. But despite the progress, aerial scouting over the open ocean remained highly unreliable. Attacks on ships under way remained rare and ineffective. Shipborne attacks against land targets required major fleet efforts for scant returns. Gunfire spotting was restricted to stationary targets. The most successful naval role for aircraft—patrolling against submarines—was tedious in practice and intangible in its results, being best measured in terms of ships not sunk rather than submarines destroyed. The official history of the British air force likely mirrored opinions in all navies in stating that "in the matter of aerial work for the navy the whole period of the war was a period of experiment rather than achievement."[43]

The British development of carrier aviation stands out, but interestingly, much of the impetus behind British efforts came from a single special use: a strike against the German fleet in harbor. The Germans emphasized shore-based aviation and particularly zeppelins, although zeppelins proved of limited utility. Torpedo bombers seemed promising but were judged not worth the bother in Germany's one sustained antishipping campaign that featured them. Facing off across the narrow Adriatic, the Italians and Austro-Hungarians deployed aircraft primarily for shore-based sea patrol and the bombing of ports. Aircraft did intervene in a surface action in the Adriatic (a rare occurrence in any era) but without measurable effect. The Russian Black Sea fleet was quite avant garde in its use of seaplane carriers, but like the British found that small numbers and poor seaplane performance minimized the effect of such operations. One lesson that failed to clearly emerge from the 1914–18 conflict was that navies had special needs, and aviators required special skills if they were to be effective over water. This important fact was overshadowed in the minds of some by the more apparent need for better aircraft.

The numbers of naval aircraft grew enormously during World War I, but those increases were dwarfed by the numbers of aircraft committed to the land war. As an example, the British air force (which combined the army and navy air services) had more than 22,000 aircraft on strength at the end of the war, with close to 6,000 supporting the land war or detailed to home defense and fewer than 3,000 allocated to naval duties. And of the naval aircraft, only about 1,300 were seaplanes or shipborne. French aircraft strengths were even more inclined toward the land war, with 6,000 aircraft in the army air forces and about 1,300 in the naval air service.[44] These proportions reflected the fact that aircraft had become a more integral feature of land than of sea warfare. Moreover, the war had seen the beginnings of strategic bombing operations, where the targets were not enemy troops but enemy infrastructure and civilians. This encouraged aviation advocates to call for independent air forces, and that would spell trouble for naval aviation in the years ahead.

Aircraft technology improved enormously throughout the interwar period, in part due to aviation's commercial applications. Speeds almost tripled, ceilings came close to doubling, typical bomber payloads more than doubled, and ranges more than tripled. Many factors contributed to these improvements, but more powerful aero engines led the way. Horsepower-to-weight ratios had doubled during World War I and doubled again by 1940, while engine outputs grew to exceed one thousand horsepower. The first jet flew in 1939. Advances in torpedo bombing, the development of dive bombing, and increasingly sophisticated bomb sights for level bombing held out the promise of improved antishipping capabilities. Only one area of aeronautics flagged. Rigid airships were largely abandoned after a series of spectacular and deadly accidents in Europe and the United States, including the crashes of *Hindenburg* and USS *Akron*, with the latter taking the life of the long-serving head of the U.S. Navy Bureau of Aeronautics, Rear Adm. William A. Moffett.

While mechanical improvements in aviation technology had a profound impact, the factor that most influenced naval air in the interwar period was the philosophy of air power, which dictated—to one degree or another—how the technology should be controlled and applied. In 1921 one of its outstanding proponents, Italian general Giulio Douhet, summarized this philosophy in a single sentence: "To conquer the command of the air means victory; to be beaten in the air means defeat."[45] In Douhet's view, Italy should pour its military resources into bombers. These would decide a war in a matter of weeks or possibly even days by destroying the enemy's air force and production centers and shattering its civilian morale with a balanced application of high explosives, incendiaries, and poison gas. Defense was futile, as air defenses would have to be spread among many potential bombing targets while the attackers could concentrate in overwhelming strength. The air theorists demanded that air forces be independent of existing armies and navies; they asserted that air assets dedicated to the support of traditional land or sea forces weakened the all-important bombing force, which in any event could support the other services if really required.[46]

This dogma inhibited the physical and intellectual development of naval aviation in several nations. The fact that during World War I aircraft had had a far greater impact supporting land than naval operations fostered a perception in some military, governmental, and even naval circles that aviation was mainly relevant to land warfare and that dedicated naval air forces were at best unnecessary and at worse a misuse of assets. Moreover, the passion of and pressures exerted by the apostles of air power, such as Douhet, Hugh Trenchard in the United Kingdom, and William Mitchell in the United States, proved seductively persuasive. They were clear about what they wanted: all aircraft under the control of an independent air force, pursuing an independent strategy. They advanced their ideas with a fervor that challenged navies' control of and even influence over their air services. Their arguments were more compelling in Europe, where the great powers were within convenient bomber range of each other, than in continent-spanning powers such as the United States or the Soviet Union or isolated nations such as Japan.

Ironically, the world's largest navy was the first to surrender its aviation assets. On 1 April 1918 the United Kingdom's political leadership amalgamated its army and navy air services to form the Royal Air Force (RAF). This was seen as a cure for the inefficiencies and duplications of effort of the army and navy in coordinating Britain's air defense and was founded upon the belief that an independent air policy, fought out in a medium without trenches or minefields, would advance victory in the current war—in fact, that air power would make possible the "devastation of enemy lands and the destruction of industrial and populous centres on a vast scale."[47] The British admiralty was divided in its response to this act, but Admiral Beatty endorsed an independent air force and "castigated the Admiralty as 'too parochial in their outlook on the conduct of the war.'" Thus, the navy accepted the loss of its air service almost without qualification, only resisting the assignment of any floating assets (such as aircraft carriers) to the new air service. The navy's contribution to the RAF was significant: 2,500 aircraft and 55,000 men.[48] As Stephen Roskill concluded, "The Board of Admiralty of 1917 . . . cannot be acquitted of a share in the responsibility for the failure to convince [the air committee] and the War Cabinet of the specialized needs of naval aviation. It was to take twenty years to rectify that failure, and it is no exaggeration to say that its repercussions made themselves felt with most serious effects throughout World War II."[49]

The British navy was quick to regret its mistake as when, for example, calls for aerial support during the 1919–20 intervention in Anatolia went unheeded, and it embarked on a campaign to regain the resource it had so readily surrendered just two years before.[50] It was not, however, until March 1939 that the navy obtained control of ship-based aircraft, and even then flying boats and land-based maritime patrol aircraft remained in the RAF. In the meanwhile, the loss of all its aviation personnel deprived the navy of the drive and expertise that naval aviation would otherwise have received.[51] In 1939 the British navy deployed seven aircraft carriers, but they operated a collection of low-performance aircraft including biplane torpedo bombers and fighters. The air force did maintain a special branch for maritime operations but by the start of World War II operated mostly obsolete flying boats and twin-engine light bombers. With respect to air force maritime doctrine, the comments of historian Christina Goulter regarding Great Britain's air force is telling: "Strategic bombing doctrine dominated the Air Ministry's thinking to the almost total exclusion of other ideas on the use of air power. . . . Rigid adherence to it meant that the very considerable number of lessons learned during the First World War about maritime aviation . . . were effectively lost and had to be relearned by the next generation of airman."[52]

The Italian navy lost control of its air assets to a new Italian air force in 1923. While not as committed to strategic bombing as its British counterpart, the Regia Aeronautica jealously guarded control of all aerial assets, and it successfully competed against the navy for scarce budget allotments throughout the 1930s (with the air force getting 19.1 percent and the navy 14.8 percent of total military expenditures in 1938).[53] The navy controlled only shipborne aviation, which consisted of cruiser and battleship catapulted-launched floatplanes piloted by air force personnel. Torpedo and dive bombers were under development but not in service by the start of World War II. The air force did not have the training to service the special needs of the navy, and cooperation at the start of the war was poor. On 18 July 1940, for example, the navy's chief of staff (COS) appealed to supreme headquarters for more aircraft to be assigned to maritime reconnaissance. The next day headquarters asked the air force COS if this could be done. The air force replied on 24 July that engaging in sterile searching over water would only decrease the force available for actually attacking the enemy. On 27 July headquarters asked the air force to assign twenty seaplanes to the navy. On 7 August the air force COS replied in a long memorandum outlining all the wear and tear that naval cooperation was causing to their men and machines and claiming that what the navy wanted would require unacceptable sacrifices in other areas. On 10 August headquarters decreed, to the navy's distress, that only five aircraft would be available.[54] The navy learned of the next major British operation via a report from an Italian commercial airliner. Only with experience did the situation improve, and by mid-1941 the Italian air force had effective torpedo bomber squadrons and better aerial reconnaissance, although it was always less than what the navy wanted.

The French government created an air ministry in 1928, a year after the navy had completed its first carrier. An independent air force followed in 1933 but in 1939 the navy regained control of its land-based aviation, operating long-range reconnaissance and torpedo bomber squadrons. Despite this, the French navy treated aviation as a low priority. France's carrier, build on a converted battleship hull, was slow and was relegated to secondary duties upon the outbreak of war. Her naval squadrons were thrown into the land fighting following the German attack in May 1940. A fast carrier, intended to operate with the Atlantic squadron for fleet protection and reconnaissance, was under construction but was never completed.[55] After the June 1940 armistice aviation played little role in French maritime operations, such as they were. At the moment of greatest need, when British and U.S. forces invaded Morocco and Algeria, a lack of fuel left French maritime reconnaissance aircraft grounded, and U.S. landing forces captured a squadron of naval torpedo bombers in its hangars.

The Versailles Treaty banned Germany from having an air force, but it created one anyway in 1935. The navy wanted its own air service but lost out in the political struggle with the megalomaniac ex-aviator Hermann Göring, who pressed for a unified air force under his control. The new service had its share of strategic bombing advocates, but Göring ultimately built a force focused on tactical support of land forces. Although the air force did include naval aviation assets, the navy had little influence over equipment, supply, or training. By the time war came, the air force owned all military aircraft and had operational control over all aspects of the maritime operations save shipborne aircraft.[56] In 1939 it maintained two squadrons of floatplanes for shipborne naval use and five squadrons of floatplanes and flying boats that operated from land bases. Germany began construction of a carrier in 1936 but never completed it.[57]

Navy–air force cooperation was never good, at least at the upper levels of command. The navy pushed for torpedo bombers, but the air force initially took the position that "bombs were much cheaper than torpedoes." Control of naval reconnaissance was also a contentious issue. Matters came to a head in a conference held on 13 December 1940. Although the navy considered that Göring's argument for retaining control had "partial factual inaccuracies and was very tendentious," the "attempt to convince General [Alfred] Jodl [COS of the armed forces high command] of naval staff's position and to revise his own opinion was not successful."[58] But as the war continued, the air force did develop specialized antishipping and reconnaissance units. The long-range scouting unit, which was intended to work with submarines in the western approaches to Great Britain, was originally ineffective because, as one German admiral put it, "Air squadrons schooled in overland fighting cannot be employed in naval warfare without further training, as the supreme command of the German air force believed. . . . The meager successes of the German air force against English sea power during the period of German air superiority are attributable to this state of affairs."[59] Admiral Karl Dönitz later spelled out the prerequisites for successful cooperation: "[T]he primary essentials to be attained were a common terminology, a common medium of communications, and above all, experience of the pilots in flying over the sea, navigation, recognition of types of ships, and their clear and correct reporting."[60] These requirements had been obvious by 1918.

The air force's attitude toward torpedoes changed in part because of successes obtained by other navies, such as the British against the battleship *Bismarck*. Even so, and despite operating floatplane torpedo bombers in the Spanish Civil War, it was 1941 before the Germans adapted the land-based He111 twin-engine bomber to carry torpedoes. Although German aviation exerted a powerful influence over certain naval campaigns—especially Norway in 1940, the Mediterranean during the spring of 1941 and the spring of 1942, and the Arctic in the summer of 1942—its overall impact was much less than it might have been. The air force's disregard of navy recommendations in the 1939–40 mining campaign (see chapter two) and its inability to maintain a sustained antishipping campaign around

Britain in late 1940 through early 1941 stand as particular failures in Germany's use of air power at sea.

The United States and Japan adopted a different course. Neither nation formed an independent air force, and their navies not only retained air elements, they nourished them. Although this result was not foreordained, there were strong pressures pushing both navies to develop larger and more capable air arms.

The U.S. Congress examined the wisdom of establishing an independent air service in the early 1920s at the urging of air power proponents such as Mitchell. Geography prevented Mitchell from making Douhet-like arguments for strategic bombing, so he instead argued that an independent air force should replace the U.S. Navy as the nation's first line of defense. Mitchell called battleships obsolete and asserted that "surface navies have entirely lost their mission of defending a coast because aircraft

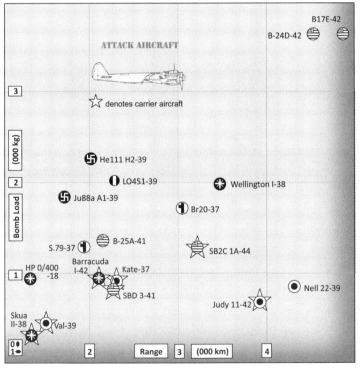

FIGURE 7.1. Bomber and Attack Aircraft. This shows the maximum ranges and maximum payloads of representative bomber and attack aircraft. Note that maximum range could not be achieved with maximum payload.

can destroy or sink any seacraft coming within their radius of operation. In fact, aircraft today are the only effective means of coast protection."[61] He tried to prove this assertion in 1921 by bombing *Ostfriesland*, an ex-German battleship serving as an anchored target, until the vessel finally sank. This stunt impressed the public but not the experts, and the Navy (and Army) retained control of their aviation assets after a bitter political battle. The Navy's victory was not absolute; it kept ship-based aircraft and shore-based flying boats throughout the interwar period, and the Marines were allowed some combat support aircraft, but the Army claimed a monopoly on all other land-based combat aircraft whether operating over land or water.[62]

Mitchell's attacks certainly energized naval officers; even air skeptics were certain that they did not want to surrender assets to an independent force. And while the mixed record of naval air in World War I meant that there was no unanimity of opinion in the Navy about the value of aviation, few felt it was worthless. In fact, there was an emerging consensus that aircraft spotting would be critical to long-range gunfire from battleships,

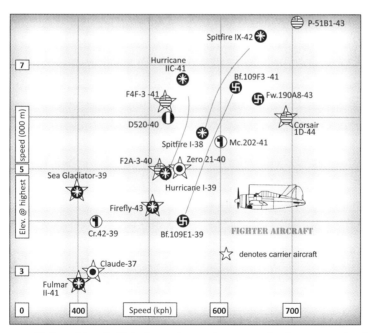

FIGURE 7.2. Fighter Aircraft. This shows the maximum speeds of representative fighter aircraft and the altitude at which each could achieve its maximum speed. Numbers after each fighter name show the year of introduction for the specific model being represented. Speed at altitude is a rough measure of a fighter's effectiveness.

particularly in the Pacific where clear weather made such engagements more likely. Whichever side had the more effective spotting would land early hits on the enemy, leading to victory in the gunnery duel. This sparked a logical train of thought. If aerial spotting was vital, then shooting down the enemy's spotters while protecting one's own was equally important. If that were the case, fighters were needed. Once a fleet needed fighters, aircraft carriers became the most efficient platform to carry them. And if the enemy also had carriers, then the best way to secure air control over a battle zone was to destroy enemy carriers with strike aircraft from friendly carriers.

While there were early debates over the relative merits of embarking the necessary aircraft on battleships and cruisers rather than carriers, carriers won the day. But getting and using aircraft carriers were complicated and expensive processes that required a venture into uncharted waters. Techniques for maintaining, arming, launching, landing, and storing aircraft in the confined space of a carrier had to be learned. Carrier aircraft needed special equipment and specific design features for catapult launches and arrested landings. Aircrew required special training. The mix of aircraft and weapons had to be decided. Tactics for carriers and their air groups had to be defined and tested. The hard-won solutions were confidential information; when Hollywood filmed flight operations for the 1931 Clark Gable film *Hell Divers* aboard the carrier *Saratoga*, the Navy required that the bottom part of the screen be blacked out to hide the ship's arresting gear. Finally, and most importantly, carriers needed to have a definite and urgent mission to justify the expense of building them and the effort of operating them and their air groups.

The U.S. Navy commissioned its first carrier, a converted collier, in 1922. While support for this class of warship within the Navy was hardly universal, development was energized by a growing realization that carriers were needed to fulfill an important strategic need. This was visualized through a series of war games conducted at the Naval War College. These allowed participants to play out a Japanese-U.S. naval war and revealed the need for large numbers of carrier aircraft, both on the front line to defeat Japanese carrier- and land-based air and in reserve to replace inevitable losses.[63] Such findings motivated the Americans to maximize the number of aircraft on each carrier and to accelerate their operational tempo. More carriers entered the fleet, and innovations such as crash barriers, flight deck servicing, and landing signal officers appeared.

Japan had its share of air power visionaries proclaiming the end of battleships, but the army and the navy were less pressured by demands for an independent air force, and the debate was largely contained within the navy.[64] The two services had cooperated in the 1894–95 Sino-Japanese war and the Russo-Japanese War and again during the brief period of active combat in World War I, but that cooperation faded in the interwar period under competition for limited budget dollars and competing strategic visions. Able to pursue its own strategy, the navy wove aircraft into its doctrine of decisive battle, envisioning (as the Americans anticipated) the use of both land- and carrier-based aviation to attrite the U.S. fleet as it advanced across the Pacific. The arms limitation treaties of 1922 and 1930 stimulated this thinking, as they regulated the construction of warships but not aircraft.[65] Both tactical precepts and operational needs caused the navy to call for very long-ranged aircraft: operationally, to deal with the immense distances of the Pacific, and tactically, to strike first by outranging the enemy.[66] This provides an excellent example of how fundamental strategies, operational constraints, and tactical requirements combined to affect technological development. The Japanese aircraft industry produced aircraft with remarkably long ranges but with weight (and durability) ruthlessly pared to the minimum. Its achievement was all the more remarkable given that Japanese aircraft engine technology lagged that of the United States, Great Britain, and Germany.

Japanese aircraft carrier development paralleled that of the United States in a number of respects. The Japanese navy came to see its carrier force first as an important adjunct to the network of island air bases in whittling down a U.S. advance, and then as a potent striking force in its own right. The Japanese navy commissioned *Hōshō* in 1922, the first carrier designed from the keel up to be commissioned by any navy; by the end of the decade, it had followed with two carriers constructed on the hulls of partly completed capital ships (as did the U.S. Navy). These allowed the navy to develop techniques and tactics for carrier operations. As discussed in chapter three, the Japanese spent more time and effort to develop effective air-droppable torpedoes than any other nation. They anticipated that these would allow aircraft to cripple or sink battleships

HMS *M2* with a hangar replacing the 12-inch gun specified in her design and carrying a Parnall Peto, sometime after 1928. The floatplane was an experimental model to meet the requirement for a two-man aircraft that could take off from the boat (a short hydraulic catapult was fitted in 1928) and stay aloft for at least an hour and a quarter. The idea was to directly marry aircraft and submarine technology and vastly expand the submarine's reconnaissance radius. After *M2* foundered in 1932 the British abandoned the concept of a submarine floatplane, leaving it to the French and Japanese to deploy operational submarine aircraft carriers. *(Wiki Public Domain)*

and carriers. Nonetheless, as the construction of its super-battleships showed, the navy viewed the advances in aircraft and carrier technology as a diversified investment; its core business remained a powerful battle line.[67] Japan's greatest innovation with respect to carrier warfare was the concept of using flattops collectively to combine their air groups into unified formations for attack or defense. This was another case where the proper use of the weapon greatly magnified its power, and at the point of its entry into World War II the Japanese navy had the world's best carrier strike force equipped with some of the world's best naval aircraft. It was, however, a brittle force lacking the industrial and training infrastructures needed to sustain itself in a prolonged conflict.

Although the British navy in 1939 was operating as many carriers as its Japanese and U.S. counterparts, the capabilities of its carrier force were much less. Its carriers were, on average, older and smaller and carried less than two-thirds as many aircraft as either the U.S. or Japanese carrier force. The loss of its naval air arm to the air force, postwar economic stringencies, and the lack of a clear strategic vision to justify the outlay of resources hobbled the development of the carrier force. In an enquiry convened in 1921 to consider the matter of aircraft at sea (the Bonar Law Enquiry), the general admiralty view was that "since (naval) aircraft could not reliably sink battleships, they would primarily perform ancillary functions to the weapons system that could, i.e., the battlefleet."[68] Carriers thus received less emphasis in British naval thinking than battleships.

By the 1930s the British navy had gone from having few potential enemies to having too many. Moreover, handling these potential enemies would require very different naval strategies. In a war with Germany or Italy, the British would have an advantage in naval resources but would have to contend with numerous land-based aircraft. These would imperil carrier attacks on enemy naval forces close to their bases. In a war with Japan, the British fleet would have to travel great distances and be more self-supporting, and carriers would have greater offensive and defensive responsibilities.

By 1937 the British were trying to cover all bases by building heavily armored carriers designed to withstand enemy air attacks at the expense of aircraft capacity. Reflecting the small size of its carrier air groups, the British navy demanded that its aircraft be multirole, considering this a reasonable compromise given its view that carrier aircraft could never hope to compete with their land-based counterparts.[69] Unsurprisingly, what it got were aircraft that were jacks of all trades but masters of none. The navy's primary carrier strike aircraft in the late 1930s, the Swordfish, served as a reconnaissance aircraft, a gunfire spotter, a torpedo bomber, and a dive bomber. The British saw the torpedo as the Swordfish's main strike weapon, in keeping with the idea that torpedoes delivered by air could best be used to "fix" a fleeing enemy by slowing one or more ships; the battleships would then close in for the kill.[70] This was a tactic better suited to attacking the Germans or Italians, which were likely to be fleeing a superior British force, than the Japanese. The British navy successfully employed its fixing tactic with torpedo bomber attacks against the German battleship *Bismarck* and the Italian cruiser *Pola*, but the list of unsuccessful attacks was much longer. Superior armor protection allowed British carriers to survive attacks that might otherwise have been fatal, as in the 1941 air attacks against *Illustrious* and *Formidable*, but these still required lengthy repairs. The failure to develop competitive carrier aircraft during the interwar period forced British carriers to rely on land-based aircraft hastily adapted to carrier use and U.S. carrier aircraft acquired through Lend-Lease.

At least the British had a naval air arm in 1939. The Germans and the Italians both rued their lack of carriers but had little hope of getting them, given the other pressing needs of their national armed forces. And given the rate at which carriers were sunk or seriously damaged, one must question how effective a single carrier would have been in the Atlantic or Mediterranean, which was a boneyard for British carriers.

It is not surprising that the most effective naval air arms of World War II belonged to the Americans and Japanese. The war they waged in the Pacific dominates the narrative of World War II aviation at sea, but of course the role of air power was much more than aircraft carriers trading air strikes in dramatic battles. The uses of aviation technology were actually very similar to those in the previous war.

EXPLOITATION: WORLD WAR II

While the core uses for aviation technology in World War II were the same as in World War I, the impact and power of aviation were far greater. This can be demonstrated with a simple statistic: whereas aircraft sank 5 Entente merchant ships of 8,039 GRT in World War I, 0.00063 percent of the total, they accounted for 820 Allied merchant ships of 2.89 million GRT in World War II, 13.4 percent of the total. What changed in the twenty years between the two wars was more than improvements in the base technology of aircraft, although such improvements were the single most important factor. It was also a matter of technological integration that enhanced mission effectiveness.

The capabilities of reconnaissance aircraft were greatly magnified when they were fitted with radar, given better and more powerful radios, and equipped with radio navigation devices to better know where they were. These tools guided the development of doctrine to improve the efficiency of air search plans and standardize the reporting of information. More powerful and effective reconnaissance was further guided by factors such as SIGINT and DF. However, this was in the best case, and these improvements did not apply equally to all nations. Even in the most advanced naval air services reconnaissance could be a hit-or-miss matter. *Scharnhorst* and *Gneisenau* (in company with several destroyer flotillas) sailed from Brest nearly to Dover unsighted by multiple layers of aerial reconnaissance, some of it radar-equipped, even though the British knew they would be coming. The Axis traffic between Europe and North Africa provides a broader example. Between November 1941 and March 1942 the Axis sailed 188 convoys between Europe and Africa or along the African coast. Signals intelligence gave British forces prenotification of 154 (82 percent) of these convoys. Even with this prenotification to help direct reconnaissance aircraft, the British attacked only fifty convoys, and only thirty (16 percent) suffered some type of damage.[71] Even as late as the October 1944 Battle of Leyte Gulf, U.S. carriers struggled to locate a Japanese decoy force that wanted to be seen.[72]

Gunnery spotting turned out to be a relatively minor factor in sea battles. There were few opportunities to use it early in the war, and radar displaced it in the war's latter stages. However, it was a significant concern of navies prior to the war because of the near-universal belief that aircraft-directed gunfire would confer a decisive advantage in long-range naval combat. Many of the same old problems dogged this practice from the very first, as during the battle of the River Plate in December 1939. British cruiser *Ajax* managed to fire a spotter aircraft into the air from her midships catapult, "a very fine evolution observing that 'X' and 'Y' turrets were at that time firing on a forward bearing."[73] But the aircraft used the wrong radio frequency, and its corrections went unheard for a half hour. Then, once properly tuned, the aircraft reported corrections to the wrong ship. Taking highly flammable aircraft into surface combat was standard practice at the war's beginning, but there are many examples of them being ignited and even providing a point of aim in night combat and the practice was generally discontinued by the end of 1942. Gunnery spotting had some successes, but there was no instance during the entire war when it materially affected the outcome of a naval action. This provides an example of a technology proving to be a dead end in meeting a specific need; by midwar a different technology, radar, was better serving the role aerial spotting was supposed to fill. Against expectations, air spotting for naval guns was more useful when the guns were targeting land targets and radar would not serve.

With respect to attacks on ships and strikes against land targets, it quickly became clear that effective attacks on ships required special techniques, training, and practice. In a typical early war example of regular bombing units used in a maritime attack role, the Italian air force sent 126 level bombers against the British Mediterranean fleet. Only seventy-six bombed the right target, with the best results being a few near-misses. Fifty others bombed the Italian fleet; they all missed as well.[74] The first German air force success against warships under way at sea came in February 1940 when they sank two of their own destroyers. This was a step backward from the Spanish Civil War when German aircraft had at least occasionally succeeded in torpedoing the right targets. Torpedoes proved one of the best ways to sink ships, and every major navy eventually developed effective torpedo bombing forces. Dive-bombing was also effective; glide-bombing—dive-bombing's less extreme cousin—was somewhat less so. Level bombing, however, while it achieved scattered successes, remained a matter of splash and dash. Only when level bombers adopted low-level attack techniques, such as skip bombing, did they begin to match the effectiveness of torpedo or dive bombers. Technological enhancements such as better aircraft and specialized weapons had a role, but training mattered more.

The power of shipborne naval aviation in attacking land targets, or at least strategic targets such as transportation networks and population centers, was inferior to land-based air with one important exception. Shipborne air's mobility, its ability to appear and disappear, gave it a power all its own, at least when applied in mass. Exploiting this mobility, carriers struck at enemy fleets in their bases and greatly reduced the ability of an enemy to keep a fleet in being safely out of harm's way. Examples include the Taranto attack (November 1940), the Pearl Harbor attack (December 1941), and the carrier strikes against *Tirpitz* in April 1944.

The Norwegian campaign in 1940 hinted at the potential effect of air power on sea power as a rain of German bombs caused some damage and more disruption, but the first campaign where air power indisputably dominated sea power came in May 1941 during the battle for Crete, when more than five hundred German and Italian aircraft savaged the British navy, sinking three cruisers and six destroyers and knocking two battleships and an aircraft carrier out of the fight. Well-equipped aircraft with

Murderers' Row. A famous photograph of five U.S. fleet carriers at Ulithi Atoll after
the invasion of Leyte. Equipped with superior aircraft flown by well-trained crews and
excellent radar permitting effective control of aerial defenses, the U.S. carrier task forces
demonstrated that quantity indeed has a quality all its own. *(Naval History and Heritage
Command, 80-G-294131)*

well-trained crews finally sank a modern battleship at sea, *Prince of Wales*,
in December 1941. For some, this signified that the age of the battleship
was coming to an end, although the torpedoing of *Jean Bart* and the mining of *Audacious* (both in 1914) had already demonstrated the battleship's
vulnerability to lesser weapons.

Merging technologies were particularly critical in antisubmarine
warfare. The case study in chapter six regarding *U-247* illustrates this
well. In 1939 aerial ASW functioned much the same as in 1918, forcing
submarines to submerge and alerting surface forces to the submarine's
presence, and perhaps, in extraordinary cases where all went perfectly,
dropping a bomb or depth charge in the submarine's vicinity. However,
by 1945 aircraft using 3-cm radar could spot a submarine from miles away;
they could drop sonobuoys to track the submarine; they were armed with

powerful weapons—improved depth bombs, rockets, and acoustic homing torpedoes—and they could provide exact locations using radio navigation tools. A submarine spotted by Allied aircraft was lucky to survive, and submarine kill rates reflected this.

Defense against aircraft focused increasingly on airborne interception, guided by radar and controlled by radio. Once the war started, navies discovered that antiaircraft fire served more to throw off an attacker's aim than to down aircraft. Greater numbers of guns provided more distraction and more kills, but with the development of the proximity radar fuze, the Allies far outstripped the Axis in enhancing the effectiveness of antiaircraft gunnery. Even those improvements paled in comparison to the ability of well-equipped carriers with well-trained crews and high-performance fighter aircraft to intercept massed enemy air strikes before they got within attack range. Japanese recognition of this led directly to kamikaze tactics, while the United States traded carrier strike aircraft for fighters in a bid to increase both their aerial interception capacity and their ability to suppress Japanese aircraft on their airfields. Carriers at first appeared as vulnerable as their detractors predicted, with six Japanese, seven British, and four U.S. carriers sunk up to the end of 1942 and more seriously damaged. But contrary to expectations, land-based air accounted for none of the losses. Moreover, increased numbers and better damage control, combined with the capabilities described above, eventually forged Allied carriers into an immensely resilient force. Carriers held the ring against land-based air, but another unforeseen development—the atomic bomb—called into question their continued usefulness.

THE TECHNOLOGY POSTWAR AND TODAY

The arrival of the atomic age raised new questions about the usefulness of navies, and the appearance of jet aircraft—heavier than their piston-engined predecessors and with far higher take-off and landing speeds—cast into doubt the ability of carriers to take the most modern aircraft to sea. But technique, technology, and geopolitics all combined to keep the carrier relevant as a platform. Technique took the form of the angled flight deck, which allowed a landing jet to overshoot its landing without smashing into parked aircraft or a crash barrier. Technology responded with the steam catapult, which generated enough power to hurl jets off flight decks at flying speeds, and the mirror landing system, which allowed them to land on the decks. The British led the way in developing all three (with the Japanese pioneering lighted landing systems before the war), but the U.S. Navy was the main beneficiary.[75] The Cold War showed that wars and near-wars would be fought without resorting to nuclear weapons, which meant that carriers could act as highly mobile means of projecting power from offshore. And the growing capability of jets and the shrinking of nuclear weapons eventually gave aircraft carriers a mission in even a nuclear conflict. Carriers have played a major role in power projection from Korea through Vietnam and the Falklands to the Persian Gulf.

Another important development was the advent of the helicopter as a multipurpose naval aviation asset. Helicopters, with their ability to take off from and land on a small platform, can be carried by ships down to the size of patrol craft. They have the weapons and sensors to find and sink a submarine or locate and at least discomfort a large warship. They can deliver troops and perform a host of functions that enhance the power of the ships carrying them. World War II had seen the centralization of at-sea air resources in aircraft carriers; helicopters started a process of partial decentralization.

ASW remains an important function, with patrol aircraft using refined versions of many of the sensors and weapons introduced in World War II. Antiship missiles have given land-based air a potent weapon against naval platforms.

Since the end of World War II the only carriers to be attacked by enemy forces were the small British flattops operating off the Falklands in the 1982 war against Argentina. They had a close call, but the enemy's inventory of Exocet missiles was limited, and defective torpedoes caused one submarine attack to fail. These results hardly invalidate the threat of nuclear submarines, hypersonic or surface-hugging cruise missiles, antiship ballistic missiles, and drone swarms, all of which threaten super-carriers. As in the interwar era, navies can only theorize about their likely effects.

WHAT THIS TELLS US

Many historians unquestioningly accept the ascendency of naval aviation as the ultimate expression of naval power. This point of view comes from the latter part of World War II in the Pacific after the fast carrier task forces of the U.S. Third/Fifth Fleets had established their absolute dominance over their foe with superior numbers, technology, and training. It has been crystalized in the idea that aircraft carriers replaced the battleship as queen of the seas (and never mind the nuclear submarine). Another and perhaps related aspect of aviation technology that merits comment is the passion it evokes. In this respect, it is the opposite of mine technology. The cult of the airplane, as expressed by such proponents as Douhet or Mitchell, profoundly impacted naval aviation. The romance and drama of being a fighter pilot, particularly a carrier pilot or a "top gun," continue to seduce. But if such symbols aid Navy recruiting, they also complicate the assessment of naval aviation as a technology. This passion exists in many forms and while it is easy to dismiss a Billy Mitchell as a fanatic, it is not as easy to spot excessive regard for the powers of aviation technology when it has been so long unchallenged in peer-to-peer combat, and the received wisdom, as expressed in budget allocations, is that the large carrier is the immutable arbiter of sea power.

When all is said and done, maritime aviation is and always has been less than its most ardent advocates would say. In 1914 and 1939 it failed to accomplish the things its supporters supposed it could do, and it is not farfetched to suppose that were a peer-to-peer war to begin tomorrow, it would again fail to meet expectations. Another point of correspondence between the dawn of maritime aviation and today is that its basic missions have changed very little even if the platforms are far more powerful. Maritime patrol—that is, intelligence—was the first mission of naval air, and it remains important, with developments suggesting that in the near term, unmanned drones will play a growing role. Antisubmarine warfare is still a major task of naval aviation. Shore-based maritime strike aircraft, with their specialized sensor suites, weapons packages, and training, are required by any nation that wishes to influence events in nearby waters, although many experts predict their strike capabilities will eventually be displaced by land-based missile systems. Strikes from the sea against land targets have been a prominent feature of the mission set of those nations that operate attack carriers, but even helicopters give nearly every navy at least a limited capacity in this regard. A new capability that has emerged since World War II is the ability of air power to deliver troops from sea to shore. A mission that has all but disappeared is that of gunnery spotting.

A large carrier has not experienced a serious attack since World War II despite intensive combat operations off the coasts of Korea and Vietnam, and in the Persian Gulf and Indian Ocean. The 1982 Falklands War and the 1988 Tanker War actions in the Persian Gulf seem to confirm that air power at sea remains paramount. The utility of even a small carrier and a dozen or so jets and helicopters in supporting expeditionary operations was a particularly striking lesson that caught the attention of several nations. In 1940 four nations operated twenty-three aircraft carriers. In 1980 eight nations operated thirty-seven aircraft carriers; in 2020 ten nations had thirty-two carriers. The aircraft carrier, as an alpha technology, has already experienced a primacy twice the length of the forty-year span of the dreadnought battleship, the alpha technology preceding it. While the United States has dominated naval aviation since World War II, China, India, Great Britain, South Korea, Italy, and Japan are all currently attempting to improve their carrier forces. This would seem to argue that the carrier will continue to be an alpha naval technology for the foreseeable future. Other trends, however, are arguing against this possibility. The latest U.S. carrier class costs about $13 billion per ship. U.S., Italian, and British carriers are operating variants of the F-35 costing $130 million per unit. Considering this amount would have purchased almost 180 first-rate fighters in 1945, it is also possible to imagine that along with carriers, aircraft are becoming too costly to risk in combat, at least in a peer-to-peer environment. Carriers today face not just the mines and torpedoes that so worried Jellicoe in 1914 but also a host of other threats, many untried but all potentially deadly.[76]

The future of naval aviation will surely be influenced by cost considerations. The development of technologies that may replace manned aviation, at least in the most demanding and deadly situations, raises other questions about the future of the large aircraft carrier and invites comparison to how the swarming kamikazes were able to swamp the sophisticated and practiced air defenses of the U.S. fleet. It is difficult to know whether the carrier has had its day, but the current crop of antiship weapons gives little cause for optimism. Navies will still require wings, but those wings may well prove to be of a new type (such as unmanned drones) flying from new platforms rather than large, expensive aircraft flying from large, expensive ships.

In World War II carriers, allied with technologies such as radar, briefly acquired the ability to defeat enemy air strikes at a distance—an ability best demonstrated in the Battle of the Philippine Sea in June 1944. However, new weapons and new methods of attack quickly challenged this ability. Moreover, undersea craft showed themselves to be potent adversaries as well. Since then, navies have continually debated whether the defenses erected around carriers are sufficient to protect them from ever more potent hazards. Perhaps not, but once again, naval aviation is not aircraft carriers, and in a future war it is not difficult to imagine that the vision of the anonymous author of the 1913 *Naval Review* article, who believed that every warship should have its own self-contained aviation component was, after all, right, even if his vision took more than a century to realize.

CONCLUSION

*How extraordinarily difficult it was to frame sound policy as long as
experience was confined to theoretical argument backed only by the
sometimes dubiously valid experience of peacetime exercises.*

—STEPHEN ROSKILL[1]

THE GENESIS OF NAVAL TECHNOLOGY

This book has examined how the world's major navies developed and
used in combat six different technologies: two weapons, mines and
torpedoes; two tools, radio and radar; and two platforms, submarines and aircraft.

These technologies had varied roots and evolved in different ways.
Naval mines began with private inventors and evolved through a process
of experimentation and improvisation by naval and shore-based establishments. Torpedo development paralleled that of mines, with torpedoes first
appearing as commercial ventures but with navies assuming the development and production roles over time. Radio also began as a private venture.
Having military and commercial applications, it evolved in both spheres
with much cross-pollination. Government funding and laboratories spear-
headed radar's development after private inventors failed to find a market
for prototype devices. Commercial growth came postwar. Early submarines were built both as commercial ventures and under government contracts. Once they proved practical, they were rapidly absorbed into normal
naval ship-building processes. With aircraft, both government-affiliated
labs and private industry advanced progress with considerable intercourse
between the two.

Although the technologies discussed in this work all have mixed
commercial, military, and scientific antecedents, navies adopted each
one for an anticipated use to meet a recognized need. This observation is

simplistic but it is also useful for understanding why technologies evolved the way they did and why certain technologies flourished in some hands and languished in others. In other words, need and use—particularly use in peer-to-peer combat—are fundamental to understanding the practical genesis of naval technologies and their employment. The key here is that need and use varied by navy.

A navy's core function is to win wars, and the role of any technology is to advance that function. Nonetheless, peacetime priorities also play an important role in the process. For example, the nuclear-powered aircraft carrier has a role to play in war, but no one can say for certain what this role would be in a peer-to-peer conflict since such a war has not occurred within the platform's span of service; its role in other wars, such as Vietnam or Iraq, has been to serve as a mobile air base supporting ground operations. Its role in situations short of war—as a means to project power and to intimidate—is, perhaps, even more influential. In nonconflict situations, it can serve both political and humanitarian functions.

Technology is endued with expectations and the promise of something more powerful, more useful, faster, cheaper—in short, something better. Naval writings warn against the dangers (especially to those with budgetary powers) of being seduced by the promise and apparent power of new technologies, especially those described as "transformative." Human nature being what it is, however, technologies trumpeted in their early stages as being transformative—torpedoes, submarines, aircraft, for example—have always attracted strong cadres of proponents, even prophets. This sets up the counternarrative of stodgy admirals who disregarded this new technology or ignored that one; this is found in the literature in multiple languages.[2] It is compelling, but false. Radar makes a fine example. Today, the utility of and need for radar in naval operations seems so obvious that one can only marvel at the obtuseness of admirals and policy-makers in nations such as France, Japan, or Italy who, in the 1930s did not throw every available franc, yen, or lira at the technology. But consider the war plans and economic situations of these nations during the Great Depression, the nature of the threats they faced, the steps they took to manage those threats, and the resources they had at their disposal. Add that to what they knew about radar and what uses seemed likely in the mid-1930s, and their decisions seem understandable, at the very least.

Time and cost are critical ingredients in the genesis of technology. Cost is usually associated with budgets and resources, but time is the dearest coin of all. Navies work in extended time scales. In 1935 a major weapons platform, such as a new battleship design, took five to seven years to develop, design, construct, and work up before it could be considered ready for operational use.[3] The first air independent submarine was prototyped in 1940, but no operational boats appeared before 1945. One consequence is that navies, especially in war, have always focused on technology more likely to return immediate results—everything else being equal—and in peace they have historically focused on proven big-ticket technologies such as battleships.

Technologies often require a certain mass before they can make any impact, much less be effective. Put simply, it takes two radios to communicate, but a network is more powerful; radar becomes decisive as powerful and easy-to-use sets proliferate in an environment of tactical aggression and numerical superiority. A single torpedo fired at a target is less than one-quarter as effective as a salvo of four. Technology favors the rich and powerful. Examples of a poor nation springing a new technology upon an unsuspecting opponent, such as the Japanese Type 93 torpedo or the Italian motorized-detachable mine, and thereby gaining an important advantage are few, and the edge is usually fleeting.

The infrastructure required to support a technology adds significantly to time and cost. Production, training, and maintenance are obvious types of infrastructure, but support also requires flexibility. Intellectual infrastructure plays just as much a role as industrial or mechanical infrastructure does. Radar required the creation of entirely new processes supported by new shipboard organizations for maximum effect. Mines, although relatively simple when viewed on a unit-by-unit basis, had to be deployed in large numbers from multiple types of platforms in just the right places and times to be most effective. Aircraft created immense logistical burdens. Mere adoption of new technologies was never enough; navies had to commit resources—always more than anticipated and often massive—to achieve worthwhile results.

A final point must be made about resources. Navies have sometimes fought with other national services for the right to develop technologies or adapt them to their special needs. For example, navies shared with other services an interest in aircraft, radar, and radio (and in the case of Germany, mines and torpedoes as well). Radio was a relative cheap technology, and services seldom clashed over broadcasting resources or airwaves. For radar, perhaps the most remarkable thing about the Allied efforts in World War II was the relative lack of competition between national armies, navies, and air forces for radar resources, at least when compared to the Japanese and Germans (Allied generosity being abetted by relative abundance, no doubt). In Japan the army and navy competed bitterly throughout the war, and the electronic warfare needs of the German air force always took priority over naval needs. Aircraft provide the strongest example of inter-service competition for control. The navies that lost the battle to retain their own aerial resources after World War I were hampered throughout the interwar years in developing, or even properly appreciating, the rapid advances in aviation and in acquiring the special skills required to operate aircraft at sea. They began the war handicapped in this critical area.

Time, talent, and money being limited, navies must place their technological bets judiciously. Navies tend to be conservative in making such decisions, and conservative tendencies can slow technical development. On the other hand, examples where excessive conservatism has prevented the adoption of a new technology are hard to find. In fact, navies have often demonstrated impressive patience with slow-starting technologies such as submarines and torpedoes. Even the British, who at the dawn of the twentieth century had the greatest stake in maintaining the status quo, explored these technologies, in part from a concern that an opposing navy could develop a decisive advantage.

The widely held notion that a new technology will in itself grant a competitive advantage is seductive. A similar idea has led navies to cherish secret tweaks or enhancements to their technologies (a faster firing cycle, a different trigger mechanism, a slightly greater gunnery range, a torpedo that can be dropped from a higher elevation), expecting thereby a measurable combat advantage. In fact, better use, especially in core technologies such as gunnery, generally gets more results than technically better tools.

Nations have a strong interest in developing technology for the war they, or their foes, plan to fight. Here, strategic vision has played a key role in choosing which technologies to develop and how to develop them. The

Russians in 1914 emphasized mine technology to counter a superior German fleet. In the interwar period, both the U.S. and the Japanese navies identified aircraft as a necessity for fighting a naval war over the expanses of the Pacific Ocean, and this spurred the development of their naval air arms. The Japanese vision of a decisive battle drove other developments such as super battleships, super torpedoes, and aircraft that achieved long ranges at the expense of durability. Strategic vision, however, is often shortsighted. For both the Japanese and Americans, carrier technology was suitable for the war that they ended up fighting, although that war did not play out as anticipated in the 1920s. Long-range torpedoes proved deadly, but never in the role they were designed to fill, nor against the targets they were designed to hit. Japan's super battleships never fought their counterparts.

USE IT OR LOSE IT

A technology must have a use; a weapon must have platforms to deliver it, tools to direct it, and a target to attack. These linkages are vital to any technology's employment and effectiveness, and they hold clues as to why some promising technologies were stillborn and others bloomed late. The potential of the torpedo, for example, was not achieved until it was paired with its best platform, the submarine, and its best target, the merchant ship. Modern examples of this dynamic abound. For example, one can ask whether it is overkill to develop expensive directed energy weapons if their best targets are drones and speedboats. Does the rail gun, a technology that is more than a century old, have a use that justifies its continued development?

Combat is a technology's acid test. Theory, practice, and simulations—the best tools available in peacetime—are critical, but a question mark hovers over any technology until it sees peer-to-peer combat. This can be seen in the examples throughout this book. The impact of mines on fleet operations was not clear until mines sank a third of the Russian and Japanese battle lines during the Russo-Japanese War. The great navies started World War I with a consensus on the best uses for submarines. In combat these uses proved nearly impossible to implement, while the merchant-killer role had barely been considered. Radio's first combat use revealed congestion and procedural and vocabulary issues that peacetime exercises had barely suggested. The flood of intelligence that radio made available to an enemy who was willing to devote the resources to exploit it came as a surprise to navies in both world wars. Radar offered great promise from the outset, but this promise was not fulfilled until navies understood its strengths and weaknesses and adapted their organizations and tactics accordingly. Expectations for aircraft were high in World War I were but not fully realized until World War II. In all cases, intense and sustained combat taught lessons that peacetime theorizing and exercises missed.

The corollary to combat as the acid test of a technology is that the lessons of combat must be learned for a technology to achieve its best use. Torpedo technology provides examples. During the Russo-Japanese War, the Japanese missed with hundreds of torpedoes in several long-range attacks against underway targets before they concluded this was not the best way to use the weapon. Radar provides more examples. The U.S. and British navies realized after lengthy use that they needed to rethink how ships received, analyzed, and translated radar information into action. The U.S. Navy led the way in this process, aided by the widespread installation of technically superior radar sets. The Navy arrived at this innovation via a bottom-up improvisation with the results reported and best practices adopted after review and scrutiny at the highest levels. Still, even with all its advantages, almost two years passed before the U.S. Navy could routinely exploit the benefits that radar conferred. The German navy fixed on the risk of active electromagnetic or acoustic devices disclosing the user's location and so developed a doctrinal approach that restricted the usefulness of radar while at the same time taking passive detection technologies, such as hydrophones, to places the British and Americans had no idea existed.

Just as cultivating bottom-up innovation has proven beneficial in extracting better results from technology, user feedback is essential to correcting problems. In World War II, both American and German sub-mariners struggled with defective torpedoes. The parallels are striking, including the difficulty that they had in convincing shore establishments that the torpedoes were flawed. One take-away is that the more compli-cated the technology, the greater the need for both exhaustive testing and the willingness to listen to feedback from users.

Feedback concerning enemy technology was also important, although such feedback can be difficult to obtain. The failure to penetrate the mysteries of superior Japanese night optics and torpedoes hobbled the U.S. Navy in night surface combat when radar should have provided an advantage. The Germans struggled with this problem in a number of guises. Widespread Allied use of centimetric radar, unsuspected by the Germans, stymied their submarines. When facing Allied HF/DF, the Germans after a time concluded that their submarines were being attacked after making radio transmissions. Headquarters, however, was slow to react, since any response would have required a complete revision of German operational doctrine. And while the German navy was meticulous about its radio encryption procedures, staff dismissed all possibility that the Allies had compromised the Enigma devices that were the bedrock of German confidence.

Conversely, rapidly recognizing or even anticipating new enemy technology had definite benefits. The Allies were aware that acoustic homing torpedoes could be developed, and they expected the Germans to deploy such a weapon. Recognition of the potential threat spawned a search for countermeasures that blunted the effectiveness of the enemy's acoustic weapons when they finally did appear. The Allied navies were also quick to deal with other German novelties. Magnetic and influence mines certainly posed problems, but their piecemeal introduction gave the Allies time to counter them. Guided weapons such as the Fritz-X and the Hs 293 were nasty surprises when the Germans debuted them, but the Allies devised effective countermeasures within weeks. The Japanese were unable to overcome the Allied radar advantage using technology, and so they resorted to unconventional approaches such as the kamikaze, which swamped the highly effective U.S. fighter direction system—at least for a time.

NEED AND USE

Determining need and use is not a simple thing. First, a perceived and an actual need are often different, but the difference is seldom clear. Think here of searchlights, more of a peril to friend than foe; likewise torpedo tubes in capital ships, and spotter floatplanes on battleships and cruisers. They most often proved to be liabilities in combat, not assets. And as recounted above, the Japanese went into World War II with the perceived need to outrange their opponents in every respect but found that out-ranging was hard to achieve in practice. There is also the matter of unanticipated need and unanticipated use. For the British navy of World War I, mines met an unanticipated need. The navy had not foreseen the need to construct mine barrages to block the transit of German submarines. Once the need was recognized, the technology was pressed into service. An example of unanticipated use is the proximity fuze. In this case, the need for more deadly antiaircraft gunfire was clear, and radar was pressed into service to improve accuracy. The better use was to apply radar technology to the shells as well so they would automatically explode when they were near the target. Radar provided both an anticipated solution (better fire control) and an unanticipated solution (the proximity fuze). Actual use is subject to so many variables that it is nearly impossible to make generalizations about any given technology that would apply to all users. But it can be said with certainty when it comes to new technology that development and use spring from need but that use is not always predicated upon original need.

Radar provides the best example of the difference between perceived and actual need, and it was late to flower due to the lack of a perceived need. Primitive radar devices were invented in the first two decades of the twentieth century, but serious development only commenced in the 1930s. Radar provided a capability that navies did not initially view as crucial. Its utility against surface targets was not apparent, and while its use as a tool for terrestrial air defense was clear, its value for naval air defense emerged only gradually. At the outset of World War II, the British navy had settled on antiaircraft guns and armor as the main defenses against air attack, while the Americans and the Japanese believed, in the Pacific context, that the best defense was a good offense, crippling enemy carriers and air bases before they could do their worst.[4] Thus, it is not surprising that the British navy came to fighter direction through informal trials despite the British air force having developed a sophisticated land-based system of radar-assisted aerial defense.

Nor is the separate development track for ship-based fighter direction surprising. There was in fact a great difference between an extensive network of fixed coastal radar stations giving an early warning of large bomber forces headed for fixed inland targets and mobile sea-based radar facilitating the distant interception of air strikes headed for the radar's base. The British navy's development of fighter direction is an example of an ultimate use differing from the original perceived need. Given its strategic mission, the German navy cultivated the offensive uses of radar, such as fire control, rather than its defensive uses, with the result that it lost a lead in radar that it never regained. The perceived need was too specialized and insignificant to justify time and resources exploring radar's other uses. In contrast, the British and U.S. navies embraced radar for its defensive capabilities and then, without an overarching plan or program, exploited its offensive uses once they better realized the potential.

In fact, uses for radar proliferated under wartime pressures. Navies first anticipated that radar would be useful for air and surface search and fire control. It would enhance the effectiveness of fleets in their traditional combat roles. And it did, but it also developed in quite different directions. The proximity fuze was one example. Effective surface search radar in escort vessels and in aircraft became a crucial tool in the Allied battle against submarines. Surface search radar aided the precise navigation of minelayers as well as station-keeping in general. The idea of radio-guided bombs and missiles had antecedents reaching back before World War I, but radar-guided weapons grew from wartime advances in the technology. These uses were not apparent in the mid-1930s when radar development started in earnest.

Unanticipated uses arise in part because technologies can interact and integrate in unanticipated ways. This is true for tools that navies employ to augment the effectiveness of platforms and weapons. And it is true of the integration of platforms and weapons as well, often in ways not envisioned when the technology was first adopted. Torpedoes made submarines practical weapons of war, even though they predated useful submersibles by a quarter of a century. They also turned aircraft into efficient ship-killers, although the road to develop that capability was long and rocky. Mines are an even older technology, but submarines and aircraft used as delivery platforms brought important new dimensions to minelaying, in both cases as a result of wartime innovations.

While such connections often enhanced the effectiveness of new technology, they also cut both ways. Submarines and aircraft both emerged as important naval technologies in World War I, with aircraft playing a vital role in limiting the effectiveness of submarines. This role would be forgotten or ignored in the interwar years, only to emerge even more forcefully in World War II as aircraft received increased capabilities from radar, sonobuoys, and acoustic homing torpedoes, above and beyond the core technology's improvements in reliability, range, and load. Mines in massive numbers became a major ASW weapon in World War I, a role not foreseen prewar. Radio and radar increased the power of aircraft in World War II but decreased it as well after navies understood how to use both tools to bolster antiaircraft defenses.

All this demonstrates the powerful effects of combining technologies and argues for the developers and users of technologies to be constantly vigilant for such links. This form of innovation can be bottom-up or top-down, but it is usually most effective if it proceeds both ways. Shipborne fighter direction, despite being the result of bottom-up innovation, was nonetheless recognized as an important development that should be nurtured. The British navy did this by establishing a central training scheme, and the U.S. Navy sent its officers there. More bottom-up innovation followed, as the two navies explored the infrastructure and procedures necessary to better use this new capacity. The U.S. Mark 24 homing torpedo is an example of a top-down development spawned by a committee-identified need to develop better ASW weapons. The Americans were able to combine naval, industrial, and academic resources to develop in short order an effective weapon that met end-user requirements. In doing so, they packaged acoustic homing, electric propulsion, and delivery in an entirely new way. Both cases illustrate the need for a constant search for new uses—from the front line to the design workshop to the research laboratory.

PRINCIPLES OF SUCCESS

This book has focused on technologies that were successful because they had a use, but their success stemmed from more than just that.

Mines were and are a successful technology because they are cheap (relatively speaking), easy to use, and effective on several levels—even the most primitive contact mine cannot be ignored by the most powerful opponent; it requires attention, and even if it is easy to neutralize, if not neutralized, it will kill. Mines' passivity is an asset, and they change geography because their impact extends beyond a single target. They do not need to explode to work—that is, they exert an impact as long as they exist.

Navies paid attention to torpedoes because they gave weak platforms the potential to sink strong platforms. But sinkings were rare until merchant ships became their target. Torpedoes were prone to malfunction in action and were easily avoided by targets capable of brisk maneuver. If they missed the target, their power was gone. Torpedoes were a technology that worked best when used correctly: in ambush, and against nonmilitary targets.

Radio was a successful technology because it took a core need, communication, and provided a tool to better meet that need. In a similar fashion, radar improved several core naval functions, including information-gathering and navigation. Submarines and aircraft succeeded by expanding the strike range of naval forces to new environments and allowed the effective deployment of new weapons, such as torpedoes, bombs, and rockets. The question, then, is: what do all these technologies have in common that made them successful?

A goal of this book was to set forth the principles that govern the successful development, introduction, and use of naval technology. Several universal, or at least very broad, principles include the following.

Expectations do not determine best use. Historically, the expectations that attend new technologies have been unrealistic. In the case of torpedoes, submarines, and aircraft, they were too high and development was slow. In the case of mines, they were too low. For radar, expectations were mostly wrong, and in the case of radio, they missed its downsides. Effective use of technology is improved by sensitivity to new uses.

Users have valuable input. This seems blindingly obvious, but militaries, being hierarchies, and scientists (and experts in general), believing that they know best, have a poor record of accepting user contributions and sometimes even suppress such contributions. The difference between the U.S. and British approaches to combat information management is one example. Both approaches had certain advantages, but the British adopted a slower, top-down development approach, while the U.S. Navy cultivated a quicker but less centralized process for learning from users. That same navy, in the same war, however, for far too long ignored complaints from submarine and destroyer crews who were fighting with defective torpedoes. In this instance, the Germans and the Americans faced similar problems and fell afoul of a similar dynamic between developers and users, but the Germans adopted a contact exploder from a captured British design within nine months of problems first surfacing, while the Americans took more than twice as long to implement a home-grown solution. Two corollaries to this principle are that users are sometimes wrong and experts *are* more often right, and that there are many good reasons why militaries must be hierarchies. These corollaries do not change the basic principle; they just provide context as to why it is difficult to incorporate user feedback in the development of naval technology.

Needs influence use. Different navies use identical technologies differently. The German approach to radar compared to Allied use is the paradigm of this principle, but examples abound in every other technology discussed in this work. The Allies had a far greater need for submarine countermeasures than did the Germans. The Germans needed guided weapons more than the Allies. The corollaries here are that a perceived need also influences use but it influences development more. British naval aviation provides a subtle illustration of this corollary. The British had a perceived need for multi-use carrier aircraft that compromised performance for the sake of serving in multiple roles: fighter/dive bombers, fighter/scouts, bomber/spotter/scouts. The other corollary is that technological development will be stunted if the need is not recognized. One example is Japanese antisubmarine warfare development and practice in World War II.

New technologies bring new vulnerabilities. Technologies, like people, have their faults. Radar and sonar emit waves that can be received by the enemy; in other words, they reveal as well as discover. This characteristic inhibited as well as directed German use of radar. For the Allies, especially if they were the stronger force, it was not as critical. SIGINT provides another example of vulnerability. The impacts of SIGINT on both sides in both world wars are still being unraveled and debated today, but what is not debated is that the consequences were serious. It appears that in both wars this vulnerability most affected the Germans. The corollary here is that vulnerabilities can take different forms, and this should influence the use of the technology. Out of respect for this corollary the Allies restricted the use of centimetric radar and the proximity fuze in areas where an example could fall into German hands, from fear that the enemy would copy it; the Germans restricted the use of the Oyster mine lest the Allies learn too soon how to deal with it.

WHAT THIS TELLS US

The story of naval technology is a story of change in all its guises: obvious, subtle, and even insidious. Physical change is easy to track—compare the appearance of HMS *Victory* to HMS *Dreadnought* to USS *Gerald R. Ford* (CVN 78). Ancillary impacts, such as those on infrastructure, are often subtle. Radio, the least intrusive of the technologies examined here, needed radio rooms, aerials, trained personnel, and a new industry to manufacture its components. New technology affects tactics: consider Jellicoe at Jutland. It changes operations: see Von Spee in the Pacific. It changes strategy: witness Japan's carrier strike at Pearl Harbor.

New technology finds new uses, it supersedes old methods, and it provokes countermeasures, all of which accelerate change. Few would have guessed in 1914 that by 1918 battleships would be supporting minesweepers and submarines rather than the reverse. Technological integration magnifies effect. During the Russo-Japanese War, torpedoes paired with new platforms such as destroyers and using new tactics had an impact, but not the impact anticipated by the majority of naval professionals. During World War I, torpedoes were integrated with a new technology, submarines, and given new missions and targets. After this, the torpedo/submarines linkup became the focus of naval warfare. By the end of World War II, submarines affected strategy to the point where Nazi Germany, chasing the promise of new sensors and propulsion technologies, would deprive the motherland of combat troops to protect its Baltic training waters. Finally, combat intensifies this process. Countermeasures foster more new technology (radar detectors), old technology used in new ways (submarine surface attacks to avoid sonar), and new tactics (kamikazes). These breed even more changes. Technology is dynamic without pause. The process does not end when new technology is introduced to a fleet; it begins. Navies must be prepared not just to seek out new technology but to facilitate the changes that will inevitably follow in its wake. They must be open to new uses and able to shed outdated methods and ways of thinking.

Where will navies look for new technologies? The most visible "new" technologies today are hugely expensive and directly related to stated military needs, such as the F-35 aircraft. This suggests that the day when advances sprang from a single inventor or even a small group is past. But this view would blind navies to innovation that can emerge from modest resources. Machine learning and drones, to name two examples, do not need huge research establishments and industrial complexes for their development. Disruptive technologies have emerged from unlikely places and will continue to do so. Navies would do well to keep broad horizons in looking for them. In the end, it is not about machines and tools; it is about the men and women who use them and the way they are used. Technology is not the weapon, the tool, or the platform; it is the application of knowledge expressed through the use of that weapon, that tool, that platform.

NOTES

CHAPTER 1. USE, DOCTRINE, INNOVATION

1. Giulio Douhet, *The Command of the Air*, trans. Dino Ferrari (Washington, DC: Office of Air Force History, 1983 reprint), 27.
2. The National Archives (TNA), ADM 1/13326, "Receipt and Handling of Enemy Intelligence in Destroyers," CO Cleveland to Captain (D) Plymouth, 26 December 1942.
3. Irving B. Holley Jr., *Ideas and Weapons: Exploitation of the Aerial Weapon by the United States during World War I: A Study of the Relationship of Technological Advance, Military Doctrine, and the Development of Weapons* (New Haven, CT: Yale University Press, 1953), 18.
4. Norman Friedman, *British Destroyers: From the Earliest Days to the Second World War* (Annapolis, MD: Naval Institute Press, 2009), 9–10.
5. Fabio De Ninno, "A Technological Fiasco: Scientific Research, Institutional Culture, and Fascism in the Italian Navy (1919–1940)," *The Journal of Military History* 84 (July 2020): 815.
6. R. W. Home and Morris F. Low, "Postwar Scientific Intelligence Missions to Japan," *Isis* 84, no. 3 (September 1993): 529.

CHAPTER 2. MINES

1. Arnold S. Lott, *Most Dangerous Sea: A History of Mine Warfare, and an Account of U.S. Navy Mine Warfare Operations in World War II and Korea* (Annapolis, MD: Naval Institute Press, 1959), 10.
2. Ralph D. Sawyer, with Mei-Chun Lee Sawyer, *Fire and Water: The Art of Incendiary and Aquatic Warfare in China* (Boulder, CO: Westview Press, 2004), 93.
3. Roger Branfill-Cook, *Torpedo: The Complete History of the World's Most Revolutionary Naval Weapon* (Barnsley, UK: Seaforth, 2014), 18–24.
4. Gregory K. Hartmann, with Scott C. Truver, *Weapons That Wait: Mine Warfare in the U.S. Navy* (Annapolis, MD: Naval Institute Press, 1991), 33. See also Robert M. Browning Jr., "Damn the Torpedoes," *Naval History* 28, no. 4 (July 2014).
5. See H. Taprell Dorling, *Swept Channels: Being an Account of the Work of the Minesweepers in the Great War* (London: Hodder and Stoughton, 1935), 27–31.
6. This section is based on Hartmann; Lott; Dorling; and Jim Crossley, *The Hidden Threat: The Story of Mines and Minesweeping by the Royal Navy in World War I* (Barnsley, UK: Pen & Sword Maritime, 2011). For harbor defense see Dion Williams, "The Defense of Our Naval Stations," U.S. Naval Institute *Proceedings* 28, no. 2 (June 1902): 181–94.

7. Historical Section, Committee of Imperial Defence, *Official History (Naval and Military) of the Russo-Japanese War* (London: Harrison and Sons and His Majesty's Stationery Office, 1910–20), vol. 1:57–59.

8. Historical Section, 1:62.

9. Norman Friedman, *U.S. Naval Weapons* (London: Conway Maritime Press, 1983), 381.

10. Historical Section, 1:65.

11. Historical Section, 1:93.

12. See Stephen McLaughlin, *Russian and Soviet Battleships* (Annapolis, MD: Naval Institute Press, 2003), 170. *Navarin* was already heavily damaged, down by the bow, and barely had headway.

13. Lott, 62; Anonymous, "Minesweeping," *The International Military Digest Annual* (New York: Cumulative Digest Corporation, 1917), 464–67.

14. Philip R. Alger, "The Employment of Submarine Mines in Future Naval Wars," U.S. Naval Institute *Proceedings* 34, no. 3 (September 1908): 1040.

15. Historical Section, 1:402.

16. "Laying of Automatic Submarine Contact Mines," Article VIII, convention signed at the Hague, 18 October 1907, https://www.loc.gov/law/help/us-treaties/bevans/m-ust000001-0669.pdf; Hartmann, 41.

17. René Greger, *The Russian Fleet, 1914–1917* (Shepperton, UK: Ian Allen, 1972), 11–12; Friedman, *U.S. Naval Weapons*, 383; Robert Gardiner, ed., *Conway's All the World's Fighting Ships, 1860–1905* (London: Conway Maritime Press, 1979), 209–10; quote, Lawrence Sondhaus, *German Submarine Warfare in World War I: The Onset of Total War at Sea* (Lanham, MD: Rowman and Littlefield, 2017), 48.

18. Hans J. Koerver, ed., *Room 40: German Naval Warfare, 1914–1918*, vol. 1, *The Fleet in Action* (Berlin: Schaltungsdienst Lange o.H.G., 2009), 274–75; Norman Friedman, *Fighting the Great War at Sea* (Annapolis, MD: Naval Institute Press, 2014), 337–38, 350.

19. David K. Brown, *The Grand Fleet: Warship Design and Development 1906–1922* (Annapolis, MD: Naval Institute Press, 1999), 136; Friedman, *U.S. Naval Weapons*, 364; Friedman, *Fighting the Great War at Sea*, 336; quote, Anonymous, "Lament for the Mine II," *Naval Review* 48, no. 4 (1964): 381.

20. Vincent P. O'Hara, W. David Dickson, and Richard Worth, eds., *To Crown the Waves: The Great Navies of the First World War* (Annapolis, MD: Naval Institute Press, 2013), 74; Friedman, *U.S. Naval Weapons*, 378.

21. O'Hara, Dickson, and Worth, *To Crown the Waves*, 35–36, 201.

22. Koerver, 274–75; James Goldrick, *Before Jutland: The Naval War in Northern European Waters, August 1914–February 1915* (Annapolis, MD: Naval Institute Press, 2015), 34.

23. Otto Groos and Walter Gladisch, *Der Krieg in der Nordsee*, 7 vols. (Berlin, Frankfurt, and Hamburg: E. S. Mittler, 1920–2006), 1:36, 133.

24. Arthur J. Marder, *From the Dreadnought to Scapa Flow*, 5 vols. (Annapolis, MD: Naval Institute Press, 2013 reprint), 2:80.

25. Goldrick, *Before Jutland*, 153.

26. Norman Friedman, *Naval Weapons of World War One: Guns, Torpedoes, and Mines of all Nations, an Illustrated Directory* (Barnsley, UK: Seaforth, 2011), 363; Marder, *From the Dreadnought to Scapa Flow*, 2:70.

27. Marder, *From the Dreadnought to Scapa Flow*, 2:245, and Julian S. Corbett and Henry Newbolt, *Naval Operations: History of the Great War Based on Official Documents*, 5 vols. (London: Longmans, Green, 1920–31), 2:140–229, provide a good overview of the Dardanelles campaign.

28. Vincent P. O'Hara and Leonard R. Heinz, *Clash of Fleets: Naval Battles of the Great War, 1914–18* (Annapolis, MD: Naval Institute Press, 2017), 126–27.

29. Greger, 18–19, 34.

30. Eberhard Rössler, *The U-Boat: The Evolution and Technical History of German Submarines* (Annapolis, MD: Naval Institute Press, 1981), 40; A. Thomazi, *La Guerre navale dans la Zone des Armées du Nord* (Paris: Payot, 1925), 83–84; quote, Dorling, 109.

31. Friedman, *U.S. Naval Weapons*, 363.

32. James Goldrick, *After Jutland: The Naval War in Northern European Waters, June 1916–November 1918* (Annapolis, MD: Naval Institute Press, 2018), 278.

33. See Paul G. Halpern, *The Battle of the Otranto Straits: Controlling the Gateway to the Adriatic in World War I* (Bloomington: Indiana University Press, 2004), for a good study.

34. Paul G. Halpern, *A Naval History of World War I* (Annapolis, MD: Naval Institute Press, 1994), 211–12, 344; Goldrick, *After Jutland*, 174; Friedman, *Fighting the Great War at Sea*, 341.

35. See O'Hara and Heinz, 235–42.

36. Dorling, 33; Friedman, *Fighting the Great War at Sea*, 346–47; Lott, 63–65; O'Hara, Dickson, and Worth, *To Crown the Waves*, 202.

37. Friedman, *Fighting the Great War at Sea*, 346.

38. Dorling, 110.

39. Dorling, 118.

40. Hartmann, 63.

41. P. E. Jenkins, "German Mines," *Journal of Naval Science* 6, no. 2 (April 1980): 107.

42. Lott, 17.

43. Anonymous, "Lament for the Mine I," *Naval Review* 48, no. 3 (1964): 282.

44. Hartmann, 60, 66.

45. Ufficio Storico della Marina Militare, *La Marina Italiana nella Seconda Guerra Mondiale*, vol. 18, *La Guerra di Mine* (Rome: Ministero della Difesa, 1988), 18:14–16; Erminio Bagnasco, *Le armi delle navi Italiane nella Seconda Guerra Mondiale* (Parma: Albertelli, 2007), 113–19.

46. Ufficio Storico, 18:38.

47. See Vincent P. O'Hara, *Six Victories: North Africa, Malta, and the Mediterranean Convoy War, November 1941–March 1942* (Annapolis, MD: Naval Institute Press, 2019), 127–29.

48. V. I. Achkasov and N. B. Pavlovich, *Soviet Naval Operations in the Great Patriotic War, 1941–1945* (Annapolis, MD: Naval Institute Press, 1981), 46.

49. Poul Grooss, *The Naval War in the Baltic, 1939–1945* (Barnsley, UK: Seaforth, 2017), 349–51; John Campbell, *Naval Weapons of World War Two* (Annapolis, MD: Naval Institute Press, 1985), 269.

50. Samuel Eliot Morison, *History of United States Naval Operations in World War II*, 14 vols. (Boston: Little Brown, 1947–85), 14:113.

51. Vincent P. O'Hara, W. David Dickson, and Richard Worth, eds., *On Seas Contested: The Seven Great Navies of the Second World War* (Annapolis, MD: Naval Institute Press, 2010), 193.

52. U.S. Strategic Bombing Survey, *Interrogations of Japanese Officials*, interrogation of Captain Kyuzo Tamura, 8 November 1945, 267.

53. Hartmann, 65; S. W. Roskill, *The War at Sea, 1939–1945*, 3 vols. (London: Her Majesty's Stationery Office, 1954–61), 1:100–2. Also, Geirr Haarr, *The Gathering Storm: The Naval War in Northern Europe, September 1939–April 1940* (Annapolis, MD: Naval Institute Press, 2013), 266–67.

54. Militärgeschichtliches Forschungsamt, ed., *Germany and the Second World War*, 6 vols. (Oxford: Oxford University Press, 2015), 2:174–75; *Fuehrer Conferences on Naval Affairs, 1939–1945* (London: Chatham, 2005), 57. Haarr, *The Gathering Storm*, 266, says sixty-nine mines.

55. John T. Mason Jr., *The Atlantic War Remembered: An Oral History Collection* (Annapolis, MD: Naval Institute Press, 1990), 43–44.

56. Lott, 68.

57. U.S. Navy, Bureau of Ordnance, OP 1673A, "German Underwater Ordnance-Mines," 14 June 1946, 3.

58. Jenkins, 111. The Japanese followed a similar practice in tolerating a bitter army/navy rivalry.

59. U.S. Navy, Office of Naval Intelligence (ONI), *Fuehrer Conferences on Matters Dealing with the German Navy*, 5 vols. (Washington, DC: ONI, 1941–45), 4:18.

60. U.S. Navy, ONI, *War Diary, German Naval Staff Operations Division*, June 1944, 76–77, 260.

61. Morison, 11:46–47, 173; Roskill, *The War at Sea*, 3/2:69, 122.

62. For this campaign, see Hartmann, 73; Lott, 223–27; U.S. Strategic Bombing Survey, 267.

63. Sherman quote: Norman Polmar et al., *Chronology of the Cold War at Sea, 1945–1991* (Annapolis, MD: Naval Institute Press, 1998), 27; Frank Uhlig, *How Navies Fight: The U.S. Navy and Its Allies* (Annapolis, MD: Naval Institute Press, 1994), 298–99.

64. Edward J. Marolda, "U.S. Mining and Mine Clearance in North Vietnam," https://www.history.navy.mil/research/library/online-reading-room/title-list-alphabetically/u/u-s-mining-and-mine-clearance-in-north-vietnam.html; Polmar et al., 142.

65. See Vincent P. O'Hara and Enrico Cernuschi, "Frogmen against a Fleet," *Naval War College Review* 68, no. 3 (Summer 2015): 119–37.

66. U.S. Navy, OP 1673A, 11.

67. Hal M. Friedman, *Digesting History: The U.S. Naval War College, the Lessons of World War II, and Future Naval Warfare* (Washington, DC: Government Printing Office, 2010), 182.

68. Brian Lavery, *Churchill's Navy: The Ships, Men, and Organisation, 1939–1945* (London: Conway, 2006), 350.

CHAPTER 3. TORPEDOES

1. Branfill-Cook, 39; Edwyn Gray, *The Devil's Device: Robert Whitehead and the History of the Torpedo*, rev. ed. (Annapolis, MD: Naval Institute Press, 1991), 53–59; W. J. Sears, "A General Description of the Whitehead Torpedo," U.S. Naval Institute *Proceedings* 22, no. 4 (October 1896): 803–38.

2. Gray, *The Devil's Device*, 46–49; Branfill-Cook, 236; Sears, 803.

3. Gray, *The Devil's Device*, 86, 93, 101.

4. Brian Ranft, ed., *Technical Change and British Naval Policy, 1860–1939* (London: Hodder and Stoughton, 1977), 24, 25.

5. David K. Brown, *Warrior to Dreadnought: Warship Development 1860–1905* (London: Chatham, 1997), 83–86, 115–17; Gardiner, *Fighting Ships, 1860–1905*, 47, 86–88, 101; Gray, *The Devil's Device*, 144; Ranft, 29–30; Murray F. Sueter, *The Evolution of the Submarine Boat Mine and Torpedo from the Sixteenth Century until the Present Time*, 2nd ed. (Portsmouth, UK: Gieve, Matthews, and Seagrove, n.d.), 297–98.

6. Brown, *Warrior to Dreadnought*, 83; Gardiner, *Fighting Ships, 1860–1905*, 26; Sueter, 297–98.

7. Herbert W. Wilson, *Battleships in Action*, 2 vols. (Annapolis, MD: Naval Institute Press, 1995 reprint), 1:65–66; Jack Greene and Alessandro Massignani, *Ironclads at War* (Conshohocken, PA: Combined Publishing, 1998), 290.

8. Branfill-Cook, 171; Gray, *The Devil's Device*, 113–14; Sueter, 316; Ranft, 27; Arthur Burke, *Torpedoes and Their Impact on Naval Warfare* (Newport, RI: Naval Undersea Warfare Center, 2017), 50.

9. Branfill-Cook, 53.

10. Greene and Massignani, 310.

11. Branfill-Cook, 173; Gardiner, *Fighting Ships, 1860–1905*, 407, 409; Wilson, *Battleships*, 1:88–89, 84.

12. T. A. Brassey, ed., *The Naval Annual 1895* (Portsmouth, UK: J. Griffin and Co., 1895), 102, 108, 112–14, 143; David C. Evans and Mark R. Peattie, *Kaigun: Strategy, Tactics, and Technology in the Imperial Japanese Navy 1887–1941* (Annapolis, MD: Naval Institute Press, 2015), 37.

13. Gray, *The Devil's Device*, 150–51; Gardiner, *Fighting Ships, 1860–1905*, 395–99; Sueter, 316–18; Wilson, *Battleships*, 1:109–10.

14. Evans and Peattie, 49.

15. Brown, *The Grand Fleet*, 21; Brown, *Warrior to Dreadnought*, 137–38, 183; Gardiner, *Fighting Ships, 1860–1905*, 206–7; Hansgeorg Jentschura, Dieter Jung, and Peter Mickel, *Warships of the Imperial Japanese Navy, 1869–1945* (Annapolis, MD: Naval Institute Press, 1999), 130–31; Sueter, 326.

16. J. H. Sypher, "Notes on the Obrey Device for Torpedoes," U.S. Naval Institute *Proceedings* 23, no. 4 (October 1897): 661.

17. L. H. Chandler, "Automobile Torpedoes: Their Use and Probable Effectiveness," U.S. Naval Institute *Proceedings* 29, no. 4 (September 1903): 887; Sueter, 306.

18. Evans and Peattie, 92, 553–54 n105; Friedman, *Naval Weapons of World War One*, 349.

19. Torpedo fire control requires the solution of a triangle composed of the line of sight to the target, the target's track relative to the line of sight, and the track of the torpedo. The triangle can be solved if the target track, target speed, and torpedo speed are known. With the triangle solved, range is only relevant to confirm that the torpedo will reach the target before exhausting its fuel. Thomas Wildenberg and Norman Polmar, *Ship Killers: A History of the American Torpedo* (Annapolis, MD: Naval Institute Press, 2010), 197.

20. Julian S. Corbett, *Maritime Operations of the Russo-Japanese War 1904–1905*, 2 vols. (Annapolis, MD, and Newport, RI: Naval Institute Press and Naval War College Press, 1994 reprint), 1:99.

21. Corbett, 1:93–101.

22. Corbett, 1:307–9; Historical Section, 1:296–98; McLaughlin, *Russian and Soviet Battleships*, 162.

23. Corbett, 1:405–13; Historical Section, 1:346.

24. Corbett, 2:105–26; Historical Section, 2:628–36.

25. Corbett, 2:294–311; Historical Section, 3:769–77.

26. Historical Section, 1:404, 3:806.

27. T. A. Brassey, ed., *The Naval Annual 1905* (Portsmouth, UK: J. Griffin and Co., 1905), 117–19, 145, 155, 167–68. For a similar view by a U.S. Navy admiral, see Wildenberg and Polmar, 32.

28. Sueter, 319, 321.

29. Eric LaCroix and Linton Wells II, *Japanese Cruisers of the Pacific War* (Annapolis, MD: Naval Institute Press, 1997), 778; Sueter, 312, 322. Gray (*The Devil's Device*, 167) says that "few [Japanese] torpedoes were fitted with gyroscopes" but cites no source for this. LaCroix and Wells write that the Japanese navy first adopted gyro-equipped torpedoes in 1897.

30. Sueter, 322.

31. Corbett, 1:100–1, 307–9, 413, 2:310.

32. Gray, *The Devil's Device*, 179; Wildenberg and Polmar, 31–32, 34–35.

33. John Brooks, *Dreadnought Gunnery and the Battle of Jutland: The Question of Fire Control* (London: Routledge, 2005), 68–70; John Jellicoe, *The Grand Fleet, 1914–1916: Its Creation, Development, and Work* (New York: George H. Doran CO., 1919), 51; O'Hara, Dickson, and Worth, *To Crown the Waves*, 24, 194; Vittorio Cuniberti, "All Torpedoes!," trans. Thomas Withers Jr., U.S. Naval Institute *Proceedings* 40, no. 1 (January 1914): 27–31.

34. Jellicoe, *Grand Fleet,* 392–95; Anonymous, "The Influence of the Long-Range Torpedo on Battle Tactics," *Naval Review* 3, no. 1 (1915): 58; Anonymous, "Notes on Fleet

Tactics," *Naval Review* 10, no. 1 (1922): 46; Yates Stirling Jr., "The Destroyer—Our Naval Weakness," U.S. Naval Institute *Proceedings* 36, no. 2 (June 1910): 477–79.

35. Marder, *From the Dreadnought to Scapa Flow*, 5:110; Gray, *The Devil's Device*, 188.

36. Campbell, *Naval Weapons*, 81, 84; Evans and Peattie, 266; Wildenberg and Polmar, 123.

37. Branfill-Cook, 56; Campbell, 202–3; Evans and Peattie, 267; LaCroix and Wells, 780.

38. Branfill-Cook, 64; O'Hara, Dickson, and Worth, *On Seas Contested*, 25; Friedman, *Naval Weapons of World War One*, 328, 330, 336–37.

39. Geoffrey Till, *Air Power and the Royal Navy, 1914–1945: A Historical Survey* (London: Jane's, 1979), 142–43.

40. Branfill-Cook, 64; Enrico Cernuschi and Vincent P. O'Hara, "Search for a Flattop: The Italian Navy and the Aircraft Carrier 1907–2007," *Warship 2007* (2007): 68, 70–72.

41. Campbell, 204; Mark R. Peattie, *Sunburst: The Rise of Japanese Naval Air Power, 1909–1941* (Annapolis, MD: Naval Institute Press, 2001), 34–39, 141–44; Wildenberg and Polmar, 82.

42. Branfill-Cook, 64; Campbell, 262, 266; Chris Goss, *Sea Eagles: Luftwaffe Anti-Shipping Units 1939–41* (London: Classic Publications, 2005), 2, 16, 49.

43. National Archives and Records Administration (NARA), USS *Yorktown*, "Report of Action of *Yorktown* and *Yorktown* Air Group on May 8, 1942," 25 May 1942, 27.

44. Branfill-Cook, 64–68; E. W. Jolie, *A Brief History of U.S. Navy Torpedo Development* (Newport, RI: Naval Underwater Systems Center, 1978), 33–34; Buford Rowland and William B. Boyd, *U.S. Navy Bureau of Ordnance in World War II* (Washington, DC: U.S. Government Printing Office, n.d.), 119–24; Wildenberg and Polmar, 71–89.

45. Anthony Newpower, *Iron Men and Tin Fish: The Race to Build a Better Torpedo during World War II* (Annapolis, MD: Naval Institute Press, 2006), 32.

46. Newpower, 30, 35.

47. Archivo dell'Ufficio Storico della Marina Militare, Regia Marina, Marisub Taranto, "Siluro inglese per aerosiluanti," 2 January 1941; Branfill-Cook, 58; Campbell, 81, 83; Hervé Coutain-Bégarie and Claude Huan, *Mers el-Kébir (1940)—La rupture franco-britannique* (Paris: Economica, 1994), 156.

48. Clay Blair, *Hitler's U-Boat War*, vol. 1, *The Hunters, 1939–1942* (New York: Random House, 1996), 1:159. Also, Gray, *The Devil's Device*, 222–23; Peter Padfield, *War beneath the Sea: Submarine Conflict during World War II* (New York: John Wiley and Sons, 1995), 58, 66–67, 81–84; Newpower, 45, 53.

49. Rowland and Boyd, 96–109; Wildenberg and Polmar, 102–13; Victor S. Alpher, "Torpedo Exploder Mechanisms of World War II: A New Perspective," *The Submarine Review* (April 2010): 83–105. For a complete history of these defects and the struggle to identify and cure them, see Newpower.

50. Ufficio Storico della Marina Militare, *La Marina Italiana nella Seconda Guerra Mondiale*, vol. 13, *I sommergibili in Mediterraneo dal 10 giugno 1940 al 31 dicembre, 1941* (Rome:

Ministero della Difesa, 1972), 31; Branfill-Cook, 59; Campbell, 204, 348; Wildenberg and Polmar, 66.

51. Newpower, 156, 176.

52. Vincent P. O'Hara, *The U.S. Navy against the Axis: Surface Combat, 1941–1945* (Annapolis, MD: Naval Institute Press, 2007), 39–44 for Java Sea and 126–27 for torpedoes against battleships.

53. United States Fleet, *Battle Experiences*, Information Bulletin No. 5 (April 15, 1943), chap. 31, 10.

54. Norman Friedman, "A Massive Torpedo," *Naval History* 33, no. 2 (April 2019): 6–7. The salvaged destroyer (*Kikazuki*) had 24-inch torpedo tubes but lacked the special facilities needed to handle the oxygen-propelled Type 93.

55. Branfill-Cook, 62; Campbell, 81, 264; Morison, 10:138–39.

56. Julius Augustus Furer, *Administration of the Navy Department in World War II* (Washington, DC: Government Printing Office, 1959), 793–95; W. J. R. Gardner, *Decoding History: The Battle of the Atlantic and Ultra* (Annapolis, MD: Naval Institute Press, 1999), 99n27.

57. Wildenberg and Polmar, 140–45.

CHAPTER 4. RADIO

1. United States Fleet, *Battle Experience*, Information Bulletin No. 5, chap. 31, 12.

2. Arthur Hezlet, *Electronics and Sea Power* (New York: Stein and Day, 1975), 31–32.

3. L. S. Howeth, *History of Communications-Electronics in the United States Navy* (Washington, DC: Office of Naval History, 1963), 20, 42, 44–45, 55, 148.

4. Daniel R. Headrick, *The Invisible Weapon: Telecommunications and International Politics, 1851–1945* (Oxford: Oxford University Press, 1991), 118, 123; Howeth, xii, 22, 32, 54–55; Hezlet, *Electronics*, 34, 41–43, 74; O'Hara, Dickson, and Worth, *To Crown the Waves*, 14, 60; Raymond C. Watson, *Radar Origins Worldwide: History of Its Evolution in 13 Nations through World War II* (Victoria, BC: Trafford, 2009), 278.

5. A. Frederick Collins, "A Review of Wireless-Telegraph Engineering Practice," *Engineering Magazine* 24 (October 1902–March 1903): 231.

6. Robert P. Bigelow, "Wireless in Warfare, 1885–1914," U.S. Naval Institute *Proceedings* 77, no. 2 (February 1951): 119.

7. Historical Section, 1:90; Corbett, 1:90, 128, 239, 300–1.

8. Historical Section, 1:154, 293; Corbett, 1:11, 148, 181, 372.

9. Historical Section, 1:371–74; Corbett, 1:283–90.

10. Corbett, 1:288.

11. Historical Section, 3:749, 752; Corbett, 2:216, 222–23, 231, 1:427.

12. Historical Section, 1:383–90; Corbett, 1:427, 434–47.

13. Corbett, 2:14–15; M. Kinai, *The Russo-Japanese War (Official Reports)*, 2 vols. (Tokyo: The Shimbashido, 1905–7), 2:14–15.

14. Hezlet, *Electronics*, 47.

15. Historical Section, 3:749.

16. Headrick, 125–32; Howeth, 202, 254; Bigelow, 122.

17. Goldrick, *Before Jutland*, 49; Friedman, *Fighting the Great War at Sea*, 90–91; Howeth, 182; Andrew Gordon, *The Rules of the Game: Jutland and British Naval Command* (Annapolis, MD: Naval Institute Press, 1996), 584.

18. Hezlet, *Electronics*, 61–62.

19. Bigelow, 124.

20. Patrick Beesly, *Room 40: Naval Intelligence 1914–18* (New York: Harcourt Brace Jovanovich, 1982), 21–23; Friedman, *Fighting the Great War at Sea*, 90n39.

21. Friedman, *Fighting the Great War at Sea*, 93; Michael Palmer, *Command at Sea* (Cambridge, MA: Harvard University Press, 2005), 233–53; Headrick, 157, 164–65; Howeth, 167, 202; TNA, ADM 189/33, HMS *Vernon* Annual Report 1913, Wireless Telegraphy Appendix, 22; Hezlet, *Electronics*, 74; O'Hara, Dickson, and Worth, *To Crown the Waves*, 15, 185, 220.

22. Hezlet, *Electronics*, 84; Bigelow, 122.

23. Friedman, *Fighting the Great War at Sea*, 64–79, 88–89; John Keegan, *Intelligence in War: Knowledge of the Enemy from Napoleon to Al-Qaeda* (New York: Alfred A. Knopf, 2003), 118–26; Halpern, *A Naval History of World War I*, 95–96; Admiralty, Great Britain, *Naval Staff Monographs (Historical)*, 19 vols., 1920–39, 1:158–65, 173; Beesly, 78.

24. Keegan, 126–27; Halpern, *A Naval History of World War I*, 74–76; O'Hara and Heinz, 87–88.

25. John Brooks, *The Battle of Jutland* (Cambridge, UK: Cambridge University Press, 2016), 140.

26. TNA, ADM 116/1341, "Grand Fleet Battle Orders," December 1915, 38–39; Brooks, *The Battle of Jutland*, 271–78, 487.

27. Brooks, *The Battle of Jutland*, 487; Goldrick, *Before Jutland*, 219.

28. Brooks, *The Battle of Jutland*, 362–63, 386, 405, 407–8; Goldrick, *Before Jutland*, 219; TNA, ADM 116/1341, 38–39, 45.

29. Brooks, *The Battle of Jutland*, 480–81; TNA, ADM 116/1341, 13, 17, 27; Admiralty, Great Britain, *Battle of Jutland: 30th May to 1st June 1916, Official Dispatches* (London: His Majesty's Stationery Office, 1920), 457–70. The times for this analysis and in the paragraph following are 1801–2100 31 May.

30. Brooks, *The Battle of Jutland*, 62–63, 296, 479, 482; Palmer, 248; Groos and Gladisch, 5:529–33. Unlike the published British signal log, the German log records only the most important (*wichtigsten*) signals. The authors have assumed that all signals from Scheer to major formations fall into this category.

31. Lawrence Sondhaus, *The Great War at Sea: A Naval History of the First World War* (Cambridge: Cambridge University Press, 2014), 245–46; Headrick, 164; Corbett and Newbolt, 5:278–81; Halpern, *A Naval History of World War I*, 427.

32. Headrick, 165; Friedman, *Fighting the Great War at Sea*, 147, 263.

33. Howeth, 210, 261; Friedman, *Fighting the Great War at Sea*, 121; Headrick, 157–59; Beesly, 59, 69–70, 254n1; Halpern, *A Naval History of World War I*, 400; Guy Hartcup,

The War of Invention: Scientific Development, 1914–1918 (London: Brassey's Defence Publishers, 1988), 124–25; Stephen McLaughlin, "Russian Naval Radio Intelligence in the First World War," Presentation, USS *Midway* Museum, San Diego, California, February 29, 2020, 5; Nikolaus A. Sifferlinger, "Austro-Hungarian and British Radio Intelligence," *Maritimes*, 31 March 2013, http://maritimes.at/en/2013/no-article-yet-2/. The accuracy numbers are an estimate based on World War II direction-finding performance. Beesly, 254n1.

34. Ivo Juurvee, "The Birth of Russian SIGINT during World War I on the Baltic Sea," *Intelligence and National Security* 32, no. 3 (February 2017): 302.

35. Keith W. Bird and Jason Hines, "In the Shadow of Ultra: A Reappraisal of German Naval Communications Intelligence in 1914–1918," *The Northern Mariner* 18, no. 2 (Spring 2018): 111. Also, National Security Agency, "The Origination and Evolution of Radio Traffic Analysis," *Cryptologic Quarterly* 6, no. 1 (Spring 1987): 23–24.

36. There is an extensive literature on the *Magdeburg* incident. A good place to start is David Kahn, "The Wreck of the *Magdeburg*," *Military History Quarterly* 2, no. 2 (1990): 97–103. SKM was replaced by the Flottenfunkspruchbuch (FFB).

37. Bird and Hines, 111, 115; Beesly, 123; Juurvee, 302.

38. Beesly, 49–53; O'Hara and Heinz, 53–59.

39. O'Hara and Heinz, 189–90.

40. Jason Hines, "Sins of Omission and Commission: A Reassessment of the Role of Intelligence in the Battle of Jutland," *The Journal of Military History* 72, no. 4 (October 2008): 1124.

41. Bird and Hines, 111–12. Quote: David Kahn, *The Codebreakers: The Story of Secret Writing* (New York: MacMillan, 1967), 277.

42. Juurvee, 302.

43. Mario De Arcangelis, *Electronic Warfare: From the Battle of Tsushima to the Falklands and Lebanon Conflicts* (Pool, UK: Blandford Press, 1985), 19; Friedman, *Fighting the Great War at Sea*, 96–97; Beesly, 95–96, 178, 181, 264; McLaughlin, "Radio Intelligence," 6–7; O'Hara, Dickson, and Worth, *To Crown the Waves*, 221–22.

44. Juurvee, 302.

45. O'Hara, Dickson, and Worth, *To Crown the Waves*, 186–87; Friedman, *Fighting the Great War at Sea*, 123, 263; Beesly, 30–31, 165–66, 274–77, 283–84. The Germans mounted two sorties to attack the Lerwick convoys. The British got forewarning of one, but not of its target.

46. Sifferlinger.

47. Howeth, 330–31; Headrick, 174, 180, 202–3.

48. Hezlet, *Electronics*, 66, 71; Watson, 24; Bigelow, 118.

49. Louis A. Gebhard, *Evolution of Naval Radio-Electronics and Contributions of the Naval Research Laboratory* (Washington, DC: Naval Research Laboratory, 1979), 96–99.

50. Howeth, 254.

51. See discussion in Alan Raven, *British Cruiser Warfare: The Lessons of the Early War, 1939–1941* (Annapolis, MD: Naval Institute Press, 2019), 248.

52. See the discussion in O'Hara, *Six Victories*, chapter two, and Vincent P. O'Hara and Enrico Cernuschi, "The Other Ultra," *Naval War College Review* 66, no. 3 (Summer 2013): 121–42, for Italian countermeasures.

53. R. A. Ratcliff, *Delusions of Intelligence: Enigma, Ultra, and the End of Secure Ciphers* (New York: Cambridge University Press, 2006), 138–39.

54. John Prados, *Combined Fleet Decoded: The Secret History of American Intelligence and the Japanese Navy in World War II* (New York: Random House, 1995),68–73; Gardner, 105, 124–28, 136–38; Keegan, 235–40, 248–49; O'Hara, Dickson, and Worth, *On Seas Contested*, 131, 172–73; Evans and Peattie, 420.

55. Kathleen Broome Williams, *Secret Weapon: U.S. High-Frequency Direction Finding in the Battle of the Atlantic* (Annapolis, MD: Naval Institute Press, 1996), 26, 37–38.

56. Derek Howse, *Radar at Sea: The Royal Navy in World War 2* (Annapolis, MD: Naval Institute Press, 1993),146; Williams, *Secret Weapon*, 90.

57. Williams, *Secret Weapon*, 178–79.

58. Williams, *Secret Weapon*, 40, 44–45, 48, 53, 200; Hezlet, *Electronics*, 229–30; Stephen Howarth and Derek Law, eds. *The Battle of the Atlantic, 1939–1945: The 50th Anniversary International Naval Conference* (Annapolis, MD: Naval Institute Press, 1994), 438; U.S. Navy, Office of Chief of Naval Operations, 20th Division of the Office of Naval Communications, G Section, *Battle of the Atlantic*, 4 vols. (Washington, DC: Department of the Navy, n.d.), 4:66–73; Government Code and Cypher School (GC&CS), Naval History, *The German Navy: Communications*, vol. 6 of 24, record group 38, box 99, 6:7–8; Raven, 273.

59. De Ninno, "A Technological Fiasco," 818; Ufficio Storico della Marina Militare, *Marina Italiana*, vol. 21, *L'Organizzazione della Marina durante il Conflitto*, 2 parts (Rome: Ministero della Difesa, 1972), 21/1:166; United States Armed Forces Far East History Division, *Operational History of Naval Communications*, Japanese Monographs, Series 118 (Washington, DC: U.S. Army, 1951), 265; NARA, GC&CS, 6:7.

60. See O'Hara, *The U.S. Navy against the Axis*, 90–91. "Roger" was a code word for "open fire" when broadcast without qualification, under the then-current signal codes.

61. United States Fleet, *Battle Experience*, Information Bulletin No. 4 (March 25, 1943), chap. 28, 72.

62. TNA, ADM 1/12248, "Reports of Proceedings, HMS *Talybont* and HMS *Wensleydale*," 24 October 1943. Also see Michael J. Whitby, "Shoot, Shoot, Shoot: Destroyer Night Fighting and the Battle of Ile de Batz," in *Fighting at Sea: Naval Battles from the Ages of Sail and Steam*, ed. Douglas M. McLean (Quebec: Robin Bass Studio, 2008), 183–238, for examples.

63. See Martin J. Bollinger, *Warriors and Wizards: The Deployment and Defeat of Radio-Controlled Glide Bombs of the Third Reich* (Annapolis, MD: Naval Institute Press, 2010), for details of these attacks.

64. Sandy Woodward and Patrick Robinson, *One Hundred Days: The Memoirs of the Falklands Battle Group Commander* (Annapolis, MD: Naval Institute Press, 1997), 120.

65. Gordon, 92. For an extended discussion of the perils of signaling, see Gordon, 583–93.

CHAPTER 5. RADAR

1. Alan Beyerchen, "From Radio to Radar," in *Military Innovation in the Interwar Period*, ed. Williamson Murray and Allan R. Millett (Cambridge, UK: Cambridge University Press, 1996).

2. Watson, 29.

3. Till, 120.

4. Robert Buderi, *The Invention That Changed the World: How a Small Group of Radar Pioneers Won the Second World War and Launched a Technological Revolution* (New York: Touchstone, 1996), 143.

5. Murray and Millett, 267, 280; Sean S. Swords, *Technical History of the Beginnings of Radar* (London: Peregrinus, 1986), 47; David K. Allison, *New Eye for the Navy: The Origin of Radar at the Naval Research Laboratory* (Washington, DC: Naval Research Laboratory, 1981), 39–40. See chapter six and the story of the Walter submarine for a parallel example.

6. Norman Friedman, *Naval Radar* (London: Conway Maritime Press, 1981), 29–32; Howse, 41.

7. Marcel Baudot, ed., *The Historical Encyclopedia of World War II* (New York: Facts on File, 1980), 406; Craig M. Payne, *Principles of Naval Weapon Systems* (Annapolis, MD: Naval Institute Press, 2006), 5.

8. Howse, 67, 71; I. C. B. Deer and M. R. D. Foot, *The Oxford Companion to the Second World War* (Oxford: Oxford University Press, 1998), 199; Buderi, 88–89; Watson, 146, 164.

9. Alan Cook, "Shipborne Radar in World War II: Some Recollections," *Note and Records of the Royal Society of London* 58, no. 3 (September 2004): 295–96.

10. Southwest Museum of Engineering, Communication, and Computation, "Morgan McMahon and Radar," https://www.smecc.org/mcmahon's_radars!.htm.

11. Alfred Price, *Instruments of Darkness: The History of Electronic Warfare* (New York: Scribners, 1978), 59; D. E. Graves, German Navy Research Report G3, "German Navy Radar Equipment, 1934–1935: Overview and Descriptive Catalogue" (Ottawa: Canadian Department of Defence, December 1990), 1–2.

12. Price, 136; Murray and Millett, 270; Erwin Sieche, "German Naval Radar to 1945," *Warship* 6, no. 21 (1982): 2–10, and *Warship* 6, no. 22 (1982): 146–57.

13. Parliamentary Debate, Commons, 10 November 1932 (270) col. 632, Lord President of the Council Mr. Stanley Baldwin.

14. Walter Kaiser, "British Radar Technology and Neville Chamberlain's Appeasement Policy," *Icon* 2 (1996): 38.

15. Murray and Millett, 287.

16. Buderi, 66; Hezlet, *Electronics*, 172–73; Watson, 258.

17. Allison, 61–63, 82–83.

18. Swords, 110.

19. Watson, 212.

20. Ufficio Storico, *Marina Italiana*, 21/1:165; Hezlet, *Electronics*, 171.

21. Ufficio Storico, *Marina Italiana*, 21/1:169; also see Watson, 343–44.

22. Evans and Peattie, 411–13; LaCroix and Wells, 773–74.

23. Watson, 317.

24. Allison, 141.

25. See U.S. Navy, ONI, *War Diary*, 28 November, 3 December, 18 December 1939; Andrew Thomas, *Defiant, Blenheim, and Havoc Aces* (Long Island City, NY: Osprey, 2012), 9; also Martin Middlebrook and Chris Everitt, *The Bomber Command War Diaries: An Operational Reference Book, 1939–1945* (Barnsley, UK: Pen & Sword Aviation, 2014), for the dates mentioned.

26. Bruce Loxton with Chris Coulthard-Clark, *The Shame of Savo: Anatomy of a Naval Disaster* (Annapolis, MD: Naval Institute Press, 1994), 284n8.

27. United States Fleet, *Battle Experience*, Information Bulletin No. 2 (March 1, 1943), chap. 10, 7.

28. George C. Dyer, *The Amphibians Came to Conquer: The Story of Admiral Richmond Kelly Turner* (Washington, DC: Department of the Navy, 1972), 1:380.

29. Loxton, 63–64.

30. U.S. Navy, *Radar Bulletin No. 1: The Tactical Use of Radar*, 1942, https://www.ibiblio.org/hyperwar/USN/ref/RADONE/index.html#VII.

31. Authors who attribute the ship's accuracy to radar include Hezlet, *Electronics*, 186–87, Roskill, *War at Sea* 1:118, Correlli Barnett, *Engage the Enemy More Closely* (London: Hodder and Stoughton, 1991), 84, and Donald MacIntyre, *The Naval War against Hitler* (London: Batesford, 1971), 13. The problem with vibration is mentioned in Norman Friedman, *Naval Firepower: Battleship Guns and Gunnery in the Dreadnought Era* (Barnsley, UK: Seaforth, 2008), 170; Eugene Millington-Drake, *The Drama of Graf Spee and the Battle of the Plate* (London: Peter Davies, 1964), 183.

32. TNA, ADM 199/787, "Action between HMS *Ajax* and Italian Destroyer Force on 12 October 1940," Enclosure No. 1, Gunnery, 7 April 1941.

33. TNA, ADM 239/138, Admiralty Naval Staff, Gunnery and Anti-Aircraft War Division, *Progress in Naval Gunnery, 1942*, 8, 83.

34. See O'Hara, *Six Victories*, 229.

35. TNA, ADM 239/140, Admiralty Naval Staff, Gunnery and Anti-Aircraft War Division, *Progress in Naval Gunnery, 1943*, 28.

36. Vincent P. O'Hara, *Torch: North Africa and the Allied Path to Victory* (Annapolis, MD: Naval Institute Press, 2015), 202.

37. TNA, ADM 239/138, 22.

38. TNA, ADM 239/138, 24–26.

39. Raymond Dannreuther, *Somerville's Force H: The Royal Navy's Gilbraltar-Based Fleet, June 1940 to March 1942* (London: Aurum, 2005), 8–9.

40. Norman Friedman, *Fighters over the Fleet: Naval Defense from Biplanes to the Cold War* (Annapolis, MD: Naval Institute Press, 2016), 112.

41. Michael Simpson, ed., *The Somerville Papers: Selections from the Private and Official Correspondence of Admiral of the Fleet Sir James Somerville* (Aldershot, UK: Scolar Press, 1996), 120; Hezlet, *Electronics*, 194–95.

42. United States Fleet, *Battle Experience*, Information Bulletin No. 1 (February 15, 1943), chap. 3, 4.

43. John B. Lundstrom, *The First Team: Pacific Naval Air Combat from Pearl Harbor to Midway* (Annapolis, MD: Naval Institute Press, 1984), 97–106, 245–51, 257–68, 303–5; United States Fleet, *Battle Experience*, Information Bulletin No. 1, chap. 3, 3; chap. 4, 5; chap. 7, 11; chap. 8, 28, 30, 32.

44. Friedman, *Fighters over the Fleet*, 125.

45. Trent Hone, *Learning War: The Evolution of Fighting Doctrine in the U.S. Navy, 1898–1945* (Annapolis, MD: Naval Institute Press, 2018), 167. See staff comments after the Battle of Cape Esperance for an example of the dynamic way rules (and tips) were devised following combat. United States Fleet, *Battle Experience*, Information Bulletin No. 3 (March 15, 1943), chap. 20, 35, and Information Bulletin No. 5 (April 15, 1943), chap. 31, 2.

46. NARA, USS *San Francisco*, "Action Report—Night Action, October 11–12, 1942," 31 October 1942, 11–12. This was bad intelligence, as it turned out.

47. NARA, USS *Boise*, "Action off Cape Esperance on Night of 11–12 October 1942," 22 October 1942, 3.

48. United States Fleet, *Battle Experience*, Information Bulletin No. 3, chap. 20, 34.

49. United States Fleet, *Battle Experience*, Information Bulletin No. 4, chap. 28, 12–13, 31.

50. See O'Hara, *The U.S. Navy against the Axis*, 126–27.

51. United States Fleet, *Battle Experience*, Information Bulletin No. 5, chap. 31, 7, 9; NARA, USS Northampton, "Report of Action with the Enemy and Resultant Sinking of U.S.S. *Northampton*," 5 December 1942, 6; NARA, USS *Pensacola*, "Report of Engagement with Enemy on the Night of November 30–December 1, 1942," 4 December 1942, Gunnery Officer Report, 1.

52. TNA, ADM 1/13326.

53. United States Fleet, *Battle Experience*, Information Bulletin No. 4, chap. 28, 56–59. See Hone, *Learning War*, 208–49, for a history of the CIC and an analysis of its benefits.

54. TNA, ADM 1/13326; Michael J. Whitby, "The Development of Action Information Organization during the Second World War," research paper, DHH 2010/5, July 1990.

55. Hone, *Learning War*, 213.

56. NARA, Commander Task Group 36.1, "Action Report—Night Engagement off Kula Gulf during Night of 5–6 July 1943," 1 August 1943, 11, and "Action Report—Night Engagement off Kolombangara during Night of 12–13 July 1943," 3 August 1943, 9.

57. Michael J. Whitby, "Planning, Challenge, and Execution: The Seaward Defense of the Assault Area off Normandy, 6–14 June 1944," 25.

58. Whitby, "Planning, Challenge, and Execution," 16.

59. Erminio Bagnasco and Enrico Cernuschi, *Le Navi de Guerra Italiane, 1940–1945* (Parma: Albertelli, 2005), 177.

60. U.S. Navy, ONI, *War Diary*, 9 June 1942, 117.

61. Francesco Mattesini, "The Italian Radar Failure in War—A Waste of Energy," Italian Maritime and Naval Documentation Association, August 10, 2019, http://www .aidmen.it/topic/1391-il-mancato-radar-italiano-in-guerra-uno-spreco-di-energie/.

62. Gaspare Galati, *100 Years of Radar* (New York: Springer International Publishing, 2016), 47.

63. Ufficio Storico della Marina Militare, *La Marina Italiana nella Seconda Guerra Mondiale*, vol. 5, *Le azioni navali in Mediterraneo dal 1 aprile 1941 al 8 settembre 1943* (Rome: Ministero della Difesa, 1970), 520.

64. John Deane Potter, *Fiasco: The Break-out of the German Battleships* (New York: Stein and Day, 1970), 92.

65. U.S. Navy, ONI, *War Diary*, 29 April 1942, 297; NARA, "Admiralty War Diary, April 1942," 722.

66. Buderi, 211.

67. Clay Blair, *Hitler's U-Boat War*, vol. 2, *The Hunted, 1942–1945* (New York: Random House, 1998), 497; U.S. Navy, ONI, "Captain U-Boats, Italy," 1942, 488, and 1943, 88, 368.

68. Watson, 245.

69. U.S. Navy, ONI, *War Diary*, 7 August 1942, 70. Emphasis in the original.

70. Correspondence with Enrico Cernuschi, 20 February 2021.

71. Louis Brown, *Technical and Military Imperatives: A Radar History of World War II* (Boca Raton, FL: CRC Press, 2017), 29.

72. Watson, 259–50.

73. See Andrew Hind, "The Cruise Missile Comes of Age," *Naval History* 22, no. 5 (October 2008): 52–57.

74. These flights are mentioned in Potter, 28–29, and de Arcangelis, 38–39.

75. Howarth and Law, 444–46.

76. Potter, 30.

77. Brian Ford, *Secret Weapons: Technology, Science, and the Race to Win World War II* (Long Island City, NY: Osprey, 2011), 251.

78. de Arcangelis, 32–33; Padfield, 285, 373; Price, 135.

79. NARA, USS *Barb*, "Report of Ninth War Patrol," 3 October 1944, 49–51, 53–58.

80. Robert Gardiner, ed., *Conway's All the World's Fighting Ships, 1947–1995* (Annapolis, MD: Naval Institute Press, 1995), 351–52, 416–17.

81. Robert D. Colvin, "Aftermath of the *Elath*," U.S. Naval Institute *Proceedings* 95, no. 10 (October 1969): 62. See also Hind.

82. Martin J. Miller Jr., "The Israeli Navy: 26 Years of Non-Peace," U.S. Naval Institute *Proceedings* 101, no. 2 (February 1975): 52.

83. Eli Rahav, "Missile Boat Warfare: Israeli Style," U.S. Naval Institute *Proceedings* 112, no. 3 (March 1986): 111.

84. Rahav, 112–13.

85. Rahav, 108; Efraim Inbar, "The Israeli Navy," *Naval War College Review* 43, no. 1 (Winter 1990): 107–8; Abraham Rabinovich, "From 'Futuristic Whimsy' to Naval Reality," *Naval History* 28, no. 3 (June 2014): 40–47; Ashraf M. Refaat, "How the Egyptian Navy Fought the October War," U.S. Naval Institute *Proceedings* 121, no. 3 (March 1995): 95. Rahav mentions maneuvering as a key defensive strategy. Inbar credits chaff. Rabinovich praises electronic countermeasures. *Contra* Refaat, another Israeli author notes that Termits could hit small targets, at least occasionally. Ze'ev Almog, "The Israeli Navy Beat the Odds," U.S. Naval Institute *Proceedings* 123, no. 3 (March 1997): 108n7.

86. Woodward and Robinson, 295–96.

87. Palmer, 312.

88. De Ninno, 820.

89. Brown, *Technical and Military Imperatives*, 83.

90. W. A. B. Douglas, Roger F. Sarty, and Michael J. Whitby, *No Higher Purpose: The Official Operational History of the Royal Canadian Navy in the Second World War, 1939–1943*, vol. 2, pt. 1 (St. Catharines, ON: Vanwell Pub., 2002), 306; LaCroix and Wells, 322.

91. Buderi, title page.

CHAPTER 6. SUBMARINES

1. Arthur Hezlet, *The Submarine and Sea Power* (New York: Stein and Day, 1967), 9.

2. Sueter, 49–59; Robert Gardiner, ed., *Conway's All the World's Fighting Ships, 1906–1921* (London: Conway Maritime Press, 1997), 387, 393.

3. Thomas Parrish, *The Submarine: A History* (New York: Penguin, 2004), 41; William Scanlan Murphy, "Dive! Dive! Dive!" *New Scientist* 7 (January 1989): 39.

4. Carl H. Hilton, "Isaac Peral and His Submarine," U.S. Naval Institute *Proceedings* 82, no. 11 (November 1956):1194–202; Gardiner, *Fighting Ships, 1906–1921*, 380–81.

5. Anonymous, "Submarine Torpedo Boat for the United States Navy," U.S. Naval Institute *Proceedings* 14, no. 1 (January 1888): 253–57.

6. Hezlet, *Submarine and Sea Power*, 9, 15.

7. Gardiner, *Fighting Ships, 1906–1921*, 312–13, 387.

8. Edwyn Gray, *British Submarines at War, 1914–1918* (Barnsley, UK: Pen & Sword Maritime, 2016), Loc. 264.

9. Gary E. Weir, "Tirpitz, Technology, and Building U-Boats, 1897–1916," *The International History Review* 6, no. 2 (May 1984): 178.

10. This is based on data from Gardiner, *Fighting Ships, 1906–1921*. For German workmanship, see U.S. Navy, ONI, *Monthly Intelligence Bulletins*, July 1919, 67; Goldrick, *After Jutland*, 46. For French design flaws, see Anthony E. Sokol, *The Imperial and Royal Austro-Hungarian Navy* (Annapolis, MD: Naval Institute Press, 1968), 98.

11. Nicholas Wolz, *From Imperial Splendor to Internment: The German Navy in the First World War* (Annapolis, MD: Naval Institute Press, 2013), 121. Also see Friedman,

Fighting the Great War at Sea, 245; Marder, *From the Dreadnought to Scapa Flow*, 1:363–64; R. H. Gibson and Maurice Prendergast, *The German Submarine War 1914–1918* (Annapolis, MD: Naval Institute Press, 2002), 25. For a discussion of the rules in place and their interpretation, see Howard S. Levie, "Submarine Warfare: With Emphasis on the 1936 London Protocol," in *International Law Studies 65: Targeting Enemy Merchant Shipping*, ed. Richard J. Grunawalt (Newport, RI: Naval War College, 1993), 28–71, and H. G. Rickover, "International Law and the Submarine," U.S. Naval Institute *Proceedings* 61, no. 9 (September 1935): 1213–27.

12. A. Gayer, "Summary of German Submarine Operations in the Various Theaters of War from 1914 to 1918," U.S. Naval Institute *Proceedings* 52, no. 4 (April 1926): 623–24.

13. See Michael Wilson, "The British 'B' Class Submarine," *Warship* 5, no. 17 (1981): 74–75. In fact, the British were selling the weapon short. In December 1914 *B11* penetrated part way up the Dardanelles and sank the old Ottoman battleship *Messudiyeh*.

14. Koerver, 55.

15. Goldrick, *Before Jutland*, 89–90.

16. Roger Keyes, *The Keyes Papers: Selections from the Private and Official Correspondence of Admiral of the Fleet Baron Keyes of Zeebrugge*, vol. 1 (London: Allen & Unwin, 1972), 19.

17. Koerver, 55.

18. Arno Spindler, "The Value of the Submarine in Naval Warfare," trans. W. P. Beehler, U.S. Naval Institute *Proceedings* 52, no. 5 (May 1926): 845.

19. Marder, *From the Dreadnought to Scapa Flow*, 2:67.

20. Keyes, 63.

21. Hezlet, *Submarine and Sea Power*, 55.

22. Sondhaus, *German Submarine Warfare*, 38.

23. Halpern, *A Naval History of World War I*, 294.

24. Halpern, *A Naval History of World War I*, 291–92; Friedman, *Fighting the Great War at Sea*, 245; Philip K. Lundeberg, "The German Naval Critique of the U-Boat Campaign, 1915–1918," *Military Affairs* 27, no. 3 (Autumn 1963): 107–8.

25. Technically, neither the British nor the Germans went as far as declaring a blockade, but the effect was similar in both cases and so the authors use the term "blockade" as a convenience.

26. H. P. Willmott, *The Last Century of Sea Power*, vol. 1 (Bloomington and Indianapolis: Indiana University Press, 2009), 258.

27. Reinhard Scheer, *Germany's High Sea Fleet in the World War* (London: Cassell and Company, 1920), 179, 186.

28. Sondhaus, *German Submarine Warfare*, 42, 49–51; Wolz, 125.

29. Marcus Faulkner, *The Great War at Sea: A Naval Atlas 1914–1919* (Annapolis, MD: Naval Institute Press, 2015), 80; Greger, 21.

30. Hezlet, *Submarine and Sea Power*, 36–37; Paul G. Halpern, *The Naval War in the Mediterranean, 1914–1918* (Annapolis, MD: Naval Institute Press, 1987), 189; Evren Mercan,

"The Impact of Allied Submarine Operations on Ottoman Decision-Making during the Gallipoli Campaign," *Journal for Maritime Research* 19, no. 1 (2017): 72; O'Hara and Heinz, 136–44.

31. V. E. Tarrant, *Jutland, the German Perspective: A New View of the Great Battle, 31 May 1916* (Annapolis, MD: Naval Institute Press, 1995), 59–61.

32. Willmott, appendices 9.7A, 9.7B. While Willmott caveats the numbers in these appendices, the authors believe the overall losses and the increased share of merchant ships sunk by submarines that they show is generally accurate.

33. Willmott, appendix 9.7B. Submarine losses and total of vessels sunk are from www.Uboat.net. Willmott says forty-eight. Marder, *From the Dreadnought to Scapa Flow*, 5:119–20, and Gibson and Prendergast, 366, report forty-six German submarines sunk between 1914 and 1916.

34. Gray, *British Submarines at War*, Loc. 2956.

35. Keyes, 43.

36. Fraser M. McKee, "An Explosive Story: The Rise and Fall of the Common Depth Charge," *The Northern Mariner* 3, no. 1 (January 1993): 48.

37. Hezlet, *Submarine and Sea Power*, 54.

38. See the discussion in David K. Brown, "Defeat in the Atlantic? Anti-Submarine Warfare 1917–19," *Warship 2002–2003* (2003): 130–32.

39. Friedman, *Fighting the Great War at Sea*, 60–61, 269.

40. Hezlet, *Submarine and Sea Power*, 52.

41. Willem Hackmann, *Seek and Strike: Sonar, Anti-Submarine Warfare, and the Royal Navy* (London: Her Majesty's Stationery Office, 1984), 15–16.

42. Hackmann, 17.

43. Hackmann, 24.

44. Jack K. Gusewelle, "Science and the Admiralty during World War I," in *Naval Warfare in the Twentieth Century 1900–1945*, ed. Gerald Jordan (New York: Crane, Russak, and Co., 1977), 116.

45. This section is based on Friedman, *Naval Weapons of World War One*; Dwight R. Messimer, *Seek and Destroy: Antisubmarine Warfare in World War I* (Annapolis, MD: Naval Institute Press, 2001); and McKee.

46. Friedman, *Naval Weapons of World War One*, 398. Messimer says the charges were 90 pounds (40.82 kg) or 156 pounds (70.76 kg).

47. Friedman, *Naval Weapons of World War One*, 397.

48. McKee, 51; Campbell, 390–91.

49. Friedman, *Fighting the Great War at Sea*, 272.

50. Hackmann, 48.

51. Hackmann, 69.

52. Hartcup, 139.

53. Lundeberg, 113.

54. Figures are from Willmott, appendix 9.7A.

55. Stephen Roskill, *Naval Policy between the Wars*, 2 vols. (Barnsley, UK: Seaforth, 2016),

2:306. Hereinafter the term sonar is used to indicate any device that transmitted sound waves and determined location and distance from the return echoes.

56. Roskill, *Naval Policy between the Wars*, 1:347.

57. Rössler, 144–45; Hackmann, 292–93. Range was highly dependent upon water and weather conditions. These ranges are from Rössler.

58. Eberhard Möller and Werner Brack, *The Encyclopedia of U-Boats from 1904 to the Present*, trans. Andrea Battson and Roger Chesneau (London: Greenhill Books, 2004), 163.

59. Hackmann, 294.

60. Hackmann.

61. Gerhard Koop and Klaus-Peter Schmolke, *Heavy Cruisers of the Admiral Hipper Class* (Annapolis, MD: Naval Institute Press, 2000), 26.

62. Rössler, 145. Also see the discussion in Howarth and Law, 430–50.

63. Geirr Haarr, *No Room for Mistakes: British and Allied Submarine Warfare, 1939–1940* (Annapolis, MD: Naval Institute Press, 2015), 70.

64. Admiralty, *The Defeat of the Enemy Attack on Shipping 1939–1945: A Study of Policy and Operations* (London: Historical Section, Admiralty, 1957), 18 and Plan 9; James Sadkovich, *The Italian Navy in World War II* (Westport, CT: Greenwood, 1994), 24.

65. Ufficio Storico della Marina Militare, *La Marina Italiana*, 21:142.

66. Admiralty, *Defeat of the Enemy Attack*, Plan 9.

67. Soviet submarine warfare regulations issued in 1939 made "attacks on the enemy's communications" the primary mission of its submarine force. O'Hara, Dickson, and Worth, *On Seas Contested*, 262.

68. Roskill, *Naval Policy between the Wars*, 2:230.

69. Carl Boyd and Akihiko Yoshida, *The Japanese Submarine Force and World War II* (Annapolis, MD: Naval Institute Press, 1995), 191.

70. See Erminio Bagnasco, *Submarines of World War Two* (London: Cassel and Co., 2000), 24. Wartime experience would show that the published characteristics of Germany's submarines understated their actual capabilities.

71. For more information on this important aspect of the anti-submarine war, see Howarth and Law, 418–29.

72. Rössler, 143–44; Campbell, 261–64.

73. Rössler, 196; Howarth and Law, 440.

74. Rössler, 146; Charles M. Sternhell and Alan M. Thorndike, *Antisubmarine Warfare in World War II* (Washington, DC: Navy Department, 1946), 159–60. Aaron S. Hamilton, *Total Undersea War: The Evolutionary Role of the Snorkel in Dönitz's U-Boat Fleet, 1944–1945* (Barnsley, UK: Seaforth, 2020), covers the development and use of the snorkel in great detail.

75. O'Hara, Dickson, and Worth, *On Seas Contested*, 75.

76. Rössler, 144.

77. This section draws heavily upon Malcolm Llewellyn-Jones, "On Britain's Doorstep: The Hunt for U-247," in *Fighting at Sea: Naval Battles from the Ages of Sail and Steam*, ed. Douglas M. McLean (Quebec: Robin Bass Studio, 2008).

78. Naval Historical Branch, Ministry of Defence, *Home Waters and the Atlantic*, vol. 1, *September 1939–8 April 1940*, CB3301(1), 31 December 1954, 71.

79. Llewellyn-Jones, "The Hunt for U-247," 279–85.

80. These were developed by the United States and were first used in July 1942 and were in full production by 1943. Their use became common by summer 1944.

81. V. E. Tarrant, *The Last Year of the Kriegsmarine, May 1944—May 1945* (Annapolis, MD: Naval Institute Press, 1994), 20–22.

82. The Germans calculated that a Type Wa2-1 Walter boat would require sixteen tons of fuel per hour of high-speed operations. This is a fuel cost of £2,720/hour. The unit cost of a Spitfire was £9,000. Also see Blair, *U-Boat War*, 2:512, for a discussion of the Walter's shortcomings. Also, Möller and Brack, 182, and Hamilton, 119–31.

83. Tarrant, *The Last Year of the Kriegsmarine*, 23.

84. Malcolm Llewellyn-Jones, "The Royal Navy on the Threshold of Modern Anti-Submarine Warfare 1944–1949," Ph.D. thesis, King's College, London, 2004, 276. Unit production would have brought the cost down.

85. For the story of Type XXI production, see Hamilton, 119–31; Adam Tooze, *The Wages of Destruction: The Making and Breaking of the Nazi Economy* (New York: Penguin Books, 2006), 612–18.

86. See Howard D. Grier, *Hitler, Dönitz, and the Baltic Sea: The Third Reich's Last Hope, 1944–1945* (Annapolis, MD: Naval Institute Press, 2007), for example.

87. Carlos E. Zartmann, "The Operations of Argentine Submarines in the Malvinas War," Naval Intelligence Support Center translation from *Marine Rundschau* (12 April 1984): 129–31. See also Sebastien Roblin, "How the Falklands War (Thanks to a Stealthy Submarine) Could Have Gone Very Differently," *The National Interest*, November 27, 2016, https://nationalinterest.org/blog/how-the-falklands-war-thanks-stealthy-submarine-could-have-18495. Fifty years in front line service is an eternity for a naval weapon.

88. Michael O'Hanlon, "A Retrospective on the So-Called Revolution in Military Affairs, 2000–2020," Brookings Institution, 2018, https://www.brookings.edu/wp-content/uploads/2018/09/FP_20181217_defense_advances_pt1.pdf.

89. German submarines sank three large British carriers while Japanese submarines sank two large U.S. carriers. U.S. submarines sank four Japanese fleet carriers. Submarines also accounted for eight small carriers (four Japanese, two British, and two U.S.).

CHAPTER 7. AIRCRAFT

1. W. Irving Chambers, "Aviation Today, and the Necessity for a National Aerodynamics Laboratory," U.S. Naval Institute *Proceedings* 38, no. 4 (December 1912): 1491.

2. Cernuschi and O'Hara, 61–62.

3. David Hamer, *Bombers versus Battleships: The Struggle between Ships and Aircraft for Control of the Surface of the Sea* (Annapolis, MD: Naval Institute Press, 1998), 2–7; W. H. Beehler, *The History of the Italian-Turkish War, September 29, 1911 to October 18,*

1912 (Annapolis, MD: The Advertiser-Republican, 1913), 31; Charles M. Melhorn, *Two-Block Fox: The Rise of the Aircraft Carrier, 1911–1929* (Annapolis, MD: Naval Institute Press, 1974), 10; Walter Raleigh and H. A. Jones, *The History of the Great War: The War in the Air: Being the Story of the Part Played in the Great War by the Royal Air Force*, 6 vols. (Oxford: Clarendon Press, 1922–37), 1:83–90. For radio, see Christina J. M. Goulter, *A Forgotten Offensive: Royal Air Force Coastal Command's Anti-Shipping Campaign, 1940–45* (London: Routledge, 1995), 5.

4. R. C. Saufley, "Naval Aviation: Its Value and Needs," U.S. Naval Institute *Proceedings* 40, no. 5 (September 1914): 1468–70; O'Hara, Dickson, and Worth, *To Crown the Waves*, 76.

5. O'Hara, Dickson, and Worth, *To Crown the Waves*, 245; Gardiner, *Fighting Ships, 1906–1921*, 307–8.

6. Michele Cosentino, "From *Elba* to *Europa*," *Warship 2017* (2017): 63–64; Peattie, 4–8.

7. Arthur Hezlet, *Aircraft and Sea Power* (New York: Stein and Day, 1970), 15–16, 20, 43; O'Hara, Dickson, and Worth, *To Crown the Waves*, 116; Viscount Hythe, ed., *The Naval Annual 1913* (Portsmouth, UK: J. Griffin and Co., 1913), 171.

8. Sokol, *Austro-Hungarian Navy*, 74.

9. O'Hara, Dickson, and Worth, *To Crown the Waves*, 297–98.

10. W. Atlee Edwards, "The U.S. Naval Air Force in Action 1917–18," U.S. Naval Institute *Proceedings* 48, no. 11 (November 1922): 1870.

11. Anonymous, "Naval Strategy—Effect of Aircraft on," *Naval Review* 1, no. 4 (1913): 260–61.

12. Raleigh and Jones, 3: appendix I, II.

13. Anonymous, "Air Power," *Naval Review* 1, no. 2 (1913): 59.

14. Rene Daveluy, "Maritime Aviation," trans. G. M. Baum, U.S. Naval Institute *Proceedings* 39, no. 3 (September 1913): 1106, 1108.

15. Felix Pietzker, "Principles of Naval Aeronautics," trans. G. M. Baum, U.S. Naval Institute *Proceedings* 40, no. 2 (March-April 1914): 389.

16. Chambers, "Aviation Today," 1491–92; Saufley, "Naval Aviation," 1462, 1470.

17. See Anonymous, "Air Power," 61, for an example of this debate.

18. See Norman Polmar, *Aircraft Carriers: A History of Carrier Aviation and Its Influence on World Events*, vol. 1, *1909–1945* (Washington, DC: Potomac Books, 2006), 23–32.

19. Raleigh and Jones, 4:24–25. The aircraft ditched and the pilot was rescued.

20. Leo Marriott, *Catapult Aircraft: The Story of Seaplanes Flown from Battleships, Cruisers, and Other Warships of the World's Navies, 1912–1950* (Barnsley, UK: Pen & Sword, 2016), x.

21. *Hermes* was laid down first, but the Japanese *Hōshō* was the first keel-up carrier to be commissioned.

22. Admiralty, *Naval Staff Monographs*, 16:18, 25, 28, 33; 17:106–7; Raleigh and Jones, 3:205; Robert K. Massie, *Castles of Steel: Britain, Germany, and the Winning of the Great War at Sea* (New York: Random House, 2003), 683; Goldrick, *After Jutland*, 67–79; Scheer, 182–83.

23. R. D. Layman, *Naval Aviation in the First World War: Its Impact and Influence* (Annapolis, MD: Naval Institute Press, 1996), 97.

24. Raleigh and Jones, 2:405–9.

25. Raleigh and Jones, 2:12–18; Admiralty, *Naval Staff Monographs*, 6:24–25.

26. Admiralty, *Naval Staff Monographs*, 4:39.

27. Admiralty, *Naval Staff Monographs*, 6:39, 42; Raleigh and Jones, 6:45–47; O'Hara and Heinz, 149. There were some instances of tethered balloons spotting fire against ship targets.

28. Michael Peck, "The First Nations to Use Aircraft to Bomb Ships Were . . . Greece and Mexico?" *The National Interest*, June 10, 2017, https://nationalinterest.org/blog/the-buzz/the-first-nations-use-aircraft-bomb-ships-were-greece-mexico-21093; Layman, 57.

29. Raleigh and Jones, 2:347, 5:412–14; Hermann Lorey, *Der Krieg in den Türkischen Gewässern*, vol. 1, *Die Mittlemeer Division* (Berlin: E. S. Mittler, 1928), 345–46.

30. Bruce Taylor, ed., *The World of the Battleship: The Lives and Careers of Twenty-One Capital Ships from the World's Navies, 1880–1990* (Annapolis, MD: Naval Institute Press, 2018), 106.

31. Raleigh and Jones, 2:64–65, 4:33; Marder, *From the Dreadnought to Scapa Flow*, 4:19–23, 236–40, 5:141–42; Till, 142. Details of the supposed victims of the second and third attacks are elusive. Layman, 62–63.

32. Rudolf Firle, Heinrich Rollman, and Ernst Gagern, *Der Krieg in der Ostsee*, 3 vols. (Berlin and Frankfurt: E. S. Mittler, 1921–64), 3:69–73.

33. Raleigh and Jones, 4:55–58; Gary Staff, *Battle for the Baltic Islands 1917: Triumph of the Imperial German Navy* (Barnsley, UK: Pen & Sword Maritime, 2008), 11–13; U.S. Navy, ONI, *Monthly Intelligence Bulletin*, June 1919, 15–16.

34. Admiralty, *Naval Staff Monographs*, 11:136–40.

35. Admiralty, *Naval Staff Monographs*, 12:133–39; Goldrick, *Before Jutland*, 237; Raleigh and Jones, 1:402–5, 2:358–61, 396–403. Not all of these raids were directed at zeppelin bases.

36. Raleigh and Jones, 6:364–67; Groos and Gladisch, 7:359.

37. Halpern, *A Naval History of World War I*, 230–31, 247–50, 252.

38. Marder, *From the Dreadnought to Scapa Flow*, 4:81–83, 270–71, 5:85, 91–95; Till, 167; Raleigh and Jones, 6:343–45. Quote: Anonymous, "The Science of Admiralty III," *Naval Review* 48, no. 1 (1964): 16.

39. Tom Le Compte, "The Few, the Brave, the Lucky," *Air & Space*, November 2008, https://www.airspacemag.com/history-of-flight/the-few-the-brave-the-lucky-45053770/?page=1, 1.

40. David Stevenson, *With Our Backs to the Wall: Victory and Defeat in 1918* (Cambridge, MA: Harvard University Press, 2011), 198.

41. Raleigh and Jones, 6:92.

42. Norman Friedman, *Naval Anti-Aircraft Guns and Gunnery* (Annapolis, MD: Naval Institute Press, 2013), 56–73; Taylor, 106.

43. Raleigh and Jones, 1:458–59.

44. Raleigh and Jones, 7:app. XLI; Enzo Angelucci, *The Rand McNally Encyclopedia of Military Aircraft 1914–1980* (New York: The Military Press, 1983), 17.

45. Douhet, 28.

46. Douhet, 21, 34, 53–58, 71–72, 94, 111, 142, 254, 390–93. Douhet took a progressively harsher line on "auxiliary" air forces over time, finally claiming that he always intended that they be abolished but that he had been reluctant to take that position initially.

47. Quote: Raleigh and Jones, 7:10. See also Roskill, *Naval Policy between the Wars*, 1:237–41.

48. Roskill, *Naval Policy between the Wars*, 1:238, 241.

49. Roskill, *Naval Policy between the Wars*, 1:241.

50. Roskill, *Naval Policy between the Wars*, 1:190–91.

51. See Thomas C. Hone, Norman Friedman, and Mark D. Mandeles, *American and British Aircraft Carrier Development, 1919–1941* (Annapolis, MD: Naval Institute Press, 1999), and Till for two excellent discussions on the effect of the British air force on the development of aviation in the British navy.

52. Goulter, xvi.

53. MacGregor Knox, *Hitler's Italian Allies: Royal Armed Forces, Fascist Regime, and the War of 1940–1943* (New York: Cambridge University Press, 2000), 26.

54. Francesco Mattesini, *Corrispondenza e Direttive Tecnico-Operative di Supermarina*, vol. 1, book 2 (Rome: Ufficio Storico della Marina Militare, 2000), 562–71.

55. O'Hara, Dickson, and Worth, *On Seas Contested*, 21–22.

56. Sönke Neitzel, "Kriegsmarine and Luftwaffe Cooperation in the War against Britain," *War in History* 10, no. 4 (November 2003): 450.

57. O'Hara, Dickson, and Worth, *On Seas Contested*, 56–58.

58. U.S. Navy, ONI, *War Diary*, December 1940, 166.

59. G. H. Bennett and R. Bennett, *Hitler's Admirals* (Annapolis, MD: Naval Institute Press, 2004), 92.

60. Bennett and Bennett, 93.

61. William Mitchell, *Winged Defense: The Development and Possibilities of Modern Air Power—Economic and Military* (New York: Knickerbocker Press, 1926), xvi, 115, 128, 132–33.

62. Mitchell, vii, 4, 14, 40, 100, 159–60, 215, 239–40; Thomas Wildenberg, *Billy Mitchell's War with the Navy: The Interwar Rivalry over Air Power* (Annapolis, MD: Naval Institute Press, 2013), 148, 151, 159–60, 168.

63. Norman Friedman, *Winning a Future War: War Gaming and Victory in the Pacific War* (Washington, DC: Naval History and Heritage Command, Department of the Navy, n.d.), 83, 92–97.

64. Peattie, 85.

65. Yoichi Hirama, "Japanese Naval Preparations for World War II," *Naval War College Review* 44, no. 2 (Spring 1991): 69–70.

66. Hirama, 72.

67. Peattie, 81–85.

68. Ranft, 112.

69. Eric J. Grove, "A War Fleet Built for Peace: British Naval Rearmament in the 1930s and the Dilemma of Deterrence versus Defence," *Naval War College Review* 44, no. 2 (Spring 1991): 86.

70. Murray and Millett, 215–16; Friedman, *Fighters over the Fleet*, 74, 79, 81.

71. See O'Hara, *Six Victories*, 26.

72. Morison, 12:191–92.

73. *The London Gazette*, "The River Plate Battle," *Supplement*, 19 June 1947, 2760.

74. Vincent O'Hara, *Struggle for the Middle Sea : The Great Navies at War in the Mediterranean Theater, 1940–1945* (Annapolis, MD: Naval Institute Press, 2009), 44.

75. Norman Friedman, *U.S. Aircraft Carriers: An Illustrated Design History* (Annapolis, MD: Naval Institute Press, 1983), 263.

76. The cost of a P-51 Mustang was $50,985 in 1945. See Marcelle Size Knaak, *Encyclopedia of U.S. Air Force Aircraft and Missile Systems*, vol. 1 (Washington, DC: Office of Air Force History, 1978), 305. That would be $730,210 in 2020 money. https://www.in2013dollars.com/us/inflation/1945?amount=50985.

CONCLUSION

1. Roskill, *Naval Policy between the Wars*, 2:398.

2. Douhet and Mitchell, to give two examples.

3. *Yamato* initial designs 1934, commissioned December 1941; *North Carolina*, 1935–41; *King George V,* 1935–40.

4. For the British navy's reliance on antiaircraft guns see Roskill, *Naval Policy between the Wars*, 2:251–52, 330n1, 332–34, 420–21.

BIBLIOGRAPHY

OFFICIAL AND PRIMARY SOURCES

Admiralty, Great Britain. *Battle of Jutland: 30th May to 1st June 1916, Official Dispatches.* London: His Majesty's Stationery Office, 1920.

———. *The Defeat of the Enemy Attack on Shipping 1939–1945: A Study of Policy and Operations.* London: Historical Section, Admiralty, 1957.

———. *Naval Staff Monographs (Historical).* 19 vols. 1920–39. http://www.navy.gov.au /media-room/publications/world-war-i-naval-staff-monographs.

Archivo dell'Ufficio Storico della Marina Militare, Regia Marina, Marisub Taranto. "Siluro inglese per aerosiluanti." 2 January 1941.

Corbett, Julian S., and Henry Newbolt. *Naval Operations: History of the Great War Based on Official Documents.* 5 vols. London: Longmans, Green, 1920–31.

Douglas, W. A. B., Roger F. Sarty, and Michael J. Whitby. *No Higher Purpose: The Official Operational History of the Royal Canadian Navy in the Second World War, 1939–1943.* Vol. 2, Pt. 1. St. Catharines, ON: Vanwell Pub., 2002.

Firle, Rudolf, Heinrich Rollman, and Ernst Gagern. *Der Krieg in der Ostsee.* 3 vols. Berlin and Frankfurt: E. S. Mittler, 1921–64.

Fuehrer Conferences on Naval Affairs, 1939–1945. London: Chatham, 2005.

Furer, Julius Augustus. *Administration of the Navy Department in World War II.* Washington, DC: Government Printing Office, 1959.

Graves, D. E. German Navy Research Report G3, "German Navy Radar Equipment, 1934–1935: Overview and Descriptive Catalogue." Ottawa: Canadian Department of Defence, December 1990.

Groos, Otto, and Walter Gladisch. *Der Krieg in der Nordsee.* 7 vols. Berlin, Frankfurt, and Hamburg: E. S. Mittler, 1920–2006.

Hinsley, F. H., et al. *British Intelligence in the Second World War.* 4 vols. New York: Cambridge University Press, 1979–84.

Historical Section, Committee of Imperial Defence. *Official History (Naval and Military) of the Russo-Japanese War.* 3 vols. London: Harrison and Sons and His Majesty's Stationery Office, 1910–20.

Keyes, Roger. *The Keyes Papers: Selections from the Private and Official Correspondence of Admiral of the Fleet Baron Keyes of Zeebrugge,* vol. 1. London: Allen & Unwin, 1972.

Kinai, M. *The Russo-Japanese War (Official Reports).* 2 vols. Tokyo: The Shimbashido, 1905–7.

The London Gazette. "The River Plate Battle." *Supplement,* 19 June 1947.

Lorey, Hermann. *Der Krieg in den Türkischen Gewässern.* Vol. 1, *Die Mittlemeer Division.* Berlin: E. S. Mittler, 1928.

Militärgeschichtliches Forschungsamt, ed. *Germany and the Second World War.* 6 vols. Oxford: Oxford University Press, 2015.

The National Archives, Kew, UK. ADM 1/12248. "Reports of Proceedings, HMS *Talybont* and HMS *Wensleydale*," 24 October 1943.

———. ADM 1/13326. "Receipt and Handling of Enemy Intelligence in Destroyers," CO Cleveland to Captain (D) Plymouth, 26 December 1942, and "Minutes of Meeting Held by DTSD on 8th June, 1943 to discuss Action Information Organisation on Destroyers."

———. ADM 116/1341. "Grand Fleet Battle Orders," December 1915.

———. ADM 189/33. HMS *Vernon* Annual Report 1913.

———. ADM 199/787. "Action between HMS *Ajax* and Italian Destroyer Force on 12 October 1940," Enclosure No. 1, Gunnery, 7 April 1941.

———. ADM 239/138. Admiralty Naval Staff, Gunnery and Anti-Aircraft War Division. *Progress in Naval Gunnery, 1942.*

———. ADM 239/140. Admiralty Naval Staff, Gunnery and Anti-Aircraft War Division. *Progress in Naval Gunnery, 1943.*

National Archives and Records Administration (NARA). United States Navy Action and Operational Reports, various dates.

———. "Admiralty War Diary," various dates.

———. Commander Destroyers Pacific Fleet. *Destroyer Night Attack Plan and Cover Letter* Attachment A to *Destroyer Torpedo Attack Instructions (Tentative) Destroyer Tactical Bulletin 4–43.* United States Pacific Fleet, 1943.

———. Commander Task Group 36.1. "Action Report—Night Engagement off Kolombangara during Night of 12–13 July 1943." 3 August 1943.

———. Commander Task Group 36.1. "Action Report—Night Engagement off Kula Gulf during Night of 5–6 July 1943." 1 August 1943.

———. Government Code and Cypher School. *Naval History. The German Navy: Communications.* Vol. 6 of 24, record group 38, box 99.

———. USS *Barb.* "Report of Ninth War Patrol." 3 October 1944.

———. USS *Boise.* "Action off Cape Esperance on Night of 11–12 October 1942." 22 October 1942.

———. USS *Northampton.* "Report of Action with the Enemy and Resultant Sinking of U.S.S. *Northampton*." 5 December 1942.

———. USS *Pensacola.* "Report of Engagement with Enemy on the Night of November 30–December 1, 1942." 4 December 1942.

———. USS *San Francisco.* "Action Report—Night Action, October 11–12, 1942." 31 October 1942.

———. USS *Yorktown.* "Report of Action of *Yorktown* and *Yorktown* Air Group on May 8, 1942." 25 May 1942.

Naval Historical Branch, Ministry of Defence. *Home Waters and the Atlantic*, vol. 1, *September 1939–8 April 1940.* CB3301(1), 31 December 1954.

Parliamentary Debates. Commons, 10 November 1932.

Raleigh, Walter, and H. A. Jones. *The History of the Great War: The War in the Air: Being the Story of the Part Played in the Great War by the Royal Air Force*. 7 vols. Oxford: Clarendon Press, 1922–37.

Roskill, S. W. *The War at Sea, 1939–1945*. 3 vols. London: Her Majesty's Stationery Office, 1954–61.

Scitor Corporation. *Technological Innovation during Protracted War: Radar and Atomic Weapons in World War II*. Prepared for Director of Net Assessment, Office of the Secretary of Defense, April 2015. https://www.esd.whs.mil/Portals/54/Documents/FOID/Reading%20Room/Litigation_Release/Litigation%20Release%20-%20Technological%20Innovation%20During%20Protracted%20War%20Radar%20and%20Atomic%20Weapons%20in%20WWII%20%20201504.pdf.

Thomazi, A. *La Guerre navale dans la Zone des Armées du Nord*. Paris: Payot, 1925.

Ufficio Storico della Marina Militare. *La Marina Italiana nella Seconda Guerra Mondiale*. Vol. 5, *Le azioni navali in Mediterraneo dal 1 aprile 1941 al 8 settembre 1943*. Rome: Ministero della Difesa, 1970.

———. Vol. 13, *I sommergibili in Mediterraneo: dal 10 giugno 1940 al 31 dicembre, 1941*. Rome: Ministero della Difesa, 1972.

———. Vol. 18, *La Guerra di Mine*. Rome: Ministero della Difesa, 1988.

———. Vol. 21, *L'Organizzazione della Marina durante il Conflitto*. 2 parts. Rome: Ministero della Difesa, 1972.

United States. Joint Army-Navy Assessment Committee. *Japanese Naval and Merchant Shipping Losses during World War II by All Causes*. Washington, DC: Government Printing Office, 1947.

United States Armed Forces Far East History Division. *Operational History of Naval Communications*. Japanese Monographs, Series 118. Washington, DC: U.S. Army, 1951.

United States Fleet. *Battle Experience*. Information Bulletin No. 1 (February 15, 1943).

———. *Battle Experience*. Information Bulletin No. 2 (March 1, 1943).

———. *Battle Experience*. Information Bulletin No. 3 (March 15, 1943).

———. *Battle Experience*. Information Bulletin No. 4 (March 25, 1943).

———. *Battle Experience*. Information Bulletin No. 5 (April 15, 1943).

———. *Radar Bulletin No. 1: The Tactical Use of Radar*. 1942. https://www.ibiblio.org/hyperwar/USNref/RADONE/index.html#VII.

U.S. Navy. Bureau of Ordnance. OP1673A, "German Underwater Ordnance—Mines." 14 June 1946.

———. Office of Chief of Naval Operations, 20th Division of the Office of Naval Communications, G Section. *Battle of the Atlantic*. Vol. 4, *Technical Intelligence from Allied Communications Intelligence*. Washington, DC: Department of the Navy, n.d.

———. Office of Naval Intelligence (ONI). "Captain U-Boats, Italy, 1942 and 1 January–30 June 1943."

———. ONI. *Fuehrer Conferences on Matters Dealing with the German Navy*. 5 vols. Washington, DC: 1941–45.

———. ONI. *Monthly Intelligence Bulletins*. 1919-23.

————. ONI. *War Diary, German Naval Staff Operations Division.* December 1939, April 1942, June 1942.

U.S. Strategic Bombing Survey. Interrogation of Japanese Officials. n.d. https://www .ibiblio.org/hyperwar/AAF/USSBS/IJO/index.html.

SECONDARY SOURCES
Books and Theses

Achkasov, V. I., and N. B. Pavlovich. *Soviet Naval Operations in the Great Patriotic War, 1941–1945.* Annapolis, MD: Naval Institute Press, 1981.

Allison, David K. *New Eye for the Navy: The Origin of Radar at the Naval Research Laboratory.* Washington, DC: Naval Research Laboratory, 1981.

Angelucci, Enzo. *The Rand McNally Encyclopedia of Military Aircraft 1914–1980.* New York: The Military Press, 1983.

Bagnasco, Erminio. *Le armi delle navi Italiane nella Seconda Guerra Mondiale.* Parma: Albertelli, 2007.

————. *Submarines of World War Two.* London: Cassel and Co., 2000.

————, and Enrico Cernuschi. *Le Navi de Guerra Italiane, 1940–1945.* Parma: Albertelli, 2005.

Barnett, Correlli. *Engage the Enemy More Closely.* London: Hodder and Stoughton, 1991.

Baudot, Marcel, ed. *The Historical Encyclopedia of World War II.* Translated by Jesse Dilson. New York: Facts on File, 1980.

Beehler, W. H. *The History of the Italian-Turkish War, September 29, 1911 to October 18, 1912.* Annapolis, MD: The Advertiser-Republican, 1913.

Beesly, Patrick. *Room 40: Naval Intelligence 1914–18.* New York: Harcourt Brace Jovanovich, 1982.

Bennett, G. H., and R. Bennett. *Hitler's Admirals.* Annapolis, MD: Naval Institute Press, 2004.

Blair, Clay. *Hitler's U-Boat War.* Vol. 1, *The Hunters, 1939–1942.* New York: Random House, 1996.

————. *Hitler's U-Boat War.* Vol. 2, *The Hunted, 1942–1945.* New York: Random House, 1998.

————. *Silent Victory: The U.S. Submarine War against Japan.* New York: Bantam, 1976.

Bollinger, Martin J. *Warriors and Wizards: The Deployment and Defeat of Radio-Controlled Glide Bombs of the Third Reich.* Annapolis, MD: Naval Institute Press, 2010.

Branfill-Cook, Roger. *Torpedo: The Complete History of the World's Most Revolutionary Naval Weapon.* Barnsley, UK: Seaforth, 2014.

Brassey, T. A., ed. *The Naval Annual 1895.* Portsmouth, UK: J. Griffin and Co., 1895.

————. *The Naval Annual 1896.* Portsmouth, UK: J. Griffin and Co., 1896.

————. *The Naval Annual 1905.* Portsmouth, UK: J. Griffin and Co., 1905.

Brooks, John. *The Battle of Jutland.* Cambridge, UK: Cambridge University Press, 2016.

————. *Dreadnought Gunnery and the Battle of Jutland: The Question of Fire Control.* London: Routledge, 2005.

Brown, David K. *The Grand Fleet: Warship Design and Development 1906–1922*. Annapolis, MD: Naval Institute Press, 1999.

———. *Nelson to Vanguard: Warship Design and Development 1923–1945*. Annapolis, MD: Naval Institute Press, 2006.

———. *Warrior to Dreadnought: Warship Development 1860–1905*. London: Chatham, 1997.

Brown, Eric. *Wings of the Navy: Flying Allied Carrier Aircraft of World War Two*. Edited by William Green. Annapolis, MD: Naval Institute Press, 1987.

Brown, Louis. *Technical and Military Imperatives: A Radar History of World War II*. Boca Raton, FL: CRC Press, 2017.

Boyd, Carl, and Akihiko Yoshida. *The Japanese Submarine Force and World War II*. Annapolis, MD: Naval Institute Press, 1995.

Bruhn, David D., and Rob Hoole. *Home Waters: Royal Navy, Royal Canadian Navy, and U.S. Navy Mine Forces Battling U-Boats in World War I*. Berwyn Heights, MD: Heritage Books, 2018.

Buderi, Robert. *The Invention That Changed the World: How a Small Group of Radar Pioneers Won the Second World War and Launched a Technological Revolution*. New York: Touchstone, 1996.

Burke, Arthur. *Torpedoes and Their Impact on Naval Warfare*. Newport, RI: Naval Undersea Warfare Center, 2017.

Cain, Anthony C. "Neither Decadent, Nor Traitorous, Nor Stupid: The French Air Force and Air Doctrine in the 1930s." Ph.D. thesis, Ohio State University, 2000.

Campbell, John. *Naval Weapons of World War Two*. Annapolis, MD: Naval Institute Press, 1985.

Corbett, Julian S. *Maritime Operations of the Russo-Japanese War 1904–1905*. 2 vols. Annapolis, MD, and Newport, RI: Naval Institute Press and Naval War College Press, 1994 reprint.

Coutain-Bégarie, Hervé, and Claude Huan. *Mers el-Kébir (1940)—La rupture franco-britannique*. Paris: Economica, 1994.

Crossley, Jim. *The Hidden Threat: The Story of Mines and Minesweeping by the Royal Navy in World War I*. Barnsley, UK: Pen & Sword Maritime, 2011.

Dannreuther, Raymond. *Somerville's Force H: The Royal Navy's Gibraltar-Based Fleet, June 1940 to March 1942*. London: Aurum, 2005.

De Arcangelis, Mario. *Electronic Warfare: From the Battle of Tsushima to the Falklands and Lebanon Conflicts*. Pool, UK: Blandford Press, 1985.

Deer, I. C. B., and M. R. D. Foot. *The Oxford Companion to the Second World War*. Oxford: Oxford University Press, 1998.

De Seversky, Alexander P. *Victory through Air Power*. New York: Simon and Schuster, 1942.

Dorling, H. Taprell. *Swept Channels: Being an Account of the Work of the Minesweepers in the Great War*. London: Hodder and Stoughton, 1935.

Douhet, Giulio. *The Command of the Air*. Translated by Dino Ferrari. Washington, DC: Office of Air Force History, 1983 reprint.

Dyer, George C. *The Amphibians Came to Conquer: The Story of Admiral Richmond Kelly Turner*. Washington, DC: Department of the Navy, 1972.

Evans, David C., and Mark R. Peattie. *Kaigun: Strategy, Tactics, and Technology in the Imperial Japanese Navy 1887–1941*. Annapolis, MD: Naval Institute Press, 1997.

Faulkner, Marcus. *The Great War at Sea: A Naval Atlas 1914–1919*. Annapolis, MD: Naval Institute Press, 2015.

Flicke, Wilhelm F. *War Secrets in the Ether*. 2 vols. Translated by Ray W. Pettengill. Washington, DC: National Security Agency, 1953.

Ford, Brian. *Secret Weapons: Technology, Science, and the Race to Win World War II*. Long Island City, NY: Osprey, 2011.

Francillon, Rene J. *Japanese Aircraft of the Pacific War*. Annapolis, MD: Naval Institute Press, 1994.

Friedman, Hal M. *Digesting History: The U.S. Naval War College, the Lessons of World War II, and Future Naval Warfare*. Washington, DC: Government Printing Office, 2010.

Friedman, Norman. *The British Battleship 1906–1946*. Barnsley, UK: Seaforth, 2015.

———. *British Cruisers: Two World Wars and After*. Barnsley, UK: Seaforth, 2010.

———. *British Destroyers: From the Earliest Days to the Second World War*. Annapolis, MD: Naval Institute Press, 2009.

———. *British Destroyers and Frigates: The Second World War and After*. Barnsley, UK: Seaforth, 2012.

———. *British Submarines in Two World Wars*. Annapolis, MD: Naval Institute Press, 2019.

———. *Fighters over the Fleet: Naval Defense from Biplanes to the Cold War*. Annapolis, MD: Naval Institute Press, 2016.

———. *Fighting the Great War at Sea*. Annapolis, MD: Naval Institute Press, 2014.

———. *Naval Anti-Aircraft Guns and Gunnery*. Annapolis, MD: Naval Institute Press, 2013.

———. *Naval Firepower: Battleship Guns and Gunnery in the Dreadnought Era*. Barnsley, UK: Seaforth, 2008.

———. *Naval Radar*. London: Conway Maritime Press, 1981.

———. *Naval Weapons of World War One: Guns, Torpedoes, and Mines of all Nations, an Illustrated Directory*. Barnsley, UK: Seaforth, 2011.

———. *U.S. Aircraft Carriers: An Illustrated Design History*. Annapolis, MD: Naval Institute Press, 1983.

———. *U.S. Naval Weapons*. London: Conway Maritime Press, 1983.

———. *Winning a Future War: War Gaming and Victory in the Pacific War*. Washington, DC: Naval History and Heritage Command, Department of the Navy, n.d.

Fulton, Robert. *Torpedo War, and Submarine Explosions*. New York: William Abbatt, 1914 reprint.

Galati, Gaspare. *100 Years of Radar*. New York: Springer International Publishing, 2016.

Gardiner, Robert, ed. *Conway's All the World's Fighting Ships, 1860–1905*. London: Conway Maritime Press, 1979.

———. *Conway's All the World's Fighting Ships, 1906–1921.* London: Conway Maritime Press, 1997.

———. *Conway's All the World's Fighting Ships, 1922–1946.* Annapolis, MD: Naval Institute Press, 1980.

———. *Conway's All the World's Fighting Ships, 1947–1995.* Annapolis, MD: Naval Institute Press, 1995.

Gardner, W. J. R. *Decoding History: The Battle of the Atlantic and Ultra.* Annapolis, MD: Naval Institute Press, 1999.

Gebhard, Louis A. *Evolution of Naval Radio-Electronics and Contributions of the Naval Research Laboratory.* Washington, DC: Naval Research Laboratory, 1979.

Gibson, R. H., and Maurice Prendergast. *The German Submarine War 1914–1918.* Annapolis, MD: Naval Institute Press, 2002.

Goldrick, James. *After Jutland: The Naval War in Northern European Waters, June 1916–November 1918.* Annapolis, MD: Naval Institute Press, 2018.

———. *Before Jutland: The Naval War in Northern European Waters, August 1914–February 1915.* Annapolis, MD: Naval Institute Press, 2015.

Gompert, David C. *Sea Power and American Interests in the Western Pacific.* Santa Monica, CA: RAND Corporation, 2013.

Gordon, Andrew. *The Rules of the Game: Jutland and British Naval Command.* Annapolis, MD: Naval Institute Press, 1996.

Goss, Chris. *Sea Eagles: Luftwaffe Anti-Shipping Units 1939–41.* London: Classic Publications, 2005.

Goulter, Christina J. M. *A Forgotten Offensive: Royal Air Force Coastal Command's Anti-Shipping Campaign, 1940–45.* London: Routledge, 1995.

Gray, Edwyn. *British Submarines at War, 1914–1918.* Barnsley, UK: Pen & Sword Maritime, 2016.

———. *The Devil's Device: Robert Whitehead and the History of the Torpedo.* Revised and updated edition. Annapolis, MD: Naval Institute Press, 1991.

Green, William. *Warplanes of the Second World War: Fighters.* 4 vols. Garden City, NY: Hanover House, 1960–61.

———. *Warplanes of the Second World War: Floatplanes.* Vol. 6. Garden City, NY: Doubleday and Company, 1963.

Greene, Jack, and Alessandro Massignani. *Ironclads at War.* Conshohocken, PA: Combined Publishing, 1998.

Greger, René. *The Russian Fleet, 1914–1917.* Shepperton, UK: Ian Allen, 1972.

Grey, C. G., ed. *All the World's Aircraft 1924.* London: Sampson Low, Marston and Company, 1924.

Grier, Howard D. *Hitler, Dönitz, and the Baltic Sea: The Third Reich's Last Hope, 1944–1945.* Annapolis, MD: Naval Institute Press, 2007.

Grooss, Poul. *The Naval War in the Baltic, 1939–1945.* Barnsley, UK: Seaforth, 2017.

Grossnick, Roy A. *United States Naval Aviation, 1910–1995.* Washington, DC: Naval Historical Center, Department of the Navy, n.d.

Haarr, Geirr. *The Gathering Storm: The Naval War in Northern Europe, September 1939–April 1940.* Annapolis, MD: Naval Institute Press, 2013.

———. *No Room for Mistakes: British and Allied Submarine Warfare, 1939–1940.* Annapolis, MD: Naval Institute Press, 2015.

Hackmann, Willem. *Seek and Strike: Sonar, Anti-Submarine Warfare, and the Royal Navy.* London: Her Majesty's Stationery Office, 1984.

Halpern, Paul G. *The Battle of the Otranto Straits: Controlling the Gateway to the Adriatic in World War I.* Bloomington: Indiana University Press, 2004.

———. *A Naval History of World War I.* Annapolis, MD: Naval Institute Press, 1994.

———. *The Naval War in the Mediterranean, 1914–1918.* Annapolis, MD: Naval Institute Press, 1987.

Hamer, David. *Bombers versus Battleships: The Struggle between Ships and Aircraft for Control of the Surface of the Sea.* Annapolis, MD: Naval Institute Press, 1998.

Hamilton, Aaron S. *Total Undersea War: The Evolutionary Role of the Snorkel in Dönitz's U-Boat Fleet, 1944–1945.* Barnsley, UK: Seaforth, 2020.

Hartcup, Guy. *The War of Invention: Scientific Development, 1914–1918.* London: Brassey's Defence Publishers, 1988.

Hartmann, Gregory K., with Scott C. Truver. *Weapons That Wait: Mine Warfare in the U.S. Navy.* Annapolis, MD: Naval Institute Press, 1991.

Headrick, Daniel R. *The Invisible Weapon: Telecommunications and International Politics, 1851–1945.* Oxford: Oxford University Press, 1991.

Hezlet, Arthur. *Aircraft and Sea Power.* New York: Stein and Day, 1970.

———. *British and Allied Submarine Operations in World War II.* Portsmouth, UK: The Royal Navy Submarine Museum, n.d.

———. *Electronics and Sea Power.* New York: Stein and Day, 1975.

———. *The Submarine and Sea Power.* New York: Stein and Day, 1967.

Holley Jr., Irving B. *Ideas and Weapons: Exploitation of the Aerial Weapon by the United States during World War I: A Study of the Relationship of Technological Advance, Military Doctrine, and the Development of Weapons.* New Haven, CT: Yale University Press, 1953.

Hone, Thomas C., Norman Friedman, and Mark D. Mandeles. *American and British Aircraft Carrier Development, 1919–1941.* Annapolis, MD: Naval Institute Press, 1999.

Hone, Trent. *Learning War: The Evolution of Fighting Doctrine in the U.S. Navy, 1898–1945.* Annapolis, MD: Naval Institute Press, 2018.

Howarth, Stephen, and Derek Law, eds. *The Battle of the Atlantic, 1939–1945: The 50th Anniversary International Naval Conference.* Annapolis, MD: Naval Institute Press, 1994.

Howeth, L. S. *History of Communications-Electronics in the United States Navy.* Washington, DC: Office of Naval History, 1963.

Howse, Derek. *Radar at Sea: The Royal Navy in World War 2.* Annapolis, MD: Naval Institute Press, 1993.

Hythe, Viscount, ed. *The Naval Annual 1913.* Portsmouth, UK: J. Griffin and Co., 1913.

Iachino, Angelo. *Tramonto di una Grande Marina.* Milan: Arnoldo Mondadori, 1966.

Jane, Fred T., ed. *Jane's All the World's Aircraft 1913*. New York: Arco, 1969 reprint.

Jellicoe, John. *The Grand Fleet, 1914–1916: Its Creation, Development, and Work*. New York: George H. Doran Co., 1919.

Jentschura, Hansgeorg, Dieter Jung, and Peter Mickel. *Warships of the Imperial Japanese Navy, 1869–1945*. Annapolis, MD: Naval Institute Press, 1999.

Jolie, E. W. *A Brief History of U.S. Navy Torpedo Development*. Newport, RI: Naval Underwater Systems Center, 1978.

Kahn, David. *The Codebreakers: The Story of Secret Writing*. New York: MacMillan, 1967.

Karau, Mark D. "'Lost Opportunities': The Marinekorps Flandern and the German War Effort, 1914–1918." Ph.D. thesis, Florida State University, 2000.

Keegan, John. *Intelligence in War: Knowledge of the Enemy from Napoleon to Al-Qaeda*. New York: Alfred A. Knopf, 2003.

Knaak, Marcelle Size. *Encyclopedia of U.S. Air Force Aircraft and Missile Systems*. Vol. 1. Washington, DC: Office of Air Force History, 1978.

Knox, MacGregor. *Hitler's Italian Allies: Royal Armed Forces, Fascist Regime, and the War of 1940–1943*. New York: Cambridge University Press, 2000.

Koop, Gerhard, and Klaus-Peter Schmolke. *Heavy Cruisers of the Admiral Hipper Class*. Annapolis, MD: Naval Institute Press, 2000.

Koerver, Hans J., ed. *Room 40: German Naval Warfare, 1914–1918*. Vol. 1, *The Fleet in Action*. Berlin: Schaltungsdienst Lange o.H.G., 2009.

Kuenne, Robert E. *The Attack Submarine: A Study in Strategy*. New Haven, CT: Yale University Press, 1965.

LaCroix, Eric, and Linton Wells II. *Japanese Cruisers of the Pacific War*. Annapolis, MD: Naval Institute Press, 1997.

Lavery, Brian. *Churchill's Navy: The Ships, Men, and Organisation, 1939–1945*. London: Conway, 2006.

Layman, R. D. *Naval Aviation in the First World War: Its Impact and Influence*. Annapolis, MD: Naval Institute Press, 1996.

Llewellyn-Jones, Malcolm. "The Royal Navy on the Threshold of Modern Anti-Submarine Warfare 1944–1949." Ph.D. thesis, King's College, London, 2004.

Lott, Arnold S. *Most Dangerous Sea: A History of Mine Warfare, and an Account of U.S. Navy Mine Warfare Operations in World War II and Korea*. Annapolis, MD: Naval Institute Press, 1959.

Loxton, Bruce, with Chris Coulthard-Clark. *The Shame of Savo: Anatomy of a Naval Disaster*. Annapolis, MD: Naval Institute Press, 1994.

Lundstrom, John B. *The First Team: Pacific Naval Air Combat from Pearl Harbor to Midway*. Annapolis, MD: Naval Institute Press, 1984.

MacIntyre, Donald. *The Naval War against Hitler*. London: Batesford, 1971.

Marder, Arthur J. *From the Dreadnought to Scapa Flow*. 5 vols. Annapolis, MD: Naval Institute Press, 2013 reprint.

———. *Old Friends, New Enemies: The Royal Navy and the Imperial Japanese Navy, Strategic Illusions 1936–1941*. Oxford: Clarendon Press, 1981.

Marriott, Leo. *Catapult Aircraft: The Story of Seaplanes Flown from Battleships, Cruisers, and Other Warships of the World's Navies, 1912–1950*. Barnsley, UK: Pen & Sword, 2016.

Mason Jr., John T. *The Atlantic War Remembered: An Oral History Collection*. Annapolis, MD: Naval Institute Press, 1990.

Massie, Robert K. *Castles of Steel: Britain, Germany, and the Winning of the Great War at Sea*. New York: Random House, 2003.

Mattesini, Francesco. *Corrispondenza e Direttive Tecnico-Operative di Supermarina*. Vol. 1, Book 2. Rome: Ufficio Storico della Marina Militare, 2000.

McLaughlin, Stephen. *Russian and Soviet Battleships*. Annapolis, MD: Naval Institute Press, 2003.

Melia, Tamara Moser. *"Damn the Torpedoes": A Short History of U.S. Naval Mine Counter-measures, 1777–1991*. Washington, DC: U.S. Naval Historical Center, 1991.

Melhorn, Charles M. *Two-Block Fox: The Rise of the Aircraft Carrier, 1911–1929*. Annapolis, MD: Naval Institute Press, 1974.

Messimer, Dwight R. *Seek and Destroy: Antisubmarine Warfare in World War I*. Annapolis, MD: Naval Institute Press, 2001.

Middlebrook, Martin, and Chris Everitt. *The Bomber Command War Diaries: An Operational Reference Book, 1939–1945*. Barnsley, UK: Pen & Sword Aviation, 2014.

Mikesh, Robert C., and Shorzoe Abe. *Japanese Aircraft, 1910–1941*. Annapolis, MD: Naval Institute Press, 1990.

Millington-Drake, Eugene. *The Drama of* Graf Spee *and the Battle of the Plate*. London: Peter Davies, 1964.

Mitchell, William. *Winged Defense: The Development and Possibilities of Modern Air Power—Economic and Military*. New York: Knickerbocker Press, 1926.

Möller, Eberhard, and Werner Brack. *The Encyclopedia of U-Boats from 1904 to the Present*. Translated by Andrea Battson and Roger Chesneau. London: Greenhill Books, 2004.

Morison, Samuel Eliot. *History of United States Naval Operations in World War II*. 14 vols. Boston: Little Brown, 1947–85.

Murray, Williamson and Allan R. Millett, eds. *Military Innovation in the Interwar Period*. Cambridge, UK: Cambridge University Press, 1996.

Newpower, Anthony. *Iron Men and Tin Fish: The Race to Build a Better Torpedo during World War II*. Annapolis, MD: Naval Institute Press, 2006.

Nofi, Albert A. *To Train the Fleet for War: The U.S. Navy Fleet Problems, 1923–1940*. Washington, DC: Government Printing Office, 2010.

O'Hara, Vincent P. *Six Victories: North Africa, Malta, and the Mediterranean Convoy War, November 1941–March 1942*. Annapolis, MD: Naval Institute Press, 2019.

———. *Struggle for the Middle Sea: The Great Navies at War in the Mediterranean Theater, 1940–1945*. Annapolis, MD: Naval Institute Press, 2009.

———. *Torch: North Africa and the Allied Path to Victory*. Annapolis, MD: Naval Institute Press, 2015.

———. *The U.S. Navy against the Axis: Surface Combat, 1941–1945*. Annapolis, MD: Naval Institute Press, 2007.

O'Hara, Vincent P., and Leonard R. Heinz. *Clash of Fleets: Naval Battles of the Great War, 1914–18*. Annapolis, MD: Naval Institute Press, 2017.

O'Hara, Vincent P., W. David Dickson, and Richard Worth, eds. *On Seas Contested: The Seven Great Navies of the Second World War*. Annapolis, MD: Naval Institute Press, 2010.

———. *To Crown the Waves: The Great Navies of the First World War*. Annapolis, MD: Naval Institute Press, 2013.

Padfield, Peter. *War beneath the Sea: Submarine Conflict during World War II*. New York: John Wiley and Sons, 1995.

Palmer, Michael. *Command at Sea*. Cambridge, MA: Harvard University Press, 2005.

Parillo, Mark. *The Japanese Merchant Marine in World War II*. Annapolis, MD: Naval Institute Press, 1993.

Parrish, Thomas, *The Submarine: A History*. New York: Penguin, 2004.

Payne, Craig M. *Principles of Naval Weapon Systems*. Annapolis, MD: Naval Institute Press, 2006.

Peattie, Mark R. *Sunburst: The Rise of Japanese Naval Air Power, 1909–1941*. Annapolis, MD: Naval Institute Press, 2001.

Polmar, Norman. *Aircraft Carriers: A History of Carrier Aviation and Its Influence on World Events*, Vol. 1, *1909–1945*. Washington, DC: Potomac Books, 2006.

Polmar, Norman, et al. *Chronology of the Cold War at Sea, 1945–1991*. Annapolis, MD: Naval Institute Press, 1998.

Potter, John Deane. *Fiasco: The Break-out of the German Battleships*. New York: Stein and Day, 1970.

Prados, John. *Combined Fleet Decoded: The Secret History of American Intelligence and the Japanese Navy in World War II*. New York: Random House, 1995.

Price, Alfred. *Instruments of Darkness: The History of Electronic Warfare*. New York: Scribners, 1978.

Ranft, Brian, ed. *Technical Change and British Naval Policy, 1860–1939*. London: Hodder and Stoughton, 1977.

Ratcliff, R. A. *Delusions of Intelligence: Enigma, Ultra, and the End of Secure Ciphers*. New York: Cambridge University Press, 2006.

Raven, Alan. *British Cruiser Warfare: The Lessons of the Early War, 1939–1941*. Annapolis, MD: Naval Institute Press, 2019.

Roskill, Stephen. *Naval Policy between the Wars*. 2 vols. Barnsley, UK: Seaforth, 2016.

Rössler, Eberhard. *The U-Boat: The Evolution and Technical History of German Submarines*. Annapolis, MD: Naval Institute Press, 1981.

Rowland, Buford, and William B. Boyd. *U.S. Navy Bureau of Ordnance in World War II*. Washington, DC: Government Printing Office, n.d.

Sadkovich, James. *The Italian Navy in World War II*. Westport, CT: Greenwood, 1994.

Sawyer, Ralph D., with Mei-Chun Lee Sawyer. *Fire and Water: The Art of Incendiary and Aquatic Warfare in China*. Boulder, CO: Westview Press, 2004.

Scheer, Reinhard. *Germany's High Sea Fleet in the World War*. London: Cassell and Company, 1920.

Sigaud, Louis A. *Douhet and Aerial Warfare*. New York: G. P. Putnam's Sons, 1941.

Simpson, Michael, ed. *The Somerville Papers: Selections from the Private and Official Correspondence of Admiral of the Fleet Sir James Somerville*. Aldershot, UK: Scolar Press, 1996.

Sokol, Anthony E. *The Imperial and Royal Austro-Hungarian Navy*. Annapolis, MD: Naval Institute Press, 1968.

Sokol, Hans H. *Österreich-Ungarns Seekrieg, 1914–1918*. Graz, Austria: Akademische Druck-u. Verlagsanstalt, 1967.

Sondhaus, Lawrence. *German Submarine Warfare in World War I: The Onset of Total War at Sea*. Lanham, MD: Rowman and Littlefield, 2017.

———. *The Great War at Sea: A Naval History of the First World War*. Cambridge, UK: Cambridge University Press, 2014.

Staff, Gary. *Battle for the Baltic Islands 1917: Triumph of the Imperial German Navy*. Barnsley, UK: Pen & Sword Maritime, 2008.

———. *Battle on the Seven Seas: German Cruiser Battles, 1914–1918*. Barnsley, UK: Pen & Sword Maritime, 2011.

Sternhell, Charles M., and Alan M. Thorndike. *Antisubmarine Warfare in World War II*. Washington, DC: Navy Department, 1946.

Stevenson, David. *With Our Backs to the Wall: Victory and Defeat in 1918*. Cambridge, MA: Harvard University Press, 2011.

Strachan, Hew. *The First World War*. Vol. 1. Oxford: Oxford University Press, 2001.

Sueter, Murray F. *The Evolution of the Submarine Boat Mine and Torpedo from the Sixteenth Century until the Present Time*. 2nd edition. Portsmouth, UK: Gieve, Matthews, and Seagrove, n.d.

Swanborough, Gordon, and Peter M. Bowers. *United States Navy Aircraft since 1911*. London: Putnam Aeronautical Books, 1990.

Swords, Sean S. *Technical History of the Beginnings of Radar*. London: Peregrinus, 1986.

Tarrant, V. E. *Jutland, the German Perspective: A New View of the Great Battle, 31 May 1916*. Annapolis, MD: Naval Institute Press, 1995.

———. *The Last Year of the Kriegsmarine, May 1944—May 1945*. Annapolis, MD: Naval Institute Press, 1994.

Taylor, Bruce, ed. *The World of the Battleship: The Lives and Careers of Twenty-One Capital Ships from the World's Navies, 1880–1990*. Annapolis, MD: Naval Institute Press, 2018.

Thetford, Owen. *British Naval Aircraft since 1912*. London: Putnam Aeronautical Books, 1991.

Thomas, Andrew. *Defiant, Blenheim, and Havoc Aces*. Long Island City, NY: Osprey, 2012.

Till, Geoffrey. *Air Power and the Royal Navy, 1914–1945: A Historical Survey*. London: Jane's, 1979.

Tillman, Barrett. *The Dauntless Dive Bomber of World War II*. Annapolis, MD: Naval Institute Press, 1976.

Tooze, Adam. *The Wages of Destruction: The Making and Breaking of the Nazi Economy*. New York: Penguin Books, 2006.

Tosti, Amedeo. *La Guerra Sotterranea: Episodi della Guerra di Mine sulla Fronte Italiana [1915–1918]*. Milan: Mondadori, 1935.

Uhlig, Frank. *How Navies Fight: The U.S. Navy and Its Allies*. Annapolis, MD: Naval Institute Press, 1994.

Warner, Denis, and Peggy Warner. *The Tide at Sunrise: A History of the Russo-Japanese War, 1904–1905*. New York: Charterhouse, 1974.

Watson, Raymond C. *Radar Origins Worldwide: History of Its Evolution in 13 Nations through World War II*. Victoria, BC: Trafford, 2009.

Whitley, M. J. *German Cruisers of World War Two*. Annapolis, MD: Naval Institute Press, 1987.

———. *German Destroyers of World War Two*. Annapolis, MD: Naval Institute Press, 1991.

Wildenberg, Thomas. *Billy Mitchell's War with the Navy: The Interwar Rivalry over Air Power*. Annapolis, MD: Naval Institute Press, 2013.

Wildenberg, Thomas, and Norman Polmar. *Ship Killers: A History of the American Torpedo*. Annapolis, MD: Naval Institute Press, 2010.

Williams, Kathleen Broome. *Secret Weapon: U.S. High-Frequency Direction Finding in the Battle of the Atlantic*. Annapolis, MD: Naval Institute Press, 1996.

Willmott, H. P. *The Last Century of Sea Power*. Vol. 1. Bloomington and Indianapolis: Indiana University Press, 2009.

Wilson, Herbert W. *Battleships in Action*. 2 vols. Annapolis, MD: Naval Institute Press, 1995 reprint.

Wolz, Nicholas. *From Imperial Splendor to Internment: The German Navy in the First World War*. Annapolis, MD: Naval Institute Press, 2013.

Woodward, Sandy, and Patrick Robinson. *One Hundred Days: The Memoirs of the Falklands Battle Group Commander*. Annapolis, MD: Naval Institute Press, 1997.

Chapters, Magazines, and Journals

Alger, Philip R. "The Employment of Submarine Mines in Future Naval Wars." U.S. Naval Institute *Proceedings* 34, no. 3 (September 1908): 1039–42.

Almog, Ze'ev. "The Israeli Navy Beat the Odds." U.S. Naval Institute *Proceedings* 123, no. 3 (March 1997): 106–8.

Alpher, Victor S. "Torpedo Exploder Mechanisms of World War II: A New Perspective." *The Submarine Review* (April 2010): 83–105.

Anonymous. "Aircraft with the Fleet." *Naval Review* 11, no. 2 (1922): 282–93.

———. "The Air Ministry: A Suggested Policy." *Naval Review* 7, no. 4 (1919): 443–45.

———. "Air Policy of the Future." *Naval Review* 7, no. 4 (1919): 446–50.

———. "Air Power." *Naval Review* 1, no. 2 (1913): 57–75.

———. "Air Service." *Flight* 5, no. 2 (May 31, 1913): 588.

———. "Correspondence." *Naval Review* 2, no.1 (1914): 73.

———. "Eddies." *Flight* 7, no. 27 (July 2, 1915): 476–77.

———. "The Fiends of the Air. The Influence of Aircraft on Imperial Defense." *Naval Review* 11, no. 1 (1923): 81–115.

———. "Four Zeppelins for the German Navy." *Flight* 1, no. 2 (January 9, 1909): 27.

———. "The Future of the Battleship." *Naval Review* 8, no. 2 (1920): 167–75, and no. 3 (1920): 368–69.

———. "Great Ships or Disaster." *Naval Review* 9, no. 2 (1921): 245–47.

———. "The Influence of the Future of Aircraft upon Problems of Imperial Defense." *Naval Review* 10, no. 2 (1922): 220–47.

———. "The Influence of the Long-Range Torpedo on Battle Tactics." *Naval Review* 3, no. 1 (1915): 56–64.

———. "Lament for the Mine I." *Naval Review* 48, no. 3 (1964): 277–83.

———. "Lament for the Mine II." *Naval Review* 48, no. 4 (1964): 380–83.

———. "Minesweeping." *The International Military Digest Annual*. New York: Cumulative Digest Corporation, 1917, 464–67.

———. "Naval Air Requirements." *Naval Review* 7, no. 3 (1919): 305–13.

———. "Naval Aviation: A Reform Required." *Naval Review* 9, no. 2 (1921): 269–73.

———. "Naval Strategy—Effect of Aircraft on." *Naval Review* 1, no. 4 (1913): 256–69.

———. "The Navy and the Air." *Naval Review* 9, no. 1 (1921): 71–73.

———. "Notes on Fleet Tactics." *Naval Review* 10, no. 1 (1922): 42–52.

———. "A Plea for a Naval Air Service." *Naval Review* 7, no. 4 (1919): 451–53.

———. "The Progress of Aircraft." *Naval Review* 8, no. 3 (1920): 408–22.

———. "The Science of Admiralty III." *Naval Review* 48, no. 1 (1964): 15–26.

———. "Some Remarks on the Evolution of Naval Warfare." *Naval Review* 1, no. 1 (1913): 53–56.

———. "Studies in the Theory of Naval Tactics III." *Naval Review* 1, no. 4 (1913): 208–23.

———. "Submarines and Aircraft." *Naval Review* 2, no. 1 (1914): 73.

———. "Submarine Torpedo Boat for the United States Navy." U.S. Naval Institute *Proceedings* 14, no. 1 (January 1888): 253–57.

———. "Torpedo Fire in Future Fleet Actions." *Naval Review* 2, no. 1 (1914): 47–57.

———. "What Changes Are Suggested in Naval Construction and Tactics as a Result of: (a) The Experience of the War? (b) The Development in Submarine and Aerial Warfare in the Future?" *Naval Review* 9, no. 4 (1921): 596–618.

———. "Wireless Telephony." *Naval Review* 9, no. 1 (1921): 159–62.

Bartlett, H. T. "Mission of Aircraft with the Fleet." U.S. Naval Institute *Proceedings* 45, no. 5 (May 1919): 729–42.

Beach, Edward L. "Our Torpedo-Boat Flotilla. The Training Needed to Insure Its Efficiency." U.S. Naval Institute *Proceedings* 29, no. 1 (January 1903): 117–59.

Bigelow, Robert P. "Wireless in Warfare, 1885–1914." U.S. Naval Institute *Proceedings* 77, no. 2 (February 1951): 117–27.

Bird, Keith W., and Jason Hines. "In the Shadow of Ultra: A Reappraisal of German Naval Communications Intelligence in 1914–1918." *The Northern Mariner* 18, no. 2 (Spring 2018): 98–117.

Brown, David K. "Defeat in the Atlantic? Anti-Submarine Warfare 1917–19." *Warship 2002–2003* (2003): 126–66.

———. "Some Thoughts on British Mines in the First World War." *Warship 2001–2002* (2002): 99–102.

Browning Jr., Robert M. "Damn the Torpedoes." *Naval History* 28, no. 4 (July 2014): 38–43.

Cernuschi, Enrico, and Vincent P. O'Hara. "Search for a Flattop: The Italian Navy and the Aircraft Carrier 1907–2007." *Warship 2007* (2007): 61–80.

Chambers, W. Irving. "Aviation and Aeroplanes." U.S. Naval Institute *Proceedings* 37, no. 1 (March 1911): 163–203.

———. "Aviation Today, and the Necessity for a National Aerodynamics Laboratory." U.S. Naval Institute *Proceedings* 38, no. 4 (December 1912): 1491–528.

Chandler, L. H. "The Automobile Torpedo and Its Uses." U.S. Naval Institute *Proceedings* 26, no. 1 (January 1900): 47–71.

———. "Automobile Torpedoes: Their Use and Probable Effectiveness." U.S. Naval Institute *Proceedings* 29, no. 4 (September 1903): 883–915.

Collins, A. Frederick. "A Review of Wireless-Telegraph Engineering Practice." *Engineering Magazine* 24 (October 1902–March 1903): 231–57.

Colvin, Robert D. "Aftermath of the *Elath*." U.S. Naval Institute *Proceedings* 95, no. 10 (October 1969): 60–67.

Cosentino, Michele. "From *Elba* to *Europa*." *Warship 2017* (2017): 63–76.

Cook, Alan. "Shipborne Radar in World War II: Some Recollections." *Note and Records of the Royal Society of London* 58, no. 3 (September 2004): 295–98.

Craven, T. T. "Naval Aviation." U.S. Naval Institute *Proceedings* 46, no. 2 (February 1920): 181–91.

Cummings, D. E. "'Aviation' or 'Naval Aviation': Which?" U.S. Naval Institute *Proceedings* 46, no. 2 (February 1920): 177–80.

———. "Use of Aircraft in Naval Warfare." U.S. Naval Institute *Proceedings* 47, no. 11 (November 1921): 1677–88.

Cuniberti, Vittorio. "All Torpedoes!" Translated by Thomas Withers Jr. U.S. Naval Institute *Proceedings* 40, no. 1 (January 1914): 27–31.

Daveluy, Rene. "Maritime Aviation." Translated by G. M. Baum. U.S. Naval Institute *Proceedings* 39, no. 3 (September 1913): 1097–109.

De Ninno, Fabio. "A Technological Fiasco: Scientific Research, Institutional Culture, and Fascism in the Italian Navy (1919–1940)." *The Journal of Military History* 84 (July 2020): 798–824.

Eberle, E. W. "The Elements of Sea Power and the Future of the Navy." U.S. Naval Institute *Proceedings* 51, no. 10 (October 1925): 1832–37.

Edwards, W. Atlee. "The U.S. Naval Air Force in Action 1917–18." U.S. Naval Institute *Proceedings* 48, no. 11 (November 1922): 1863–82.

Ferguson, J. N. "The Submarine Mine." U.S. Naval Institute *Proceedings* 40, no. 6 (November 1914): 1697–706.

Fiske, Bradley A. "Air Power." U.S. Naval Institute *Proceedings* 43, no. 8 (August 1917): 1701–4.

———. "Electricity in Naval Life." U.S. Naval Institute *Proceedings* 22, no. 2 (April 1896): 323–428.

———. "Torpedo Plane and Bomber." U.S. Naval Institute *Proceedings* 48, no. 9 (September 1922): 1473–78.

FitzSimonds, James R. "Aircraft Carriers versus Battleships in War and Myth: Demythologizing Carrier Air Dominance at Sea." *Journal of Military History* 84 (July 2020): 843–65.

Friedman, Norman. "A Massive Torpedo." *Naval History* 33, no. 2 (April 2019): 6–7.

Fuller, J. F. C. "What Changes Are Suggested in Naval Construction and Tactics as a Result of: (a) The Experience of the War? (b) The Development in Submarine and Aerial Warfare in the Future?" *Naval Review* 10, no. 1 (1922): 73–104.

Gayer, A. "Summary of German Submarine Operations in the Various Theaters of War from 1914 to 1918." Translated by W. P. Beehler. U.S. Naval Institute *Proceedings* 52, no. 4 (April 1926): 621–59.

Grove, Eric J. "A War Fleet Built for Peace: British Naval Rearmament in the 1930s and the Dilemma of Deterrence versus Defence." *Naval War College Review* 44, no. 2 (Spring 1991): 82–92.

Gusewelle, Jack K. "Science and the Admiralty during World War I." In Gerald Jordan, ed., *Naval Warfare in the Twentieth Century 1900–1945*. New York: Crane, Russak, and Co., 1977, 105–16.

Hilton, Carl H. "Isaac Peral and His Submarine," U.S. Naval Institute *Proceedings* 82, no. 11 (November 1956): 1194–202.

Hind, Andrew. "The Cruise Missile Comes of Age." *Naval History* 22, no. 5 (October 2008): 52–57.

Hines, Jason. "Sins of Omission and Commission: A Reassessment of the Role of Intelligence in the Battle of Jutland." *The Journal of Military History* 72, no. 4 (October 2008): 1117–54.

Hirama, Yoichi. "Japanese Naval Preparations for World War II." *Naval War College Review* 44, no. 2 (Spring 1991): 63–81.

Holler, Roger A. "The Evolution of the Sonobuoy from World War II to the Cold War." *Journal of Underwater Acoustics* (January 2014): 322–46. https://apps.dtic.mil/dtic/tr/fulltext/u2/a597432.pdf.

Home, R. W., and Morris F. Low. "Postwar Scientific Intelligence Missions to Japan." *Isis* 84, no. 3 (September 1993): 527–37.

Hunsaker, J. C. "The Navy's First Airships." U.S. Naval Institute *Proceedings* 45, no. 8 (August 1919): 1347–68.

Inbar, Efraim. "The Israeli Navy." *Naval War College Review* 43, no. 1 (Winter 1990): 100–11.

Itani, Jiro, Hans Lengerer, and Tomoko Rehm-Takahara. "Japanese Oxygen Torpedoes and Fire Control Systems." *Warship 1991* (1991): 121–31.

Jackson, John P. "Employment and Tactics of Aircraft in Naval Warfare." U.S. Naval Institute *Proceedings* 48, no. 8 (August 1922): 1263–97.

Jenkins, P. E. "German Mines." *Journal of Naval Science* 6, no. 2 (April 1980).

Juurvee, Ivo. "The Birth of Russian SIGINT during World War I on the Baltic Sea." *Intelligence and National Security* 32, no. 3 (February 2017): 300–12.

Kahn, David. "The Wreck of the *Magdeburg*." *Military History Quarterly* 2, no. 2 (1990): 97–103.

Kaiser, Walter. "British Radar Technology and Neville Chamberlain's Appeasement Policy." *Icon* 2 (1996): 29–52.

Lapointe, E. "Aviation in the Navy." U.S. Naval Institute *Proceedings* 38, no. 2 (June 1912): 627–56.

Lautenschläger, Karl. "The Submarine in Naval Warfare, 1901–2001." *International Security* 11, no. 3 (Winter 1986/87): 94–140.

———. "Technology and the Evolution of Naval Warfare." *International Security* 8, no. 2 (Fall 1983): 3–51.

Le Compte, Tom. "The Few, the Brave, the Lucky." *Air & Space*. November 2008. https://www.airspacemag.com/history-of-flight/the-few-the-brave-the-lucky-45053770/?page=1.

Levie, Howard S. "Submarine Warfare: With Emphasis on the 1936 London Protocol." In *International Law Studies 65: Targeting Enemy Merchant Shipping*. Edited by Richard J. Grunawalt. Newport, RI: Naval War College, 1993, 28–71.

Llewellyn-Jones, Malcolm. "On Britain's Doorstep: The Hunt for U-247." In *Fighting at Sea: Naval Battles from the Ages of Sail and Steam*. Edited by Douglas M. McLean. Quebec: Robin Bass Studio, 2008: 241–88.

Lundeberg, Philip K. "The German Naval Critique of the U-Boat Campaign, 1915–1918." *Military Affairs* 27, no. 3 (Autumn 1963): 119–30.

Marolda, Edward J. "U.S. Mining and Mine Clearance in North Vietnam." https://www.history.navy.mil/research/library/online-reading-room/title-list-alphabetically/u/u-s-mining-and-mine-clearance-in-north-vietnam.html.

Mattesini, Francesco. "The Italian Radar Failure in War—A Waste of Energy." Italian Maritime and Naval Documentation Association, August 10, 2019. http://www.aidmen.it/topic/1391-il-mancato-radar-italiano-in-guerra-uno-spreco-di-energie/.

McKee, Fraser M. "An Explosive Story: The Rise and Fall of the Common Depth Charge." *The Northern Mariner* 3, no. 1 (January 1993), 45–58.

Meacham, James A. "Four Mining Campaigns: An Historical Analysis of the Decisions of the Commanders." *Naval War College Review* 20, no. 6 (June 1967): 58–129.

Mercan, Evren. "The Impact of Allied Submarine Operations on Ottoman Decision-Making during the Gallipoli Campaign." *Journal for Maritime Research* 19, no. 1 (2017): 63–75.

Milford, Frederick J. "U.S. Navy Torpedoes, Part Two: The Great Torpedo Scandal, 1941–43." *The Submarine Review* (October 1996). http://www.geocities.ws/pentagon/1592/ustorp2.htm.

Miller Jr., Martin J. "The Israeli Navy: 26 Years of Non-peace." U.S. Naval Institute *Proceedings* 101, no. 2 (February 1975): 49–54.

Moffett, William A. "Naval Aviation." U.S. Naval Institute *Proceedings* 53, no. 10 (October 1927): 1081–83.

Murphy, William Scanlan. "Dive! Dive! Dive!" *New Scientist* 7 (January 1989): 36–41.

National Security Agency. "The Origination and Evolution of Radio Traffic Analysis." *Cryptologic Quarterly* 6, no. 1 (Spring 1987): 21–40.

Neitzel, Sönke. "Kriegsmarine and Luftwaffe Cooperation in the War against Britain." *War in History* 10, no. 4 (November 2003): 448–63.

O'Hanlon, Michael. "A Retrospective on the So-Called Revolution in Military Affairs, 2000–2020." Brookings Institution, 2018. https://www.brookings.edu/wp-content/uploads/2018/09/FP_20181217_defense_advances_pt1.pdf.

O'Hara, Vincent P., and Enrico Cernuschi. "Frogmen against a Fleet." *Naval War College Review* 68, no. 3 (Summer 2015): 119–37.

———. "The Other Ultra." *Naval War College Review* 66, no. 3 (Summer 2013): 121–42.

Partala, M. A. "The Origins of Radio Intelligence in the Russian Fleet in the Russo-Japanese War, 1904–1905." Translated by Stephen McLaughlin. *Izvestiia SPbGETU "LETI"—Seriia Istoriia nauki, obrazovaniia i tekhniki*, no. 1 (2007): 7–15.

Peck, Michael. "The First Nations to Use Aircraft to Bomb Ships Were . . . Greece and Mexico?" *The National Interest*, June 10, 2017. https://nationalinterest.org/blog/the-buzz/the-first-nations-use-aircraft-bomb-ships-were-greece-mexico-21093.

Pietzker, Felix. "Principles of Naval Aeronautics." Translated by G. M. Baum. U.S. Naval Institute *Proceedings* 40, no. 2 (March-April 1914): 389–401.

Rabinovich, Abraham. "From 'Futuristic Whimsy' to Naval Reality." *Naval History* 28, no. 3 (June 2014): 40–47.

Rahav, Eli. "Missile Boat Warfare: Israeli Style." U.S. Naval Institute *Proceedings* 112, no. 3 (March 1986): 107–13.

Ramsey, DeWitt C. "The Development of Aviation in the Fleet." U.S. Naval Institute *Proceedings* 49, no. 9 (September 1923): 1395–417.

Refaat, Ashraf M. "How the Egyptian Navy Fought the October War." U.S. Naval Institute *Proceedings* 121, no. 3 (March 1995): 94–97.

Rickover, H. G. "International Law and the Submarine." U.S. Naval Institute *Proceedings* 61, no. 9 (September 1935): 1213–27.

Roblin, Sebastien. "How the Falklands War (Thanks to a Stealthy Submarine) Could Have Gone Very Differently." *The National Interest*, November 27, 2016. https://nationalinterest.org/blog/how-the-falklands-war-thanks-stealthy-submarine-could-have-18495.

Ruge, Friedrich. "German Minesweepers in World War II." U.S. Naval Institute *Proceedings* 78, no. 9 (September 1952): 995–1003.

Saufley, R. C. "Naval Aviation: Its Value and Needs." U.S. Naval Institute *Proceedings* 40, no. 5 (September 1914): 1460–72.

———. "The Work Ahead of Naval Aviation." U.S. Naval Institute *Proceedings* 41, no. 2 (March 1915): 505–12.

Sears, W. J. "A General Description of the Whitehead Torpedo." U.S. Naval Institute *Proceedings* 22, no. 4 (October 1896): 803–38.

Sieche, Erwin. "German Naval Radar to 1945." *Warship* 6, no. 21 (1982): 2–10, and *Warship* 6, no. 22 (1982): 146–57.

Sifferlinger, Nikolaus A. "Austro-Hungarian and British Radio Intelligence." *Maritimes*, 31 March 2013. http://maritimes.at/en/2013/no-article-yet-2/.

Spindler, Arno. "The Value of the Submarine in Naval Warfare." Translated by W. P. Beehler. U.S. Naval Institute *Proceedings* 52, no. 5 (May 1926): 835–54.

Stirling Jr., Yates. "The Destroyer—Our Naval Weakness." U.S. Naval Institute *Proceedings* 36, no. 2 (June 1910): 469–80.

Stone, Ellery W. "The Poulsen Arc." U.S. Naval Institute *Proceedings* 46, no. 7 (July 1920): 1049–73.

Studd, R. G. "Changes in Naval Construction and Tactics Which Suggest Themselves as the Result of War Experience and the Future Development in Submarine and Aerial Activity." *Naval Review* 9, no. 3 (1921): 420–38.

Sypher, J. H. "Notes on the Obrey Device for Torpedoes." U.S. Naval Institute *Proceedings* 23, no. 4 (October 1897): 655–61.

Turner, R. K., and T. D. Ruddock. "Gun Defense against Torpedo Planes." U.S. Naval Institute *Proceedings* 48, no. 10 (October 1922): 1687–95.

Van der Veer, Norman. "Mining Operations in the War." U.S. Naval Institute *Proceedings* 45, no. 11 (November 1919): 1857–65.

Voitoux, Gabriel. "New Weapons and Old Ones." U.S. Naval Institute *Proceedings* 49, no. 10 (October 1923): 1635–41.

Weir, Gary E. "Tirpitz, Technology, and Building U-Boats, 1897–1916." *The International History Review* 6, no. 2 (May 1984): 174–90.

Whitby, Michael J. "The Development of Action Information Organization during the Second World War." Research Paper. DHH 2010/5, July 1990.

———. "Planning, Challenge, and Execution: The Seaward Defense of the Assault Area off Normandy, 6–14 June 1944." Unpublished paper.

———. "Shoot, Shoot, Shoot: Destroyer Night Fighting and the Battle of Ile de Batz." In Douglas M. McLean, ed., *Fighting at Sea: Naval Battles from the Ages of Sail and Steam*. Quebec: Robin Bass Studio, 2008, 183–238.

Williams, Dion. "The Defense of Our Naval Stations." U.S. Naval Institute *Proceedings* 28, no. 2 (June 1902): 181–94.

Wilson, Michael. "The British 'B' Class Submarine." *Warship* 5, no. 17 (1981): 74–75.

Woodhouse, Henry. "The Aircraft's Part in Beating the U-Boat." U.S. Naval Institute *Proceedings* 44, no. 12 (December 1918): 2727–38.

———. "The Torpedoplane: The New Weapon Which Promises to Revolutionize Naval Tactics." U.S. Naval Institute *Proceedings* 45, no. 5 (May 1919): 743–52.

Zartmann, Carlos E. "The Operations of Argentine Submarines in the Malvinas War." Naval Intelligence Support Center translation from *Marine Rundschau* (12 April 1984): 129–31.

Presentations

McLaughlin, Stephen. "Russian Naval Radio Intelligence in the First World War." Presentation, USS *Midway* Museum, San Diego, California, February 29, 2020.

Websites

Library of Congress. "Laying of Automatic Submarine Contact Mines." Article VIII, convention signed at the Hague, 18 October 1907. https://www.loc.gov/law/help/us -treaties/bevans/m-ust000001-0669.pdf.

Mason, Geoffrey B. "HF/DF or HUFF DUFF—High Frequency Radio Direction Finding in Royal Navy Warships." Naval-History.net, 1992. https://www.naval-history .net/xGM-Tech-HFDF.htm.

Southwest Museum of Engineering, Communication, and Computation. "Morgan McMahon and Radar." https://www.smecc.org/mcmahon's_radars!.htm.

Woolrich, R. S. "Fighter-Direction Materiel and Technique, 1939–45." Navigating and Direction Officers' Association. http://www.ndassoc.net/docs/nd-assoc-fighter -direction.pdf.

World War I Naval Combat. worldwar1.co.uk.

INDEX

Aboukir (Great Britain), 162
acoustic mine. *See* mine types
Action Information Organization (AIO),
     136–37. *See also* combat information
     center (CIC)
AD104. *See* mine types
Admiral Hipper (Germany), 129
Adriatic Sea, 163–64, 197, 205, 210; and
     mines, 30, 35
Ainsworth, Walden, 74
air power, 222, 228; and application of, 224,
     229; in Germany, 216; in Japan 219; and
     philosophy of, 211–13
aircraft carriers, 213, 227; and Axis, 222;
     and evolution of, 199–201, 218; and
     Great Britain, 220–21; and Japan, 206,
     219–20, 226, 235; and survivability
     of, 104, 132, 226, 229–30; and United
     States, 218–19, 224. *See also* aircraft
     types: carrier aircraft; seaplane
     carriers
aircraft types: Beaufort, 174; Blenheim,
     126; Caproni, 205; carrier aircraft, 68,
     200, 203, 210, 213, 218–22; F-35, 229,
     244; FW200, 142; He111, 215; Liberator,
     184–85; S.79, 110; Schütte-Lanz, 196;
     Short 184, 205; Sopwith Camel, 200,
     206; Sopwith Cuckoo, 205; Sopwith
     Pup, 200; Sutherland, 185; Swordfish,
     184–85, 221; Wellington, 126, 142
Airship No. 1 (Great Britain), 194
Ajax (Great Britain), 128, 223
Akron (United States), 211
Alberich. *See* countermeasures
Alexandria, 41, 49
Alexandrovski (Russia), 155

Algeria, 178, 214
Algerié (France), 124
Alstitt, Samuel, 155
Amatol. *See* explosives
American Revolutionary War, 18–19, 154
Amethyst (Great Britain), 55
ammonia perchlorate. *See* explosives
Amphion (Great Britain), 30
Amrum Bank. *See* mine barrages and
     minefields
Amur (Russia), 25
Anglo-American cooperation. *See*
     cooperation
antisubmarine warfare (ASW), 168–73,
     181, 191, 225; and aircraft, 207–8, 228;
     and the Falklands War, 189; and radio,
     103; and sonobuoys, 186, 205, 240; and
     tactics of, 161, 184–85; and weapons of,
     76–77, 174–76, 186. *See also* France. *See*
     radar detectors
Aquidaban (Brazil), 56
Arab-Israeli Wars, 7, 148–49
Arghetto. *See* radio types
Argus (Great Britain), 201
Ark Royal (Great Britain), 130, 152
Army Air Forces. *See* United States
artificial intelligence, 2, 7
Asdic. *See* sonar
ASV Mark II. *See* radar types
ASV Mark XI. *See* radar types
Atlantic Conveyor (Great Britain), 149
Attentive (Great Britain), 205
Audacious (Great Britain), 30, 255
Augaur. *See* radio stations
Axis: and African traffic, 182, 223;
     and intelligence, 106; and naval

missiles, 111, 148–49; and Bat, 143;
   and Exocet, 149, 227; and Fritz-X
   (Ruhrstahl PC 1400FX), 111, 237;
   and Gabriel, 148; and Harpoon,
   149; and Hs 293, 111, 237; and
   OTOMAT, 149; and P-15 Termit,
   147–48
Mitchell, William, 7, 216–17, 228. *See also*
   air power
Miyako (Japan), 27
Mk 24 Tigerfish. *See* torpedo types
Mk-37. *See* torpedo types
Mk VIII. *See* torpedo types
Moltke (Germany), 34, 165
Monitor (United States), 148
Moon Island, 34
Morocco, 178, 214
Morse code, 82, 130
Mussolini, Benito, 124

Nauru. *See* radio stations
Naval Research Laboratory, 123
Naval War College, 50, 218
Navarin (Russia), 27
Nelson (Great Britain), 42, 123
Nelson, Horatio, 10, 114
Neptune, Operation, 138
New Ironsides (United States), 20
New York (United States), 123, 127
Nimitz, Chester, 50, 137
Nitrocellulose. *See* explosives
Nordenfelt, Thorsten, 155
Nordenfelt I (Greece), 155
Nordenfelt II (Ottoman), 155
Nordenfelt IV (Russia), 155
Noreen Mary (Great Britain), 184
Norfolk (Great Britain), 129
Normandie (France), 123
Normandy, 138–39, 184. *See also* Neptune,
   Operation
North Sea, 30, 64, 203; and intelligence,
   96–99, 101; and mines, 37; and
   submarines, 90, 159–60

North Sea Barrage. *See* mine barrages and
   minefields
Northern Barrage. *See* mine barrages and
   minefields
nuclear power, 1, 4, 7, 15, 49, 188. *See also*
   submarines
nuclear weapons, 4, 19

Obry, Ludwig, 59
Obry device. *See* inventions
Ocean (Great Britain), 33
Okinawa, 42, 145
Orkneys. *See* mine barrages and minefields
Osa-class (Egypt), 148
Oslo Report, 76
Ostfriesland (Germany), 217
OTOMAT. *See* missiles
Otranto, Strait of, 35
Otranto barrier. *See* mine barrages and
   minefields

P-15 Termit. *See* missiles
P200. *See* mine types
Pacific, War of the, 14, 56
Pacific Fleet. *See* United States (U.S.)
   Navy
Panama Canal, 91
paravane. *See* minesweeping
Pathfinder (Great Britain), 161
Pearl Harbor, 206, 224, 243
Peattie, Mark, 42
Peral, Isaac, 155
Persian Gulf Tanker Wars, 7, 48, 149, 229
Petropavlovsk (Russia), 26
Philippine Sea, Battle of the, 132, 230
picric acid. *See* explosives
Pietro Micca (Italy), 54
Pietzker, Felix, 198
plan position indicator (PPI), 132, 134, 139.
   See also radar
Pluton (France), 40
Pobeda (Russia), 26
Pola (Italy), 221

65; and France, 54, 56; and impact of, 3, 78–79, 224, 239, 231, 243; and Japan, 8, 56–57, 61–64t; 67–68, 73–74, 79; and Russia, 54t, 78; and Russo-Japanese War, 60–64; and submarines, 156–57; and World War I, 64–66, 162, 205–6; and World War II, 70–74, 136–38, 174. *See also* France; Germany; inventions; Italy; torpedo types
Trafalgar, Battle of, 6, 10, 114
traffic analysis. *See* intelligence
Trenchard, Hugh, 116, 212
trinitrotoluene (TNT). *See* explosives
Triple Alliance, 30
Triple Alliance, War of the, 20
Triumph (Great Britain), 164
Tsingtao (Qingdao), 90, 196
Tsushima, Battle of, 6, 37, 62–64, 84–86, 93
Turner, Richmond K, 127
Turtle (United Colonies), 19, 154
Type 21. *See* radar types
Type 21 GO dentan. *See* radar types
Type 271. *See* radar types
Type 276. *See* radar types
Type 279. *See* radar types
Type 282. *See* radar types
Type 284. *See* radar types
Type 285. *See* radar types
Type 286. *See* radar types
Type 286M. *See* radar types
Type 79X. *See* radar types
Type 79Z. *See* radar types
Type 91. *See* torpedo types
Type 93. *See* torpedo types
Type 97. *See* intelligence
Type D. *See* depth charge types
Type VII submarine, 174, 187
Type VIIC submarine, 184
Type XVIIB submarine, 187
Type XXI submarine, 187–88
Type XXIII submarine, 187
Typex. *See* intelligence

U-12 (Austria Hungry), 163
U-13 (Germany), 160
U-15 (Germany), 160
U-17 (Germany), 164
U-18 (Germany), 162
U-19 class (Germany), 157
U-20 (Germany), 162
U-205 (Germany), 142
U-21 (Germany), 161, 164
U-247 (Germany), 184–86, 225
U-2511 (Germany), 187
U-35 (Germany), 66
U-570 (Germany), 174
U-68 (Germany), 171
U-794 (Germany), 187
U-9 (Germany), 162
UC-2 (Germany), 34
United States: and aircraft carriers, 218, 227–29, 235; and Army, 194, 217; and Army Air Forces, 45, 47; and ASW, 171–72; and mines, 37t, 40, 43, 46–48, 50; and naval aviation, 195, 197, 200, 212, 226, 229; and radar, 116, 123, 125, 127–38, 145, 236; and radio, 82–83, 87, 103–4, 108–10, 123; and submarines, 147, 156, 160t, 176t, 179, 181–82; and torpedoes, 53, 55, 60, 67t, 68t–72, 76, 80. *See also* cooperation
United States (U.S.) Navy: and Destroyer Squadron 18, 139; and direction-finding, 107; and innovation, 137, 241; and missiles, 143, 148–49; and night surface combat, 237; Pacific Fleet, 72, 137; and Third/Fifth Fleet, 228

V-80 (Germany), 186
vacuum tube. *See* inventions
Valiant (Great Britain), 129, 131
VB. *See* intelligence
Vella Gulf, Battle of, 138
Veracruz, 83, 197
Vernon (Great Britain), 29, 35
Vesuvius (Great Britain), 53, 54t

ABOUT THE AUTHORS

VINCENT P. O'HARA is an independent naval historian and the author of thirteen works, including *Six Victories: North Africa, Malta, and the Mediterranean Convoy War, November 1941–March 1942*, and *Clash of Fleets: Naval Battles of the Great War, 1914–18*, with Leonard R. Heinz. He holds a history degree from the University of California, Berkeley, and lives in Chula Vista, California.

LEONARD R. HEINZ worked for many years as a financial services lawyer while maintaining an active interest in military and naval history. He has written articles and designed wargames on naval topics. He holds a history degree from the University of Pennsylvania and lives in Corrales, New Mexico.